THE
FALCON
AND THE
SNOWMAN

A True Story of
Friendship and Espionage

ROBERT LINDSEY

THE LYONS PRESS
Guilford, Connecticut

An imprint of The Globe Pequot Press

The Lyons Press is an imprint of The Globe Pequot Press.

Originally published in hardcover 1979 by Simon and Schuster, New York

Printed in Canada

1 2 3 4 5 6 7 8 9 10

The Library of Congress Cataloging-in-Publication Data is available on file.

ISBN 1-58574-502-2

THE FALCON AND THE SNOWMAN

To Sandra,
MY STAFF OF LIFE

WHAT FOLLOWS IS A TRUE STORY. THE NAMES OF CERTAIN CHARACTERS HAVE BEEN CHANGED IN ORDER TO PROTECT THEIR PRIVACY.

THE FALCON AND THE SNOWMAN

1
A HALO OF SMOG hung over Mexico City on the morning of January 6, 1977, obscuring the mountains beyond the city with a brown membrane of moist soot. Christmas decorations, remnants of *Posada,* the city's most festive celebration, still clung to many of the buildings on the Paseo de la Reforma, the broad boulevard that sweeps proudly from the Old City to Chapultepec Park, a Latin American Champs-Elysées.

It was the Day of the Three Kings, and, as was the tradition, children throughout the capital of Mexico were opening their Christmas packages. Under an elm tree along Reforma, an organ-grinder cranked out the repetitious strains of a Strauss waltz, entertaining tourists beside the statue of Cuahutemoc, the last of the Aztec emperors, while his assistant, a small boy, scurried about, cap outstretched, soliciting coins.

Behind the glittering window walls of the office towers that loomed over the tree-lined boulevard, secretaries were beginning to grow anxious, restless for their two-hour midday *siesta* to begin. At the National Pawnshop, *Monte de Piedad*—the Mountain of Pity—people stood waiting their turn, holding musical instruments and cartons containing anonymous family treasures.

A taxi, one of the salmon-colored sedans that loiter outside the big downtown hotels which cater to foreign tourists, threaded its way through the clotted queues of cars, trucks and buses on Reforma. Just as it was about to be swallowed up in the whirlpool of traffic swirling around the entrance to the park, the passenger in the back seat of the cab leaned forward and told the driver to stop. He was a small, chunky man. So small, in fact, that when he got out of the taxi someone seeing him from behind might have guessed that he was a grade-school pupil

9

on his way home to one of the grand houses concealed behind high walls on the side streets in the neighborhood. But when he turned around, a stranger, expecting to see a child, would have seen a moustache and the weathered complexion of a man who four days earlier had turned twenty-five and who, indeed, looked older than that. Although he was short, he had broad shoulders and a thick torso that seemed out of proportion to the rest of his body; brown hair flopped over his forehead and curled around his ears, landing half an inch above the collar of a brown sport coat; above his bushy moustache there were turquoise eyes that seemed at once too large and more moist than they should have been.

He walked three blocks to Calzada de Tacubaya, a wide expressway now almost hopelessly congealed with late-morning traffic, and turned toward a three-story white building. It was a big, brooding fortress of a place half hidden behind trees with a forest of radio antennae bristling from the roof and a plaque on an outer wall that read:

EMBAJADA
DE LA UNION DE LAS REPUBLICAS
SOCIALISTAS SOVIETICAS

It was the Soviet Embassy. He walked along the sidewalk in front of the wall and then paused; through a row of iron bars, he studied a small guardhouse set back from the street for several moments. Then he scanned the upper floors of the main building. For a moment he thought he saw a curtain jiggle at one window and the face of a man looking at him; but the face vanished suddenly. After a full minute, he started walking again. But before he took more than a few steps, he saw a limousine slowing to enter the compound and he rushed to intercept it. But the car didn't stop and it quickly disappeared behind a wall. He lit a cigarette, looked around and casually lobbed a ball of paper through the iron bars.

Before he could walk thirty paces, a Mexican policeman ran up and ordered him to halt. He protested that he was a tourist from California who had gotten lost while seeing the sights of Mexico City. But two hours later he was under arrest at the Metropolitan Police Headquarters of Mexico City, accused of murder.

As he waited to be questioned, he could recall his first visit to the Embassy. It had been simple then: He had presented himself to the clerk at the reception desk in the guardhouse, thrown down the com-

puter programming cards and said, "I have a friend with socialist lean-
ings who would like you to have some information." The clerk shook
his head and said he didn't speak English and left to get someone who
did.

He had sat in the stark lobby of the building, his feet barely reaching
the floor, looking up at a portrait of Lenin on the wall. When he was
sure no one was watching him, he raised the Minolta that he had hung
around his neck to look like a tourist and snapped a picture. *Who
knows?* he thought. *Someone might be willing to pay for a photograph
of the inside of the Russian embassy.*

Twenty minutes later he met Okana.

Vasily Ivanovich Okana was listed with Mexican authorities as a
vice consul of the Soviet foreign service. He was in fact a member of
the Soviet intelligence service, the KGB. At that first meeting, the
American had not been much impressed physically by the slender man
in the poorly fitting black suit. Later he had learned that beneath the
baggy suit was the muscled physique of a fitness fanatic.

"These are interesting," the thirty-eight-year-old KGB agent had
said in English as his fingers played with the computer cards. "But
what are they?"

He was only a courier, he replied, but it was his understanding that
they had something to do with what people called "spy satellites."

2   THE PALOS VERDES PENINSULA is in Southern California. From the air it looks like the jagged prow of a
huge ship trying to escape from the rest of North
America. It rises like a rocky, slab-sided Gibraltar at the southern
entrance to Santa Monica Bay and at sunset glows with soft shades of
orange reflected by thousands of Mediterranean tile roofs. Nine miles
long and four miles wide, the mountainous Peninsula lifts up and away
from the table-flat Los Angeles basin, establishing physical and social
isolation from the freeway culture of that city. The isolation was cre-

ated eons ago by geological forces and by centuries of sedimentation, erosion and waves that sculpted a land of scalloped coves, terraced cliffs and rocky headlands above lonely beaches strewn with pebbles and driftwood.

For centuries its remoteness resisted efforts to populate the Peninsula. It was like a vast feudal grazing land, producing hides, tallow, beef and, later, vegetables tended by immigrant tenant farmers from Japan. But after World War II, when Los Angeles was becoming the prototype of modern urban sprawl, more and more people who had emigrated to that city became disenchanted with its version of the California Dream, and many began to colonize The Hill, as its inhabitants came to refer to their refuge from the sprawl. As time went on, the Palos Verdes Peninsula became a prestigious address, and as it did, many colonizers of The Hill began to look down, in more than one way, on the people who lived below on the flatlands of the basin.

The immigrants to The Hill were, for the most part, college-educated people from out of state who had come to California with little more than their brains and their ambition. And they had found success that allowed them to afford a place on The Hill. They were achievers who accumulated money, most of them, not through inheritance or bloodlines but through their own talents, drive and ambition. Many prospered in the aerospace industry at companies like North American Aviation, Douglas Aircraft, Hughes Aircraft, TRW Systems and other firms that built airplanes, missiles, space satellites and electronic gadgetry down on the flatlands. In the years after the war, aerospace ballooned into a prosperous industry as specialized and concentrated as Detroit's, and Palos Verdes became its Bloomfield Hills.

Others came to The Hill after making a bundle as lawyers, doctors or businessmen. The common denominator of the colonizers was success. Palos Verdes didn't have any industry of its own. But a fortune could be made there in real estate; building lots that sold for $1,000 in the fifties were commanding $10,000 in the early sixties and almost $100,000 by the middle seventies, when even a modest home on The Hill cost $150,000 and $300,000 did not buy an opulent one. The earliest real estate promoters had tried to entice flatlanders to The Hill by merchandising it as a kind of transplanted Côte d'Azur. Homes visible from the sea, they decreed, had to have Old World red tile roofs, and even the names they gave to the neighborhoods on The Hill sounded like a Mediterranean melody—Malaga Cove, Portuguese Bend, Lunada

Bay, Montemalaga and Abalone Cove. The rule about the red tile roofs was relaxed in later years, but on some days, when the sky was especially clear and the ocean especially blue, it was not difficult for the inhabitants of The Hill to imagine that they were gazing out on their own Riviera and their own Capri, the rocky island of Catalina anchored twenty-one miles offshore.

. .

Andrew Daulton Lee was born in 1952; Christopher John Boyce, a year later. Their parents were among the first wave of people who settled the Peninsula in the fifties and early sixties. The Lees bought a rambling ranch house with a putting green in the backyard on Lunada Bay, across the street from the Pacific Ocean. The Boyces were not quite as prosperous and bought a home in a pleasant but slightly less prestigious neighborhood farther from the sea.

The two families were among the charter parishioners of the new Catholic church, St. John Fisher, that was built in 1961 to serve the growing Peninsula population. Boyce and Lee were among the first students at the parochial school that was built next to the church, and they were among the first altar boys to serve Mass there.

There is nothing in their school records, or in the memories of their friends or teachers, to indicate that they were anything but two devout Catholic boys growing up in happy, warm families in one of the most affluent suburbs in America, living one version of the American Dream and facing nothing but the brightest of futures.

3 DR. DAULTON BRADLEY LEE had grown up a long way from The Hill in a small farm town in Illinois where his father was the local dentist. It was not a poor family, but during the Depression it was not a wealthy one either. As long as anyone could remember, he had been regarded as a young man driven by high ambition—an ambition, he later said, that he had inherited from his father.

After graduating from high school, he left the farm town to attend a small college in Eureka, Illinois. But World War II intervened, and a few weeks after Pearl Harbor, his National Guard unit was mobilized. He was sent to an infantry training base in Tennessee, where he applied for a transfer to the Army Air Corps, hoping to become a combat pilot. He scored high marks on the screening test and immediately was accepted for flight school. After preliminary flight training in Alabama, he was ordered to Davis-Monthan Air Base, which had been hurriedly bulldozed out of sand and sagebrush near Tucson, Arizona.

Second Lieutenant Daulton Bradley Lee was a handsome man who had brown curly hair, stood more than six feet tall and had a style about him that made his leather flight jacket and trailing silk scarf look as if they had been designed expressly for him. He had not been at Davis-Monthan long before he met a coed at the University of Arizona in Tucson.

It was a fast wartime romance. After dating for four months, he married Anne Clark in November, 1942, before the altar of Ss. Peter and Paul Catholic Church in Tucson. The following August, he was on his way to Europe.

Anne Lee had been born in Montana but had moved with her mother and father—a physician who specialized in heart disease—to Long Beach, near Los Angeles, as an infant, and she considered herself a native Californian. A beauty who would keep her good looks long after she had lost her youth and her hair had turned prematurely gray, she had enrolled at the university with plans to become a teacher. But after her husband went overseas, she dropped out of college and moved back to her parents' home in Long Beach, where a daughter was born the next year.

Her husband, meanwhile, was distinguishing himself in the air: flying B-24 bombers over Italy, Daulton Lee had become a lieutenant colonel by the time he was twenty-three, and when the war was over, he came home with the Distinguished Flying Cross, the Air Medal and the Croix de Guerre with palm—and his old ambition. Before the war he had thought about becoming a doctor, and encouraged by his father-in-law, he enrolled in the Medical School at the University of Southern California in Los Angeles, where he got high marks, and then decided to specialize in pathology.

While he was still in medical school, though, the couple experienced a major disappointment: Mrs. Lee learned she could not have any

more children. They wanted a son, and in 1952 they heard through friends that an infant boy might be available for adoption. In those days, before the pill and other advances in birth control, it was easier to adopt a child than it would become in the future. That winter they brought home their second child and named him Andrew Daulton. (As the years went on he preferred to be called Daulton, after his father.)

Not much was known of the child's natural parents except that they were of Polish and Lithuanian ancestry and were blue-collar workers. "They were educated people in technical fields; they had an electronics type of education," Anne Lee, his adoptive mother, would recall later. Although his natural parents had been married, theirs had been a stormy marriage, and they had gone to the divorce courts before his conception to obtain an interlocutory divorce decree. Under California law at the time, a year's waiting time was necessary before an interlocutory decree could become final, and if the couple engaged in sexual relations during that year the decree became invalid. It was during this twelve-month waiting period that Andrew Daulton Lee was conceived. Still determined to dissolve their marriage, his parents decided not to reveal his conception to the court, and he was placed for adoption.

When Daulton was two years old, Mrs. Lee procured a booklet that had been written to help adoptive parents explain the circumstances of their children's birth. She settled Daulton onto her lap and told him how she and his father had yearned for a child, and when at last they had seen Daulton they had loved him and selected him over all other children. And, she recalled later, he had seemed to accept the fact of his adoption as easily as if she had been teaching him how to tie his shoes. Eventually, the Lees decided they wanted more children, and in 1954 they adopted another sister for him, Mary Anne, and in 1958, a brother, David. Meanwhile, as the family grew, Dr. Lee was becoming increasingly successful—and prosperous—in his field.

Along with other pupils at St. John Fisher, Daulton was indoctrinated in a brand of Roman Catholicism somewhat harsher than that which would prevail a few years later following the winds of liberalization that blew from Rome during and after the tenure of Pope John XXIII. His was a religious training rooted in a doctrine that to commit a mortal sin meant risking eternal damnation in the fires of hell. But he accepted it and was a regular communicant at St. John Fisher.

Daulton learned other lessons at home. His father, whose childhood had not been materially bountiful, assured Daulton that he was deter-

mined to give his own children some of the things that he had missed; and indeed, whether it was toys, clothing or travel, Daulton enjoyed a childhood of abundance, financed by the growing wealth of his father. When he was eleven, his parents sent him to Southern California's most exclusive summer camp—Gold Arrow Camp, in the High Sierra mountains, where his camp-mates included the sons of comedian Jerry Lewis; Otis Chandler, the publisher of the *Los Angeles Times,* and other prominent and wealthy people. By David Strick, the son of movie director Joseph Strick, who shared Daulton's cabin, he was remembered as a tough competitor, generous and likable, but troubled by his size—"A Mickey Rooney character," he called him. "He was a plucky guy who sort of walked with a swagger, I think, because he was conscious of his shortness. When we had a water fight, he stayed in it until the end and never wanted to give up. When his parents sent him a box of candy," Strick recalled, "he walked around and gave some to everybody before he ate any; he loved to give gifts; everybody else who got something from home hoarded it."

Daulton was an unspectacular student at St. John Fisher, but he discovered in grade school that he had a talent most of his classmates didn't have: he could make things with his hands better than almost anyone else. With a hammer and saw and modest materials, he could fashion a tree house, a go-kart or other toys that became the envy of his friends.

A lot was made in the Lee household of Dr. Lee's rise from the obscure Illinois farm town to a position of importance near the top of the Peninsula's medical hierarchy. A lot was made also of his war record. Daulton lost count of how many times his father's decorations and his picture in uniform were taken out of a closet to be shown and admired by the family; and of course, there was the oft-told family legend that Daulton would recall many years later with still a trace of awe: "He was a lieutenant colonel when he was twenty-three, one of the youngest in the Air Corps. His commanding officer told him, 'I'd like to make you a general—you deserve it—but I'd get too much flak if I made you a general at your age.' "

Perhaps it is difficult under the best of circumstances to be the son of a doctor in America: Society elevates physicians to pedestals regardless of their faults; men and women with lesser occupational status pay deference to them, inducing in some physicians a sense of exaggerated self-importance and impatience in others that is extended be-

yond medicine to encompass whatever they do. In a social milieu where ambition is a religion and money is the ultimate laurel of success, the shadow may be cast even larger on a young son by his father because, of all the professions, his is one of the most richly rewarded. If it is difficult, then, under the best of circumstances for a son to shape his own identity in the presence of such a shadow, what if the father is a war hero who stands more than six feet tall and the son, at maturity, is only five feet two? What if the son is adopted, not natural-born; if he is bright but not academically driven? What if the father is handsome and athletic and his eldest son is not?

When he was a child, there was talk of Daulton's following his father and becoming a physician, but as Daulton grew older, Dr. Lee became increasingly bitter over what he saw as the coming of socialized medicine. "Medicine's a dying profession," he repeatedly told his eldest son. "Those bureaucrats in Washington are killing the practice of medicine as we know it." Rather than press his son to become a doctor, he gave this advice to Daulton:

"Do whatever you want in life, but whatever you decide to do, be the best at it."

When Daulton was still in grade school it was decided that someday he would attend Notre Dame, the famous Catholic university in South Bend, Indiana. His father told him frequently that it had been his childhood dream to go to Notre Dame, with its rich traditions of scholarship and football excellence, but his family couldn't afford it because of the Depression. Things would be different for Daulton and David, he said: their family had the money, and his sons could have what he had been forced to miss. Daulton and his father also dreamed of how someday he would play football for the Fighting Irish.

Unfortunately, Daulton stopped growing when he was in the fifth grade. As his classmates kept growing taller, and he did not, he became defensive about his stature and seemed uncomfortable around taller friends. Years later he could still recall the kind of questions that would embarrass him then: "People would ask me, 'How come you're so short and your dad is so tall and your brother is six inches taller?' " It was a question that was doubly painful because, obliquely, it raised the issue of his adoption. When Daulton became depressed, his mother would tell him, "Don't worry all the time about size; there have been lots of people who were short and have done marvelous things." Daulton had other troubles, too. He worried that his ears were too big, and

as a youngster he began to develop serious problems with acne on his face and body.

It was a problem that would haunt him for years.

. .

Daulton went out for Little League baseball, and his father coached the team. "He was a dogged little guy," remembered Msgr. Thomas J. McCarthy, the first pastor of St. John Fisher, who often celebrated Mass with Daulton serving as altar boy on one side of him and Christopher Boyce on the other. "Daulton was small, but he made up for what he lacked in natural ability with moxie." The priest noticed one thing in particular about Daulton's participation in sports: he seemed preoccupied with proving himself to his father. When he struck out or dropped a ball, the first thing Daulton usually did was look over in the direction of his father to see if he was watching. Later on, Daulton took up golf in hopes of sharing another of his father's interests, but Dr. Lee almost always won, and Daulton's inability to beat his father was a source of laughs for the family.

After Daulton was graduated from St. John Fisher in the spring of 1966, he enrolled at Palos Verdes High School, a complex of low-slung buildings topped with red tile roofs styled vaguely, de rigueur, like a Spanish mission; the school was about a mile from the Lee home and only about 200 yards from a bluff overlooking the Pacific. Students could look out and see ships passing by. It was a school where, on the average, at least 90 percent of each year's graduating class went on to college and where the student parking lot was usually crowded with Cadillacs, Corvettes, Mercedes-Benzes, Porsches and other expensive cars. The following year, Christopher John Boyce followed Daulton to Palos Verdes High.

. .

Chris's parents had also grown up far from The Hill. His mother, Noreen, was the product of an Old World Irish Catholic family from Ohio, one in which the Sacraments were observed and Mass was an obligatory joy on Sundays. Under the influence of the sisters at the parochial school that she attended, Noreen Hollenbeck decided as a child to become a nun, and at eighteen she entered a convent operated by the Ursulines, an order devoted to the education of young girls. But eighteen months after entering the convent, she decided that she was

18

not suited for the cloistered life after all and elected not to take her final vows. She left the convent but not the Church. Then, as in the future, seldom did a day begin for Noreen Hollenbeck without Mass and Holy Communion. The young girl who had wanted to become a nun had the stunning good looks and the sturdy, ample frame of an Irish country girl, and it was not long after she left the convent that Charles Eugene Boyce fell in love with her.

Boyce was a native of Colorado who had a natural gift for athletics and a keen academic mind, two qualities that had presented him with a dilemma: after he was mustered out of military service following World War II, he could not choose between becoming a lawyer and becoming a professional baseball player. Although he wasn't a Catholic, he enrolled at Loyola University, a Jesuit college near Los Angeles, on the G.I. Bill, playing semipro baseball as a sideline while choosing his plans for the future. A pitcher, he was good enough to be recruited by the New York Giants' farm-club system, but an elbow injury ended what could have been a promising career in baseball. In 1948, after three years of prelaw at Loyola, he decided to enroll in the Southwestern School of Law. After graduation, he was recruited by the Federal Bureau of Investigation. He remained in the bureau for almost two years, dealing with the potpourri of cases that came the way of a young agent stationed in those days in the New York City and New Haven offices—bank robberies, fraud, forgeries and the epidemic of espionage scares during the McCarthy era. Attracted by the prospect of a better-paying career in industry, he resigned from the bureau in 1952 and took a job helping to oversee plant security for an airplane manufacturer in Southern California, which he now considered his home.

Charles Boyce was a tall, rugged man whom some people called cold but who could warm up to a new acquaintance after a while. He loved cigars, tended to have strong convictions on most things and was wont to advance his convictions with what a longtime friend called "a very strong personality." Although he was not a Catholic, his bride had asked him for a promise to raise their children as Catholics, and he had agreed. They would have nine children—four boys and five girls: what some neighbors would refer to as "an old-fashioned Catholic family."

Chris was the first of their children, and he plunged into his mother's faith with as much zeal as she had herself. He devoured his catechism

and, long after many of his classmates had resigned as altar boys, pulled himself out of bed before dawn to serve Mass. Father Glenn, a St. John Fisher priest, became one of his best friends. He was a middle-aged Irishman with a brogue as thick as porridge who could be merciless with Chris in the confessional and then go out and kick a football with him, still wearing his black cassock. Amid Chris's emerging piety there was a measure of the troublemaker, but Father Glenn was tolerant and, most of the time, put up with this facet of his personality. Sometimes while Chris was serving for Father Glenn, he inconspicuously dragged his feet at the communion rail to charge himself with static electricity; then, with calculated glee, gave a shock on the chin to friends with the communion plate. Father Glenn was suspicious about the sparks but never figured out their origin.

Chris fell deeply under the priest's spell, and the seeds of Catholicism that his mother had planted in him were fertilized and nurtured by Father Glenn.

It was faith rooted not only in the doctrines and traditions of the Roman Catholic Church but in an especially severe moral code. Like the Church itself, Chris began to view moral questions in black and white, and without much tolerance for deviation. One day, a priest from St. John Fisher told his father, "You know, I think Chris is more conservative than Cardinal McIntyre."

It was a reference to Cardinal James Francis McIntyre, who for years ruled the Archdiocese of Los Angeles with a medieval style of orthodoxy that, for a long time, froze out many of the reforms that swept the church elsewhere during the 1960s.

As was expected of Chris by his church, he treated authority figures —his parents, the priests and sisters at St. John Fisher, other adults he met—with deference and respect. He wholeheartedly embraced the doctrine that God had delegated to the Pope infallible authority over His flock, that the Pope had delegated some of his authority to the bishops, priests and nuns and that members of the flock obeyed the decisions of the Church hierarchy because they were *right* decisions.

Chris's acceptance of authority was reinforced by his father. Like many men attracted to law enforcement, Charles Boyce was conservative politically. And, like the Church, he tended to view things in black and white. He believed in obedience to constituted authority, loved his country and tried to pass on this loyalty and love to his eldest son. For the father, it was love guided by the America-right-or-wrong

ethos that galvanized his country during World War II; his son eventually would judge America by a different kind of standard.

•   •

As the eldest of nine, Chris became the leader of the Boyce clan and was idolized by his brothers and sisters. During his grade-school years, the Boyce family continued to grow while his father was climbing as a security executive in the defense industry. But while he took on more responsibility at work, he wasn't an absentee father: Charles Boyce taught his son how to tie fishing flies, coached the baseball team at St. John Fisher, tutored him in football and helped mold a will to compete and win on the playing field. He also passed on to his son a love of history, especially military history. When he was a child, they spent hours together talking of ancient wars and battlefields; when Chris was thirteen his favorite book was *Lee's Lieutenants,* and he dreamed of fighting himself in the expanding war in Vietnam as soon as he was old enough. His father was an ardent supporter of the war and could not understand why anyone opposed it. Once, when his father got into a bitter argument over the war with another coach of a Little League team, Chris passionately rooted for his father from the sidelines, sure that he was right.

While Chris was still in grade school, friends began to notice that he had an unusual trait: he liked to take risks. When he carried a football, for example, they noticed he ran head-on into waiting tacklers and kept squirming to get away when other runners would have given up; when he climbed trees, he could usually be counted on to climb higher than other kids and go out on the farthest, weakest limb.

Test scores confirmed his teachers' suspicions that Chris had a brilliant mind. He scored 142 on an I.Q. test, and he seldom got anything but an A on his school exams. His academic passion was history, especially ancient political and military history. Outdoors, his passion became bird watching and hiking in the wilderness. He was particularly interested in birds; his father, noticing the interest, gave him a book on falconry, the sport of hunting game with birds, and he began to read more about the subject. Years later, his eighth-grade teacher, Sister Jean-Marie Bartunek, looked back on her year with Christopher Boyce and described him as the kind of pupil every teacher lived for—smart, curious, hardworking, compassionate and articulate: "He was interested in everything! Science, debating, journalism, music, art; he liked

to write poetry and talk on any subject, and he was a natural leader. He was a wonderful, sensitive, happy and intelligent boy who came from a perfect family.''

In his last year at St. John Fisher, Chris was elected student-body president and delivered the graduation address. The previous year he had discovered a second passion besides history—debating and public speaking—and he had harbored hopes of attending Loyola High School, a Catholic school operated by the Jesuits in Los Angeles that frequently turned out champion debating teams. But the family decided that Loyola was too far from The Hill, and he went to Palos Verdes High School instead. Monsignor McCarthy, who had watched Chris mature from a slightly shy altar boy to the brightest star in the school, would, years later, think back on the young student he knew: ''He was one of the finest boys I'd ever met or taught,'' he said. ''I don't think I've ever known a boy with such idealism.''

4 CHRISTOPHER JOHN BOYCE arrived at Palos Verdes High School in the autumn of 1967. It was an era of assassinations, an unpopular war, flower children, LSD, festering disenchantment with old standards and challenges from the young to parental assumptions. It was a time when the privileged kids who drove home from Palos Verdes High in sports cars and Cadillacs learned to watch, with everyone else, nightly TV reports of body counts and napalming in Vietnam, race riots and political dissenters beaten back by police clubs. The Vietnam War had been a fact of American life since the early sixties, but until now Chris had been only a spectator of the war on the nightly news. As a high school freshman, he responded to his instinctive interest in history and public affairs and began to follow the war more closely and form his own judgments about it. He also began to think—and form judgments—about other things, too.

It is impossible to pinpoint the exact moment when Chris began to rebel against the assumptions of his father's generation and to shape

his own view of the world, the human condition, nationalism and the future of his planet.

Perhaps a trip he made to Mexico with his classmates from the sixth grade at St. John Fisher had been first to cause something to stir. The class left The Hill before dawn in a caravan of station wagons led by Sister Jean to deliver food, medical supplies and Christmas packages to a rural village in Mexico; it was a routine Saturday charity mission for parochial schools in Southern California those days. It was a one-way drive of less than four hours from his doorstep in Palos Verdes. But the economic chasm that separated his town and the village stunned Chris and moved him to tears. The caravan rolled into the village and he saw unpaved streets, shacks made of sticks and cardboard, open sewers; he looked into the faces of some of the children and then looked away quickly—their faces were disfigured and glazed by ugly red scar tissue, the result of fires ignited by fallen candles in their paper hovels. Years later, Chris would recollect:

"There were thousands of them, their flimsy shacks bending in the wind. They were lining the highway and in the ravines and on the hillsides. The children stood by the side of the road wearing only filthy underclothes. Here and there a dozen or so crouched around cooking fires. Their dreams were empty, but they were still people, just forgotten have-nots. I promised myself then that I would never forget—if nothing else, I would never forget.

"I had been taught that Mexico was a democratic nation, but what spirit of liberty existed in the cardboard hovels? They had had nothing —no hope, no future—and they had stood wan and emaciated. They had not even retained the bruised dignity of peasants. I wondered: Were we in no way responsible for what existed ten miles beyond our borders? Will no authority take responsibility for all of mankind; will the Third World always just be an abscess? Most frightening, I wondered, wasn't it in America's best self-interest to perpetuate its disproportionate consumption? Had we based our system on permanent inequity?"

•   •

Perhaps something else stirred in Chris one night during the summer of 1965 when his father took him to St. John Fisher, which sat atop one of the highest points on the Peninsula, and, together, they looked out toward Los Angeles. It was a rare night: wind had pushed aside the layer of smog that usually blanketed the city, and every light below

was like a star; it was as if they were examining a diorama from behind a sheet of glass. They had come to St. John Fisher to watch the black ghetto of Watts burn.

As they looked down from the shelter of Chris's classroom at the orange glow and columns of billowing smoke rising from the riot-torn ghetto, a jeep sped by. He imagined an army of blacks and their flames advancing on The Hill toward his own home. But he was reassured later when his father bought a shotgun in case the family had to deal with the threat from below.

Other events also may have stirred Chris's doubts, but if there was anyone who had first ignited them, it was Robin.

Robin arrived at Chris's home in Palos Verdes on a Saturday morning in 1967 with hair to his waist, beads, a windowless Volkswagen van, "roaches" in the ashtray and a hooded falcon named Mohammed on his wrist.

Like Daulton, Robin was the son of a wealthy doctor from The Hill. He had heard from a mutual friend who lived up the street from Chris that there was a teen-ager in the neighborhood who had an interest in birds. He knocked at the Boyce front door and asked, "Is Chris here?"

Chris took one look at his falcon and was never the same.

To Chris's dad, Robin was an alien: "the original weirdo," he would call him later. But his father cooked the stranger scrambled eggs, and Chris probably would always remember the meal: a member of the subculture sitting down to breakfast with the rock-hard conservative, the former FBI agent who still wore a gun under his arm to work. They're like people from different planets who speak different languages, he thought. Chris, as best he could, tried to interpret for them. The square kid of fifteen with a flattop haircut who wanted to become a priest looked first at the happy, nonconforming twenty-one-year-old and then at his forty-three-year-old father and wondered at the dichotomy: Who was right? he asked himself.

If there was ever a moment when Chris discovered the curious, horrible ambiguity that would haunt his life, this was it. Other people, he thought, may have a single identity, but not me. Chris from then on could not—or would not—make a choice.

• •

Robin asked Chris if he wanted to see Mohammed fly.

As they drove away in the van to fly Mohammed that first morning, Chris looked out the window back at his home. Years later, he would

still recall the silhouette of his father in an upstairs window and the intensity of the feelings he felt stirring inside him that day.

They flew Mohammed under an overcast sky on one of the terraced Palos Verdes hills that swept gently down toward the Pacific and then plunged, with a final steep dive, to a cauldron of turbulent white surf. It was wild and beautiful there then, before the subdividers came with their bulldozers. The string beans had just been harvested, and there was a smell of damp soil in the air.

Hooded, Mohammed sat on Robin's wrist listening for the sounds of the field, the brass bells on his feet tinkling softly as he waited.

Robin whispered in his ear and stroked his wings and clenched fist to calm the bird. A lark called from across the field, and Mohammed shuddered. Gently, Robin removed the leash and swivel from the jesses strapped around the bird's feet and, with his teeth and free hand, slid off the hood. The bird waited no more than an instant. Mohammed sprang off his fist and pumped his wings rapidly to gain altitude, climbing higher and higher as Robin and Chris scrambled across the field noisily to flush the larks. Then Mohammed selected one of the fleeing larks; he suddenly plunged in the power dive that falconers call a "stoop." Contact seemed imminent. But then the lark lurched and it escaped the diving talons of the falcon. Mohammed quickly regained altitude and came down for a second attack; this time he slammed into the lark with a clanging of bells. There was an explosion of feathers, and the lark fell like a stone.

Mohammed was back on Robin's gauntlet a few minutes later, savoring breast of lark. Resting in the field after the hunt, smoking his first joint in the company of a friendly stranger and his bird, it occurred to Chris: They are one; this strange young hippie has his own peace.

Robin died in a freak accident nearly two years later—fatally burned by blazing hashish oil he was preparing for sale. He lingered for three days in the hospital before dying; he left behind a wife and children— and Chris's respect.

There was an article in the paper about the fire and the young drug pusher's death, which Chris's father showed him. From then on, falconry was anathema to his dad.

•   •

Robin had clearly been an important factor. But what about Rick?

Rick was the archetypal California surfer—big, wiry, glue-footed on the boards, a potential South Bay champion. He spent every hour he

could on the waves beneath the Palos Verdes bluffs, locked into curls, practicing his kickouts and coming up smiling even when he was "wiped out." Rick was outgoing, happy—and before he had really begun to shave, a Marine.

Rick hadn't been in Vietnam long when a land mine blew off most of his right leg. After he came home on a creaking artificial leg, he and Chris sometimes went down to the bluffs to watch the surfers and check out the size of the combers. Eventually Rick managed to learn how to walk pretty well, without much sign of a limp, but his missing leg—and the nationalism that, in Boyce's mind, had removed it—sickened Chris.

"No cause or 'just' war for peace, for honor, for freedom, for the people, for property; not Crazy Horse's charge at the Little Big Horn, nor Pickett's nor the Tet Offensive, nor Thermopylae, nor the Inchon Landing, nor the Alamo, nor even Château-Thierry and the Bulge, nor any of them were worth tearing off Rick's leg and his manhood," Chris would say many years later. "I didn't believe it then and I don't believe it now, and someday everyone won't."

At sixteen, Chris had decided to reject nationalism and everything for which it stood.

5 THERE WAS NOT MUCH for young people to do in Palos Verdes. The calculated isolation from the freeways of Los Angeles was a virtue to those who sought its serenity, ocean breezes and unpolluted air. But for adolescents, the town offered no youth clubs, bowling alleys or skating rinks and not even a movie theater until the early seventies. There was little public transportation on The Hill. Kids growing up there, for the most part, were left to their own resources to find entertainment and excitement.

Marijuana had been around for decades in Southern California, popular among some of the people who worked in the movie industry and in the Los Angeles Mexican-American *barrio*. But in middle-class

Anglo communities, pot had been a taboo, especially so in a community like Palos Verdes that perennially voted Republican, went to church on Sundays and didn't experiment with new life-styles because most of the people there had already found what they wanted. Sharing a quick cigarette in the school rest room or a can of beer on a Saturday night was an acceptable forbidden fruit, but not drugs. This began to change in the middle sixties.

Robin hadn't been the only son of Palos Verdes to wander off The Hill and disappear into the Haight-Ashbury, the mountains of Big Sur or some other enclave of dropouts and return with full beard, long hair, a drug habit, a drug business with which to support himself and a falcon on his wrist. There was a small cult of people like him; there were Leroy and Weird Harold and Jon and a dozen more. Jon was Robin's partner, and he could make leather hoods for falcons as fine as any crafted by the artisans of Elizabethan England.

They were a nomadic breed, mostly from wealthy families—contemptuous of many of the indigenous values of Palos Verdes; hedonists who loved the wilderness for its solitude and marijuana for its psychic solace and who found a curious way of banking the money they made from selling marijuana, hashish, LSD and cocaine: they invested it in rare Oriental rugs from Turkey, Persia and the Caucasus Mountains of Russia. Prices for the rugs were skyrocketing, and who'd expect a hippie to have a fortune in nineteenth-century carpets?

Moreover, Robin and his friends weren't the only ones who returned to the Peninsula with values challenging those imparted by the parents on The Hill.

College students who had left The Hill for Berkeley, Stanford and elsewhere came home with samples of pot and other drugs—and advice to younger brothers and sisters to turn on. "It's no worse than alcohol," they said, usually with a reference to their parents' nightly cocktail hour. Some of the returning college students and dropouts like Robin discovered that substantial amounts of extra spending money could be generated by the sale of a few marijuana cigarettes to the well-heeled kids on The Hill. This lesson was not lost on some entrepreneurial-minded students at P.V. High, including the eldest son of Dr. Lee.

At first the flow of illicit drugs into the community was little more than a trickle. But by the end of the sixties, the trickle had become a torrent. Experimentation expanded beyond pot to barbiturates, am-

phetamines, LSD, hashish, peyote, cocaine and heroin. From the high school, drugs filtered down to the junior high schools of Palos Verdes and even to some of the elementary schools. Not every young person in Palos Verdes used drugs, but the social pressure was such that junior high pupils who didn't pop pills or blow weed were called "lame" and ostracized by many of their classmates.

By the mid-seventies, like a wave that had crested, the drug epidemic had peaked. But in the years when Daulton and Chris were passing into manhood, drugs were as much a part of high school in their affluent community as history and biology, pep rallies and football games.

Inexplicably, a generation of parents did not realize what was happening to their children. Perhaps they didn't try to know. Lethargy, glazed watery eyes, erratic behavior—somehow, they missed the symptoms, and some didn't learn that their children were helplessly dependent on drugs until they were dead from an overdose; or, some didn't know until their children were scratching off their clothes and screaming from the hallucinations of a nightmarish experience with LSD; or they did not know until the children were just *gone*—runaways swallowed up by the adolescent underground, pursuing the capricious gods that they found in a pill, a snort, a joint or a fix.

The Palos Verdes schools tried to snuff out the drug epidemic, but they didn't have much success; when two-way mirrors were installed in the rest rooms for teachers to monitor drug sales and the lunchtime pot smoking, the kids went elsewhere; eventually, the junior highs cancelled most evening social events because it became impossible to have a dance or a class party without a mantle of sweet-smelling marijuana smoke in the air. "You could go to the schools and they were selling drugs on the street corner," Dr. Lee would recall later of those times.

• •

It was becoming clear to everybody, Daulton included, that he would not go to Notre Dame, because he wasn't making the grades that his parents insisted that he must earn to get into a selective university. Virtually the only time Daulton managed to bring home an A or B on his report card other than for Woodshop was when he gave it to himself. He erased a D or F on the report card, substituted a B or A and used a photocopying machine to produce a report card that was welcomed at home.

When things went poorly at school or he became depressed, Daulton could always find escape with his tools in the family garage. From a shop teacher at P.V. High who had recognized his skills and encouraged him, Daulton learned how to turn raw lumber into spectacular boxes of inlaid walnut, oak, ebony and teak; and as he got better, he crafted delicate bowls and inlaid tables and cabinets inspired by the work of artisans of eighteenth-century France who became his heroes.

When Daulton came home from school one day during his junior year after a session with his counselor, his mother noticed that he seemed unhappy and asked if anything was bothering him; Daulton confessed he was having troubles with his college-prep classes, and said that he had admitted this to his counselor that morning before asking him for advice about a possible career in woodworking. He said the school official had ridiculed the idea:

"You live in Palos Verdes; you don't work with your hands, you work with your brain."

Years later, Daulton still remembered this confrontation with bitterness:

"He couldn't understand why somebody would want to work in a shop with all that sawdust and create a piece of art out of wood. That's how I looked at it; it was an art. Louis the Fourteenth period pieces are some of the most highly prized furniture in the world."

Although his counselors insisted that Daulton was more than intelligent enough to be college material, school simply didn't interest him. "Maybe I was bored; I knew the information was in the books if I really needed to know it," Daulton said, looking back on his failed high school career. "I saw all those kids trying to get grades and saw the pressures from their parents; if I'd found a reason to pursue a different course I might have gotten involved with it, but I was just content to move out of high school and get started on something else."

As Dr. Lee continued to make more money, the family increasingly could afford to indulge a taste for fine art objects, which began to fill their home. Dr. and Mrs. Lee traveled frequently to Europe and the Far East, and they honed a taste for fine art initially acquired from her parents. Sharing the interest with their four children, they discussed it at meals, went as a family to inspect projected purchases and often took family outings to museums to see new exhibits. None of the children was more interested in the art—or in other material things of life—than Daulton. Listening carefully, he became more knowledgeable about his parents' collection, and when new friends visited he

gave them a tour of the home, explaining proudly the finer points of each item of Oriental art or other objet d'art.

Daulton was not like the members of his generation who rejected the materialism of their parents. Indeed, he repeatedly told his brother and friends that when he was older he wanted to live exactly like his parents. In fact, Daulton had already found an enterprise that made him believe he could be just as wealthy as his father without having to work as hard.

It was to bring him not only money, but a kind of power he had never imagined possible.

• •

Daulton was introduced to marijuana as a high school freshman, and before long, pot had become more than a Saturday-night substitute for a six-pack of beer. He began arriving late for midmorning classes, his eyes glazed—or not showing up at all; he became not only a user of pot but a proselytizer who eagerly solicited friends to drop by his home after school for a joint. After a year or so, he graduated to cocaine. He had discovered that a pinch of coke in a nostril was a marvelous psychic potion; it made him feel euphoric and eased the emptiness he felt about his size, his nagging failure to satisfy his father and a pain that increasingly weighed heavily on him—an inadequacy he felt with girls. Every doubt was exorcised—at least for a few hours—in the euphoria of self-confidence that the drugs yielded. After his first joint, Daulton was never the same again.

"Maybe you could call us the idle rich," Daulton would recall of those years later. "We weren't opulent rich, but it was a group where you had all the money for everything you needed. Money wasn't at the level of scrounging; you had money for cars, concerts, yet you still had extra money to spend. We were the idle rich, like the ancient Inca priests who kept the coca leaves for themselves and kept them from the masses."

• •

Chris and Daulton had been friends but not buddies at St. John Fisher. After they both went out for the same football squad at Palos Verdes High, their friendship thickened as their common origins at the parochial school pushed them together—Catholics needed friends in a high school where most of the other students had spent years together at the same public elementary schools. Neither was large enough to

make the varsity or junior varsity football squad—Chris stood five feet eight; Daulton was just a shade over five feet—but both made the backfield on the "C" team, the school's third team for smaller players. One day after practice, Daulton showed Chris some pictures that he'd taken of several barn owls. Since his encounter with Robin, Chris had been reading everything he could find about birds—and was fascinated when Daulton showed him a zoo of predatory birds that he was keeping in his backyard. Tethered to perches beside the Lee family's putting green were more than a dozen owls, hawks and falcons.

Their friendship began to flourish even more after that day, mostly because of this mutual interest in falconry, and soon they were best friends.

No one ever satisfactorily explained Daulton's unusual interest in animals. Besides his collection of birds of prey, he kept a pair of piranha fish in a tank at his home for a while and entertained friends by dropping goldfish into the tank to be eaten by the piranhas; later on, he bought a pair of armadillos to keep as pets.

Daulton's experiences with predators were not always successful. Once, he took Chris to a field near the top of the Peninsula to show him a new red-tailed hawk he had bought. She was a big bird, weighing perhaps forty-five ounces. Chris noted that the bird gripped Daulton's gloved hand like a vise, and he sat down at the edge of the field to watch as Daulton cast off the bird with a wave of his hand. When she was airborne, the bird started to lumber back ominously toward Daulton. He threw out a lure of pigeon meat used to train falcons, and the big bird hit it like a train. But she didn't stop; she bounded off the lure, caromed into Daulton's face and clamped her big hind talon into his gums. Meanwhile, her other three talons spread across his left cheek from his nose to his ear, while she held her other foot poised in reserve, as if looking for an opening through Daulton's flailing arms. Chris, twenty yards away, yelled solicitous advice to his friend, but the hawk clung tenaciously to Daulton's face while blood seemed to spring out of it in all directions.

After Daulton finally managed to shake the bird off, he gave her away.

• •

Daulton was graduated from Palos Verdes High School in June, 1970, with the minimum number of credits needed for a diploma. Because his parents still wanted him to try college, Daulton enrolled at

Allan Hancock Junior College in Santa Maria, about 150 miles north of Los Angeles, in September, 1970. The Lees had hopes that he might be able to turn his life around, get respectable grades at Hancock and transfer to a four-year college. But nothing at Hancock inspired Daulton, and he dropped out of college the following winter.

Besides, Daulton had other plans: he had decided to become a full-time professional dope pusher.

When he was in high school, Daulton had watched how handsomely the older pushers lived and had been impressed: they had new cars or vans, wallets stuffed with cash and plenty of girls. And they didn't have to work very hard. There was something else, too. After one of his suppliers recruited him as a runner to deliver pot at P.V. High, Daulton made a pleasant discovery: for the first time, he was *somebody*. The tall, leggy blondes whom he'd admired but who had spurned him while choosing oversized, blue-eyed surfers began to select seats near him in the cafeteria and show enthusiasm for his boasts. Because of his access to drugs, *they* courted *him*. Daulton was a perceptive student of human nature, and he was pleased by what he saw in the eyes of the daughters of doctors, aerospace executives and businessmen.

And Daulton decided to take advantage of the curious hunger: if he became interested in a girl, he offered her a free joint or, if he liked her a lot, cocaine, which was more expensive. A pattern developed: First, he created a dependency by giving away drugs to girls; then he waited for them to ask for more. It was as if he were playing them like game fish until they were hooked. Once they were hooked, he demanded payment—in the back seat of a car. In a way, Daulton might have imagined the transaction as a form of pure capitalism: he provided drugs to fulfill a need, while they paid in a currency he wanted: attention and sex.

•   •

Daulton and, to a lesser extent, Chris had grown up with just about everything a rich society could bestow on its young men. They had money, good schools, a good family and a good future. They had everything—including boredom.

As younger brothers often do, David Lee had grown up worshiping his older brother, and he was a spectator who witnessed at close hand the processes that shaped his brother. "There was too much bore-

dom,'' he would recollect about the years he and Daulton were reaching maturity. "There was not enough to do, and the people were so rich . . . A big dealer would come around and he seemed like a big shot. There was nothing else to do, and some of the people got stuck, like my brother.''

As an apprentice pusher, Daulton learned quickly, and after a while he decided to hang up his own shingle. He carefully studied other pushers' methods, learned where to obtain drugs from wholesale dealers and began to recruit teen-age students as his runners. Whatever Daulton's problems were with a textbook, he proved to have a natural flair for business. Before long, he was making several hundred dollars a week at his new trade and had begun a climb that would make him one of the most successful drug dealers on the southern rim of the Los Angeles Basin. He was becoming, in the jargon of the times, a snowman—snow, as in the snowy-white grains of cocaine.

6 CHRIS WAS HAVING MORE DIFFICULTY than Daulton charting the course of his life. The straight A's that he had earned at St. John Fisher had begun to deteriorate in high school into a mediocre record of mostly C's; he could usually count on good marks in history, speech or athletics, but he rarely showed much interest in math, languages or sciences.

His parents thought they knew the reason for the change in Chris: Andrew Daulton Lee.

At the beginning of his junior year, they decided to transfer him to Rolling Hills High School, which was on the other side of The Hill, on a slope that faced the city of Los Angeles rather than the ocean.

The school-district boundary lines were drawn in such a way that most of the wealthiest communities on The Hill sent their children to Palos Verdes High School. The students who went to Rolling Hills High were, for the most part, indisputably prosperous, but more middle-class. The Boyces lived in a neighborhood where their children could attend either of the schools.

33

By the end of Chris's sophomore year, they had decided they didn't like some aspects of the atmosphere at P. V. High. They were troubled by the ostentatious wealth displayed by some of Chris's friends, but mostly they were upset by what they saw as an aimless lazy pursuit of pleasure by some of the rich kids there.

More than any of Chris's other friends, they disliked Daulton. They suspected he was involved with drugs, and they saw something sinister in the short, scruffy, long-haired youth who drove up to their house in his parents' blue Cadillac, and it made them worry; they were sure he had something to do with the changes they'd seen in Chris. Chris's mother urged him to drop his friendship with Daulton: "You're known by the people you associate with," she said. But then, as later, Chris possessed a strong loyalty to friends he had made, and his parents' strategy did not work. Even after Chris went to the new school, they continued to see each other frequently, to fly their falcons and go trapping together.

. .

Like most of his contemporaries, Chris now used marijuana regularly, but it didn't become the obsession that it became for Daulton; indeed, most older people who knew him probably would have been amazed to know that he had ever smoked even one joint. To most people in the adult world who knew him, Chris remained a sort of quintessential clean-cut American teen-ager with good manners, brains, ambition and religious piety. He worked part-time as a delivery boy for a liquor store after school, was idolized by his brothers and sisters, and faithfully led his family to Mass every Sunday. As they had for years, friends kidded Chris that someday he would become the first American Pope.

But unbeknownst to them or his mother, a storm was brewing over his faith in Catholicism. It began with a burst of atheism that flared about the same time his pubescent voice was deepening. Before long, the atheism had burned out, but it was replaced by doubts of the divinity of Jesus. This was a fundamental crisis for the teen-ager; his church didn't leave any room for doubt that Jesus was the Son of God. *It was the cornerstone of the Catholic faith.* Without it, Chris wasn't a Catholic.

Until then, Catholicism had been a joy for Chris. Many, maybe most, other children in the parish found church discipline, required attendance at Sunday Mass, confession, the Rosary and other church

rituals a wearisome, if necessary, obligation. Not Chris; the church had been *fun* for Chris as far back as he could remember. His enjoyment of church had perhaps begun when he was only six, when he went to Mass with his mother and his baby sister, Kathy, and in front of them there was an old woman who was wearing a mink scarf flung over her shoulders. It was the kind of scarf with the minks' stuffed heads on it. Chris was so tiny that he couldn't see over the woman and beyond the pew, and so his eyes focused on the tiny faces of two dead minks in front of him. After a while he became curious, and reached out and tweaked one of the minks on its nose. His sister giggled at the sight, and Chris began to giggle too; soon his mother joined them and all three were laughing out of control. The woman in the mink scarf turned around and looked at the woman and her two children. Chris's mother quickly grabbed the children and herded them out of the pew and up the aisle, and they all hid behind the baptismal font, still laughing. From then on, Chris associated the Church with good times.

As he grew older, he discovered other pleasures in the Church. He liked the ritualistic world of sisters and priests. His teachers convinced him that the Church, as well as America, was filled with and led by men of honor and selfless goodness; at the age of ten, he fell in love with his nun, and the Baltimore Catechism had become his definitive guide to his beliefs and behavior; he was embarrassed slightly when his mother's temper occasionally flared in a Gaelic oath, and as a child, he occasionally was ashamed that his father was an Orangeman, a non-Catholic Irishman. But he was devoted to his mother and his father—who, he rationalized, mitigated his heresy by going to Mass on Christmas and the Holy Days.

The Church was the family's link back to Ireland and to the ages, and it seemed a natural choice for Chris when, in the third grade, he decided to become a priest—and eventually a saint. When all else failed, Chris was told, when evil and barbarians ravaged humanity, it had been the Church that stood firm and saved Christendom. Church and—later—the Constitution: these were the absolute truths in his home, and if anyone doubted either, he was a heathen.

Sometime during his years in high school, Chris developed what he would later call "a terminal case of 'Prove it!' " "I wondered," he said later, "were there any absolute truths? I decided probably not, except that hate was a universal trait; but surely Catholicism would be my last refuge."

But the more he read history and science, the more he wondered if

he had been hoodwinked. Reality was not like the Baltimore Catechism. He asked himself, Why don't modern Catholics lay down their
military burdens like St. Paul and the converted Christian martyrs in
the Roman legions to live at one with Christ? Now they went to war
and killed—like Catholic Bavaria for Hitler and Catholic South Vietnam. It wasn't something new; hadn't Catholic Popes called for the
Crusades to reconquer the Holy Land? Chris decided there had been a
widening gap between the original teachings of Christ and the teachings
of his church since the second century.

It was a realization that Chris did not take lightly. He began to
wonder if he had been *betrayed*, made a fool of. He began to question
the rationality of accepting as infallible the word of the Pope, and as he
read more about the papacy, he wondered if the Vatican was not just
another selfish political power center wrapped in jewels, hypocrisy and
ritual. Once his doubts surfaced, they cascaded out; he was troubled
by Church teachings on the Virgin Birth, by stories of barbaric murders
during the Spanish Inquisition, by the secondary place of women in the
Church and other elements of Catholicism. Yet he could not be sure.
The stitches of faith sewn in his conscience by his mother, Father
Glenn, Monsignor McCarthy and the sisters at St. John Fisher did not
all rupture at once. Some were sewn too tightly. On one side of his
mind was the awakening of reason challenging dogma; on the other
side, the dogma, well entrenched, continued to tug and nag at his
conscience.

A panic began to engulf Chris regarding his future. Years earlier he
had decided to become a priest. Now he was nearing the end of high
school, when he should be making plans to enter the seminary. Yet the
foundations of his faith were rocking beneath him.

At the same time he was experiencing this crisis of conscience, the
nightly news was haunting him in a different way.

• •

The revulsion toward war and what he saw as its roots that had
begun to flower in his mind was fertilized by the drumbeat of the
televised casualty reports from Vietnam and his reading of history
books and biographies that he brought home from the school library.
Chris concluded that Vietnam was part of a long continuum of history:
they were all the same, from Carthage to the Central Highlands, mindless wars of man butchering man for idiotic concepts of patriotic pride.

36

Just as he had begun to suspect he had been hoodwinked by the nuns and priests, Chris began to wonder if he had been betrayed also by his country and its teachings of liberty and justice for all. He decided America was living a lie: its citizens *were* afforded liberty and freedom, but to protect these freedoms, didn't it encourage repressive dictatorships around the world where such freedoms were forbidden? Modern America, he decided, was like ancient Athens. It provided liberty and parasitic prosperity to its citizens while exploiting its empire of slaves on the Aegean.

In the recesses of his mind, Chris no longer thought of himself as an American. He rejected nationalism as a fundamental evil of mankind and as something that conflicted drastically with his—and, he felt, God's—vision of, and hope for, One World, a "universal state." That state, Chris hoped, would come someday, but not before there was a final battle of nationalistic giants.

. .

As Chris continued to develop his own concepts of the world, he realized that he was growing farther and farther apart from his father. By the end of his senior year he felt they agreed on very little. They still shared a love for history and sports and tradition, and they continued to go fishing together regularly in the High Sierras, and his father never missed seeing a game in which Chris competed. Theirs was never a stormy father–son relationship. Chris could recall being spanked by his father only once in his life, and there were seldom harsh words between them. But there were few overt signs of affection between them, either. Chris had become his mother's son.

Eventually, Chris would reject virtually all of the attitudes of nationalism and patriotism that were so fundamental to his father. But for the most part, he kept his heresy to himself; no one knew how deep were the doubts that tormented him.

In June, 1971, Chris was graduated from Rolling Hills High School, 367th in a class of 505, with plans to enroll the following September at Harbor College, a two-year, blue-collar college in the port town of Wilmington, not far from the base of The Hill. When his parents asked what he intended to do with his life, Chris said he had two possible careers in mind—the priesthood and law.

But Mrs. Boyce was worried. She had noticed that he had begun to miss Mass, and occasionally doubts about some aspect of the Church

surfaced in his conversations with her. She decided to seek the advice of Monsignor McCarthy, for whom she had a special reverence, and the compassionate priest quieted her doubts.

"Look, Noreen," he said. "These are turbulent times he's going through; don't worry. It happens to a lot of young men; there was a time I wouldn't go near a church when I was young either. Chris will come back."

• •

When he was frustrated about his faith or his future, Chris retreated to falconry. It became not only a hobby but an obsession that consumed his every spare moment. He devoured every book he could find on falconry and plunged into its history, lore and traditions with the fervor of a religious zealot. To Chris falconry was a bridge to ancient history; in his fantasies he began to see himself as part of a continuum that had begun with kings in Persia, Egypt, China and medieval England. Flying a falcon in exactly the same way that men had done centuries before Christ transplanted Chris into their time. His greatest pleasure was to trap a passage (a falcon in its first season and juvenile plumage) that had followed its parents from the eyrie and learned to hunt and then coax it to become his own partner in the hunt. It was a strange transaction: a man offering himself to a bird. It usually began with an offer of the warm breast of a partridge or pigeon to the tethered bird; a quick, cautious jump to the wrist and then a slow courtship and free flight; and finally a kind of marriage between man and animal.

Daulton never shared the full intensity of Chris's passion for falconry, but the sport was a bond that kept them together long after other classmates drifted away and found new interests off The Hill. If it had not been for this bond they would probably have gone their separate ways. Instead, the two friends spent one or two weekends a month traveling to the Mojave Desert of California and into the mountains beyond to photograph birds, set traps and take turns holding a rope while the other, the rope tied to his waist, descended a cliff to inspect the eyrie of a bird. And when the day was over, they usually lit up a joint and passed it between them. It was in these moments at the end of the day that Chris loved to let his mind roam: he imagined how a falcon must feel as it soared above him with eyes so powerful they could find a tiny prairie dog scooting through sagebrush from two thousand feet; or how the bird felt in a stoop, diving at 150 miles an

hour at a helpless pigeon. As the vapors of the drug eased into his lungs, setting in motion a biochemical chain reaction in his brain, Chris retreated even deeper into his fantasies. He imagined himself a Renaissance prince flying a huge falcon while wearing flowing robes of satin. And then he might turn to a different fantasy—a vision of himself flying his falcon while dressed in a tuxedo. One day, he told Daulton, he would do just that.

7

"ANDREW DAULTON LEE?"

"Yes," the defendant replied.

Daulton looked up at Judge Allen Miller of the Los Angeles County Superior Court in Torrance, California, on February 4, 1972. The previous October, he had been busted for selling marijuana to a high school student. The district attorney's office had reduced the charge to possession—rather than sale—of a marijuana cigarette. But it was a serious offense nonetheless.

Three years later, the California Legislature would downgrade possession of small amounts of marijuana to a misdemeanor. It would be treated no more seriously than a traffic ticket. But when Daulton went to court, the stigma that had cloaked marijuana use for so long in middle-class America had not yet dissolved. Possession of marijuana was a felony, punishable by a year in prison or more.

Still, the winds were changing; the courts had seen hundreds of young men and women like Daulton, many of them from the well-off families of the Palos Verdes Peninsula, brought up on drug charges. The early ones had gone to prison. But society was beginning to question whether the punishment being meted out fitted the crime.

Judge Miller glanced at the stubby young man before him who had been convicted of possessing marijuana and noticed that he had no other arrests on his record. His lawyer appealed for a second chance, saying Daulton had just enrolled at Whittier College—a respected school whose alumni included Richard M. Nixon. If the judge was

lenient, the lawyer said, Daulton could start a new life at Whittier the following day.

"Full-time schooling in Whittier?" the judge asked.

"Full-time," the lawyer responded.

"Well, that's pretty good. Do you have a job—do you intend to have a job on the outside?"

"I intend to get a part-time job," Daulton said.

"I'll make this a misdemeanor by sentence," the judge said. "One year in County Jail."

Daulton's spirits plummeted. But then the judge added: "I'll suspend the sentence and place you on probation for a period of three years." There would be a $150 fine; an agreement that Daulton would have to avoid illicit drugs and drug users; periodic reports to probation officers—but no jail sentence.

"Mr. Lee, I don't know what the drug situation is out at Whittier. But if it comes to my attention, very frankly, that you continue to use marijuana or dangerous drugs, and it probably would if you had another bust, I can advise you that I'll give you at least six months in the County Jail for violation of probation. I'm just indicating to you that it may not be worth your while to continue to smoke marijuana."

Daulton looked at the judge as sincerely as he could and said he was off drugs for good.

• •

Daulton dropped out of Whittier the following spring, continuing the pattern he had begun on his graduation from Palos Verdes High two years earlier in June, 1970. During the two years, he had tried three colleges—Hancock and Whittier and Harbor, briefly—and a half-dozen jobs. He had started jobs as a deliveryman, as a telephone sales solicitor, as a cabinetmaker, as a shipping clerk and as a skin diver in a marina, where he helped clean and repair yachts. But none of the jobs paid nearly as much as he could make from pushing drugs. And the work was harder. Daulton liked full-time jobs even less than he liked college, and inevitably, he drifted back to what he knew best—drug dealing.

His arrest in October, 1971, had slowed the momentum of the entrepreneur from Palos Verdes. But soon after Judge Miller gave him probation, he went back to work trying to enlarge his business. And for a while he did very well indeed: by the summer of 1973, a year after

he left Whittier, Daulton had a drug business that was grossing $1,000 to $2,000 a week. Daulton had always had a streak of generosity, and now that he had really big money he was no different; most weeks, he spent hundreds of dollars throwing parties for friends at which he bought the drugs, and he could be counted on to pick up the tab for expensive dinners. One night he took three girls to a mosquelike Moroccan restaurant on Sunset Boulevard in Hollywood, seated them all around him on pillows resting on the floor and joked that he felt as if he had a harem. The bill for the night was almost $250.

He slept until eleven or so most mornings, showered, made a few phone calls to his runners and then played handball or tennis for an hour or two. There'd be a few sales in the afternoon, then dinner at a restaurant near the Peninsula, and a party at night, and at three or four he'd get to bed. Every few weeks there was a trip to Mexico or San Diego, just across the border from Mexico, to replenish his inventory. It was a period that Daulton would recall later with the kind of affectionate nostalgia that people reserve for recounting the best years of their lives:

"It was before the era of the rip-off; I sold marijuana and hashish that was the finest in the world—hashish from Afghanistan, the finest flower tops from Mexico. I was selling weed at the time for a hundred and fifty dollars a pound when you could buy a kilo [2.2 pounds] for that much. People were telling me, You're out of your mind, you're overpriced. But within six months everybody was coming after me; they said they were willing to pay because I had the best product.

"I had a clientele you wouldn't believe: older, more sophisticated people. I had the best product, and the best, cleanest highs. And in those days you could trust the people you were dealing with. The way it was then, we were into getting high first, making a profit second. Later, the whole thing got out of proportion. It became cutthroat, rip-offs, anything goes. When I first got into it, well, it broke down to a very legitimate business; it was illegal, but it was a very legitimate kind of business."

Eventually, Daulton was admitted to The Brotherhood, a measure of social acceptance in his milieu at least equal to his parents' acceptance by the Palos Verdes Country Club. The Brotherhood was a drug cult founded by Dr. Timothy Leary, the onetime Harvard lecturer who in the late nineteen-sixties became an advocate of LSD and other drugs. Daulton would describe his association with The Brotherhood

later as almost a religious experience, with drugs as its god: "We were just a tightly knit group of people who were aligned in the distribution of a high quality of drug. We weren't talking about the overthrowing of governments; we were just talking about a different awareness, of viewing things from a different perspective. We didn't want to hurt anybody."

Except for Chris, Daulton was by now spurning former classmates who had opted to lead conventional lives. "It was hard to find anything in common with people who worked all day," he would explain. "They were all hooked to the grind of working eight to four, coming home, getting drunk every night, waking up with a hangover and going to work. I was sleeping late, playing handball, traveling; I had money, women when I wanted them; you couldn't ask for a better life."

Early in 1973, Daulton moved out of his parents' home into an apartment in Torrance, a city on the flatlands north of the Peninsula, with Aaron Johnson, another product of The Hill whose father earned $200,000 a year as vice president of a steel company. A muscular blond athlete who always had a string of girls pursuing him, Johnson, like Daulton, had abandoned college and was making his living by selling drugs. The two soon agreed to become partners. Daulton also formed an occasional partnership with Barclay Granger, another friend from Palos Verdes High.

On the last day of July, 1973, with business thriving and Daulton enjoying himself as never before, a shaggy youth with shoulder-length hair and an unkempt beard approached Johnson in a bar and said he wanted to buy ten pounds of marijuana. When the new customer later showed up at their apartment to pick up the weed, Johnson said he would go after the merchandise and left with an empty shopping bag for one of the places where he and Daulton stashed their inventory. Daulton stayed behind and was chatting with the new client when cops —so many he couldn't count them—shoved their way into the apartment. Suddenly, the new "customer" pulled out a revolver and announced he was a police officer. When Johnson returned, he and Daulton were taken to jail, and samples of marijuana, hashish, hashish oil and peyote found in Daulton's bedroom were seized by the police. Within two days, he and his friend posted bail of $5,000 apiece—not much money for the prosperous drug traffickers—and they were released. Unruffled, they resumed business as usual.

Four days later, the fourteen-year-old brother of Barclay Granger offered to sell a gram of cocaine to a bearded undercover policeman in

Huntington Beach, a town on the coast south of Long Beach. The policeman expressed delight at the quality of the cocaine, asked for more and arranged to buy an additional twenty-three grams for $1,300 on July 12. Granger's brother made the delivery, was arrested and led the police to his brother and Daulton, who had been using the fourteen-year-old as part of a cadre of youthful runners. Granger and Daulton quickly posted $10,000 each and were released on bail for the second time in two weeks.

Daulton had now been arrested twice while he was on probation for his 1971 arrest. His parents warned him that he would have to go to jail. Daulton said that the arrests, both of them, were a frame-up. "Don't worry," he said. "I'll beat it."

He was wrong.

"I beg the court to let me continue probation," Daulton wrote Judge Burch Donahue of the Los Angeles County Superior Court early in 1974. With the help of his attorney, Daulton had managed to postpone the moment of reckoning on the two new arrests for almost six months. But he had finally run out of delaying tactics and faced the revocation of his probation. He pleaded for mercy: "I have a deadly fear of the violence and homosexuality in jail; too many people have told me of it," he wrote.

But Judge Donahue, who had taken over Daulton's case from Judge Miller, said two felony arrests for selling dangerous drugs while the defendant was on probation was too much. He revoked Daulton's probation and sentenced him to serve one year in the Los Angeles County Jail's minimum-security work camp, the Wayside Honor Rancho.

If Daulton behaved himself, the judge said, he might consider a reduction in the sentence at some point in the future. But first, he said, Daulton would have to show a will to rehabilitate himself. Daulton entered the jail farm on March 7, 1974.

• •

While Daulton had plunged into drug dealing so profitably, convinced that he had found his life's calling, Chris was still groping for his direction in life. In January, 1972, he enrolled at Harbor Junior College—an episode of mononucleosis had made him miss the previous semester—and he earned a B-plus average, suggesting he had rediscovered some of his old academic prowess. But Chris, still unable to resolve his religious doubts, felt disoriented. In the summer of 1972,

he made a pact with himself: he would give the church one year; if it would save his faith, he would gladly become a priest.

He decided that the best place to resolve his doubts was under the influence of the Jesuits, the most intellectual of the religious orders. In September, 1972, he entered Loyola University, the Jesuit institution that his father had attended. If the Jesuits could subdue the devils that were nibbling at his beliefs, he told himself, he would enter the priesthood the following year and devote his life to God and the Church.

These were fast-moving times in America and in the world, and Chris continued to devour the news reports on television and in the newspapers. There were President Nixon's visit to China, the departure of the last American ground troops from South Vietnam and, from Chile, reports of troubles within the administration of President Salvador Allende. Chris avidly followed news of the presidential campaign and President Nixon's landslide victory over George McGovern and the reports beginning to emerge from Washington suggesting that the Nixon Administration might be attempting to hide some politically embarrassing secrets. There were other stories in the paper, although Chris did not notice all of them, including the dispatches from Australia noting that after twenty-three years of rule by the Liberal and National Country parties, the Labour Party, led by Edward Gough Whitlam, had been elected to run the country.

As Chris lost himself in texts on religious philosophy, metaphysics and history, the news began to turn increasingly sour. The nation's Vice President resigned after pleading no contest to accusations of tax evasion. Daniel Ellsberg and Anthony Russo were prosecuted for attempting to alert the public to corrupt policies pursued by the United States Government during the Vietnam War. There were reports that America had secretly bombed Cambodia. After the fall of the Allende government in Chile, there were ugly rumors that the Central Intelligence Agency might have had a hand in his death. And throughout the year, the cancer of Watergate continued to spread.

In June of 1973, Chris left Loyola. The experiment had failed. He told friends that he was now an agnostic. Once again, he told himself, he had to decide what he was going to do with the rest of his life.

• •

The following September, he found a happiness that had eluded him before. He enrolled at California Polytechnic State University in San

Luis Obispo, a semirural community about two hundred miles north of Los Angeles. Cal Poly was best known as an agricultural and technical school; it wasn't noted for history and prelaw studies, the curricula Chris selected. But he chose Cal Poly less for its academic strengths in these fields than for its proximity to Morro Bay, a town on the Pacific Coast twelve miles from the campus that was the site of a Federal sanctuary for peregrine falcons, which are among the largest and most prized of falcons. For Chris, it was a kind of earthly paradise. He would spend days at a time watching and photographing the birds.

The protected sanctuary was on Morro Rock, a giant monolith shaped like half an egg that rises out of the sea close to shore. He bought a rubber raft and rowed to the base of the rock to admire at close range the grace and ageless elegance of the predators and their instinctive skill so perfectly shaped by eons of evolution. He watched a pair of older birds train their young to hunt by killing a duck, picking it up and then dropping it in front of the young birds—an exercise that helped them to practice catching prey in midair. The coastal mountains behind Morro Bay were to Chris another refuge from what he increasingly thought of as the honky-tonk culture of Southern California orbiting around Los Angeles. He camped alone among the oaks and pines and studied prairie falcons nesting in the coastals, and thought, what better pursuit in life could there be than to study these birds? Professors in the History Department at Cal Poly encouraged him to apply for a Federal grant to finance a study of the history of falconry. The idea excited Chris. He envisaged an odyssey that would take him to Asia and Europe, to old castles, temples and archives, from the Pyrenees to above the Arctic Circle, where the great Arctic gyrfalcons flew. But the grant was not approved, and Chris, disappointed, decided to leave Cal Poly the following June. Gnawing at him was the implicit pressure that society wanted more out of him.

Several years later he would say of the year he spent on Morro Bay: "Why I didn't stay there I'll never know. I guess I was guilty about being so happy and felt that if I didn't at least try entering The Establishment I would have been forever locked in prejudices of my own making. How dumb."

•   •

After school ended in June, he told his parents that he'd decided to quit college for a while, bank some money and make some decisions.

Then he'd return to college in a year or two, probably to become a lawyer. His father said he would see what he could do about helping him to find a job. Maybe, he said, Chris might even find a job that he would like for its career possibilities and he could end his seemingly aimless wandering.

In the aerospace industry, as in many industries, there is a kind of informal "old boy network" that arranges jobs for the sons and daughters of members of the network. A company executive may not be able to hire his own son because it would invite charges of nepotism; but what is wrong in calling a friend who's an executive of another company and asking a favor? Such arrangements can work reciprocally without charges of nepotism.

Chris's father decided to ask a friend at the Hughes Aircraft Company if he might have any openings. But the friend, with an apology, said he couldn't help.

Then Chris's father called a friend who worked for TRW Defense and Space Systems Group in nearby Redondo Beach. This friend said he might be able to.

8 WHEN HIS FATHER TOLD HIM about the job, Chris didn't know what kind of work people did at the dozen or so buildings marked "TRW" that sprawled over a sizable portion of Redondo Beach, one of the coastal cities that hug the rim of the Pacific north of the Peninsula. The fathers of several of his friends in Palos Verdes had worked at TRW when he was in high school. But the only thing Chris recalled about the company was that it had something to do with computers or electronics—like a lot of the industries that provided work for fathers on The Hill.

To Chris it didn't matter what business the company was in. He just wanted to work awhile, save some money and, eventually, return to college. His father told him the job would probably be in the mail room —a boring prospect, Chris thought, but a satisfactory economic bridge

before going back to school and making a decision about what to do with his future.

In the middle of June, 1974, Chris made an appointment to see his father's friend. He drove to one of the several TRW compounds in Redondo Beach and presented himself at a reception desk; he signed his name on a visitor's card, and after a clerk made a telephone call to confirm his appointment he was given a badge allowing him to enter a limited portion of the plant under the guidance of an escort.

The complex looked much like the aerospace plant where his father worked—really more like a college campus than a factory. There were modern buildings fronting on wide expanses of grass and lots of trees; there were no smokestacks. On the top of several of the buildings were curious igloo-shaped white superstructures that puzzled Chris.

Inside the plant, he walked past rooms that seemed to stretch endlessly into the distance. Each room was illuminated by a ceiling of white fluorescent lights that glowed without shadows and seemed to sap the room of any color; inside each room there was a panorama of bobbing heads hunched over engineering drawing boards. Elsewhere in the plant, there were cavernous rooms with high ceilings, cranes and men in overalls working on glittering metallic hardware of the space age, seemingly without dust, dirt, grease or smoke.

The interview went well. His father's friend was a husky, warm man in his late forties who wore horn-rimmed glasses. The man had a lot in common with his father: he lived on The Hill, had a big family—eight children—and had served in the FBI. The man even knew Chris's uncle; they had served together in the bureau. The gregarious, beefy administrator liked the sober and intelligent youth sitting before him. He told Chris that the chances were good he could have a job at TRW, but first he would have to go through the usual Personnel Department application procedures; and he would have to pass a routine Government security check.

When Chris left his office, the TRW executive already knew exactly what job Chris was to have. But he didn't say anything about it, and Chris was not to know what was on his mind for another four months.

•   •

On July 16, Chris sat at a table in a TRW personnel office, a job application before him, and with a ball-point pen filled in his name, address, date of birth, educational background and job history (two

47

jobs as a janitor, one as a pizza cook, one as a waiter and another as a liquor delivery boy), listed the members of his family and gave several neighbors as references. At the bottom of the application was a request:

"Tell us anything else about your work interests, experience, abilities, or career interests which may be helpful in evaluating your qualifications. Include any special skills such as typing and shorthand speeds, business machines, etc."

Chris answered with candor, admitting he was job hunting at TRW only as a brief expedient before taking up more important things:

"I am delaying my prelaw studies at Cal Poly, San Luis Obispo," he wrote, "for financial reasons and seek employment to correct this situation, determined to work until September, 1976. I am also a licensed California falconer presently flying an Accipiter Cooper."

. .

Two days after Chris wrote out his job application at TRW, Andrew Daulton Lee sat down at the Wayside Honor Rancho and wrote an application of a different kind.

In pencil Daulton carefully printed a message to Judge Burch Donahue of the Los Angeles County Superior Court:

"The reason for my request for a modification in my sentence is for an education purpose. I feel the time I have spent here has given me mental as well as a physical advantage in returning to an educational pursuit. I am aware that my incarceration has helped me to evaluate my life and made it possible for me to formulate plans for the future. I was majoring in business and economics at the time of my sentencing and I would like to be able to return to school this upcoming semester."

Daulton listed his occupation on the application as "scuba diver and cabinet maker."

At Wayside, Daulton had taught some of the other prisoners some of the things he knew about woodworking. Fellow prisoners also taught him some wrinkles about drug dealing that he hadn't known before, and most important, he had met some people who promised to help him make a connection with major drug wholesalers in Mexico, something he had been trying to do for four years.

. .

Christopher John Boyce went to work for TRW on July 29, 1974. His title: General Clerk. His salary: $140 a week. He was twenty-one years old.

On his first day at work, he was photographed and fingerprinted, completed more forms from the Personnel Department and was given a security badge for admission to the plant. The picture on the badge was of a smiling, untroubled young man looking out curiously through a slick plastic film, the kind of picture that might have been taken by an automated camera in an amusement-park arcade.

As he was processed through the Personnel Department, he was handed brochures describing the company's health-insurance and pension programs, a statement of policy on holidays and days off, and a wallet-sized booklet designed to explain to new employees the espionage laws of the United States. Along with other "new-hires" who had joined TRW that Monday, he was summoned to a classroom for a security briefing. They were told that working in a defense plant would seem different to them from any place where they had worked before. Badges were required to get onto the plant premises and should never be lost; no personal guests were allowed, and official visitors had to be approved by Security and be escorted when they were on the plant premises. It was possible, they were told, that they would have to deal with sensitive defense information, and for this reason an in-depth government security check would be made on each of them. Above all, they were told, their work at TRW would be guided by the fundamental rule of the defense industry in protecting sensitive information—the "need to know" rule. It stated: only persons with a specific, job-related *requirement* to know about certain classified work would be given access to it; to others, even in the same office, the information would be off limits. This rule, the new-hires were told, was essential to prevent the spread of secrets.

The briefing completed, Chris was handed a piece of paper on which he acknowledged he had been advised of these rules. "I shall not knowingly and willfully communicate, deliver or transmit in any manner classified information to an unauthorized person or agency," he pledged.

His first assignment was in Classified Material Control, a department responsible for regulating the flow of secret documents through the plant. Many documents, he was told, had to be locked in safes and could be taken out only with the signatures of a handful of designated

people given need-to-know authority. These documents could be transported within the plant only by armed guards. Precise records, his supervisor explained, had to be kept each time one of the secret documents was examined by anyone; the movement and second-by-second location of the data, which ran into tens of thousands of documents, were logged in computers and monitored. It was a dull job, mostly paper shuffling. Chris was not cleared to handle the documents themselves; he helped record their movement around the plant and processed applications for security clearances and issued badges.

On the first Friday after he started work, Chris received a notice to report to Building E-2 at 8:30 A.M. for another briefing. Other new employees hired that week crowded with him into a classroom, and a young woman appeared at the front of the room and introduced herself.

"Good morning," she said. "I am here to present the extremely important subject of industrial security, a subject which is of mutual interest and concern to you and me.

"Why? Because, one, as citizens of the United States we have a moral responsibility to protect the government's classified information; and two, as employees of TRW Systems Group, we are bound by a security agreement that obligates TRW to the Department of Defense to protect and safeguard classified information generated by or furnished TRW in the performance of its many classified contracts.

"You might respond to my vindication on security by stating that our formidable military strength should deter the aggressive efforts of the Soviet and satellite nations," she said. "I agree.

"But the security provided by the Air Force's Strategic Air Command, the Army's Special Forces, the Navy's Polaris missiles and the Marine Corps's readiness is a defense against an overt and outright attack." What the employees of TRW and other defense contractors must guard against, the voice droned on, is "an insidious effort by Communist agents to get government secrets that are covert." And she began to list examples of how careless, foolish Americans had been duped by Soviet agents.

"One individual worked for Convair in San Diego," the young woman said. "He had been contacted and agreed to furnish secrets for a price. The FBI got on to him after a while, but couldn't figure out how he was getting the volumes of material out. It was one of those plants that you don't carry anything in without having it searched and you fill out thirty forms to carry something out, and then copies go to everyone from the president to the janitor.

"His way was a simple one: he ran Xerox copies and put them in a contractor's envelope, prepared a contractor's label and mailed them to his contact on the East Coast via the company mail. He slipped up, though, when he put a wrong address on one package and it was returned marked, 'No such address.' They opened it to see who it was from and found classified information. And they nailed him.

"Russians use all sorts of gimmicks to get acquainted with Americans," she said. "They cultivate their friendship and then use them in whatever manner possible." She told the new employees about a woman who worked "at a local defense plant" who went to West Germany on a vacation in 1966 and was befriended by a "local German boy when she stopped into a local beer garden to sample the beer." When the woman returned to Los Angeles, the security-briefing officer continued, a Russian exchange student in this country tried to contact her, but "fortunately the girl reported the incident to Security."

When the lecture was over, the new TRW employees watched a film reinforcing the warnings of Communist agents: *Security Is Your Responsibility*. Chris then signed another document acknowledging that he had seen the film and had been advised of America's espionage laws and of the menace of Communist agents.

• •

On the day Chris was hired, TRW granted him access to "confidential" defense information, as was the standard procedure for new employees in the defense industry. Confidential is the lowest of the three basic levels of classification used by the United States to guard military information. It is information deemed less sensitive than "Secret" or "Top Secret" data.

Although his father's friend had still not told him, he had bigger things in store for Chris than a Confidential clearance.

Chris received a new set of forms to complete in early August, asking for further information about his past. Once again, he listed his name, his place and date of birth and his parents' place and date of birth. But this time he gave a detailed description of each of the jobs he had held. He gave his physical description—five feet eight inches tall; 150 pounds; brown hair, blue eyes; he noted that he was a member of no organizations, that he had never traveled outside the United States and that he had no relatives residing out of the country. It was the biography of a young high school graduate without anything very distinctive about it.

On August 8, unbeknownst to Chris, these forms and copies of other papers collected in his file during the processing of his application were placed in a pouch and sent to Langley, Virginia. The destination was the Central Intelligence Agency.

Federal investigators had already begun to look into Chris's childhood, his high school years and his tentative tries at college. Government agents interviewed neighbors of the Boyces' in Palos Verdes and sent questionnaires to his former employers. Except for indications of drift in his life—three colleges in three years and seven jobs in two years—there wasn't much to draw attention to the young man for those preparing his security-clearance file.

The investigation uncovered no criminal record and determined that Chris had a good credit rating. A neighbor who taught school in Los Angeles was interviewed and, the investigator reported, gave Chris the highest praise. "He has known subject Boyce approximately 18 years" and "vouches for subject's integrity and knows of no reason why subject could not get a Government clearance."

Apparently, no one during the investigation mentioned Chris's affection for marijuana. Or if anyone *did* mention it, perhaps the investigators concluded that occasional use of marijuana had become so common that it was not enough reason to deny a security clearance to an otherwise qualified young man. The investigation of Christopher John Boyce was perhaps as thorough a look into the background of a twenty-one-year-old from one of America's most privileged environments that his country could expect, except for one thing: it did not look into his mind and discover the conflicts and disillusionment that were bedeviling him.

• •

Judge Burch Donahue, who had been crippled as a youth, rolled his wheelchair into a courtroom in the Los Angeles County Superior Court annex in Torrance on September 6. Before him was Daulton's hand-printed note from the Wayside Honor Rancho. Trying to look harmless, Daulton was sitting with his lawyer, Kenneth Kahn, who quickly launched into a persuasive appeal to the judge on behalf of his client: Daulton had spent six months at Wayside, he said, and he had no bad marks on his record. Now he deserved a second chance and wanted to enter Harbor College, the junior college below The Hill that Chris had attended for a semester. He reminded the judge that he had said at

Daulton's last hearing that he might be released early if his behavior was good in prison.

"I did indicate that back in February, with reference to schooling, as long as the conduct was satisfactory," Donahue acknowledged.

"I want the young man to understand this: I want a copy of his class schedule at Harbor, and I expect fifteen units *plus*. Do you understand that, young man? Some fellows enroll and quit as soon as I let them go to school. . . ."

"Yes," Daulton replied.

"So the modification will be granted as to time served. All other terms and conditions are to remain the same."

The months at Wayside hadn't been wasted, Daulton told his parents. He said he'd made some new friends and had had some time to work with his hands in the prison woodshop.

Once Daulton was out of jail, however, he lost no time in going back to his old business.

• •

The same week Daulton was released from jail, Chris passed his initial security check at TRW.

A few days later, while he was visiting the Lee house on a Saturday night after a day of flying hawks in the desert, Mrs. Lee asked Chris what he was doing on his new job. "I push papers around and sweep the floors," he said.

On the job, Chris's politeness and intelligence and his willingness to work were already impressing his superiors at TRW. On September 24, the company was informed by the Department of Defense that it had approved Christopher John Boyce, Badge No. 6944S, for access to Secret information.

This broadened the contributions Chris could make in Classified Material Control, but he still regarded the job as boring. Besides, it wasn't yielding as much money as he wanted. He wanted more money —not only for school the next year, but to buy a sports car, a British Triumph roadster. In mid-October, a friend told him about a part-time job that was open in Westchester, a community on the edge of Los Angeles International Airport not far from Loyola University. The job, tending bar in a pool hall, paid only $60 a week for four hours a night or so. But figuring this would bring his total weekly pretax income to a respectable $200 a week, he took it.

53

Chris was a quick study and a good listener. He deduced from remarks made by one of the secretaries in the office that TRW had a different job in mind for him eventually, but nobody would give him the details when he brought up the subject.

Early in November, TRW received a classified message from the CIA. It said that Christopher John Boyce had been cleared for a Special Projects Briefing.

On November 15, he was summoned to Building M-4, and for the first time he heard about Project Rhyolite and the Black Vault.

9 "RHYOLITE IS A MULTIPURPOSE covert electronic surveillance system. . . ."

Chris's head felt ready to burst. His muscles tingled, and every neuron in his body was supersensitized to what was happening around him. Before leaving home he had swallowed two amphetamine tablets. "Whites" had been a casual element of his life since high school. But lately he wasn't using pep pills only to get high; he needed them to stay awake. Without the pills, he couldn't keep alert after a long night of tending bar. His moonlighting job was becoming more and more tiresome; some nights he spent more time breaking up fights among the customers than he did drawing glasses of beer for them.

That morning, he had been told that he was being given another assignment and would have to undergo a special briefing for the new position. He had been instructed to report to Section 1986 in Building M-4—a building conspicuously off limits to most TRW employees. Situated between a big expanse of parking lots and rolling green parkland, the M-4 complex consisted of a low, mint-green-colored building and a towering concrete-gray annex topped by one of those big white igloos that mystified Chris.

He was about to discover what was under the igloo.

He obtained a special pass to show at two guard checkpoints before reaching Section 1986, a cluster of offices in M-4. The briefing began,

and Chris struggled to dampen the drug-induced sense of euphoria. The briefing officer was Larry Rogers, whose comings and goings around the plant had had a quality of mystery; something to do with a classified project.

In a voice that lowered noticeably as he began, Rogers told Chris that the work in this section of the plant involved secret projects, and he explained that Chris had been specially cleared by the government to work on them.

Chris, noticing what he thought was a curious glint of suspicion in Rogers' eyes, wondered if Rogers knew he was high; he tried to look straight ahead and concentrate.

Rogers ordered Chris never to discuss with anyone the briefing he was about to give; never to divulge to anyone the existence of the projects of which he was about to hear, or discuss with anyone the kind of work he was to do; and never to mention to anyone not cleared for the projects their code names or the fact that they were clandestine operations of the Central Intelligence Agency.

In fact, he ordered, never mention to anyone—his family, his girl-friends, any outsiders—that the CIA had any relationship whatsoever with TRW, or that his salary was being paid by the CIA under a contract with TRW. *What the hell is he talking about?* Chris wondered.

Rogers then introduced Chris to what he called "the black world. . . ."

Orbiting satellites, he went on, were to a large extent taking over much of the work of human spies for the United States. And, he continued, TRW was one of a handful of American companies in the business of developing and manufacturing the satellites used by the CIA to collect secret intelligence information from space. Chris, he said, had been selected to serve on the team that operated some of these satellites. . . .

•   •

Chris had stumbled into one of the most secret of all American espionage operations—an invisible intelligence bureaucracy supervised from the White House by the National Security Council and entrusted with the responsibility to ferret out and analyze secrets about the Soviet Union, China and other countries. Cameras carried in the satellites could photograph missile bases, airfields, submarine pens, harbors and other defense installations from a hundred miles or more in space with such clarity that they could pinpoint a single man walking

alone on a vast desert. Sensors in the satellites were not blinded by the dark; radar eyes and heat-sensing infrared sensors penetrated clouds and dark skies and made photos almost as sharp as those made during a clear day by normal cameras.

The espionage bureaucracy of which Chris had become a part was officially invisible because the United States did not admit it existed. Thousands of people worked on this national program to gather strategic intelligence information, each with a special security clearance more exclusive than Top Secret, and with special security apparatus designed solely for the satellite systems to ensure that Russian agents or spies of other countries couldn't penetrate it. Men and women assigned to the operation were forbidden to admit to anyone without a similar clearance—including their wives and husbands—that they worked on the program or, indeed, that such satellite surveillance even occurred. There were occasional discreet official references to some of the agencies that were involved in the operation, such as the National Reconnaissance Office or the Committee of 40, a group of senior government officials with authority to order espionage operations and plan satellite missions. But such mentions were rare and usually purposefully opaque. It was the position of the CIA that in an era when annihilation of the United States was potentially only minutes away—the time it would take for a fusillade of nuclear missiles to lunge from Russia, arc through the fringes of space and rain H-bombs on America —no intelligence operation was more vital than the satellite patrols in space, because they enabled the National Security Council and the President to maintain minute-by-minute surveillance of Soviet military operations and preparations for war and, hopefully, prevent a surprise attack. (The satellite eyes were not turned off after they passed over the Soviet and Chinese borders; indeed, they could—and did—take photos of activities in any country of interest to the NSC.)

A new breed of spy—a robot in space—had been created, and Chris was now about to help operate it from the earth.

There were essentially three components in the national satellite intelligence-collection system that, to enhance secrecy, were narrowly compartmentalized so that specialists working in one area wouldn't, under normal circumstances, have access to secrets involving the other elements. One component was assigned to build and operate the satellites; the second was responsible for collecting and initially processing the data (the "product" in CIA parlance) sent to earth by the satellites;

56

the third was a massive, on-the-ground program to analyze the data to measure their military, economic or political significance. There were more than a dozen different types of satellites, each with its own project code name, mission and method of operating; each system might have three or four or more different satellites peering down from space ◀ at any one time, each sending back "product" for analysis. The code name that was applied to encompass the extraordinarily tight security procedures for all of these different systems was "Byeman."

During the briefing, Chris smiled after Rogers kept referring to the satellites as "birds." The word was like a switch. It made his thoughts drift as if they had been lifted up on the wings of his falcon with its darting eyes that could spot a rabbit trying to find shade beneath the flimsy shadow of a desert cactus; and then he thought of the satellite: men watching men using eyes in space. It was Big Brother, a 1984 world. A "byeman" is a man who works underground—and that was what Chris had become.

• •

Project Rhyolite (RH was the code preferred for everyday use) was one of the systems in the family of intelligence-collection satellites developed by the United States. It had been developed by TRW to eavesdrop electronically on foreign countries, especially the eastern Soviet Union, China and Soviet missile test ranges in the Pacific. It was a "bug"—much like the listening devices detectives plant on telephones to eavesdrop on private conversations—except that it was a listening device on the missile-launching tests of the two countries and on their telecommunications system—and on several other nations whose communications traffic the United States might want to monitor.

Chris was to learn that each satellite carried a battery of antennas capable of sucking foreign microwave signals from out of space like a vacuum cleaner picking up specks of dust from a carpet: American intelligence agents could monitor Communist microwave radio and long-distance telephone traffic over much of the European landmass, eavesdropping on a Soviet commissar in Moscow talking to his mistress in Yalta or on a general talking to his lieutenants across the great continent; a computer was programmed to hunt electronically for certain key words or phrases of special interest to U.S. agents, who could use the satellite to pinpoint Soviet and Chinese defense radar systems

and learn the frequencies, pulse rate and other specifications of the radar systems that would be vital if the United States ever wanted to jam the transmitters during a war; and equally important, the satellites provided the means to monitor tests of the latest Communist ballistic missiles, including the newest multiple-warhead systems and defense-penetration devices, by intercepting telemetry signals from the missiles that were intended for Soviet engineers on the ground. Data from Soviet satellites could also be intercepted.

Chris was told he had been assigned to work in a communications vault that was the nerve center for this system of international espionage—a code room linking the TRW plant with CIA Headquarters and Rhyolite's major ground stations in Australia. The continuing disclosures about the secret world fascinated Chris, and he was especially intrigued by what he saw as a bizarre contrast between the mechanical spies he had been told about and the location of the ground stations. The Rhyolite earth stations had been planted in a world that was about as close as man could find now to the Stone Age; they were situated near Alice Springs in the harsh Outback of Australia, an oasis in a desert where aborigines still lived much as Stone Age men did thousands of years ago.

Under an Executive Agreement between the United States and Australia, Chris was told, all intelligence information collected by the satellites and relayed to the network of dish-shaped microwave antennas at Alice Springs was to be shared with the Australian intelligence service.

However, Rogers told Chris, the United States, by design, was not living up to the agreement: certain information was *not* being passed to Australia. He explained that TRW was designing a new, larger satellite with a new array of sensors; the Australians, Rogers emphasized, were never to be told about it; anytime Chris sent messages that would reach Australia, he must delete any reference to the new satellite.

Its name was Argus, or AR—for Advanced Rhyolite. Whoever in the CIA had selected the cryptonym must have enjoyed his choice, because it was appropriate. In Greek mythology, Argus was a giant with one hundred eyes . . . a vigilant guardian. With its array of sensors, the Central Intelligence Agency's Argus was mythology's giant brought to reality. It is not known whether the author of the code name knew the mythological fate of Argus. Ultimately Argus was slain by Hermes, the god of commerce, cunning and theft . . . the patron of thieves and rogues.

Chris was vaguely troubled by the revelation that one of America's closest allies was being deceived by the U.S. Government, but he let the thought slip away and accepted an invitation to go to lunch with some of the other TRW employees assigned to Rhyolite. The group included Rogers; Gene Norman, a thin, balding black man, and Fred Young, a taciturn engineer who he later learned was a former CIA agent who had been assigned to the agency's secret war in Laos and had used his pull in the organization to get a job on the TRW program when the war ended. Chris realized the lunch was to be a celebration of sorts, to mark his induction into their secret society.

His mind was still numb from the effects of the "whites" as he crowded with the others around a table at The Hangar, a dimly lit beer joint two blocks from M-4 that was a hangout for TRW workers. Hamburgers were ordered along with a pitcher of beer. The pitcher was soon empty, and they ordered one after another. Like lodge brothers introducing a new member to some of the inner secrets of their private fraternity, the older men gave Chris their observations about various bosses on the project, some opinions about the CIA residents who worked undercover at TRW and some thoughts on the women in M-4. Someone mentioned Laurie Vicker.

"She'll screw anybody; be careful," Norman said with a laugh, and the others leered agreement. "She's kinky," Rogers added, as if it were a warning, and Chris wondered what he meant specifically.

All four began to feel the effects of the beer after a while, but Norman was the least successful in concealing it. Slurring his words, he devoted ten minutes to recounting how, when he was in Vietnam, he and another Marine had raped a woman near a paddy field while her husband was kept back at rifle point. Chris had heard of such incidents, but never at first hand. He sat back with his glass of beer cradled between his hands and stared at the stranger as he added further details to his spicy narrative. What kind of group have I gotten into?, Chris asked himself.

By the time they arrived back at the plant, the four men had finished seven or eight—nobody was sure—pitchers of beer. Each paid extra attention to the challenge of not stumbling as they walked past the guards.

• •

After lunch it was time for Chris to see the Black Vault.

Concealed in an obscure cluster of offices in M-4, it was a tiny

59

fortress within a fortress that was separated from the rest of the plant by a steel vault door—the same kind, Chris noted, that banks used. Beneath the floor and around the vault, he was told, were thick blankets of concrete, and the vault door could be opened only with a three-number combination known by three people; even knowing the combination did not ensure entry, because behind the main door was another door that required a key.

The vault was located beyond a wall of an office used for processing classified data that was decorated in aerospace-industry bland, with squares of asphalt tile on the floor; wall panels painted turquoise; ceilings surfaced with squares of acoustical tile and the omnipresent fluorescent lights.

Seated at a desk near the vault door Chris saw a girl of about thirty with coarse black hair that seemed to have been combed recently without much effect. She was plump, with a large bosom, but not pretty enough to warrant a second glance. She was a "systems analyst"—an expert, he was told, on computers. Norman led Chris over to the desk and introduced him to Laurie Vicker. As they shook hands, Laurie looked Chris over, and a shameless look of interest flickered in her eyes that didn't escape him.

Off to one side of this office, Chris noticed a long room with walls lined with filing cabinets, each with a locked steel bar running down the center.

Beside the khaki-colored door of the vault, signs warned, NO ADMITTANCE, and RESTRICTED AREA: ENTRY BY PERMISSION ONLY. A smaller notice ordered no one to enter the vault without a clearance, and there was a sign-up sheet on which persons entering or leaving the vault were required to log the time.

Only six people were cleared for access to the vault, Chris was told, and he was to be one of them. People called it the Black Vault, Norman explained, because Black was a catchall term the intelligence community applied to any covert intelligence operation; Air Force officers assigned to the project, for example, called themselves the "Black Air Force"; "spooks" was another affectionate expression for operatives on CIA projects. Another TRW employee translated another euphemism; whenever "Special Programs" or "Special Project" was mentioned, it was likely to involve espionage.

It was time to enter the vault.

Chris was led past the threshold and discovered a room that was

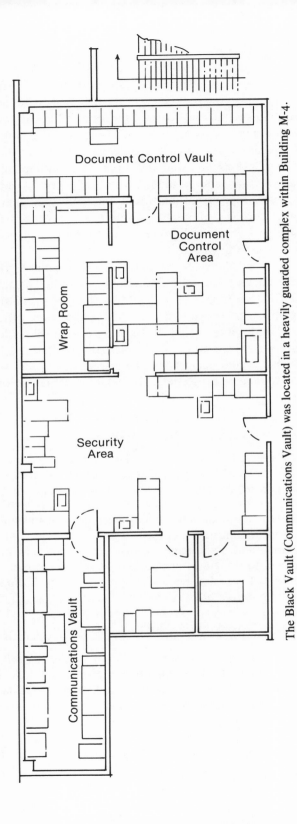

Document Control Vault

Document
Control
Area

Wrap Room

Security
Area

Communications Vault

The Black Vault (Communications Vault) was located in a heavily guarded complex within Building M-4.

long and narrow—maybe fifteen feet long, no more than five feet across. Flimsy red carpeting covered the floor; the dropped ceiling was veneered with sound-absorbent tile; folders, binders and books were stacked around the room in no apparent order. There were also a floor safe and several filing cabinets, two clocks showing *different* times of day, a table and a chair. Along one wall was a machine that looked to Chris like a teletype machine, and on the opposite wall were two similar machines with keyboards. About midway in the vault was a set of drapes that prevented anyone who might be walking by from seeing in when the vault door was open, and also provided a barrier between two people working within the vault.

Norman said Chris would have to have a "Crypto Briefing" from the National Security Agency before he worked in the vault. The NSA outranked even the CIA when it came to dealing with the transmission of classified information, he explained, and the NSA briefing officer wouldn't be at the plant until next month. Because of that, he added, he couldn't tell him everything about operations in the vault.

At the close of what would seem later like a long day, Chris was handed a two-page statement by Rogers. The statement, CIA Form 2441, read:

SPECIAL PROJECT SECRECY AGREEMENT

I acknowledge that I have been indoctrinated in the Project identified below and thus have received highly classified information related to United States intelligence collection activities. I am aware that the unauthorized disclosure or negligent handling of such information could seriously affect the national defense and that the transmission or revelation of such information to unauthorized persons could subject me to prosecution under the Espionage Laws. I have been informed that approval for access to Project information may only be granted by Project Headquarters. I have also been informed that extraordinary security measures and controls have been established to protect Project information and that access to such information is restricted to those who "must know" based on their present position or functional use.

I realize that a briefing of this scope and depth, which identifies sponsorship, reveals codewords and admits to the ultimate intelligence application of the Project, is given only to those individuals who have been specifically approved for the above identified Project at the high-

est level and that this type of information may not be divulged to individuals with lesser levels of access.

Having reviewed the above security requirements, I pledge that I will never publish or reveal, by any means, classified Project information to unauthorized persons. Along with this pledge, I recognize and accept the fact that I have a personal and individual responsibility for the protection of all such information in my possession no matter where generated or how acquired and agree to abide by the security requirements and regulations established for the Project.

There was an additional pledge not to visit Communist countries without prior approval. The agreement concluded by identifying Projects Rhyolite and Argus as the subjects of the security agreement. Chris signed it, and the agreement itself was marked SECRET.

Just before quitting time, Norman gave him one more quick tour of the vault. He spun the combination of the Diebold floor safe and reached in and showed Chris a handful of papers that he said contained codes for the cipher equipment the NSA was to brief him about later.

"These are probably worth twenty thousand dollars a month to the Russians," he boasted, a conspiratorial grin on his face. Chris just looked at the ciphers, not knowing what response was expected of him. He decided the black man was a braggart.

After work, Chris found his Volkswagen in the parking lot. But before getting in, he decided to puff a joint. He lit up one that had been in the car and watched the passing crowds of TRW workers, not yet sure that he liked the aerospace industry.

He spotted Laurie Vicker in the crowd walking toward him, and as she approached, looking for her car, a flash of recognition appeared in her eyes. She recognized the odor of the smoke coiling out of the joint, smiled at Chris and kept on walking.

The next day Laurie was wearing a low-cut dress that revealed a substantial panorama of cleavage. Before noon, she came into the vault; Chris was momentarily by himself, and she invited him to have lunch with her at her boyfriend's apartment; the boyfriend was out of town working, she explained, with an inviting smile.

Chris couldn't avoid admiring her breasts as she leaned over the desk where he was working. But there was something coarse about her that subdued any lust he might have felt. He declined the invitation— the first of many she would tender, even after she got married.

10 ON DECEMBER 12, 1974, a National Security Agency officer arrived from Washington and began to brief Chris on the crypto equipment. Secret messages, he explained, sometimes had to be broadcast over the open airwaves, which meant foreign agents could intercept them. The United States was able to prevent potential enemies from discovering the contents of its most private military and diplomatic messages, he continued, by using a highly sophisticated system of classified codes and transmission methods developed by the NSA. The secrets, he emphasized, were secure only as long as the methods used to encode and decode them were secure. Thus, he went on, extreme precautions had to be taken to protect the communication methods and the codes. The Government, he continued, had established a level of security clearance for people assigned to work with the crypto systems that was even more selective than Top Secret, and Chris had been approved for this most exclusive of clearances.

The NSA officer then launched into an explanation of how the system worked.

Computers, he said, now did most of the work of encoding and decoding. Before messages were released to the airwaves, telephone lines or teletype circuits, the computers scrambled them into a kaleidoscopic babel of electronic pulses. They were so complex that would-be code breakers would have to analyze millions of possible combinations of signals before finding a pattern. The coding instructions for the encryption machines were the most precious secrets about the system. He showed Chris a list of numbers; it was marked TOP SECRET/NOFORN, which he said meant no distribution to any foreign countries. This key list, he said, was used in setting the codes on the machine; the coding instructions—called ciphers—were changed daily by all of the stations using the system, and they all had copies of the same designated code for each day. The broadcast frequencies on which the messages were transmitted also were changed frequently.

64

The official instructed Chris in how to operate the communications gear in the Black Vault, and, despite an acute absence of mechanical aptitude, he caught on quickly: after all, it was about as easy as using a typewriter.

When the briefing was over, Chris signed an agreement pledging not to divulge to anyone the crypto information he had been given. Incredible as it would seem later, the $140-a-week college dropout now possessed a Top Secret clearance from the Department of Defense, a Strategic Intelligence–Byeman clearance from the CIA and a crypto clearance from the NSA; they would give him access to the nation's most secret cryptographic systems and some of its most secret espionage operations. He was three months short of his twenty-second birthday.

•   •

Over the next few months, Chris began to learn more about the history of TRW and the new world that he had entered. It was a world that, for the most part, had come into being in 1952, one year before he was born.

American intelligence agents that year began to receive disquieting reports from agents in Eastern Europe that the Soviet Union, initially with the help of captured Nazi scientists, was developing rockets capable of hurling a payload weighing several hundred pounds over a distance of several thousand miles.

U.S. officials suspected that the Russians were also trying to develop a hydrogen bomb. The possibility that sometime soon the Soviets would be able to rocket H-bombs through the fringes of space and drop them on New York or Los Angeles startled the few people in Washington who knew the secret.

Early in 1954, after the agents' reports of rocket research were confirmed, a hastily appointed Pentagon advisory panel sent a scientific study to President Eisenhower concluding that it was feasible—and urgent—for the United States to begin development of its own intercontinental ballistic missile to counterbalance the Soviet threat. Given a massive amount of work, the technology would be available, the panel said, to reduce the size of an H-Bomb so that it could be delivered by an ICBM—*if* the United States could develop an ICBM. The President gave his go-ahead, and a crash program matched in urgency only by the World War II Manhattan Project, which produced the atomic bomb, began to develop a strategic long-range missile.

Within a few weeks a group of Air Force officers wearing civilian clothes landed at Los Angeles International Airport and began searching for a command post from which to direct the secret project. They chose an abandoned Spanish-style Catholic church and connected parochial school in downtown Inglewood, a middle-class town near the airport and about thirty minutes by car from Palos Verdes, where many of the scientists, engineers and military men who were to converge on the old school would eventually choose to live.

Because the urgency to develop the weapon was so great, the Pentagon decided that it couldn't rely on conventional military command and engineering organizations. In an innovation, it decided to sponsor the establishment of a private corporation to manage the project, recruit engineering and scientific talent, and oversee design, testing and deployment of the ICBM on a parallel basis with the Air Force. Two engineer-entrepreneurs, Simon Ramo and Dean Woolridge, were chosen to head the task, and they founded the Ramo-Woolridge Corporation, to direct the project, in 1953; five years later, after a merger with Thompson Products, Inc., the company changed its name to the Thompson-Ramo-Woolridge Corporation, and later it became the TRW Corporation.

Under the stewardship of TRW, the United States would more than close the Soviet lead in missile technology. It began developing the Atlas, Titan, Thor and Minuteman missiles and started initial design of the nation's first espionage satellites.

• •

In the summer of 1956, a new high-altitude reconnaissance plane, the U-2, which had been developed secretly in another part of Southern California by the Lockheed Corporation, began to fly clandestine missions over the Soviet Union to search for additional data about the Soviets' missile project.

The U-2 began to bring back photographic images of a tableau that, like Stonehenge or the aqueducts of ancient Rome, would become a distinguishing artifact of a particular age in the history of man. They were scenes, photographed vertically from great distances, of new roads in remote areas, of land shaved bare of vegetation, of trucks and new buildings, and evidence of human activity around tall structures called gantries. The photos were evidence of missile-launching pads under construction.

In August, 1957, the Soviet Union announced it had tested a "super-long-distance intercontinental multistage ballistic missile" that had flown at an "unprecedented altitude and landed in the target area." Six weeks later, on October 4, Moscow announced that, using the ICBM as a rocket booster, the Russians had launched history's first artificial satellite, Sputnik I.

Both launchings had come sooner than American officials had expected, and they added urgency to the American project.

Two things happened in 1960 that altered history even more. On May 1, a U-2 piloted by Francis Gary Powers was brought down over the Soviet Union. The effectiveness of the prized source of intelligence had vanished just when the United States most needed data about the progress being made on a Soviet weapon with the potential to destroy American civilization within half an hour.

The second event was closely related to the first and occurred on August 10. After twelve failures, the Air Force recovered a capsule over the Pacific that had been sent back to earth from an orbiting satellite called Discoverer. The cover story used to describe Project Discoverer was that it was a scientific venture to test the effects of space flight on monkeys and other animals; in fact, its mission was to bring back espionage pictures from space. It was a test bed for an *unmanned* U-2; instead of operating from fourteen miles above the earth, like Francis Gary Powers, it would spy from one hundred miles or more in space while traveling at a speed of 17,000 miles an hour.

The idea of using satellites for aerial reconnaissance had been proposed to the Pentagon in 1946 by the Rand Corporation. In 1953, the year Chris was born, the CIA hired Rand to study further the feasibility of satellites for espionage.

Although it would be five years before the Atlas and Thor missiles would be available to launch satellites into space, in a secret report called Project Feed-Back, Rand envisaged a push-button era of espionage; from their lofty vantage point in space, Rand concluded, satellites could photograph Russian defense installations and troop movements, ferret out Soviet radio transmissions and, with heat-sensing infrared detectors, detect an enemy's missile launches. Such a warning of a missile rising from the Siberian wasteland, CIA officials were told, might give the United States enough time to launch a counterattack. Thus, the possibility that such a warning could be sounded might in itself ensure national survival: the certainty that America

would know of a surprise attack and would have time to launch a devastating nuclear counterattack, Pentagon theorists said, should deter a first strike against the country because such an attack would become suicidal.

In the summer of 1955, the CIA, through the Air Force, gave Lockheed a contract to develop the first U.S. photoreconnaissance satellite, called Samos, and a companion system that was to detect the fiery plume of a rising missile with infrared heat sensors. Its name was Midas. The success of the Discoverer 13, after so many failures, established that it was possible to recover photographic film from a satellite speeding at five miles a second through the distant reaches of space. While it was developing this system to lob cassettes containing film back from space, Lockheed was also pressing ahead with another system; it would send strategic intelligence photos back to earth electronically via high-resolution television transmissions.

A year after the Discoverer 13 success, the White House, on advice from the CIA, clamped a secrecy lid on all satellite espionage operations. It became forbidden even to acknowledge the existence of such systems.

Meanwhile, the Soviet Union had begun to develop its own reconnaissance satellites, and a curious kind of international gentlemen's agreement evolved: Each side knew the other had such satellites, but tacitly both agreed to say nothing publicly about the other's espionage efforts in space. Each side knew what the other was doing, but they found no value in airing it publicly, because it would just trigger a response in kind. However, for all the superficial good manners regarding each other's space spies, learning about each other's capabilities —and vulnerabilities—in satellite espionage became a principal preoccupation of the intelligence services of the two countries, the CIA and the KGB.

By the early 1970s, no KGB agent had ever penetrated the U.S. satellite operations.

Meanwhile, satellites became as indispensable to modern generals as spears were to ancient warriors. Their surveillance capabilities became a cornerstone of American defense in the nuclear era, as well as a promising tool in the search for a stable peace. The satellites were eyes in space that could photograph and inventory the number, locations and types of missiles deployed by the Soviets, and thus allow U.S. negotiators to enter Strategic Arms Limitation Talks (SALT) with

prior knowledge of the extent of the Soviet arsenal and determine if the Russians were living up to any SALT agreement. Likewise, the Russians could monitor U.S. land-based missiles the same way.

Satellites could eavesdrop on telecommunications around the world and maintain a vigil in space to warn of a possible attack; and if deterrence failed, satellites would be ready in space to report on the accuracy of missiles by locating and counting the mushroom clouds that would billow into the sky during a nuclear war.

The United States built a global network of tracking stations to control the satellites and receive information from them. Headquartered in a huge windowless structure beside a Lockheed plant in Northern California, the network spanned the globe with stations in Alaska, Hawaii, Guam, Iceland, Australia, the Seychelles Islands off Africa and other secret locations. From this command post, Air Force operators could guide the satellites by remote control, much as if they were in the cockpit of a plane.

Along with Lockheed, TRW became the CIA's principal supplier of Black Satellites.

.   .

Besides learning more about satellite espionage, Chris in his initial months on the job began to know some of his associates better. Gene Norman, he learned, had worked at TRW for seven years, including five in Special Projects. He both liked and felt repelled by him. Gene seemed to enjoy assuming the role of an older brother teaching Chris the ways of the world. There was nothing racial about the tension that Chris began to feel toward his black co-worker. Chris felt no racial bias toward anyone. But Norman's values were not always consistent with those of the new code-room clerk, who still carried with him substantial vestiges of the moral code he'd assimilated at St. John Fisher.

Norman made much of his two years as a Marine in Vietnam. To Chris he often acted as if he were *still* a Marine. He never stopped talking about the camaraderie of Marines under fire, and he was forever polishing his dark cordovan-colored shoes.

Norman loved to drink beer, smoke pot and ogle women's breasts; Chris discovered this one night after work when Norman took him to a place near the plant called The Buckit. At noon and in the late afternoon, it was usually jammed with employees from the half-dozen or so defense plants in the area, CIA men from the Project and person-

nel from the sprawling nearby Air Force Space and Missile Systems Organization complex, which had evolved from the old secret organization that began in the Inglewood parochial school.

The Buckit offered inexpensive food, cheap beer and nonstop dancing on two runways by young women wearing G-strings, shoes and nothing else. Intelligence analysts who spent the morning reviewing photographs of Soviet missile pads taken from space could relax at noon by studying the bobbing breasts of young girls. Over beer, and against the noisy background of strident recorded music and customers' cheers and whistles at the girls, Norman regaled Chris, as he had earlier, with stories from Vietnam—about the whores, the combat and the constant killing, giving Chris a much more personal view of the war than he had received via the nightly news. One of Norman's favorite stories was how he and other Marines had taken Viet Cong soldiers up in a helicopter and then tossed them out—sometimes if they didn't answer their questions, sometimes after they did. Chris didn't believe the stories at first. But as they were repeated with additional horrifying details, he began to believe them, and it gave him still another perspective on his country.

Another person whom Chris could not help getting to know better was Laurie Vicker. She was apparently a whiz at computers, but she didn't seem too bright to Chris. Whenever her work load was light, or she just got a whim to do so, she came into the vault and tried to make conversation with him. Laurie wanted more than anything else to get married and move out of the home of her parents. She liked marijuana, Valium and amphetamines; the last, she said, were necessary to dampen her appetite so that she could lose weight.

During these first few weeks Chris learned other things about Laurie: she liked her sex in threesomes and, sometimes, accompanied by pain, and she delighted in talking about it. She said she enjoyed wearing black leather outfits during her sex and flogging men who got their sexual kicks that way. Chris wasn't sexually interested at all in the lusty, overweight girl; she was too coarse for him, and her graphic invitations to join her group-sex sessions embarrassed him. But, as he discovered, he was clearly in the minority.

. .

Each station in the Central Intelligence Agency network of which Chris was now a part had a designator, or "slug," that identified it. It

was an address cited on each message. For instance, CIA Headquarters in Langley, Virginia, appropriately was called "Pilot"; TRW was "Pedal"; Canberra, the capital of Australia, was "Casino." Chris learned that he was to operate two cryptographic systems between TRW and the CIA headquarters and, with Langley as an intermediate relay point, to Australia and other stations around the world.

The first of the machines was the KW-7. It worked exactly like a teletype machine except for one thing: when Chris typed a message on the keyboard, a computer scrambled the sequence of letters, words and sentences he typed into an incoherent stream of electronic pulses. Conversely, when messages arrived from Pilot, the machine reversed the process, transforming incoherent pulses from the CIA into plain English. The messages sent over this encoded teletype system were called TWX's, like ordinary teletype messages. The second machine he operated, the KG-13, scrambled voices into meaningless gibberish to prevent eavesdropping on telephone and radio conversations between TRW, Langley and any other stations plugged temporarily into the circuit. When TRW or CIA representatives needed to hold what they called a "secure" conversation, certain not to be penetrated by the KGB or other foreign agents, they spoke over the KG-13 from the vault or from an upstairs command post in M-4 called the War Room. It was the room where day-to-day operations of TRW satellites built for the CIA were directed and where executives and CIA representatives congregated during crises. In both machines, the ciphers had to be changed daily. It was one of the systematic precautions taken to prevent enemies from getting access to the messages. Every so often, usually every three to six months, a new supply of ciphers arrived. The National Security Agency dispatched an armed courier to TRW with the ciphers, and they were locked in the Diebold floor safe. Chris learned how to change the ciphers each day by repositioning key settings on the machines. Soon, he was told, the NSA would be changing to a new system of computer punched cards. Under the new system, the cards were to come in booklets of thirty-four—thirty-one cards for successive days in the month and three for emergencies or other contingencies.

• •

Chris's life in the vault began to settle into a routine. A few minutes before 7:30 A.M. each weekday, he showed his Special Projects badge

to a guard, then passed two more guard checkpoints before reaching the outer office in front of the vault. Before attempting to open the vault, he telephoned a TRW guard to announce his intention to do so, so that the guard could temporarily disconnect the main vault alarm. Then he worked the combination, opened the vault door and, using a key, opened the inner door. He switched off another alarm, opened the Diebold and then chose the designated cipher for the day. After he set the cipher and turned on the machines, there was a "good morning" contact with the CIA operator at Pilot. Then he tore up the previous day's ciphers and placed them in a bag, where they would be stored for several weeks before being ground up into pulp by a high-speed electrical blender in the vault.

His next step was to collect the messages for TRW that had accumulated during the night and then make copies for the CIA resident officers at the plant and senior TRW project officials. One copy of each message—about fifty or sixty flowed through the vault each day—was retained in the vault for a year. Anyone with access to the code room could thus look back on a full year of the CIA's decoded secret mail.

After copying and distributing the TWX traffic, Chris began sending outgoing messages and arranging conversations via the secure voice link. His was a job more or less like that of a switchboard operator who linked callers in telephone conversations around the world.

As the days went on, the young man who had grown up on the Palos Verdes Peninsula intent on becoming a Roman Catholic priest, and who had found his happiest days walking in the woods near Morro Bay, plunged deeper into the new world that had been revealed to him —the CIA espionage and its deception, Gene Norman's tales of butchery in Vietnam, and Laurie's continued attempts at seduction.

Chris disliked Norman, but kept his aversion to himself. They had to work closely together and their shifts coincided, and inevitably, circumstances brought them together a lot. They began to lunch regularly at The Hangar or The Buckit, where Norman's favorite subject of conversation—aside from the Vietnam War, of course—was a hypothetical plot to sell some of the ciphers to a foreign country. It was a joke, but they fantasized how they might pull off the caper as they went through successive pitchers of beer. The best approach, they agreed, would be to sell the stuff to a Russian or Chinese embassy in a foreign country.

Chris occasionally rode with Norman on courier runs to the CIA's West Coast Office, which, unmarked, filled the basement of a high-rise

office building near Los Angeles International Airport, and Norman occasionally dropped by the bar and pool hall where Chris worked at night. Chris was supposed to close the bar at 2 A.M., but he got so tired of breaking up fights among the patrons on some nights that he sometimes closed early. After a while, even amphetamines didn't keep him awake when he arrived for work in the vault, and on the day before Christmas, 1974, he quit.

•   •

Because the vault was off limits to guards and even to most senior executives at TRW, Chris discovered it was used as a kind of private playpen by the select group that was allowed inside. When traffic with Pilot was slow, Norman, Laurie and a handful of their friends came in for cocktails, or to gossip or play Risk, a game distantly related to Monopoly. When the liquor they hid in the vault ran out, Chris or somebody else went on what they all called a "booze run" to a nearby liquor store, carrying the liquor into the plant in a briefcase or other container as if it were classified data bound for the code room. The guards never asked any questions. Morning visitors to the vault could expect vodka–and–orange juice; afternoons, there was often peppermint Schnapps, red wine or daiquiris whipped up in the CIA's document-destruction blender. The vault became an increasingly popular place.

•   •

As 1975 began, the domestic political pot was reaching a boil in Australia, the destination for many of the messages from Pedal. And in certain components of the United States Government, uneasiness was mounting about the political heat Down Under.

In 1968, Australia and the United States had signed an agreement providing for the establishment of CIA bases at Pine Gap and Murrunger, near Alice Springs in Central Australia, about two thousand miles northwest of Sydney. The bases sprawled over more than four square miles of bush country. Their function was to control and gather data sent back from space by spy satellites. But the Australian public had never been informed that this was the purpose of the bases. Although there had been occasional speculation in the Australian press that they had a military function that might invite a Soviet attack on Australia in the event of a U.S.–U.S.S.R. war, officially the Australian Government described the bases as "space research stations" operated by the

U.S. Defense Department jointly with Australia. The impression was left—purposefully—that these remote bases were dedicated to the peaceful pursuit of knowledge about the universe.

Despite probings by the Australian press, no one had ever publicly made a connection between the CIA and the facilities. This was highly satisfactory to the CIA, which regarded the listening posts as crucial to American intelligence operations.

An upset victory in 1972 by the Australian Labour Party and the election of Gough Whitlam as prime minister sent jitters through the CIA. The agency feared that a left-leaning government in Australia might reveal the function of the bases or, worse, abrogate the agreement and close down the facilities.

Because of these fears and apprehension that the KGB might find it easy to penetrate a labor government, the CIA decided to limit the information it made available to the Australian Security and Intelligence Service, the Australian CIA. To the American CIA, there were high stakes involved in the bases, and not surprisingly, it meant to keep them. Despite professions of loyalty from Whitlam to the American–Australian alliance, apprehension about an anti-U.S. shift in Australian policy continued to grow within the Central Intelligence Agency.

And in the minds of certain officials within the CIA, these fears were soon validated. One of Whitlam's first acts after becoming prime minister was to tweak the United States by withdrawing Australian troops from Vietnam, and in 1973 he publicly denounced the American bombing of Hanoi, enraging President Nixon.

Meanwhile, strident demands for official explanation of the American bases were being voiced increasingly by some members of the Labour Party. The CIA, convinced that the future of facilities vital to the security of the United States was jeopardized by a potentially unfriendly government, placed the highest priority on ensuring the survival of the bases and secretly poured money heavily into the opposition Liberal and National Country parties. The CIA wanted Whitlam out.

• •

As he worked at his new job, Chris wasn't aware of such machinations more than eight thousand miles away. But one day, while looking over encrypted TWX traffic from Langley, he read with fascination the

details of one slant of the American intelligence offensive in Australia. Telex messages reported that several strikes were threatened in Australia that, it was feared, might disrupt movement of equipment and personnel to Alice Springs, and thus delay improvements being made at the CIA bases. In the messages, Chris made the discovery that the CIA was planning to block the strikes. Its agents had infiltrated the leadership of Australian unions, and Pilot reported that it expected agents working for the CIA to be able to prevent the strikes or, as they had done in the past, at least minimize their potential damage to the intelligence agency's operations.

The discovery that America was tinkering with the internal affairs of a friendly country was another shocker for Chris.

It would not be the last one.

As further messages flowed back and forth before him, Chris realized Australia wasn't the only ally being deceived by the agency. And he realized that U.S. spy satellites were used to spy not only on potential enemies such as Russia and China but on "friendly" countries such as France and Israel.

Chris decided he hated the CIA, its projects and its dishonor in the name of "national security." He saw its operations as part of a *pattern*. It was a pattern that included Vietnam, Spiro Agnew, Richard Nixon and more. In Chris's mind, it was part of a pattern that went back centuries, to every other senseless battle of national states. If the CIA was doing this to Australia, Chris asked himself, wouldn't it have engineered Allende's death in Chile?

The spooks whom Chris knew in the CIA accepted Chris as one of their own: he was now part of what they called "the intelligence community." But he was repelled by any thought that he shared in the guilt, and he began to think carefully about how he might strike back.

11 FOR DAULTON the new year had also begun with a discovery, but of a different kind. After almost five years of trying, he had finally found a contact in the Mexican Mafia, a mother-lode source of drugs operating out of Culiacán in the Mexican state of Sinaloa. Culiacán was the hub of Mexico's booming trade in marijuana, cocaine and heroin. It was a violent and savage place that almost overnight had begun to enjoy a gold rush rooted in brown gold—brown Mexican heroin. The gold rush had been triggered unintentionally by Richard M. Nixon.

In 1974, under intense pressure from the Nixon Administration, Turkey, which, via France and Central America, had been America's principal source of heroin, prohibited the cultivation of opium poppies. The crackdown in Turkey crimped the supply, and sent prices soaring on the streets of New York, Detroit, Los Angeles and other cities.

The owners of great expanses of land in the Sierra Madre mountains of Mexico east of Culiacán, who had been supplying America with much of its marijuana, began to help fill the breach. Later on, Thailand, Cambodia, Burma and other countries in Southeast Asia would also help meet the demand; but for now, Southeast Asia was in a state of upheaval left by the Vietnam War, and there were not yet any substantial lines of supply for opium from these areas to the United States. Addicts regarded the brown heroin from Mexico as inferior to the refined white heroin from Turkey. But it was available when the Turkish supply dried up—and it was relatively easy to smuggle into America over the little-guarded U.S.–Mexico border.

Daulton had made a good, if unspectacular, living selling marijuana and cocaine. Now, like the growers in the Sierra Madre, he decided to move into the heroin trade.

Unfortunately, he also became addicted to his product.

• •

By late in 1974, Culiacán was a Latin-flavored blend of frontier-era Dodge City and Prohibition-era Chicago. Millions of dollars flooded into the poor agricultural center. Over tortuous routes, opium grown on the remote slopes of the Sierra Madre was brought down on week-long trips via mule trains to the city of 360,000 and refined in laboratories in and near Culiacán. Mexican Federal troops periodically mounted offensives to smash the illicit commerce. But *mordida*— bribes—often encouraged officials to be lax in enforcement, and officials who weren't lax, or newspapermen who investigated the traffic, usually found assassination squads waiting for them. The bars, cafés and hotels of Culiacán, and the town houses and sprawling haciendas built by Mexican drug millionaires outside town, became trading floors for a commerce that generated more than 80 percent of America's heroin. Stakes were high, but so were profits. Gangs of rival growers and dealers fought and killed for control of the traffic; they drove Cadillacs and Lincolns that had been stolen in the United States and armed themselves with guns, automatic rifles and machine guns smuggled across the border, and hardly a day passed without at least one gang murder.

It was this world that Daulton entered late in 1974. Through a friend, another pusher, he was introduced in Los Angeles to a young man from one of the ten families that controlled most of the Culiacán drug trade. For Daulton, it was like the discovery of an old prospector finally seeing the glint of gold in a mountain of quartz. Pot and coke were profitable, but neither promised the profits of heroin. Offering automatic pistols to his new acquaintance as gifts of introduction, he ingratiated himself first with this family and later with a second one. At last, he told himself, he had his own predictable source of supply.

When Daulton had been an apprentice in the trade, he bought his merchandise from another pusher in Los Angeles, surrendering, to his regret, part of the profit; occasionally he had made a connection with a minor-league Mexican dealer and had driven his own load over the border from Tijuana or some other border town, the drugs hidden behind a panel in the trunk of his car. But Daulton had for a long time dreamed of bigger things. Now that he had a sure source of drugs, he began to make some changes in his way of doing business. (Years later, when he was asked to describe his business operation, he did so with the pride of an entrepreneur who had opened a tiny corner store and had built it up into a chain of supermarkets.) At first, after he made

his initial contact in Culiacán, he paid couriers—"mules"—to bring heroin and cocaine over the border. Although, like other dealers, he recruited as mules young women who sometimes secreted plastic bags of cocaine or heroin in their vaginas while entering the United States, Daulton didn't like this method: it didn't bring in enough dope each trip to satisfy him. So he developed his own stable of mules. There was an old Mexican near Tijuana who would drive a big load of pot across the border in his jeep for $500, and he used him a lot. There was Ike, a middle-aged hippie who had lost a leg in a car accident and had a cocaine habit. Ike was waiting for an insurance settlement from the accident, mostly to support his passion for cocaine, and he ran coke across the border for Daulton. Customs agents in Los Angeles noticed how frequently he arrived from Mexico, and without any success they began to shake him down, opening the lining of his suitcase and searching him thoroughly. They never discovered that he was standing on the cocaine, hidden inside his artificial leg.

Daulton's most satisfying method to bring over the dope, however, was not in a hollow leg, but in a commercial airliner—either doing it himself or using a mule. The method was deceptively simple: Like all the other passengers, he'd book a seat on one of the airlines that flew between Mexico and the United States and then board his plane with plastic packages of cocaine or heroin hidden beneath his shirt. After the plane took off, Daulton got up from his seat and walked down the aisle to the lavatory, entered and closed the door. Using a screwdriver, he pried open a panel in the bulkhead of the plane behind the toilet-tissue dispenser or paper-towel receptacle or elsewhere and then stowed the packages of dope and retightened the panel. After the plane landed in the United States, he cleared Customs, opening his bag for Customs agents. Because he had studied airline flight operations, he knew exactly where the plane was headed next after refueling. Daulton or one of his associates simply bought a ticket on this flight, and when the plane was airborne somewhere over the United States, another trip was made to the lavatory and the dope was removed from its hiding place. "It never failed," Daulton would reminisce later.

Still, there was an element of risk—always the chance that a shipment that had cost several thousand dollars might be intercepted. And as his sales grew, Daulton wanted more volume; so he devised a scheme to serve as an on-the-spot jobber of marijuana, cocaine and heroin in Mexico. Using his contacts with the Mexican growers in

Culiacán, he became a middleman, buying drugs and reselling them to dealers from Los Angeles, Chicago, New York and other cities. These dealers flew to Mexico and transported the contraband themselves over the border or hired their own mules. "I could buy the stuff fairly cheap because of my contacts with my associates," he recalled. "I made a profit when I sold it in Mexico, and I didn't have to take any risks; it was a sweet way of operating." His volume doubled, then tripled.

Changes were occurring in the drug business, however, that made Daulton feel uncomfortable and long for the old days. There was a new phrase in the American lexicon—"rip-off"—that had originated with drug dealers to describe a practice of dishonor among thieves: a deal for a drug buy was made; an appointment was made to exchange money and drugs; but at the appointed time, the seller produced a gun and took the money—or the buyer flashed a weapon and stole the merchandise without paying for it.

The essence of the rip-off was to promise and not deliver; it was a process Daulton and Chris would come to know well.

• •

Because of the growing hazards of rip-offs and his busts by undercover narcotics agents, Daulton began carrying a gun. He liked his new image. When he returned from Culiacán, he regaled his friends about the drug wars. He boasted that he was tight with the Mexican Mafia and told of murders he had witnessed and the close scrapes from which he had escaped. His friends in Culiacán, he bragged, often invited him to go to their ranches in the mountains by mule. But, he said, he was too smart to risk getting caught in the crossfire of raids between warring growers. Once, he bragged, one of his suppliers in Mexico had badly needed more weapons to carry on the drug wars, and, he said, he had delivered scores of automatic rifles stolen from an Army base in Texas to cement his relationship.

"I wasn't into revolution," Daulton said of the gunrunning scheme years later. "But I saw how those people in Mexico were being oppressed. You're talking about people in the mountains where the only cash crop is opium, like Cambodia and Laos; you're talking about people whose families for generations have been growing weed, and you've got the local *Federales;* half the time they're buying it from them and the other half busting them, and the people are unarmed.

They wanted guns; that was the only way they could take care of the law. Law isn't done in the courtroom there; it's done in the street.''

Daulton rented a beach house on the Mexican coast to live in when he was out of the country, and when he came back to Palos Verdes he resumed his easy life at his parents' home. Each time a load came in from Mexico, he bankrolled cocaine parties for his friends; he put the coke on a coffee table and invited everybody to "dig in.'' He had what he wanted most—money, power over people, travel and high living. Daulton judged himself happy and far more successful than any of his former classmates at Palos Verdes High. Although he longed for a serious relationship with a woman, he eventually gave up trying to romance girls and continued to buy them. Friends rarely saw him with a date at one of his own parties, and when he arrived in Mexico, one of the first things he usually did was take a cab to a brothel.

Daulton worked hard to cultivate what he thought of as his new image and to impress his circle of school dropouts, addicts, pushers and drug-abusing teen-age castoffs from broken homes in Palos Verdes that he was a *somebody*. Once, when Andy Boyer, with whom he'd served time at the Wayside Honor Rancho, came by his house to buy marijuana, Daulton acted as if the visit were a reunion of old college classmates comparing notes on postgraduation careers, and he were the one who had succeeded. He whipped out a wallet with an inch-wide wad of cash and led Boyer on a tour of some of his hiding places where he cached his drug inventory—concealed drawers in a cabinet he had built, the head of a straw horse mounted on a wall in his room and a spot behind a ventilation grille. And then he boasted to Boyer that he'd made the big time—he had cracked the Mexican Mafia.

But for all of Daulton's successes, two shadows loomed over his life: his increasing addiction to heroin, and the possibility that he might have to go back to jail.

A few weeks after Judge Donahue freed him from Wayside, Daulton had abandoned his classes at Harbor College and begun missing appointments with his probation officer. Suspecting he was dealing again, the probation officer warned Daulton that probation would be revoked unless he got a full-time job. Daulton had been ducking his P.O. because it would mean taking a urine test, and that would reveal that he was using drugs again—an infraction that in itself could mean a return to jail. Daulton had addicted dozens of friends to drugs, and now he had addicted himself to heroin, a drug that he boasted would never

ensnare him. He didn't inject heroin, but snorted it—lodging a few grains in a nostril and sucking it in until euphoria overtook him.

• •

Honoring his multiple pledges of secrecy, Chris at first did not mention to friends his new job in the vault. But after a while, as the weekly round of drug parties went on as usual, Chris began to drop hints to Daulton about it. At first, he said that he had a new assignment he couldn't discuss; then one night he casually mentioned to Daulton that he'd been to the local CIA headquarters in the basement of the Tishman Building near International Airport that day, but said slyly he couldn't say anything more about it. After Chris rented a small cottage not far from the TRW plant, he tantalized his friend with another hint: TRW, he said, had made him get a telephone because he had a new job that gave him more responsibility. Daulton, ever curious, pressed his friend to explain what was going on. All he got was knowing smiles and once an enigmatic reply: "I'm working with birds."

By the beginning of 1975 there was no doubt where Daulton was in life: he was fully submerged in the drug culture and hypnotized by its easy life. Chris, on the other hand, was trying to inhabit two universes. By day he played his role in the high-stakes game of espionage-from-space. By night he rejoined the bored youths of Palos Verdes and Daulton's loutish cadre of jobless drug cronies from the beach cities north of The Hill, partying and getting high. Ostensibly, the two friends were as different as the sun and the moon. Chris was intense, hard-working, an introspective young man who his parents said was going to become a lawyer: Daulton was by now the self-styled racketeer, with long unkempt hair and a scruffy goatee, who sometimes carried a gun, talked in a swagger and gave away drugs to addict the unaddicted.

• •

One Saturday night in January, there was another party at Daulton's home. As usual, beer, pot and cocaine were supplied by the generous host.

After midnight, everybody had left except Chris. He and Daulton were complaining about the world they had inherited—about Watergate, Vietnam, air pollution, corruption in big business and government, and other assorted perceived evils. Daulton saw in these evils a larger force that was the source of his own problems. Political crooks

81

like Nixon were beating the law, but not he, even though selling drugs was a victimless crime that filled a legitimate public need. "It's a hell of a lot better than people who go on welfare," he declared smugly. He complained again how the courts were hassling him, trying to send him back to jail for a victimless crime. But, he told Chris emphatically, he wasn't going back.

The conversation turned to Chris's job, and for the first time, details about life in the Black Vault came out: Chris told his friend what he did in the vault, about the CIA's satellites and how they spied from space with eyes so fantastic they could isolate a single man on a desert. Outrage at what he regarded as a mindless arms race that would inevitably lead to a horrible nuclear holocaust and what he saw as his own role in it welled up in him, and he bitterly assailed man's suicidal pursuit of nationalistic pride.

His mind disoriented by cocaine, Chris foggily traced the similarities he found so fascinating between the lifeless espionage robots with which he worked at TRW and the flight and eyes of falcons. As Chris described the globe-circling orbits of Rhyolite satellites, his narrative shifted seamlessly into a description of his falcon sweeping through the air, and Daulton couldn't follow from one moment to the next whether he was talking about real birds or man-made ones.

• •

By the following weekend, Chris had come to a decision.

There was another party at Daulton's, and like the one the week before, it ended with the two friends alone in Daulton's living room stoned on cocaine. But it wasn't the drug that induced what Chris was about to do. The cocaine was only a catalyst: It served to sharpen Chris's ability to see exactly how corrupt his country's morals had become; how the United States was living a lie, preaching democracy while propping up dictatorships, toppling democratically elected governments and murdering and maiming in the name of blind nationalism. It gave him insight into the whole cancerous tapestry of perverted American principles. What he was about to do had been taking shape in his mind for many months—perhaps since his first briefing about the Black Vault and its dirty tricks. He had decided he had no choice but to do what he was about to do.

Chris had weighed the possibility of making his proposal to Daulton on the same ground of contempt that animated his own actions. But he

knew instantly this wouldn't work. Once, perhaps, he mused, it might have, but not now. And so he appealed to the motive that he knew would energize Daulton's will more than any other.

Chris told his friend that he had a business proposition.

In his job at TRW, he explained, he was handling classified government information that, according to a friend at work, Gene Norman, would be worth at least $20,000—maybe $50,000—every month to the Russians or the Communist Chinese. He said he and Norman had even discussed how they could do it and had agreed the best approach would be to go to a Communist country's embassy in a third country—such as a Chinese Embassy in Africa, or the Soviet Embassy in Havana or Mexico City—and offer the material for sale.

Chris then proposed a partnership: he would obtain old classified documents and Daulton would sell them to the Russians or Chinese.

Daulton laughed at the idea.

"Man, you're crazy," he said, rejecting the proposal without taking it seriously.

"I'm telling you, we could make hundreds of thousands of dollars," Chris said enticingly.

Daulton didn't say anything, then tentatively rejected the idea again. But Chris knew his friend well. He knew his friend couldn't turn down a mother lode like this, and he was right.

12

THE OPPORTUNITY TO DIVERSIFY his business with a new line of merchandise couldn't have come at a more opportune time for Daulton. His drug business had experienced several setbacks: he had lost almost $10,000 to a rip-off after he posted front money for a drug buy that went sour and the potential seller stole his money; he had lost several thousand dollars when the Mexican Government devalued the peso and his deposits in Mexican banks, where he kept some of his operating capital, shrank overnight. And he had developed such a consuming dependency on heroin and cocaine that it was costing him $500 a week.

It was time to get out of drugs and into something else, Daulton told his brother philosophically one night in the spring of 1975. It was not like it used to be—rip-offs, undercover narcs all over the place, the Federal Drug Enforcement Administration peeking around every corner. What he really wanted to do, Daulton said, was save enough money to buy a legitimate business that the two of them could run.

"I'm a good businessman," he boasted to David Lee. The two adopted sons of Dr. Lee had been close since childhood; even though Daulton was several inches shorter, David looked up to his brother, who was four years older, and Daulton had done his best to look after him; David was one of the few people to whom he would not supply drugs, although he had constantly tried to recruit David as a partner, and David had said he wanted no part of it.

The idea of buying a business interested the brothers and they became enthusiastic; they talked about starting with one business and building up a chain—maybe pizza parlors, a hardware store or something like that. One of the brothers mentioned the Golden Cove Delicatessen two miles from their home; it was for sale. David said he'd look into buying the deli, and Daulton said he would look into raising the capital. But Daulton had one further thought for his brother: "Stay in school and work hard; don't blow your life like I've blown mine."

. .

In mid-March, Daulton went to a faded yellow stucco apartment house located in Redondo Beach a few blocks from the Pacific surf. Apartment E, on the second floor, was rented by a sometime business partner of Daulton's, Danny Patrick, and they used it as a command post for their drug business.

About four o'clock in the afternoon, one of their customers, after telephoning in advance, knocked on the apartment door and introduced Daulton and Patrick to a ragged-looking man in his mid-twenties and described him as a newcomer to the Redondo area who wanted to buy some cocaine.

Daulton welcomed the stranger because he had the recommendation of an old customer, and he and Patrick quickly told him that he wouldn't find any purer product in the entire South Bay.

Daulton lit up a marijuana cigarette and passed it to the two youths. They took a puff and the joint was passed back to Daulton and Patrick, and then back to them. It was a scene worthy of a Western movie—

Indians making friends amid wisps of smoke while a pipe passed from man to man.

The stranger seemed anxious and said he wanted two pounds of cocaine, some of which he would sell to his own clientele in Orange County. After the first buy, he said, there would be others. The news delighted Daulton, always looking for avenues to increase his volume. As they negotiated a price, Chris arrived in the apartment after ending his shift at the TRW plant, and he immediately took some puffs from a newly lit joint. The stranger said he wanted to get down to business. "Let's see how good your stuff is," he said.

Patrick said that he had some high-quality cocaine hidden outside the apartment but didn't want to go for it until it was dark. "Too many cops around," he said.

Finally, after dusk turned into night, Patrick said it was safe to go out. He left and a few minutes later returned with a clear plastic bag —the kind used to keep sandwiches fresh in lunch boxes. It was bulging with white powder.

"There's a full ounce there," Patrick said. "It's the best you'll get anywhere in L.A."

Patrick dug out a small spoon from his pocket and plucked a few granules of cocaine from the bag and handed it to the newcomer, expecting him to stick it in a nostril to savor its effects. Instead, the new customer said he wanted to test its purity, and dropped the sample into a glass vial filled with fluid that he produced from his pocket and shook it up. Defensively, he said, "I just don't want to get ripped off; I don't know you guys yet." As he continued to shake the vial, the liquid became milky. It was confirmation that the substance he had been handed was indeed cocaine.

"Why don't you snort some?" Patrick inquired. "Try it. It's good stuff."

"I didn't come here to party," the new customer said.

There was a silence in the room.

Daulton, Chris and Patrick looked at each other.

"I gotta go," Chris said. "I think I hear my mother calling." He got up and left the apartment.

"Are you a narc?" Daulton demanded.

"No," he said, brushing off the question with a laugh. "I just want to see if this is good stuff or not."

The answer satisfied Daulton and Patrick, and they relaxed. Eagerly

anticipating the profit from a two-pound sale, they offered him another sample to take with him. "Try it," Daulton said, confidently predicting that it would convince him they offered a quality product. The man shook hands with Daulton and Patrick and said he would be calling them to arrange for delivery of his purchase. He said he had a partner lined up to help finance the deal, but would have to wait a week or so to get the cash.

Ten days later, the same stranger knocked again on the front door of the two-bedroom apartment. Patrick opened the door a crack and saw his familiar face . . . and then he saw that the new customer was holding the shield of a Los Angeles County Sheriff's Department deputy in one hand and what looked like a search warrant in the other.

"Cops!" Patrick shouted.

He tried to slam the door in the deputy's face. But the undercover officer was stronger and forced it open. From behind him, a raiding party of five other narcs poured into the tiny apartment while several others stood guard outside.

Daulton and one of his "runners" had been sitting at a table sorting cocaine, marijuana, amphetamines and other drugs. They looked up and saw Patrick, still screaming "Cops," race past them toward the rear of the apartment, with shouting police officers in pursuit.

Charging out of his chair as if it were spring-loaded, Daulton ran toward the bathroom while Patrick sprinted past him into a bedroom. Patrick struggled to lock the bedroom door, but it wouldn't lock, and one of the detectives forced it open.

Cornered, Patrick looked around, spread his arms and leaped head-first through the window of the second-story bedroom. The window exploded with projectiles of glass. For a moment, Patrick was suspended in air, a halo of glittering shards encircling him, as if he were held there by the strings of a puppeteer. Then suddenly he fell to the ground, landing beside a staked-out policeman who was already wiping blood from a wound in his arm ripped open by a spear of glass.

The undercover narc looked out in disbelief from the window. Then, wondering where to look for Daulton, he heard the sound of a toilet flushing. He forced his way into the bathroom and saw Daulton, his square head canted downward and looking at a spiral of gurgling water in the toilet bowl.

The inventory of heroin, cocaine, marijuana, LSD and amphetamine tablets found in the apartment was carted off to a Sheriff's Department substation as evidence, dealing Daulton's business another financial

setback. Patrick, daubed with his own blood from scalp to shoes, managed to walk after his plunge, and he, Daulton and the surprised, newly hired runner were booked on charges of selling cocaine and possession of marijuana, methamphetamine, LSD and opium. The bail was set at $15,000.

At the substation, Daulton turned on his most cunning self. He had to. There was no possibility he could raise $15,000. Various partners owed him at least $20,000. But he knew they wouldn't be able to raise it on short notice. His only chance was to talk his way out of the crisis. And so he began.

"I've had it with this drug shit," Daulton told the undercover narc who had busted him, and he seemed genuinely contrite. "This fuckin' dope shit has ruined my life."

Daulton knew that the man who had set him up and arrested him was the one who would decide what charges would be brought against him, and so he decided he had to bargain with him to stay out of jail. Daulton also knew that all narcs lived by their informants—every time he had been busted it was because of a snitch—and he correctly appraised the ambitions of the deputy sheriff.

"Let me out of here and I'll help you," he said, offering himself as an informant.

The cop said he was interested and offered to make a deal: he would drop some of the charges, so bail would be only $10,000. He crossed out "$15,000" on the booking sheet with an "X" and replaced it with "$10,000." But, he emphasized, Daulton would have to help him.

"I can't get ten grand," Daulton said. "I don't have it. No deal."

"Okay," the cop said, and he wrote "$15,000" on the booking sheet again and crossed out "$10,000."

"You want to get out of pushin'? I can help you," the cop said. "But I can't let you out of here, no way."

Daulton poured it on some more: In jail, he said, he wouldn't be of any use to the detective. Outside, he could do plenty.

The cop said he would give it some more thought. He left the room, and Daulton waited out his decision.

An hour passed and the detective returned. He said he believed Daulton meant what he said about being finished with narcotics and that he believed he really wanted to help. He had decided, he said, to reduce the charge to "Being Present Where Marijuana Was Being Smoked."

Once again, the detective crossed off the $15,000 bail, and the next

morning, Daulton was released from jail. His bail had been lowered to $500.

• •

Although Daulton had used his wily persuasiveness to get out of jail again, he still had other problems.

The Los Angeles County Probation Department officer who was supervising the parole that had been granted to him following his arrest in 1971, and had been extended after his two arrests in 1973, had filed a report with Judge Donahue in early March recommending that the probation be revoked.

Andrew Daulton Lee simply refused to submit to the supervision of probation, the P.O. told the judge. The defendant, he said, had been given repeated opportunities to get a job or stay in college, but had spurned every opportunity and almost always missed appointments with his probation officer.

Two days after Daulton was released from jail, the undercover policeman who had made the deal with him came by his house to collect. He laid out a blueprint by which he hoped to nail a prominent Los Angeles criminal lawyer, who specialized in defending clients from the underworld, and a professional football player, a former Los Angeles Ram. Both, the cop claimed, were up to their ears in the drug business. But he needed help to get some evidence. The cop, it seemed to Daulton, was salivating at the prospect of the big collars, and the thought repulsed him. But he agreed to help set up cocaine buys with the two men which would be monitored by the detective, and agreed to be wired with a listening device. The cop left Daulton a very happy man.

"I'm not going back to the slammer," Daulton told his friend and occasional business partner, Aaron Johnson, the next day. He had begun to suspect that Johnson himself was working as an informer; indeed, he wondered if their own 1973 arrest hadn't been set up by Johnson. Too many of Johnson's friends were being busted. But he didn't express this concern to Johnson or tell him about the deal he had just cut with the Los Angeles County Sheriff's Department. But he admitted to Johnson that he was worried about his P.O.'s report.

When Daulton had made the deal with the narc, he had intended to go through with it. It had to be done to get out of jail, he reflected. But

after he thought about it, he decided that it was too risky. His life wouldn't be worth anything if he became a snitch. Besides, it was against his principles.

The next morning, Ken Kahn, his lawyer, called Daulton and gave him more bad news: The Los Angeles County District Attorney's office said that on the basis of the Probation Department report, it intended to petition the court to order Daulton's return to jail—not the County Jail, but the State Prison. Kahn said a hearing had been scheduled for early April before Judge Donahue to consider the petition and the damning Probation Department report.

Daulton hung up and decided that he had to leave the United States. He would *not* go to jail. And, he thought, the Russians might provide the key to his survival.

• •

The two friends sat in easy chairs near each other in the room at Daulton's home that his father used as a den.

"Okay, one more time: what do I do when I get there?" Daulton asked.

"Get a telephone book, look up the address, hop in a taxi, pass the place, get off several blocks away, case it; walk in like you own the place and then give the stuff to the first security officer you see and stall until they get someone who can read it. Simple," Chris said.

"It ain't that simple," Daulton said.

"You're wasting my time. Good-bye," Chris replied.

"Okay, okay. Sit down. What about my money?" Daulton said.

"The air fare is in the envelope," Chris said. "Your flight leaves at eleven. That's four hours from now."

"No, I mean *my* money."

"Take it up with them," Chris said.

"But how do I know?" Daulton said. "It's my ass that's being risked, ya know."

"Put yourself in their place," Chris said. After all, he said, Daulton was about to offer the Russians American defense secrets.

"Now, remember, don't give 'em my name, because if you do they won't need you."

"I've thought about that," Daulton said. "Want a gin-and-tonic?"

Chris accepted the offer, and Daulton asked his father, who was in a nearby room, to fix them a drink.

As he did, they hunched over a typewriter and Chris tapped out a message:

Enclosed is a computer card from a National Security Agency crypto system. If you want to do business, please advise the courier.

. .

Two days later, the undercover agent who had arrested Daulton called the Lee house to talk over the planned setup of the ex–football player and the mob attorney. Dr. Lee answered the phone, and the detective, who had met the physician at the jail after Daulton's arrest, said he imagined Dr. Lee must be very happy that his son was getting out of drugs.

"I think he really means it," the sheriff's detective said. "Did he tell you he's going to work for us?"

Dr. Lee hadn't heard this item of news and said so.

"Well, he is," the detective said. "He'll really be able to do some good."

"If he is, I don't know how he's going to do it," Dr. Lee said. "He just left to live in Mexico."

It took a few moments for the cop to realize that he had been victimized. His first reaction was disbelief; then he asked Dr. Lee if he had a telephone number in Mexico for his son. When the physician said he didn't have one, the narcotics officer politely said good-bye and hung up. But he vowed to himself that this wouldn't be the end of things.

. .

Chris returned to work in the Black Vault, and as he operated the encrypted teletype machine, he sometimes looked up from the keyboard, stared blankly at the wall and wondered what forces he had set in motion.

13

WHEN CHRIS WAS TWELVE, he had taken possession of his own field, forty beautiful acres in Palos Verdes; he never took legal possession of it, but took possession of it in his mind. He shared the field with a wizened old Mexican tenant farmer named Rosco; Rosco looked after the neat rows of beans that grew on one part of the field while Chris assumed the responsibility of looking over the creatures that populated the land.

He knew where they all lived—the diamondback rattlers beneath the yellowed Palos Verdes stone; the pheasant that roosted in the eucalyptus trees; the mallards that rested in the winter and the red-winged blackbirds that fed on polliwogs in the marsh. He knew the quail and the barn owls that nested in the gnarled stump of a tree not far from a wild hive of bees. He saw where shrikes had impaled the mice they caught on cactus needles and even found which burrow a skunk and her four offspring, following in single file, disappeared into each morning. He had gotten to know a red fox with a gimpy front foot, and Chris named it—what else?—Gimpy. One morning he had found the fox dead on Hawthorne Boulevard, and after school that day at St. John Fisher, he had picked up the carcass of Gimpy, pedaled his bike to the glen that he had prowled and left it there in a better resting place.

Chris knew every inch of his forty acres, every wild flower as well as every creature. Even after he had gone on to high school he still came down to the field every now and then to watch the cottontails come out at dusk. As his faith in the institutions in which he had invested his trust waned, his field remained a constant in Chris's life.

When he was sixteen, Chris discovered surveyors quartering the field. His stomach tightened, and he knew what to expect.

• •

Several months later, he crossed the field a last time and paused to inspect a hummingbird's dainty nest in the crotch of a snag hidden in

tall grass; in it he saw a hummingbird incubating two tiny eggs. The ground shook and Chris had to step aside, and he watched an earthmover rumble forward with a cloud of gray-white smoke. The maternal courage of the hummingbird held her in her nest until the last moment, and then she fled from the trembling snag in an iridescent blur. Then the tiny nest disappeared beneath the machine.

Chris took his grief home with him and was lectured by his father on the prerogatives of ownership, free enterprise and the construction boom. But he silently rejected all of it and went brooding to his room. Chris decided no one should own that field or any field anywhere: man, he decided, had been given the earth in trust; it was not his chattel. He decided that the concept of private property was a thing of tragedy, an evil to be abolished.

A couple of mornings later, in an American History class, Chris listened to a lecture that reviewed the extermination of Indian tribes in the conquest of the West and the conquest of half of Mexico that left Chicanos as pariahs in what had been their own country. However, the teacher said, America had changed and matured; it was defending free expression around the world and fighting for peace in Vietnam. After class, Chris angrily slammed his text, *Triumph of Democracy,* into his locker.

But he didn't brood for long.

That night, he enlisted two friends on a mission; they bought nine ten-pound bags of sugar, and after dark they began lugging it to his field. Before long they were scratching from poison sumac and taking cactus needles in the shin. When Mike, one of his friends, tripped for the third time in the dark, he said, "Whose idea was this, anyway?"

"Pretend you're in 'Nam," Chris said.

"At least they don't have cactus in the jungle," Mike said, picking up his thirty pounds of sugar.

A half hour later they peered over a canyon wall at the construction company's fenced equipment yard and saw the silhouette of a guard.

"Let's get out of here!" Mike said.

Chris and the other friend grabbed him.

"You didn't tell me about a guard," he said.

"He's asleep," Chris whispered.

"Then why isn't he lying down?" Mike wanted to know.

"They always sleep sitting up; that's what my father says," Chris said with authority.

Before Mike had a chance to challenge the logic, his friends were moving through a hole in the fence, and very soon all three of them were assaulting the earthmovers, trucks and trenchers with sugar.

Chris poisoned three bulldozers, emptying his sacks of sugar into their gas tanks, making sure not to spill the sugar and leave evidence.

Fifteen minutes later, the trio met at the fence and climbed down the canyon through the brush and cactus, whooping like Iroquois.

The assault delayed the defiling of Chris's field for two weeks. But in the end the field perished.

Chris visited it years later after he had begun to work at TRW. There were silver Eldorados and bronze Mercedes-Benzes and imported olive trees in place of the eucalyptus and beans; there were clipped hedges and instant lawns grown elsewhere and laid out like carpeting on his field in front of ranch and ersatz–Spanish-style homes. He spotted two matrons wearing sunglasses and tennis outfits carrying their rackets down a circular driveway to a black Porsche and swinging lumpy thighs onto red leather.

Somewhere, he thought, beneath it all was his poor raped field, and he thought of wild blossoms growing between fallen columns in the bleached ruins of Carthage.

14

"WHO IS YOUR FRIEND?" Vasily Ivanovich Okana asked the American who walked into the Soviet Embassy in Mexico City during the first week of April, 1975, and announced that he had brought information about "spy satellites."

The KGB agent studied the stranger with a cautious smile. When Okana was apprehensive or unsure of a situation, as he was now, his charcoal eyebrows tended to bob up and down spontaneously like a pair of rafts on a choppy lake. Daulton, trying not to be distracted by the motion of the eyebrows, replied that he could not identify his friend, who had a sensitive job working for the American government.

The friend, he said, wanted to defect to the Soviet Union but had a wife and two children and did not want to leave them behind. Elaborating on the brief note Chris had typed, Daulton said they had a proposition for the Soviet Union. His friend was motivated by a belief in the future of socialism, while he was a fugitive from the police on a trumped-up charge. They were prepared to deliver American defense secrets to the U.S.S.R., but expected to be paid well for them.

There was no expression on the Russian's face when Daulton had finished his short sales pitch.

Without seeming to demand it, Okana asked Daulton if he had any personal identification. Daulton pulled out his wallet and offered his driver's license. The agent made a note of his name and address and then handed the license back to him, making a complimentary remark about Southern California.

"Would you like vodka?" he asked. Daulton said he would enjoy it, and Okana left the office where he was conducting the interview and came back a few seconds later. Within a few minutes a male servant brought in two large bottles of vodka and a bowl of iced caviar.

The Russian said that he had once served in the United States and had polished his English there; Daulton noticed that the bobbing of his eyebrows had subsided somewhat, but there was still an apprehensive look behind his gray eyes. Daulton explained that what he had brought was only samples of the kind of information that his friend could make available to the Soviet Union. He stressed that his friend was personally involved in the operation of spy satellites and had unlimited access to secrets that he was sure the Russians would want to buy.

Leaving Daulton with a drink in his hand, Okana excused himself, taking the computer programming cards and a twelve-inch length of paper tape used in the KG-13 and KW-7 crypto machines that Chris had given to Daulton.

When he returned twenty minutes later, Okana carried a piece of notepaper in one hand and, referring to it, began to probe Daulton about reconnaissance satellites. From his conversations with Chris, Daulton knew enough to convince the Russian that he had more than a casual knowledge of such satellites and a secret CIA post somewhere near Los Angeles.

Okana poured another glass of vodka for his guest and invited him to sample more caviar. Then he left the room for another conference somewhere else in the embassy. This time when he returned, he

handed Daulton an envelope containing $250 in American currency—
enough, he said, to finance a return trip from Los Angeles to Mexico.

Okana was warm now and smiling continuously, although the nervous bobbing of his eyebrows reappeared from time to time to distract
Daulton. Okana said that he and his associates were very much interested in the proposition made by Daulton and his friend, and they
looked forward to a mutually profitable enterprise. And then he gave
Daulton instructions to meet him at a Mexico City restaurant on his
next trip and told him they would use passwords at future meetings.
Daulton would be asked:

"Do you know the restaurant in San Francisco?"

And Daulton was to reply:

"No, but I know the restaurant in Los Angeles."

Okana said they would also use code names to reduce the possibility
of detection. Daulton, he said, was to be known as "Luis," and he
would be called "John."

The meeting was over, and Daulton shook hands with the KGB man.

"*Adios,* John," Daulton said.

"*Adios,* Luis," Okana said.

And with that, a curious commerce between the Union of Soviet
Socialist Republics and two young men from a wealthy suburb in California had begun.

• •

According to their plan, Chris was standing near a telephone booth
that night in Hermosa Beach, another one of the beach communities
north of The Hill. At nine o'clock the phone in the booth rang, and he
went inside and closed the door.

"Hello," he answered.

"Hello, Mr. Philippe?" inquired a telephone operator with a Latin
accent.

"Yes," Chris said.

"One moment please, Mr. Philippe. Your party is on the line, Señor
Gómez."

He heard Daulton's voice:

"*Gracias. Buenas noches,* Señor Philippe."

"Good evening, Señor Gómez," Chris replied. "How's Señora
Gómez?"

"Fuck if I know. You were right. My uncle says 'Hi.' "

"Simple?" Chris asked.

"Like hell."

"Simple," Chris said with I-told-you-so self-assuredness.

"You're crazy," Daulton said, trying to deflate the self-assuredness. "Now do me one favor. Don't get fired, and stay off those damned cliffs until I get back there. Man, this is going to blow your—"

Chris hung up the phone and walked down to the edge of the ocean, breathing the salt air. He looked back at the night lights of Hermosa, the alleys and the shadows, and he turned to the luminescent Pacific surf in search of guidance. But its indifferent pounding mocked him. What are these? he asked himself. Misgivings?

Chris had only half-expected Daulton to go through with it.

"It's too late, my friend," Chris whispered aloud to himself as the white foam of the churning surf rolled toward him from the dark ocean. "We're over the Rubicon."

．．

The next day Chris drove his Volkswagen as fast as he could to the serenity of the Mojave Desert, its lonely sandscape of sagebrush and Joshua trees at once hostile and inviting to him. The enormity of what he had embarked on weighted him down. With luck, he thought, it would last a few months. He told himself that he had launched himself on a path that was certain to lead to his destruction. The blood pounded at his temples because of the knowledge of what he had unleashed.

Chris parked the Volkswagen where the pavement ceased, and he hiked into the mountains to the first prairie falcon eyrie that he had ever found. He shouted into the desert and sobbed and shook his fist and consigned himself to the only God he knew, to nature around him, to all the cannon fodder that would ever be squandered, to the death of the nation-states and to the rocks under his feet. He wept until he decided that he had no qualms. And then he went home, resolved to let them have it right between the eyes.

15

THE EVENING that Chris was alone in the desert, Daulton sat down in his $40-a-day room in the Hotel El Romano Diana in Mexico City and composed a letter to his brother, David, who was attending college in Idaho. He apologized for leaving without a formal good-bye, but said he had no choice but to flee. "Sometimes," he said, "freedom is more important than one's country."

Daulton said he was excited by the prospect of life as an expatriate which loomed ahead of him and that he hadn't faced such an interesting challenge in years. Each man has only so many years to live, he said, and he wasn't going to waste his being hassled. Besides, he went on, there was no way he could ever burn one of his associates in the drug trade—it was against everything he had ever learned in the Brotherhood.

There was a happy eagerness about the letter; Daulton said he was thinking about getting a sailboat and might even take a trip to the Caribbean. He urged his brother to read a book called *Paper Trip,* which told how to procure identification papers, and asked him to investigate whether there was a Federal warrant—as well as a state warrant—out for his arrest. If the Feds were also looking for him, he suggested, it might make a difference in his plans to come back to the States. He did not mention his visit with the Russians, but said:

"Hey, you could really help out if you got into a *good legal situation* because the bucks are going to be flowing in one month. . . ."

• •

With the wheels now in motion for his new enterprise, Daulton decided to see some of Mexico. He flew to Puerto Vallarta, a resort on the Bay of Banderas west of Guadalajara that had been a somnolent fishing village with a reputation for spectacular sailfishing jealously guarded by sport fishermen until a few *gringo* artists discovered its

serenity during the 1950s. A few years later Richard Burton and Elizabeth Taylor stayed there while he made a film, *The Night of the Iguana,* nearby, and very soon Puerto Vallarta was a fashionable stop for jet setters and would-be jet setters.

Lately, Daulton's stomach had been giving him trouble—he was convinced he had an ulcer—so he decided to relax several days on Los Muertos Beach in Puerto Vallarta and uncoil some of the tension that had been tightening inside him. On the day in mid-April when Daulton had been ordered to appear before Judge Donahue to defend himself on the District Attorney's petition to send him back to jail, he was happily lying on his back under the Mexican sun, drinking a margarita and enjoying the cool salty breezes that swept in from the Pacific.

After he was rested and tan, he made his way back leisurely to Mexico City for a brief meeting with Okana. As prearranged, they met for dinner on April 23 in a Mexico City restaurant, where they exchanged the passwords. Okana was plainly interested now in the offer made by Daulton, and the young American was slightly surprised by the magnitude of his eagerness. He said he had been in touch with his friend and that deliveries of information would begin shortly.

Daulton was a dutiful son, and that night he placed a call to his parents in Palos Verdes to let them know that things were going fine for him. The Lees led a busy social life, and perhaps that was why they had not always been totally informed about Daulton's affairs since his feet-first plunge into the drug underworld.

Despite his problems with the law, Daulton's parents remained as loyal to him as any loving parents would. Their hope was that someday he would grow out of it.

When he called home that evening, Daulton said that except for some trouble with his stomach, he was in good health and having the time of his life. He said he was doing a lot of sight-seeing and enjoying himself thoroughly, but Daulton didn't mention his new business venture. His mother chided him about the missed court appointment, but Daulton told her not to worry about it.

The same evening, he wrote a letter to his younger sister, who was attending the University of California at its Santa Cruz campus south of San Francisco. Like his earlier letter to David, it blended optimism and apprehension, hinting cryptically of a Big Deal. "I'm sitting on cash that makes all my years of deals look like peanuts," he con-

98

fided, without elaborating. "I should have gone international years ago."

It was a warm letter which indicated the close relationship between brother and sister. Daulton colorfully recounted some of the details of his trip to Puerto Vallarta and promised someday to give his sister a guided tour; he had been getting so much practice speaking Spanish, he joked, that he was beginning to forget his English! As if to assure his sister that he was not suffering in exile, Daulton said he'd just had a sauna and a massage after returning to Mexico City and the previous week he'd gotten a haircut, shave and manicure.

Daulton disclosed that he was planning a quick trip to the States and at that time he would give her his car—it wasn't any good to him anymore, and it was better to give it to her than sell it at a giveaway price. He warned her not to mention his plans for the trip to anyone, because he didn't know how large a dragnet the cops had out for him. Glumly, Daulton wrote that he'd gotten some bad news from Los Angeles: the D.A. was going to re-try him "on some shit" and wanted to send him back to the prison farm "or worse." Daulton made clear that under no circumstances would he go back to jail. He advised his sister, "Keep in school, this organized crime shit is expensive when you add up the alka seltzer."

There was, he added, one big plus about his move to Mexico: "I got that dog off my leg, the one (brown dog) that kept biting me for $300 a week."

Daulton had a second thought, and on the back of a page of the letter he scrawled, "I haven't felt so good in 10 years."

The same night, he wrote another letter to David Lee. All was well, he said. The following day, April 24, he was planning to fly up to Mazatlán to further burnish a tan that was already unbelievable. Someday, he said, over a glass of good brandy, he would show David the pictures he'd taken on his Mexican odyssey and fill him in on some of his experiences. He repeated the earlier report to his sister about the massage and sauna and last week's haircut, shave and manicure and said that he had bought a new suit—a tailor-made one—as well as several new shirts and a pair of shoes. If all went well, he said, he would be seeing David fairly soon, probably no later than the middle of June. "Study hard so I can put 20,000 into a legit business with you; I think I'm too hot to open a store."

On the back of the letter, Daulton wrote a postscript: "I've got a

money maker going and it is in no way related to my past foolishness (narco). So don't worry about my trying to smuggle los contrabandos en los Estados Unidos.''

• •

A curiously idyllic period in Daulton's troubled existence had begun. Although the threat of jail still loomed over him, and it was too risky to return to Palos Verdes, he had settled easily into the life of expatriate beach bum. His fear of confinement ebbed away, and he dreamed of the dollars that would be rolling in soon from the new scam. It had taken him three days in Mexico City and a pinch of cocaine to muster the courage to go to the embassy. But when he had gone there he had seen something in the eyes of Okana that made him feel comfortable, even excited. *The rip-off should work.*

16 IN REARING NINE CHILDREN, Noreen Boyce had become an expert at diagnosing childhood ailments, nursing cut fingers and looking after an occasional broken bone. She could tell by now, she thought, when a member of her brood was attempting to tell a white lie or was troubled by something in school. She had had less experience, however, with the effects of alcohol and drugs on them.

But one evening she noticed that Chris was acting strangely—his eyes were red and he didn't seem himself—and she wondered if he might have been drinking. Chris didn't come by the house much these days, but that wasn't unusual; in fact, he had visited home so seldom in the last year that his parents had begun to refer to him as "the mystery man." When Charles Boyce came home from work at night, one of the first things he was likely to ask his wife was "Anything new from 'the mystery man'?"

This evening as they talked in the kitchen, Chris seemed to be a little more willing to talk about his life than usual, and his mother suspected

that it might have had something to do with drugs or liquor. Something was bothering Chris, and she tried to ferret it out.

Chris shook his head as if to say he couldn't tell her about the mysterious problem, and then said, "Mom, I'm going to have to do something that may embarrass Dad."

"Chris," his mother replied quickly, "Don't do it, please. If it's anything serious, it could kill your father."

"Mom, I'm sorry. I have no way out."

His mother pressed him to explain what he meant, but Chris didn't answer, and after a while Mrs. Boyce all but forgot the incident.

•   •

The CIA man had a proposition for Chris.

Ray Slack, who supervised the movement of classified information for the agency on the West Coast, said the CIA needed an experienced security specialist to work at a classified facility eighty miles from Las Vegas. Slack said he was impressed by Chris's performance at TRW and suggested he consider working directly for the agency in a career assignment. The CIA was a good place to work, he added, and there might be bigger and better things in the future. Chris said he would consider it.

"I think I'll take it," he told Gene Norman afterward, adding that it meant a good pay increase.

But several days later he told a surprised Norman he'd thought it over and had decided to reject the offer.

"It's too far from everything," he said, and the work schedule was rugged—round-the-clock shifts for three or four days before any time off. Besides, he added, "It's too far from any women."

What Chris did not say was that he thought he was falling in love.

He had seen Alana MacDonald for the first time on a Friday night in November at the pool hall and bar. Sitting with three girlfriends, she was in the shadows just beyond the glare of the lights that bathed the pool tables—a blond five-foot-two teenybopper, Chris decided. Even in the shadows, her tan complexion surrounded by her blond curls seemed perfect, if vaguely defiant. But definitely underage, Chris decided. She was trying to look like a sophisticated twenty-one-year-old but could have passed for fifteen.

"I.D., please," Chris had said to the four girls.

"You poor thing," Alana said with a smile that dismissed the young

bartender. "Run along and get me . . . let me see . . . a Bud will be fine."

"I.D. or out," Chris ordered.

"I'm not leaving," she retorted, then pulled a wallet out of her purse and handed Chris a driver's license that certified she was twenty-three. It belonged to her sister.

"Twenty-three. *Sure*," Chris said.

"Twenty-four in two months," she said tartly.

The other girls also had I.D.'s that Chris decided were either forged or borrowed. But as far as he was concerned, it didn't matter; they had established that they met California's minimum drinking age of twenty-one, and he was protected if any state investigators came calling, as they did often enough.

"Make that four Buds, bartender," the blonde demanded. Smiling, she pulled a cue stick from a rack on the wall to enforce the order. She would be giving orders to Chris for the next two years. Alana stayed late that night at the bar with her friends, and about midnight, Chris asked for her telephone number. They went out the next weekend and almost every weekend after that.

Lana, as he began to call her, was a Christian Scientist. She went to Bible-reading class promptly at ten o'clock every Sunday morning and firmly believed that faith, not doctors, cured illnesses and injuries. For the fallen Catholic, who had grown up under the long shadow of Rome, her faith was sometimes spooky. One day he noticed small warts on her left hand and suggested that she go to a dermatologist to have them removed. She scolded him for heresy, and several days later the warts were gone, prompting Chris to say it was voodoo. Who ever heard of praying for the demise of a wart? he asked himself. When he wanted to get under Lana's skin, Chris fell on the floor and writhed in pain and pleaded for a doctor. But she learned after a while to pointedly ignore his performance, and he stopped.

Lana was a bicycle nut who loved to pedal all the way from Palos Verdes to Santa Monica and back, an excursion of twenty miles or so that left Chris with aching thighs for a week but left Lana making plans for even longer trips. And she was a Stevie Wonder nut who would dance to his records around Chris's house, clapping her hands and snapping her fingers as if she were one big wiggle. Lana was embarrassed by dirty stories, but at the beach she wore a bikini that would fit in a pocket. There wasn't an ounce of fat on her, and she nagged

Chris about his mania for junk food and a double chin she perceived to be developing above his thin neck.

Lana loved to cook, and she loved babies—human or otherwise. Everything was *her* baby: she had two miniature mutts that could almost fit in the palm of her hand—they were her babies; her car—an old Rambler—and her dozens of house plants were her babies; and when they went fishing and she hooked a big slimy bass and finally got it into the boat, she said, *"Poor baby."*

Chris was usually addressed as "You stupid," or something similar. "You stupid," she'd demand, "why aren't your dishes done?" "You stupid, why don't you do your laundry?" For Chris, domestic responsibilities were only minor considerations. "She threw superlative tantrums," he recalled later, "and I was always trying to unwrap myself from around her little finger. Sometimes I would take her for granted and there would be hell to pay."

Chris tried not to become too attached to Lana in those early months. But that didn't fit into the plans for her baby. She had just turned eighteen when they met; but as Chris would say, "The little monkey was twice as together as I was; she was the practical one and I was the dreamer."

Chris introduced Lana to the wilderness and falconry, and together they explored as much of the West as they could reach on the weekends he could get away from work and she could spare from her studies at junior college. They rode down the Colorado River on a raft, hiked into the backwoods to spot falcons, cooked dinner over campfires in the desert and began blending their lives.

The fact that Lana was a Christian Scientist vaguely troubled Chris's mother, but she noticed that Lana had an electric personality that complemented Chris's introspective moodiness and that she was well liked by Chris's sisters—so well that it seemed she had become another member of the family. After a while, Chris's parents said they could see marriage on the horizon.

•   •

A few days after Daulton's second visit with the Russians, Chris signed out for a week's vacation. He filled out a form at TRW noting that he planned to travel outside the country. It was an official formality, required even though he was going only sixty-five miles across the Mexican border, on a camping trip with Lana and a couple with whom

they had occasionally double-dated: Hank Lyle, a fellow falconer and friend from high school who now worked as an airline ticket sales agent, and his girlfriend, Sandy Jones, who was a friend of Lana's. Their destination was Estero Beach, a wide expanse of sand that stretched into the Pacific from beneath a brow of rocky cliffs near the Mexican town of Ensenada. As they headed south, Chris remembered the first time he had made a trip with Hank.

It had been a treasure hunt and had even begun with a treasure map: A few days after their graduation from Rolling Hills High, they had set out for Texas in the Lyle family's station wagon and, behind it, a trailer crammed with empty cartons labeled BEKINS VAN AND STORAGE COMPANY. Chris had informed his father that he and Hank were going to Colorado to pick up some free furniture promised by a friend.

The truth was that Chris and Hank had left on a peyote expedition. A friend of Hank's who wasn't interested in the information himself had met an old man, a family friend, who had said he knew a place in Texas where wild peyote cactuses grew as thick as wheat on the plains of Kansas and had given him a map showing him the way. Peyote is nature's LSD—a plant that produces buttons containing a natural hallucinogenic drug like lysergic acid. Only Indians who used the drug for religious reasons were permitted legally to grow or harvest it. Although the only drug Chris used at this stage of his life was marijuana, the idea of finding a treasure of peyote that could be sold for a profit excited him; besides, what better way was there to celebrate graduation?

After a two-day drive, the two friends followed the old man's map south through Texas to a desolate patch of desert within sight of the Mexican border river, the Rio Grande. And just as the old man had said, the peyote was there—acres and acres of it, growing wild in the desert!

They harvested the stuff for four days—four days in which the afternoon temperatures climbed to over 100 degrees. Methodically, but not pushing themselves, they cut down the plants, broke off the buttons and filled the Bekins boxes with their treasure; for appearances, they had marked each box with a word or two, such as DISHES, TOOLS and LINENS. And on one, DAULTON'S TOYS. One afternoon while Chris was running back to the station wagon with a load, he heard a sound something like a machine gun off to one side of him. He looked down and saw a rattlesnake uncoil and lunge. It missed him, but he felt it bite

on the gunnysack of peyote flung over his back, and he then saw it fall away.

•   •

On the fifth day, when Hank had gone back with a load to the station wagon, Chris looked up and saw a cloud of dust rising on the horizon against a low backdrop of cactus, and the cloud seemed to be moving toward him. He squinted and soon realized that it was a U.S. Border Patrol jeep. Somebody had seen him and probably figured that he was a Mexican illegal alien who had swum the Rio Grande. That somebody was in a hurry to catch him.

The only clothes Chris had on were boots and Levi's—no shirt, no underwear. In that heat, that was all he had wanted. When he saw the speeding jeep and looked down at the peyote cactuses all around him, Chris began running. Hank was nowhere to be seen. Chris sprinted as fast as he could in the direction of a rolling formation of ravines more than a mile away. The ravines, he knew, would slow the jeep.

He reached the first gully just one hundred yards ahead of the jeep, which was trailing behind it a rooster tail of dust, and kept on running. He thought he was safe. But somehow, the jeep found a way into the ravine and was closing the gap fast. It was close enough for Chris to see two men in the jeep, and to decide he must do something fast or get caught. At the top of the next ravine he threw himself to one side, into the trough of the wide rut, hoping they would pass him by. He lunged into the air and unfortunately flopped onto a cactus. Bleeding, he lay on the ground and poked his head to one side of the needles and saw the jeep approach and speed past him; if the Border Patrol agents had looked down, they would have seen a bloodied, grinning fugitive.

After a couple of minutes, the Border Patrolmen realized they had passed their quarry and turned back. But by then it was too late. Chris had run in the opposite direction down the trough of a gulley out of the sight of his pursuers. The last thing Chris heard was a shouted voice somewhere in the distance: "He must be over there!"

•   •

Chris and Hank had agreed beforehand that if their idyll in the peyote field was interrupted by any lawmen, it would be each man for himself. Figuring that Hank had seen the Border Patrolmen and was headed for home in a hurry, Chris, without a shirt or money, began his

way back to The Hill. He would later say that the six days in which he found his way home had been one of the richest periods of his life. In a way, it was a rite of coming of age. He eventually found his way out of the field and located a highway and hitched a ride with a truck driver. He was a Cajun from Louisiana with such a thick accent Chris couldn't determine what he was saying most of the time. But he took Chris to the border town of Laredo and was sufficiently taken with him to give him one of his own shirts. In Laredo a gray-haired Mexican driving a huge, gasping old truck that could barely reach a top speed of thirty miles an hour picked him up, gave him a few dollars and took him to San Antonio. And in San Antonio Chris got a ride with a tourist who took him all the way back to Southern California, where, to his surprise, he beat Lyle home. His companion had figured that Chris had gotten lost in the desert and had hunted for him for five days before giving him up for dead, a victim of the desert sun. He had phoned home with a report of Chris's disappearance, and his parents had told the Boyces.

Chris's parents had filed a missing-person report with the police, but had also concluded that he was dead. When he walked in the door of his home in Palos Verdes, however, he did not receive the kind of reception one might expect from someone who was returning from the dead. His father somehow knew *everything*. Chris never figured out how he had done it, but his father, who had done some investigating after the report from Lyle, knew all about the map, the peyote and the secret mission to find it. Charles Boyce was more furious than Chris had ever seen him before, and he gave Chris an order: he was going to join the Marines.

Chris, in no position to argue, accepted the order in silence. But after a few days, his father's ire had cooled, and Chris told his mother that he didn't want to be a Marine. She interceded, as he had expected, with his father, and his parents agreed that perhaps it would be better if he went to college that fall. But they assured him he would be on probation.

Chris never again saw all that peyote they had picked. Lyle had dumped it somewhere beside a road in Texas.

Now, in Mexico, Lyle and Chris laughed and reminisced about the trip as they sat around their campfire on the beach with Lana and Sandy Jones. They swam and fished and cooked their catch over the open fire; they slept in tents; and Chris forgot about the events he had set in motion.

When the vacation was over and the two couples were driving back home, Chris told Hank of a dream. He said that he wanted to drive his Volkswagen to Road's End in the Yukon Territory in Canada—the end of civilization—and then push ahead into the wilderness toward the North Pole. Chris had already modified the VW to handle the terrain. Indeed, it was a strange-looking machine: it was painted bright yellow; the hood had been removed and replaced with a squat, blunt-nosed front end with two bug-eye headlights; the factory fenders had been removed and replaced with tiny glass-fiber brows; and there were plump, oversized tires, special lights and heavy-duty springs all designed for off-road use.

When he finally reached the north country, Chris told Hank, he would spend months studying the Arctic falcon—a giant species as regal as the peregrine—before it became extinct.

Beyond that, Chris said he was still undecided about what he wanted to do with his life; probably he would return to college, go to law school and maybe join the FBI like his father.

17

ON MAY 18, 1975, Daulton arrived in Mexico City for his third meeting with the Russians.

At the previous meeting, Okana had instructed Daulton to rendezvous with him on the eighteenth at 6 P.M. near the Polyforum on Avenida Insurgentes Sur. Daulton knew the location well. It was one of Mexico City's major artistic landmarks. The Polyforum had been executed by the Mexican muralist David Alfaro Siqueiros as "an atheistic temple—not to adore God but to adore man." A fusion of blazing color and sculpture, it was a vast amphitheater of art with a three-dimensional mural that depicted Siqueiros' concept of "The March of Humanity," and a rotating turntable on which hundreds of people at once could view the circular work of art.

Shoppers, store clerks, tourists from the hinterlands and well-dressed businessmen left little room on the sidewalk for the short man from California as he approached the structure. But Daulton managed to thread his way through the early-evening crowds and find a fence to

lean against which Siqueiros himself had designed. He studied the crowds for Okana but saw only a collage of Mexicans in a hurry. Suddenly, amid the brown faces, a familiar black suit caught his eye, and Daulton looked up from the pumping hips and shoulders and saw the athletic figure of Okana striding toward him.

The Russian greeted his new spy warmly and they exchanged the passwords. They shook hands and blended quickly into the throngs of shoppers and tourists that seemed omnipresent in Mexico City, regardless of the season. The short American wearing brown slacks and a light-brown jacket and the Russian in his dark suit continued their walk along Insurgentes. They looked around them, studying the crowds as they walked. Okana again brought up his interest in knowing the identity of his friend, and, for a reason that Daulton never fathomed, he asked casually if his friend was black. Daulton repeated that he could say only that his friend held an important position with an American firm that produced spy satellites. But he wasn't black, he assured him. His friend, he repeated, believed in socialism and wanted to help the Soviet Union; this was only the beginning; many more secrets would be forthcoming, he promised tantalizingly.

Daulton slipped him ten KW-7 cipher cards, and Okana looked pleased. After they had walked a few more blocks, Okana pointed out a restaurant they had just passed and said he would meet Daulton there at eight o'clock that night. Quickly, Okana flagged down a taxi and was gone with the cards that Daulton had delivered.

Promptly at eight, Okana arrived at the Villa Nova Restaurant and found Daulton waiting for him. Okana requested a table against a far wall and seated himself so that he could watch the entrance. There was something about Okana's nervousness—maybe it was the bobbing eyebrows again—that Daulton found humorous; it reminded him of himself as he kept an eye out for narcs.

Apparently, the Russians had examined the cipher cards since their earlier meeting.

Okana said that he and his associates were pleased with the delivery; a few moments after they sat down, he gave Daulton an envelope. Daulton felt it, but couldn't resist looking inside; there was a deck of $100 bills, but he couldn't tell how many.

"To peace," Okana said, and they both raised their glasses.

Okana stressed that his country had great admiration for Daulton's friend who was doing such a service for the cause of peace.

After they ordered dinner, Okana removed a piece of paper from the inside pocket of his suit coat and began to read a list of questions in English that he said he would like Daulton's friend to answer. The questions were pointed and specific: Exactly what kind of facility does the friend work in? Who are his superiors? What kind of encryption machines are employed, the model and serial numbers? On what radio frequencies and band width are the messages broadcast? Exactly what satellites are manufactured at the plant where the friend works? What are their functions and orbital parameters? The list went on. . . .

Okana seemed to be playing a game with him. When he mentioned Daulton's friend, there was a spark in his eye that seemed to be saying, There isn't *really* a friend, is there? *You* work in the defense plant, don't you? Though the Soviet agent never said he believed that Daulton and his friend were one and the same, Daulton was sure that Okana believed it anyway. Daulton painstakingly copied the list of questions on a sheet of blank paper given him by the Russian, and then the conversation turned to talk of war and peace, and Okana said he was certain that in Daulton's lifetime, the Soviets would rule America.

Okana said they needed a method for Daulton to alert the Soviet delegation at the embassy when he was in Mexico City and wanted to arrange a meeting.

The KGB agent removed a spool of white surgical adhesive tape from a pocket and handed it to Daulton. He said he should use it to make a mark on the first Tuesday of the month to signal his arrival; the marks were to be made in the shape of an "X" on lampposts near certain intersections in Mexico City that would be monitored by the Russians. If the utility poles were marked with the tape, the Russians would expect a meeting the following day.

The X's, he explained, were to be taped exactly one meter above the ground at one of six locations that Okana pointed out on a map of the city. There was a site near the Polyforum at Dakota and Insurgentes, another at Insurgentes and Concepción, another at Dakota and Filadelfia, and so forth. To guide him to the spots, Okana presented him with pictures of each intersection that looked like color postcards which tourists in Mexico City would send home to family and friends.

If the Russians observed a mark at one of the intersections, they would expect Daulton at 6 P.M. the following evening at a location that would be predetermined and changed from time to time. Neither party was to wait more than fifteen minutes if the other didn't appear. If

either party missed a meeting, there would be a backup rendezvous at ten the following morning. He told Daulton *never* to go to the embassy unannounced.

• •

The cipher cards that Daulton sold on May 18 had been given to him by Chris several days earlier, after Daulton had made a quick round-trip flight from Mexico. Chris had wanted to know every detail of what had occurred during the first two meetings.

"I don't believe it," Chris said. "I didn't think you'd pull it off."

"They really want the stuff; they're crazy for it," Daulton said. Daulton said he had received $3,000 for the delivery, and he split it evenly with Chris, although Chris traded in part of his share for some cocaine. Daulton then flew back to Mexico.

18

DURING HIS INITIAL BRIEFINGS, Chris had been told that beneath the bulbous white dome atop M-4 was the High Bay Area, a place where TRW conducted some of the final checkout tests on new satellites and stored them until they were shipped to Cape Canaveral, in Florida, or Vandenberg Air Force Base, up the California coast. These were the two American bases from which spy satellites were launched into space.

As a new employee assigned to Special Projects, he had been taken on a tour of the High Bay Area and had seen several launch-ready satellites and mock-ups of the espionage spacecraft. But he had not been much impressed. They looked like lumpy, shiny boxes perhaps half the size of a railroad boxcar. However, he was told that when they were up in space the satellites looked much different from these bland objects; they had to be packed into tight boxes like this so that they could fit in the narrow nose of a launch booster during their ascent; in space, they opened like an accordion.

Chris wanted to see what a Rhyolite payload looked like when it was unfurled in space, and he had been told he could do so once or twice a

year when a standby satellite that was kept in reserve was opened and examined so that engineers could be certain it was ready—no one ever knew when another bird would be needed. Launch frequency depended on how long existing satellites already in space survived the searing heat of the sun's rays, the pounding of micrometeorites and other hazards. One TRW payload already in orbit was supposed to have a life of two years, Chris was told, but it had been working for almost four years, causing jokes around M-4 that the company had made it *too* reliable. After all, the company wanted to sell another one to the CIA.

The High Bay Area was jokingly referred to as "Sherwood's Forest" when the satellite was opened, and Chris learned why. What he had thought was an unimposing box had been opened into a massive creature—a concave dish that measured at least seventy feet across. It was the main antenna of the satellite, and it was backed and supported by a framework grid that reminded Chris of the back of steel bleachers at a high school football field.

The High Bay Area was an enormous vertical cavern topped by the igloo covering. The satellite glistened eerily in the glow of floodlights and bristled with strange appendages: there were large panels of steel-blue solar cells reaching out from the main structure, reflecting the lights as if they were a constellation of tiny stars, and there were several lesser antennae and other gadgets whose function was a mystery to Chris.

Chris studied the machine, one spy looking at another, and then walked away—thinking again of the similarities between the bizarre machine and the eyes and ears of his falcons.

• •

Chris had long since decided that there was a wide gap between reality and the government-mandated "tight security" regarding the satellites so zealously preached in the security briefings. "Security at TRW is a joke," he told Daulton. Supposedly, Special Project employees cleared for a particular system were allowed to discuss their project only with other people specifically cleared for the same project. But he discovered that not everyone followed the stricture. One day, for example, an acquaintance told Chris about a secret project at M-4 to build a new satellite that would be used to shoot down other satellites with a superhigh-energy laser beam.

It was a weapon out of science fiction, evoking images of robot surrogates of man battling each other with light beams in the dark and cold vacuum of space tens of thousands of miles from Earth. The project was so secret that the Air Force had set up a special communications vault at TRW to handle traffic for this project exclusively; lie-detector tests had been required of all the Air Force officers assigned to it. Although Chris didn't know it at the time, it was one of the highest-priority satellite programs in the country—nor did he know that Soviet engineers were simultaneously developing the same kind of system.

While looking over traffic from Pilot one day, Chris discovered an item that made him smile: A TRW employee on this project had stolen components for the laser gun and taken them home. It seemed that he was planning to go into business for himself to manufacture the lasers at his own company. He had been caught, the laser components were returned from his garage and he was fired. But Chris laughed out loud at the angry protest from Pilot about TRW's failure to prevent parts for the secret project from being carted out of the plant.

· ·

Chris was drinking more now than ever before in his life, and much of his drinking was done in the Black Vault. Drinking was a routine fact of life there, and as the frequency of parties behind its steel door increased, the handful of people allowed inside found ever more ingenious ways to smuggle booze to the TRW inner sanctum. Sometimes they used the courier pouches set aside for carrying Central Intelligence Agency and National Security Agency documents; sometimes they used the case for a large camera that was used to make pictures for Project security badges. When the CIA hired a new clerk—a stunning if not very bright blonde—she was invited in for a drink on her first day on the job. She hadn't had much experience with alcohol, and after several vodka–and–orange juices she was so drunk that she couldn't walk out of the vault without leaning on Laurie Vicker.

It was not an auspicious beginning, but she managed to hold on to her job, and it was not long before she had moved in with an engineer who worked on one of the black projects. Once, the couple threw a party for Special Projects people that lasted two days and was considered a total success—except for the complaints of neighbors who protested about the sexual couplings that took place on the front lawn of the couple's home.

Drinking and security violations weren't the only goings-on that bemused Chris about the gap between his security briefings and reality. He got to know an employee named Huey who showed porno movies in the plant at lunchtime; another who worked in the High Bay Area and sold bets on baseball games; and another who took bets on the horse races over the secure telephone lines in the TRW War Room.

Meanwhile, Laurie Vicker announced that she was getting married soon. But that didn't stop her from continuing her attempted seduction of Chris, which he continued to resist. Gene Norman had found a sideline job—selling Amway household cleaners and other products out of the Black Vault by telephone and to TRW employees. He encouraged Chris to join him to make some extra money, and between handling secret messages, Chris also sold Amway merchandise.

Chris was also getting to know better the CIA residents at the plant and some of the agency's employees who worked in the West Coast Office. With few exceptions, he was frightened of them. "When they talked about nuclear war," he would recall years later, "they didn't think in terms of *if* there will be a war, but *when* there will be a war." Their casualness about a nuclear holocaust horrified him. For the most part, he thought the CIA spooks were cold, self-righteous, right-on Americans.

A lot of the CIA men, Chris thought, reminded him of his father.

19

DAULTON OFFICIALLY BECAME a fugitive on May 27, 1975, when Judge Donahue, after giving him a second chance to appear in court and explain his refusal to cooperate with probation officers, issued a bench warrant for his arrest. Daulton got the news from his family by telephone in Mazatlán.

He had expected it and wasn't troubled, because as he lay on the sand Daulton could compliment himself on having pulled off his smartest business deal ever: the Russians were now bankrolling his drug business.

Following the May 18 meeting with Okana, he began what was to become a routine trading circuit: the Russians gave him money for documents from the Black Vault, and he invested his share of the proceeds (and eventually, more than his share), in Culiacán or Mazatlán, in marijuana or heroin. If it was done right, Daulton knew, $10,000 from the Russians might be turned into $50,000 or more in Los Angeles.

The capitalistic symmetry of the transactions delighted Daulton, and he was convinced from his first visits with the Russians that they would buy anything as long as the flow of goods from the vault continued. There was one problem with the arrangement, however. He was growing tired of life on the run in Mexico. He was beginning to grow tired of the spicy Mexican food and the unpurified Mexican water that was hard on his stomach; he was tired of the ubiquitous mariachi bands and was homesick for people who spoke English.

Returning to Palos Verdes and the beach towns near the Peninsula was out for now because of the warrant for his arrest. But he decided he would be safe in Santa Cruz, the seaside university town in Northern California where one of his sisters lived.

He arrived in Santa Cruz in early June after a flight via Los Angeles and San Jose under the name of Theodore Philip Lovelance—one of several alter egos Daulton had adopted using counterfeit identification papers arranged for by friends in the narcotics underworld. Two days after moving in with his sister, he applied for a driver's license at the California Department of Motor Vehicles branch office in Santa Cruz under the name of Lovelance. On the line of the application where he was to list his height, Daulton, who had never been taller than five feet two, attested that he was five feet five inches tall. Perhaps it was a mistake made in haste; perhaps he had a document from the real Lovelance noting that as his height; or perhaps it was the fantasy of a man creating an alter ego that in his mind was more appealing than his own. Whatever, the DMV clerk did not notice the discrepancy, and he got the license; it was only later that the lie about his height precipitated a crisis.

Daulton had become Theodore Philip Lovelance by paying $200 to the girlfriend of a young hippie who, like Robin, had died in a fire; for the $200 he got the boyfriend's birth certificate and all the other documents that had certified the existence of Theodore Philip Lovelance. It was a trick he learned while reading *The Paper Trip*. Lovelance was

the complete alias; Daulton even wore a high school graduation ring with the dead man's name engraved in it.

.   .

After three weeks in Santa Cruz, Daulton flew to Los Angeles and arranged by telephone to meet Chris after dark in an alley in Hermosa Beach. He said he was expected in Mexico City in a few days and wanted something to deliver. Chris promised to give him something, and two nights later they met in the same alley and Chris handed him about twenty sheets of 8½-by-11-inch paper with typing on them. Daulton noted the word "Rhyolite" on one sheet.

.   .

On the first Tuesday in July, Daulton arrived in Mexico City and placed several X's on lampposts along Avenida Insurgentes Sur. At six o'clock the following evening he found Okana waiting for him at the Polyforum. Although they instantly recognized each other, Okana wanted to play by the rules (he enjoys it, Daulton thought) and asked, "Do you know the restaurant in San Francisco?"

"No, but I know the restaurant in Los Angeles," Daulton said.

They walked the same route they had taken during the last meeting. Before long a dark limousine of a make Daulton didn't recognize squeezed out of the six lanes of traffic on Insurgentes and stopped at the curb to pick them up. The driver was a huge man in a black suit who, even from the back seat, reminded Daulton of a large, hairy bear.

"Speak English," Okana whispered to Daulton after he had started to say something in his broken Spanish.

After Daulton and Okana climbed into the back seat, however, the driver didn't seem to be particularly interested in listening. He shoved the car into low gear and accelerated it as if he were in a road race. Daulton soon realized that he wasn't driving the limousine like a race car because he wanted to get somewhere in a hurry: he was trying to make sure they weren't being tailed. The black car careened around corners with a squeal of tires, went a block or two, then turned again and repeated the maneuver. They weaved in and out of traffic for twenty minutes, and as they did Okana constantly checked the rear window. Finally, the car began to slow at a park several miles from the center of town.

As the limousine stopped, a European man emerged from the

shadow of a tree. Daulton vaguely recognized him and decided he might have seen him on that first day in the embassy. The man got into the back seat with Daulton and Okana and offered his handshake with a smile, saying that he was delighted to meet "Comrade Lee."

The man was introduced to Daulton as "The Colonel." He didn't know it at the time, but he was meeting a general. Mikhail Vasilyevich Muzankov was listed on the roster of the Soviet mission as a consular official. But in fact, he was a general in the Red Army and the senior official of the KGB in charge of terrorism in the Western Hemisphere.

Muzankov was about fifty, a tall and beefy man with blue eyes and a craggy complexion that made Daulton think of a seafarer. He had two features that especially etched themselves in Daulton's memory. One was his iron-gray hair. The color of stainless steel, it was lush and cropped like an expensive bristle brush. The other was his front teeth. They were stained yellow and brown by nicotine, and the two most prominent ones were made of steel. When The Colonel smiled, the only thing Daulton could see was a mouthful of glittering metal.

Later that evening, Daulton was introduced to the driver, a dour man named Karpov. In future months Daulton would come to realize that Karpov was not what he appeared to be—an attentive servant—but an officer in the KGB. But he didn't know that yet, and he wondered at the size of the man. In his black uniform, Karpov towered over the woodworker from California by more than a foot, an enormous trunk next to a stump; his eyes reminded Daulton of coal, and his hands were massive paws with thick, puffy fingers.

Okana explained that The Colonel would also be dealing with Daulton from now on, and Daulton wondered if there was a changing-of-the-guard under way; was he being handed off from one case officer to another? Daulton studied the man and was impressed by his air of self-assuredness and the reaction of the other Russians to him. There was a palpable deference to him, and he seemed more polished than the other KGB agents. Years later Daulton would try to remember the first impression that Muzankov made on him and he would pick a simile from the world he knew best: "It was like the difference between a dealer who was used to dealing in ounces compared with one who won't handle anything smaller than kilos. He was up there at the top."

Karpov dropped the three of them at another park, and they sat shoulder to shoulder on a bench with Daulton in the middle, watching

a man selling balloons walk by, his merchandise a geyser of colors above his head.

Daulton handed the Russians the material Chris had given him.

There were more cipher cards and copies of several TWX messages between Pilot, Pedal and Moreno—the code name for the base at Alice Springs.

After inspecting the documents briefly, Steely Teeth gave them to Karpov, who had reappeared after parking the embassy car. Daulton had tried to make conversation with him in English, but the chauffeur shook his head.

With Karpov now in possession of the documents, Steely Teeth suggested that he, Daulton and Okana adjourn to a nearby restaurant for drinks, dinner and a celebration. The Russians were all smiles.

Karpov appeared at the restaurant just as coffee was being served. He said something in Russian to Steely Teeth, who told Daulton they would like to have more time to examine the documents. Would it be possible for him to see them again the next day?

At ten the following morning, Daulton was waiting at a bus stop near the Old City at a spot where he had been told to expect Karpov. The chauffeur was prompt and took Daulton on another high-speed trip through the narrow streets of the Old City, circumnavigating the Zócalo, Mexico City's huge central square, and then plunging into alleys and seemingly getting lost in the byways of the city until the car arrived at the embassy with Daulton flattened on the back seat to avoid being seen.

He was led into a room deep inside the embassy and greeted by Steely Teeth.

Caviar and bottles of vodka were waiting on a table next to a tape recorder. Okana wasn't there, but Karpov sat in a corner quietly watching Daulton. Under interrogation by The Colonel, Daulton told what he knew about the satellite operations. Again, he refused to identify his source. But he did his best to raise the Russians' expectations of what he would deliver in the future.

"I'm sure I can get what you want next month," Daulton said, and this seemed to please the KGB men.

Steely Teeth said the operation was going well, but that additional information was required pertaining to the TRW satellites. Daulton sensed that someone, outside the circle of Russians he had met, was being consulted each time Karpov or The Colonel left the room and

came back with new inquiries. He suspected they might have brought a technical specialist from outside Mexico City.

Steely Teeth said they wanted as much technical data about the satellites as Daulton's friend could obtain, but particularly they wanted details of the infrared sensing instruments employed on TRW satellites. He also asked for copies of instruction manuals for the use of components of the satellites, the tables-of-contents of official publications dealing with the space vehicles, names of the people who worked with his friend, pictures of the place where the friend worked and photographs of the satellites. Still more data were needed, the Soviet agent continued, about the methods of transmission—especially the frequency and band widths—used in the system that employed the ciphers.

Daulton slowly took notes on the questions and said optimistically he thought he could get what was wanted. After a while, Karpov came into the room and handed Daulton an envelope containing scores of $100 bills.

Before Karpov took him back, Steely Teeth advised Daulton he was foolish to bring the documents physically to Mexico City; instead, he should photograph them and return them quickly to where his friend had found them. This would reduce the risk, he said.

They said good-bye and agreed tentatively to another meeting the following month.

．．

Daulton had told his brother, David, that he was embarking on a scam to sell something to the Russians even before his first connection with the Soviets, and he had said that when it was over he would be wealthy.

More than anyone else, Dave knew that Daulton liked to spin tales that cloaked him in importance. He had long observed at close hand the demons that haunted Daulton because of his size and looks, the humiliation that girls bestowed on him and his failure to please his father. Even when Daulton came home boasting that he now knew the Russians would "buy anything," Dave was skeptical. But as Daulton made more trips to Mexico and returned home with envelopes stuffed with brand-new American currency, Dave began to suspect that there might be some truth to Daulton's crazy claim that he and Chris were pulling off a scam involving the Soviet Union.

Several months after Daulton started his periodic trips to Mexico City, Dave joined a group of Palos Verdes high school students on a tour of Eastern Europe.

The tour proceeded normally until the delegation reached Kiev, the ancient city in the Ukraine. After David unaccountably became ill with a high fever and nausea, he blamed the attack on too much beer and sausage when the group had visited Poland. But a Russian doctor who was summoned to his hotel said he had a serious viral infection and he'd have to be hospitalized while the group continued without him.

At a Kiev hospital, David had a visit from the group's English-speaking guide, Ira Mironenko, who worked for Intourist, the Soviet tourist agency. He had noticed her during the tour and thought once or twice that she was trying to catch his eye. She had seemed to go out of her way to choose a seat next to him in the opera and had purposely rubbed against him as they left. David had been flattered by the attention and interested in the possibilities.

When the girl arrived at his bedside he was even more encouraged. Ira visited him three times, staying several hours each time and asking to know all about America. She seemed particularly interested in Dave's family, and when he said he had a brother she inquired at length about him.

David felt he had made a conquest. They agreed to exchange letters; but after he was back in the United States, he wrote to Ira and she did not reply. He would never know why she had asked so many questions, or whether her interest was in him or in Daulton.

20

THE FIRST THING men noticed about Carole Benedict was her figure. She had blond hair the color of straw and blue eyes, but her hair and face were usually overlooked during the first glance. For as long as she could remember, whether she was rushing to class through the corridors at Rolling Hills High or stretched out on a blanket on the sand at Redondo Beach,

Carole had seen men and boys, out of the corner of her eye, studying the lines and motion of her breasts. (Some of the football players who pursued her in high school calculated that she taped out at thirty-eight inches before the end of her junior year.)

By the time Daulton met her in 1973, there was already the hint of tarnish on the looks of a girl whose shape, straw-colored hair and beauty were of the stuff which the myth of the California Girl (the girls of California were *all* supposed to look like that) relied on for perpetuation.

Carole was the daughter of a lawyer who lived in the most exclusive part of the status-conscious Peninsula, the rural enclave of Rolling Hills. It was the kind of place that real estate ads referred to as "horse country." It was isolated from the rest of The Hill by fences and guards at gates who made sure that only residents and their authorized guests entered the three-square-mile community-within-a-community of wooded high ground and $400,000-and-up homes. To live in Rolling Hills was to live "behind the gates." In a world where some people chose their Mercedes-Benzes or Jaguars as much to communicate to neighbors their continuing upward economic climb in life as they did for transportation, living "behind the gates" represented the Peninsula's supreme validation of having risen very high indeed.

Carole Benedict had everything material that she wanted. But for years, her family had been ruptured by bitter combat between her mother and father. It was a turbulent union that would eventually dissolve in divorce, and Carole gravitated from her troubled home to Barclay Granger.

If Carole epitomized Madison Avenue's fantasy of the California Girl, Granger's tanned, rugged beachcomber looks were a perfect complement. Barclay never looked better than when he was on a surfboard, his long brown hair streaming in the wind like the trailing scarf of an aviator, his knees slightly bent and arms outstretched, gliding beneath the curl of a six-footer while the gremmies—the girls who followed the surfers—watched in awe from shore.

As a high school student he haunted the beaches up and down the California coast, pursuing the best waves and dreaming of someday riding the biggest waves of all at Sunset Beach in Hawaii. Girls were never a problem for Barclay; they hovered around him like kids surrounding an ice cream vendor on a hot day at the beach. His life was nonstop surfing, sex, drinking and drugs. And even though some of his

friends died of overdoses, Barclay merely regarded this as "part of the territory."

When his friends at Palos Verdes High scattered after graduation to enter college or go to war, to begin careers or marry, Barclay clung to his waves. His father—a business executive who was divorced from his mother—like Daulton's father tried to interest his son in college. Barclay tried a semester at Harbor College but didn't survive even its relaxed academic standards. The only thing he wanted to do was surf. For a while, he found a compromise between work and play—a job at a shop that shaped long planks of lightweight foam plastic into surfboards; but he didn't like the *work* part of this compromise.

Carole's parents didn't approve of Barclay, who was more than three years older than she was. But they were distracted by the final throes of the dissolution of their marriage, and Carole was edged into a side room of their lives. A few weeks before her seventeenth birthday, Carole moved in with Granger, who tried to support both of them on the sporadic earnings he made shaping surfboards. But that didn't bring in enough money, so Carole got a part-time job selling women's clothing in a dress shop.

Like Daulton, Barclay resisted the discipline of a regular job. And as with Daulton, the easy money of drug dealing seemed exactly what he was looking for.

He managed to find a reliable supply before Daulton did, and for a while Daulton had acted as a subcontractor to him, selling marijuana, for which he got a cut of the profit. Later, Daulton found his own source and they teamed as partners; they diversified into cocaine and, eventually, heroin until some weeks they were grossing more than $3,000. Their timing was lucky: just when many customers on The Hill had become bored with pot, they had found a source of coke, and then heroin. Coke was a more expensive high than pot—$20 or more a pop compared with $2—but they found plenty of buyers who could afford it.

Daulton saw a lot of Carole and Barclay during the spring and summer of 1975. During his quick trips from Mexico or from Santa Cruz for a deal, he often stayed at their apartment, making his deals over the telephone, keeping the windows shaded and the doors locked.

After the arrest warrant was issued, Carole thought she noticed a change in Daulton. He still boasted of the big deals he was going to pull off, and still entertained lavishly at his cost-be-damned parties that had

become a legend on The Hill. But, as she would recall, "He wouldn't relax: he was nervous all the time and always complaining of trouble with his stomach."

Meanwhile, stresses had begun to appear in the fragile relationship that Carole and Barclay had built for themselves in the small Redondo Beach apartment. Now that she had a steady job, she suggested that Barclay give up pushing drugs, get a real job and then marry her.

Carole believed she was still in love with Barclay, but their apartment was often a battleground, not only over his drug dealing and her fears that he would have to go to jail, but over her suspicions that he was seeing other girls. They were suspicions, unfortunately for Carole, that were justified.

Daulton had fancied the well-built girl, who was four inches taller than he was, for several years, and he was not unaware of the troubles she was having with Barclay. He placed a call to her from Mexico and suggested that she and Barclay come down for a holiday—or, he added, if she wanted to come alone, that would be fine too. Daulton said he needed a mule to carry money—someone to carry cash across the border. The most he could bring over the border, he explained, was $5,000; any amount over that had to be declared to Customs officers. So all she had to do for a free holiday in Mexico was carry that amount for him—and there was nothing illegal about it.

In truth, Daulton had more in mind for Carole than carrying money.

Several times Carole had seen Daulton flashing stacks of $100 bills that he had explained casually he had obtained in Mexico. She'd wondered about the source of all this money but had decided he was probably just doing well in his drug business.

Barclay told Carole he couldn't go to Mexico now because he was scheduled to appear in court within a few days to answer charges on another drug bust. But, he said, she should go and have a good time without him.

Barclay was glad to see Carole off on the plane to Mexico. He had found another interest: her name was Darlene Cooper, and she was yet another teen-age refugee from Palos Verdes.

Darlene had been one of the original "groupies"—the teen-age girls who systematically pursued rock-music stars in the sixties like quarry in a fox hunt, sneaking into their hotels and trying to seduce them and, after succeeding, comparing their scores with one another like frontier bounty hunters. Darlene's family was well-to-do, and she had all the

money she needed to finance expeditions to New York, Chicago, San Francisco and other cities on rock stars' concert tours. Darlene was a well-organized camp follower and, according to the gossip heard on The Hill, had one week boasted of bedding at least one member of every group listed on *Billboard* magazine's chart of the top five best-selling single records.

Darlene constantly wove fantasies about her future. Some of her friends had told her that she was tall enough and pretty enough to become a fashion model, especially when she bleached her hair and it came out a stunning blend of gold and ivory, and Darlene began to dream of going to New York City and becoming a model. But that wasn't her only dream. Darlene admired the rugged looks of Barclay Granger, and the day that Carole left to see Daulton in Mexico, Darlene went to bed with Barclay.

Carole's destination was Mazatlán, which had been an obscure fishing village on the Gulf of California in Mexico until the mid-sixties, when travel agents and tour operators, and then tourists, discovered its turquoise waters and beaches with sand like granules of snowy-white sugar. These days, jets were bringing *gringos* by the thousands every week, most of them from Southern California, on charter flights to Mazatlán, where a week under the sun (including hotels and air fare) cost just under $200. For Daulton, Mazatlán had attractions besides sun and sand. It was within driving distance of Culiacán. As the gang warfare there became more intense, and the U.S. Drug Enforcement Administration began having success in deploying undercover agents to fight the drug trade, some of the Culiacán drug traffickers began using Mazatlán as a safer base of operations. Lost amid the hordes of tourists who jammed the high-rise hotels that had sprouted like sunflowers along the edge of the ocean, Daulton could conduct business as well as enjoy himself.

Carole landed at the Mazatlán airport and took a taxi eight miles north of the city to the Camino Real Hotel. As usual, Daulton had chosen to live in the most expensive hotel in town. Perched on a promontory overlooking the Pacific, the city's busy port and nervous tourists floating past beneath huge billowing yellow-and-red parasails towed through the air by speedboats and long tethers, the Camino Real was Mazatlán's newest hotel. Carole located him near the pool; he had a drink in his hand, and mentally she noted that Daulton might have been right—it *did* look like a good life.

Daulton, who was registered as Ted Lovelance, lived with Carole in the hotel for four days, and it was the start of a curious romance. For years Daulton had dreamed of getting the big-busted girl into bed—one friend joked he'd probably spent $5,000 at it—but despite uncounted gifts, expensive dinners and drugs, he hadn't succeeded. In Mazatlán, Daulton would believe that the tall, willowy, sexy girl was falling for him, and he later boasted in detail of their nights spent in bed at the Camino Real. Carole, in the blank, empty gaze that often characterized her, later said their relationship had been mostly platonic. But during the stormy final months of her affair with Barclay, and for a short time after that, she used Daulton to lean on.

On the night of Carole's arrival, they celebrated with margaritas and dinner at Señor Frog's, a noisy Mazatlán restaurant where seafood was served family style on long tables, while a tinny mariachi band strolled past and serenaded the diners. Afterward, they went for a swim in the hotel pool before going to bed. It was probably one of the happier episodes in Daulton's frequently tormented life.

They hired a car the next day and went sight-seeing like tourists along the spectacular curving shoreline near Mazatlán. They lunched on the jumbo shrimp for which Mazatlán is famous, then visited an arcade of shops that promoters had built to cater to the growing number of American tourists who visited the resort.

Carole admired a leather jacket in one shop, and Daulton immediately bought it. When she admired jewelry at another shop, he bought that for her too.

After they went swimming, with Carole wearing a bikini that caused one distracted American tourist to fall into the pool, Daulton returned to the arcade and spent $800 on an Oriental cloisonné vase and some pottery for Carole. During their shopping trips and at meals, she observed that the wad of cash in Daulton's wallet seemed inexhaustible; and later, she discovered why: whenever he ran out of cash, he merely picked out more from a suitcase in the room. Carole asked where the money came from, and Daulton boasted that he'd found a profitable new enterprise—selling stolen securities in Mexico.

The idyll over, Daulton bought an airline ticket to Los Angeles for Carole and kissed her good-bye.

• •

The reason Daulton had so much cash at Mazatlán was that three days before he met Carole at the Camino Real he had made another

delivery in Mexico. Chris had supplied him with another batch of month-old key-list ciphers that were supposed to have already been destroyed and copies of TWX messages regarding Rhyolite.

Along with the documents, Daulton gave the Soviets a personal message from Chris. It was in code, about thirty numbers printed on a 3-by-5-inch file card. Chris had devised the code during a quiet moment in the vault. The code was based on the number seven. Starting backward, he took the letters of the alphabet and assigned each a number based on seven. Z, the last letter of the alphabet, was assigned 7; Y was 14; X, 21; W, 28, and so on. And then he reversed the digits. X became 12; W, 82; and so forth. At the end of his coded message was the telephone number of a pay phone in Hermosa Beach, the town north of Redondo Beach. Chris had told Daulton that they needed a means to communicate with the Russians from the United States and suggested in the note that the KGB men in Mexico call the number at a specified hour—he gave them a day and time—if they had any messages. What Chris didn't say to Daulton was that he was trying to set up an independent channel of communication so that he could deal with the Russians himself and not have his fate so wrapped up in the whims of his friend. He figured the Russians could easily crack the simple code, and later he found out that he was right.

•   •

Chris's message was one symptom of mild stresses that had begun to develop in the partnership.

Unlike Daulton, Chris was not motivated in their joint enterprise by economic reasons. But he believed the Russians must be paying more for the documents than Daulton was reporting to him, and he didn't like being made a fool of. In truth, Daulton by now had received more than $10,000 from the Soviets and Chris had received only about $3,000 of it.

But money was only a minor cause of the fissures beginning to form in the espionage alliance.

The reality of what he had initiated was now tangible to Chris: *I have become a Soviet spy*. It had begun as a whim. It had started as an almost instinctive gesture of protest against a system of corrupt morality that he had despised, and he had given little thought to where it might lead. Indeed, until he received the call from "Señor Gomez" confirming that Daulton had made contact with the Russians, Chris had only half-believed his friend would have the nerve to go through

with it. Now, not only was he beginning to have misgivings, but Chris was disturbed by the increasing enthusiasm Daulton was showing for the enterprise. At first he had seemed panic-stricken at the prospect of entering the den of the KGB. Now, it seemed, he was beginning to *enjoy* it.

Daulton was also beginning to grow uneasy, but for different reasons. He sensed that Chris might be holding back documents on him, and this troubled Daulton. The Russians were a gold mine richer than any he had ever mined—they were there for the *taking*. And they had to be mined for all they were worth.

But in late August, Daulton realized that he had been wrong. When he told Chris that he was ready for another trip, Chris gave him a file of papers marked TOP SECRET and RHYOLITE and Daulton decided that he didn't have any reason to worry. In this delivery were TWX messages regarding the CIA's secret manipulations of the internal affairs of Australia.

They met at Daulton's house, where Chris gave him the material and Daulton bragged at length about his four days with the beautiful Carole Benedict, and her beautiful breasts. They shared a joint and had a game of chess, and before parting Chris had a final message for Daulton: "Remember, don't tell 'em my name."

"Don't worry," Daulton reassured him. "They think you're black —did I tell you that?"

"Let 'em think it," Chris said as he left the Lee house.

Chris decided that if he had misgivings, there was no turning back now.

21

FOR THE RUSSIANS, learning the identity of Daulton's source had become an obsession. Apparently satisfied now that the diminutive American who delivered the documents was not himself employed in a sensitive government job, they continued to press Daulton for his friend's name. In September, Daulton gave part of it to them.

He arrived in Mexico City on the first Tuesday of the month and, as instructed, taped X marks on one of the designated rows of lampposts. The Russians, in giving Daulton directions for a meeting, always used the twenty-four-hour clock; 1800 hours, for example, was 6 P.M. The following evening, at 1800 hours, he was waiting at a park that had been designated for this meeting on his last trip. Okana arrived a few minutes later with Karpov, but without The Colonel. The Colonel was now his regular case officer, but Okana was still in the picture. After an exchange of the passwords and the usual stroll beneath the trees, Daulton slipped the documents to Okana, who in turn passed them to Karpov. The chauffeur drove away, apparently headed for the embassy to assess the quality of the material. Okana and Daulton went to a restaurant, and after they had ordered a drink, they were joined by The Colonel, his shiny teeth flashing a friendly smile. Daulton greeted him with his first name: "Mikhail!" he said warmly.

Okana, Daulton decided, was deceptively slight. He had informed Daulton that he worked out by lifting weights and said he tried to run several miles daily; from the way the Russian carried himself, Daulton was beginning to realize that his body was mostly muscle. He also noticed that Okana had some capitalistic traits: he appreciated French food and old wines and fussed when his dinner wasn't prepared to his liking. Daulton would recall later: "He'd order fifty-, sixty-dollar bottles of wine. I bet he was telling his control that I had expensive tastes and he had to order good wine to keep me happy."

"Now tell us who this mysterious friend of yours is," Okana said near the end of the meal after brandy had been ordered. The Soviet Union, he said, was prepared to pay Daulton much more money— "hundreds of thousands of dollars"—if the Russians were sure the material he provided was authentic and they knew the source.

Daulton was now very nearly drunk and tried to keep up his resistance, but the promise of more money tantalized him. And when they gave him yet another business-size envelope fat with cash, part of his resistance finally melted.

"His name is Cristobal," he said.

Cristobal's father, Daulton went on, was a former agent of the FBI who now was director of security for a large American defense company. He had helped Chris get a job highly placed in the security field at TRW. He repeated that Cristobal was disgusted with his government and wanted to help the Russian cause. Daulton spelled out a few more

specifics of the job and what he knew about the function of the code room in handling messages between the CIA Headquarters, Australia and other countries. The two KGB agents exchanged smiles and seemed visibly delighted at this confirmation that they had penetrated one of America's most important satellite espionage operations at such a key location. Okana ordered more brandy.

But Daulton was not finished. His courage mobilized by wine, brandy and cocaine he had snorted before the meeting, he took the offensive: attempting to be his most persuasive, he said the Russians were paying him too little for the risks he was taking. True, his friend was motivated by ideology, he reiterated. But he was a fugitive from the law—on a phony, trumped-up drug charge, to be sure, but he was still a fugitive—and he deserved more cash for the risks he was having to take.

Steely Teeth laughed and brushed off his protests as if to say, "Don't worry. You'll get all the money you can spend." The Soviet Union was very generous with people who helped it, and there would be great rewards, he said glowingly.

Daulton, now more confident than ever, made a new proposal: on a future trip, he would exchange some information for an agreement by the Russians to carry ten kilos—twenty-two pounds—of cocaine from Lima, Peru, to the United States. There was no risk to the Russians, he said, speaking quickly, and it would augment what he considered his inadequate payments from them.

The two Russians exchanged blank looks with each other and responded to the proposition with silence. Daulton pressed the idea aggressively. The Russians had "nothing to lose." After a few more moments of silence, The Colonel said they would think it over.

Changing the subject, Okana expressed concern over Daulton's continuing practice of bringing actual documents and cipher cards from the code room. He said there would be much less risk if Cristobal photographed the documents, returned them and then passed the film to Daulton. He suggested that Daulton buy a miniature camera, a Minox-B, which was smaller than a package of cigarettes. Such a camera, he said, could be purchased in California; its negatives were small, but they could be blown up as large as the original documents.

The long evening ended after midnight, and Daulton arranged to see them again the following day.

Karpov dropped him off at the Holiday Inn—a transplanted bit of

America located in the *Zona Rosa,* the Pink Zone, of Mexico City. A rectangular area of a dozen blocks or so off the Paseo de la Reforma, the Zona Rosa was to Mexico City what Picadilly was to London and King's Cross was to Sydney—a neon-bathed hub of nightlife, restaurants, bars and shops.

As he entered the lobby, Daulton would recall later, he spotted a brunette woman who looked European standing at one side of the cavernous room, and he admired her dark good looks and her figure, which was shown off to good advantage by a white sweater. It was not unusual to see women alone at night in Mexico City, but they tended to be streetwalkers who didn't loiter inside the better hotels. Daulton thought he might have seen the woman earlier in the day, but he couldn't remember where, and he wondered if she had been following him. As Daulton moved toward an elevator, she began to walk in the same direction, and as the elevator door opened and he went in, the woman picked up her stride so that she could get in before the door closed. She smiled at Daulton, and when he reached his floor, the woman grabbed his arm and went into his room with him. Years later Daulton said of this incident: "I guess the Russians sent her to keep an eye out on me, but she didn't say anything and we just enjoyed ourselves in bed."

• •

The next morning Daulton was sitting on a bench in the Parco Popular when he heard the loping stride of a runner behind him on the grass. He looked around and saw a smiling Okana in a blue jogging suit, his face flushed and moist from perspiration.

Daulton didn't mention the woman and Okana didn't either.

The Russian walked with Daulton and expounded the rewards of jogging, a calling for which the American did not have much enthusiasm, but he listened patiently. Then the agent turned to business.

He said the latest delivery had been analyzed, and while some of the information was excellent, the Russians needed the frequencies on which the messages were broadcast.

"I know, I know," Daulton said. "I'm working on them; I'll have them next month."

Perhaps it would be a good idea, Okana added, if Cristobal made a trip to Mexico City so that they could all confer and experts in the field of communications could discuss his work. The last thing Daulton

wanted to do was bring Chris to Mexico City. Then, he realized, the Russians wouldn't need *him* anymore. But he didn't express his concern; he said he would speak to his friend about a visit. But he added that he doubted if he would want to take the risk. Then perhaps, Okana added, he could go to California and visit his friend. Daulton did not reply to that.

There was one more thing, Okana said. He needed receipts to prove that he had paid money to Daulton. Okana gave Daulton several pieces of paper with cash figures on them, and Daulton initialed them, wondering if all government bureaucracies were the same, whether the Russian (like some Americans) would cheat on his expense account and doctor the receipts to get some extra money for himself.

. .

Using an alias to get through Customs and Immigration formalities at the airport, Daulton returned to Los Angeles. He divided the $5,000 he had received with Chris and debriefed him on the trip. Daulton was more enthusiastic than ever about their joint venture; Chris said he was surprised it was still going on. "Man, they love this stuff," Daulton said. "They're crazy for it."

Daulton said the Russians wanted him to photograph the documents —and were beginning to put more pressure on him for the frequencies and for answers to some of the questions he'd brought back for Chris earlier. Casually, Daulton mentioned something Chris hadn't known: before the earlier deliveries, he had made copies of some of the documents that he'd sold to the Russians. They were stored in a secure place, Daulton said; maybe they could sell them again—to China. Chris said nothing, but did not miss the meaning of this disclosure to himself: somewhere there were copies of documents from the Black Vault that could implicate him in espionage.

Chris agreed that it would probably be safer to use a camera to photograph material in the future. But as for sending the frequencies, he said the Russians would take what was delivered.

"Fuck 'em," he said. "We'll give them what we want to give them and that's all."

22

"I'VE GOT TO BUY a spy camera," Daulton said to Barclay Granger as they cruised in Barclay's car along Hawthorne Boulevard. The spine of the Palos Verdes Peninsula, the boulevard began at the ocean and rose over The Hill to the flatlands and the edge of the vast urban sprawl of the Los Angeles basin.

"You're crazy," Granger said.

"No, I mean it; I need a baby camera," he said. He muttered that it had something to do with his new business—selling stolen securities —but wouldn't answer any questions from Barclay about his intended purpose for the camera. Granger suggested that they check a shop in the Peninsula Shopping Center in Palos Verdes, Finley's Jewelry Store. When they got there, there was a Minox-B right in the window.

A clerk at Finley's explained that the camera had belonged to one of the partners in the store, had hardly been used at all and was being sold at a cut-rate price of $155. The clerk couldn't find the instruction book for the camera, but said he would look for it. Daulton paid cash for the camera and left his telephone number so that he could be called when the instruction manual was found.

After the youths left the store, the clerk noticed that one of the accessories he had shown them—a stand for copying documents—was missing. Puzzled, he called Daulton's home, but Daulton said he didn't know what had happened to it.

Daulton liked gadgets, and during the next few days he spent hours playing with the tiny camera, photographing snowlike piles of cocaine and whipping it out of his shirt at parties and taking a picture of surprised friends, saying, "Look at my spy camera." Daulton had always loved to boast about his adventures—real or imagined—and began to drop hints that he was leading a double life. The pothead who had bragged about gunrunning and the Mexican Mafia now hinted that he was dealing with the Russians, working as an agent for the CIA.

When he told his story, it was often to friends who, like himself, were floating on coke or horse or pot, and for some of them his tales became integrated into the fantasy of their drug trips. Years later, several could not recall whether Daulton had actually told them about the Russians or if the story was something they had imagined while high.

Friends not submerged in the drug culture believed his stories even less. A neighbor whom he had grown up with on Paseo del Mar, the oceanfront street where the Lees lived, and who had gone East to college dropped by to see Daulton, and was immediately presented with an espionage novel, *The Matlock Paper* by Robert Ludlum. Daulton insisted his old playmate should read it. "It's all real," he said with a knowing expression. The neighbor, recalling the little boy who had told tall tales almost all his life, laughed it off. "A small-man complex" was the excuse he later gave for disregarding Daulton's hints of intrigue and danger.

• •

Betsy Lee Stewart was one of the few girls in Palos Verdes who had a genuine affection for Daulton—a sisterly kind of affection. Betsy was twenty, a tiny blonde with blue eyes who dreamed of becoming an airline stewardess. She and Daulton had become acquainted in high school, and although they never dated, they shared an affection for the outdoors and took long walks together on the high bluffs overlooking the ocean. They remained close after high school—close enough for each to be able to confide troubles to the other.

There was a touch of the protective mother bear in Betsy Lee. She was troubled by how some of the Palos Verdes girls—including Darlene Cooper and some of her other friends—manipulated Daulton to get free drugs. She was annoyed when they came on to Daulton, sweet and feigning interest in him to get pot or other drugs, and then ridiculed him behind his back, calling him a "creep," or "the Polack shrimp." When he didn't have drugs, they simply ignored him. But Betsy didn't ignore him.

Following graduation, she watched his descent into a life-style orbiting around narcotics and the rootless fraternity of long-haired louts and drug pushers who gravitated to the older beach communities north of Palos Verdes, and she took on Daulton as a sometime rehabilitation project. Believing she could do something for him, she spent countless

hours trying to boost his ego and tame emotional stresses that she attributed to his size, his adoption and his fear of being used.

Shortly after Daulton returned from a trip to Chicago to buy new identification papers, Betsy and Daulton met at a party at the home of a mutual friend in Palos Verdes. The party, in October, 1975, would last two days, and the refreshments would include all of the illicit narcotics available on the Peninsula in those days.

Betsy Lee hadn't seen the Minox yet, so Daulton pulled it out of his shirt pocket and told her with a conspiratorial expression that he had a new job—spying on the United States for the Russians. Betsy Lee loved the little camera, and Daulton said he would buy her one for Christmas, but she ignored the claim he was a spy as another of his coke-induced fantasies.

"You don't believe me?" he said, almost in a whisper.

"Sure I do, sure," she said.

Then he said, "I'm only kidding. I made it up."

A few moments later, Daulton seemed to get angry and reversed himself again.

"It's *true*—you don't believe me; I *am* a spy; I see the Russians all the time."

The party rolled on; more postadolescents from Palos Verdes High, along with more beer and drugs, arrived at the sprawling bluff-top home that looked out at the island of Catalina.

After midnight, Daulton was thoroughly stoned on cocaine. He said he badly needed to talk to Betsy Lee, and they went off by themselves.

Daulton confessed to her that he was afraid he was addicted to heroin. He said he was putting on a front: he told his friends that he could take it or leave it—but in fact, he couldn't.

"I don't want to be a junkie," he said, grabbing Betsy Lee in a way that frightened her.

He broke into tears and said he desperately needed someone to love; he embraced her and said it again and again, the tears rolling down his face. He said none of the girls except Betsy Lee cared anything about him except for his dope, and he repeated that he needed someone to love and to love *him*.

Betsy Lee had always suspected Daulton had a crush on her, but she wasn't prepared for the avalanche of affection and emotion that cascaded out of him. Kindly, she said she would work with him to kick

the heroin and no matter what happened, she would always be his friend.

But she made it clear that she was talking about friendship, not love.

Daulton said he couldn't possibly get off drugs without her help; he said he couldn't live without drugs unless he had someone to lean on. Touched, Betsy Lee said, "We'll do it together," wondering if his addiction might not be as much psychological as it was physical.

For the next few days, they met several hours a day at her house or his, and talked over his problems. And as they did, he began to spill out more about his new business operations in Mexico City. But Betsy Lee still couldn't believe the crazy picture of this sad friend working as a spy, and she ascribed it to madness induced by narcotics.

After a few weeks, Betsy Lee gave up the effort to liberate Daulton from his addiction; it was just taking too much of her time, she said, and just stopped calling him.

Many months later, however, after Betsy Lee knew that many of Daulton's ramblings about spies and Russian agents and stolen documents had been true, she would look back on the period when he was trying desperately but unsuccessfully to get off drugs, and say:

"It was so sad. He had really heavy emotional problems. He was confused; and I don't think he knew what he was doing. I think he just thought he could get away with something, make some money and feel important."

• •

Daulton eventually gave the Minox and tripod to Chris, and a few weeks later Chris handed Daulton four rolls of film and said the Russians should pay $50,000 for the pictures.

The next day, the first Tuesday in November, Daulton got an early-morning Mexicana Airlines Boeing 727 flight from Los Angeles and flew to Benito Juárez International Airport in Mexico City—a bustling, noisy confluence of air routes from around the country and a microcosm of its peoples: farmers from the interior, wealthy businessmen from Guadalajara and other cities, uniformed soldiers home for leave, and others.

Daulton had never had higher hopes about scoring with the Russians than on this trip.

After a limousine ride to the María Isabel–Sheraton Hotel and a quick shower, he hailed a taxi and taped X's at an intersection south-

west of Chapultepec Park. At six the following evening he was waiting near the Bali Restaurant for The Colonel to arrive. But he didn't show up, which puzzled Daulton because the Russians had never missed a meeting.

He had dinner by himself and returned to the hotel. Following the backup plan, he went to the Bali the next morning at ten. Fifteen minutes went by and still The Colonel didn't show.

Even though he had been told never to go to the embassy on his own, Daulton decided to go there and investigate. He had film that was worth thousands, and he wanted the cash to front a drug buy in Culiacán. Daulton looked into the guardhouse and didn't recognize any of the faces he saw. But he noticed that each time an automobile left or arrived at the embassy, a gate was opened.

It was a foolhardy idea, he thought, but why not? Daulton was high on coke he'd snorted to fortify himself, and it urged him on; the next time a car passed, Daulton strode matter-of-factly onto the grounds of the embassy and, bypassing the guardhouse, he entered the main building, startling a guard. He said that he wanted to see Colonel Muzankov, and pointed to his own front teeth with lips opened wide to make the guard understand whom he wanted to see. He was ordered to wait, and a few moments later Steely Teeth appeared and escorted him to what appeared to be a small office.

He scolded Daulton for coming to the embassy, but Daulton protested that he had made the mark and no one had met him.

"Where did you make the mark?" the Red Army general inquired of his spy, and Daulton told him.

"That was the wrong street," he said. Daulton had placed the adhesive marks on lampposts a full block from where they were supposed to be.

The Colonel good-naturedly brushed it off, as if to say, "No matter." Then he asked what new information Daulton had brought.

Daulton reached into his pocket and handed him the four cartridges of film Chris had given him. Karpov, the chauffeur, came in a few minutes later, smiled slightly at Daulton (intimidating him as usual) and took away the film to be developed.

A servant arrived and placed caviar and full bottles of vodka in front of Daulton and his case officer. From past experience, Daulton knew that it was the custom for each man to finish his own bottle at one sitting, and he braced for the challenge.

135

It was not yet eleven in the morning, but the two men began drinking the vodka, chasing it down with mineral water.

"To peace," the Russian said, as usual.

"To peace," Daulton agreed.

As they waited for the film to be developed, the level of vodka in their respective bottles continued to descend, and Steely Teeth asked the latest news about Cristobal. Daulton said his friend felt it would be foolish to come to Mexico as requested because he feared his superiors might hear of the trip, and that might blow the whole thing. But Daulton announced he had brought the "best" package of information so far and he knew the Russians should be happy.

"It's what you want," Daulton said.

"Es goot," his comrade said, clearly anxious for the work in the darkroom to be finished.

The Russian, whose bottle of vodka was emptying faster than Daulton's, said he was optimistic that from now on this would be a mutually beneficial operation for all—his country, Daulton and his socialist friend.

"Es goot," Daulton mimicked, saying that his friend had told him the information he had brought today should be worth $50,000.

As they waited, the Russian emotionally assailed the government of Mexico, saying that it was run by and for the rich, that there was such poverty that it was only a matter of time before the Mexican people overturned their government and embraced Communism.

Daulton asked if any decision had been made on his request to carry cocaine in the diplomatic mail, and the man shook his head, as if to say it was out of his hands. He had recommended acceptance of Daulton's proposal to higher authorities, he said reassuringly, but had not heard from them.

Daulton admired a Russian-made rug in the office with knowledgeable appreciation and told the agent he had a collection of Oriental rugs. The Russian replied with a grin that if that was the case, he must have a Russian rug, because the finest carpets in the world came from the Caucasus Mountains in his country.

At that moment, the door opened and Karpov came in carrying a stack of photographs which he placed in front of The Colonel.

• •

Daulton lounged back in his seat, waiting for The Colonel to praise the pictures. But except for the slick sound of the glossies' slapping

together as the Russian turned from one to the next, there was silence. After a while, Daulton squinted across the table to see what he was looking at.

The first few pictures seemed dark. The Colonel frowned and went on without saying anything. He paused at several on which Daulton could see, upside down, some typewritten text, but the images looked gray and some of the lettering was fuzzy. Then there were more dark prints, and the Russian sighed.

Daulton sensed things weren't going as well as he had expected.

Steely Teeth lit a cigarette, and except for the rhythmic slapping of the glossies, there was more silence in the room. He flipped over one picture and stared at it for a long time, then turned it vertically, then horizontally again, as if he were attempting to decipher something.

Daulton rose slightly out of his seat to see what it was that interested him. Vodka and cocaine had left their mark on Daulton, and he had to struggle to bring his eyes into sharp focus.

What he saw puzzled him. He thought he saw the curves of a woman.

He looked again and decided that he could definitely see the nipples of a woman and, below them, a triangle of pubic hair. He shook his head, trying to shake off the effects of the coke, and looked again.

Daulton was sure now that he was looking at a photograph of a nude woman. The Colonel also studied the picture, but he didn't say anything. Daulton decided that *he* had better not say anything either.

The KGB officer turned over another picture from the stack and Daulton saw a nude man and a nude woman. It looked as if they were fucking on a bed. Daulton shifted uncomfortably in his chair and avoided the Russian's eyes.

There was more silence.

The Colonel turned another picture, then another and another. They were all nudes.

Muzankov picked up the pictures and slammed them down hard in front of Daulton so that they slid across the table and almost landed in his lap, and then he let loose with an angry tirade in Russian.

Daulton didn't know what he was saying, but from the look on his face he knew what he meant. He fought to conceal his surprise and fear and said with a hastily mobilized smile that his friend must have sent the pictures as a joke.

Unfortunately, the KGB man did not enjoy the joke. He studied

Daulton for a long moment, then began looking at the remaining pictures in the stack of more than one hundred exposures.

Some were "goot," he said. But too many, he said, were overexposed.

"Look at *thees*—terrible," he said of one group of glossies.

"*Basura*"—garbage—he said of another.

Daulton's friend, he implored, must practice; he was not a good photographer yet. It was essential that he obtain instruction from Soviet experts who could meet him in Los Angeles, Mexico City or somewhere else. It was necessary, the Russian repeated, for his friend to become a better photographer.

He pointed out more examples of bad photography—documents that were fuzzy or shot from out of range—and he said the camera should be placed exactly forty centimeters from the documents that were being photographed.

Daulton, once again, said his friend couldn't leave America without taking a risk because his employers required him to inform them each time he left the United States. "Then *you* should come to Vienna," the Russian said. The Russians would pay for the trip, he continued, and Daulton could get photography lessons and other training; he, in turn, could coach Cristobal.

Daulton heard him out, but refused to commit himself.

"What about the money?" he said, undaunted by the dressing down and the embarrassment over the nudes. Chris had said this delivery was worth $50,000, and he was determined to get it.

The Soviet agent laughed and said most of the photographs were worthless. But when he saw Daulton about to protest, he assured him that he would be paid something for the shipment, and if the quality improved, future shipments would be worth much more. Daulton relaxed and vowed to himself to have a serious talk with Chris about his nude pictures.

The two men tossed down more glasses of vodka; lunch was brought in; and the Russian said they should move ahead with plans for the Vienna trip. Daulton, beneath his alcoholic haze, wondered whether the Russians might be planning to spirit him away permanently to Eastern Europe, but he tried not to reveal his wariness. Whether he made the trip, he told the Russian, depended on some business problems he had to deal with in the United States, and he repeated he would let him know his decision later.

The Colonel said they needed some means of direct communication

when Daulton was in America and gave Daulton a list of three pay telephones and their numbers in California—one in a parking garage in San Francisco, one in Santa Monica across from a statue of the Blessed Virgin Mary and one at Grauman's Chinese Theater in Hollywood, the theater with the footprints of famous movie stars cast in concrete near the entrance. He simply ignored Chris's proposal for a telephone drop in Hermosa Beach. Daulton was given a list of times when he was supposed to be waiting near each phone for a call. The Colonel also asked if there was an address in California where the Russians could send mail to him without being detected. Daulton suggested a mail drop at the home of his sister in Santa Cruz. The Colonel explained how the mail drop was to work:

From time to time the Russians would send him a picture showing the Pyramid of the Sun. One of Mexico's most famous landmarks, the pyramid was a huge archaeological ruin a few miles from Mexico City that had been built 2,400 years ago by an ancient Mexican culture.

The postcards, the Russian said, would be mailed to him at his sister's address inside an envelope. But he emphasized that the message on the card would be less important than the date listed on it: Daulton was to add seven days to the date to determine when the next meeting was to occur. The meeting would be at 1800 hours on the designated day, or if for any reason this meeting was missed, it would be at 1000 hours the following morning.

Daulton brought up the money again, insisting the material he had brought was worth at least $5,000. Without a word, the Russian handed Daulton an envelope containing $6,500—$5,000 for the delivery, and $1,500 to finance a trip to Vienna. But he reiterated his concern that the quality of the photography had to be improved. He urged Daulton again to ask his friend for data on TRW's infrared sensors and to see if he could obtain ciphers for the coding machines several months ahead of when they would be used. For each package of the advance ciphers, he said, there would be a premium payment of $10,000.

They were the kind of parting words Daulton liked to hear.

• •

"It doesn't matter what we send them; they'll pay for it," Chris insisted when Daulton complained about the nudes. Chris explained that he had photographed pictures in a copy of *Hustler* magazine that someone had left in the vault.

"Big joke; it's my fuckin' ass that's on the line, fucker," Daulton

said angrily. "I'm risking my life. Big fuckin' joke; it wasn't funny." But, correctly, Chris pointed out that Daulton had returned with another envelope filled with cash, and that in itself, he said, proved his point. Daulton said he had to agree, and they both burst into smug laughter. Daulton could not forget the eager look on the Russian's face. Nevertheless, he said, "*Please* try to get something good next time." Then he filled Chris in on more of the details of his trip. They passed a joint back and forth and decided that since Daulton had a code name, Chris should have one too. Daulton thought of one, and they agreed on it: "Falcon."

23 FAR FROM PALOS VERDES, Redondo Beach or Mexico City, the simmering political dispute in Australia over the American bases near Alice Springs was coming to a boil in October of 1975.

Whether or not the controversy over the secret bases was fueled by facts leaked to Labour Party members or the press by the KGB— information the KGB had purchased in Mexico City from two young Americans—is a matter for conjecture. But one thing was obvious: politically damaging hints about the CIA's activities in Australia were coming from somewhere and threatening to ignite a fire storm that might consume the bases politically.

Cables flew back and forth between Canberra and Washington. On the day following Whitlam's speech, senior Australian military and intelligence officials in Canberra briefed Queen Elizabeth's governor-general, Sir John Kerr (who had a personal background in military intelligence during World War II), and advised him of the CIA's grave apprehension that public discussion of the facilities could be disastrous.

On November 10, 1975, five days after Daulton's latest delivery in Mexico City, the Australian Security Intelligence Organization received a message from its liaison officer with the CIA in Washington.

Repeating expressions of concern voiced previously by the U.S. intelligence agency over public discussion of the bases, he said he had just returned from a meeting with senior CIA representatives and, attempting to summarize its contents, he reported:

CIA IS PERPLEXED AS TO WHAT ALL THIS MEANS. DOES THIS SIGNIFY SOME CHANGE IN OUR BILATERAL INTELLIGENCE SECURITY RELATED FIELD. CIA CANNOT SEE HOW THIS DIALOGUE WITH CONTINUED REFERENCE TO CIA CAN DO OTHER THAN BLOW THE LID OFF THOSE INSTALLATIONS IN AUSTRALIA WHERE THE PERSONS CONCERNED HAVE BEEN WORKING AND THAT ARE VITAL TO BOTH OUR SERVICES AND COUNTRIES, PARTICULARLY THE INSTALLATIONS AT ALICE SPRINGS.

Nevertheless, members of the Labour Party were increasingly raising public inquiries and making pointed comments about the mysterious facilities. Late in October the Government revealed that construction of the bases had not been supervised by the U.S. Department of Defense, as claimed by the previous government, but by a CIA official, whose name became public. It was revealed during inquiries by Labour Party members that not even senior members of the Australian Foreign Ministry had been told the exact function of the bases.

But the mystery over the purpose of the bases in the Australian desert was not the only one being talked about regarding the CIA.

Prime Minister Whitlam began to charge in public that the American intelligence organization—which at that time was incurring growing international notoriety over its suspected machinations in Chile—had tampered with the Australian political process by secretly channeling funds to his opponents in the Liberal and National Country parties—politicians who had supported the American bases. Whitlam demanded an investigation by the Australian Defense Department to identify, once and for all, the real purpose of the bases.

In early November, the Prime Minister said in a speech that he had confirmed reports the CIA had indeed built the facilities. This official acknowledgment of the CIA's role in Australia intensified the crisis atmosphere within certain components of the CIA, where it was feared the political brouhaha could explode and force closing of the bases. The threat was perceived as anything but a minor matter. Within the National Security Council, the bases were considered absolutely vital to America's survivability in an era of nuclear warfare, not only be-

cause of Projects Rhyolite and Argus but because of other satellite espionage systems that were considered indispensable to the country's efforts to keep a constant eye on Soviet military preparedness.

The message from Washington concluded with a warning that if public discussion of CIA operations and facilities in Australia continued, the United States might see fit to stop sharing its intelligence information with Australia. (At the time, Australia had thought it was receiving *all* of the information from the satellites.)

What other steps the CIA took to protect its bases and ensure a friendly government in Canberra are not known.

On November 11, Prime Minister Whitlam had scheduled another speech in which he was to discuss the CIA and the mysterious installations in the Outback.

But he never got a chance to deliver it. On that day, Governor-General Sir John Kerr removed him from office.

24

ROBERT LANGSTROTH, a twenty-eight-year-old Vietnam veteran who found a job with the Palos Verdes Estates Police Department when he came back from the war, was at the wheel of a city police car about six o'clock on a Saturday night three weeks before Christmas in 1975. It was nearly dark, with only an orange-and-rose haze still lingering over the Pacific as he guided the black-and-white Dodge past the oceanfront homes lining Paseo del Mar.

Langstroth had just rounded a curve near the Lee family's silver-gray home when he saw a red sports car about fifty yards ahead of him and noticed that the red reflector was missing from one of the car's taillights. He decided to stop the car and advise the driver, thinking he probably wasn't aware of it.

Switching on his red lights, Langstroth moved in behind the sports car.

Daulton looked in his mirror and was startled by the glowing double

red eyes behind him. He speed-shifted the MG into second without hesitating and jammed his foot on the accelerator. By the time he was at the first corner, the roadster was doing 80. Daulton took this corner without moving his foot off the gas; the police car, its siren screaming, however, stayed right behind him, and the two vehicles roared through the neighborhood of some of Palos Verdes' most expensive homes.

When he reached Palos Verdes Drive, a four-lane divided highway that hugged the ocean, Daulton turned right without stopping and picked up speed, missing an oncoming station wagon by eight or ten feet. When Langstroth followed him around the corner, he had even less room to spare.

With open road ahead of him, Daulton floored the agile roadster, and was soon careening at more than 100 miles an hour along the curving drive that clung to a rocky bluff high above a stretch of turbulent white surf.

Langstroth saw a small package sail out of the speeding car; but before he could react, the MG swerved off the highway into the dirt center divider strip, digging up such a cloud of dust that for a moment Langstroth lost the red car in his headlights. The policeman now expected the driver to make a quick U-turn on the divider strip, and he slowed to loop around behind him.

But instead of slowing and turning in the opposite direction, Daulton gunned the engine and headed south again—going the wrong way in the one-way lane.

Sitting beside Daulton in the car, Peter Frank begged for him to stop. A high school friend and fellow falconer, Frank had been visiting Daulton at his home when Daulton suggested they go for a ride in the MG, which was owned by his brother, David.

Rocketing south on the northbound road, Daulton said he couldn't stop.

"They've got a warrant out on me," he said.

At that moment Frank saw a Pontiac headed directly at them and shouted, "Turn, turn!"

Daulton yanked the steering wheel and the car bounced back into the divider strip, out of the path of the Pontiac, and skidded crazily in the dirt. The MG shuddered as Daulton pressed the accelerator and tried to get it moving again in the loose dirt. As the car's wheels groped for traction and momentarily spun, Frank opened the door and threw himself out.

Langstroth saw a young man with shoulder-length brown hair, wearing Levi's and a blue Levi jacket, but lost him as he sprinted in the direction of the ocean cliffs.

Daulton finally managed to get the car under control and back onto Palos Verdes Drive, and tried to lose the policeman by using the sports car's maneuverability to turn sharply into a residential neighborhood.

Langstroth saw him make the turn, and started to follow, but the police car was traveling at almost 100 miles an hour. He fought the wheel to stay with the MG, but his prowl car was too heavy and was going too fast, and it went into a long, sweeping skid.

Langstroth spotted another car headed directly at him. It was northbound on Palos Verdes Drive. The driver had begun to heed the red light and siren and was pulling to a stop. But the wheels of Langstroth's patrol car were locked and he was skidding, and there was nothing he could do except wait for the impact. The police car slammed into the other vehicle and spun around. But Langstroth discovered his car was still operable, and he picked up the pursuit.

Once again Daulton was headed south in the northbound lanes. Northbound cars, bewildered by the sight of Daulton's approaching headlights and the flashing red lights behind them, peeled off onto the shoulder like birds scattering from the sight of a man with a gun. At the foot of Hawthorne Boulevard, just where it slopes down and ends at the ocean, Daulton turned left and began to climb up the slope in the direction of Los Angeles. Then, in another try to lose the cop, he made a sharp turn and veered onto a steep incline leading to a residential side street.

This time Langstroth was ready and stayed right behind him. For Daulton, the turn was a mistake: he had to slow the MG to 60 miles an hour as it rose up the hill, and the more powerful engine in Langstroth's car began to close the gap.

Still, Daulton gave no sign of abandoning his run. The policeman decided there was only one way he could stop the fugitive. He accelerated the police car and aimed it directly at the rear of the laboring MG.

He struck it, and Daulton's car was rammed into a curb. He wasn't hurt, but he was stopped.

When the police discovered that the fleeing suspect had a wad of bills totaling $302 in his pocket, Daulton was booked for armed robbery and reckless driving. Daulton scoffed at the robbery charge and said he could settle everything.

Detectives were called to the Palos Verdes Estates Police Station from their homes and took the case over from the uniformed division. Daulton told the detectives that his name was Ted Lovelance and that he was a resident of Santa Cruz; he identified himself with his driver's license. He explained that he had been traveling down the coast from Santa Cruz to San Diego and in order to enjoy the scenery had passed through Palos Verdes Estates, where he had picked up a hitchhiker. He didn't know the hitchhiker's name, but he remembered that he wore Levi's and had shoulder-length hair. Everything had been normal, he continued, until the police car tried to stop him; when the red lights went on, he said, the hitchhiker had drawn a gun and told him to lose the patrol car. After that, Daulton said, he had had no choice but to obey out of fear for his life.

"Why didn't you stop when he jumped out?" a detective asked incredulously.

"I wanted to get as far away from that guy as I could."

"What about the money?"

"It's for my vacation."

Another detective who was standing by during the questioning picked up the driver's license and took a second look at Daulton. The license said the driver was five feet five. He noticed that Daulton was several inches shorter. The detectives conferred in another room, and one recalled that there was a felony warrant outstanding for a drug pusher who was quite short—just like this suspect.

After a check of the files, a detective returned to Daulton and asked him to roll up the sleeves of his shirt to the elbows. Daulton silently complied.

The officers saw a panorama of inflamed skin. The blotches weren't drug-injection puncture marks, as the cops thought, but evidence of Daulton's old problem with acne. But they didn't believe it was acne.

"Are you a hype?" a policeman asked. Daulton repeatedly denied that he was an addict, but the red scars on his arm worked against him.

Finally, Daulton admitted his real name.

The robbery charge was dropped, and he was booked for reckless driving, resisting arrest, driving under the influence of a controlled substance and displaying a fictitious driver's license and as a fugitive wanted for violation of probation on drug charges.

Four days later, Daulton was out of jail.

He posted $2,500 bail, including $500 borrowed from Chris, who

extracted an I.O.U. in exchange for the loan for which he would be repaid after the next delivery to the Russians. Judge Burch Donahue said he would take up the case again in early January. Until then, at least, Daulton was back on the streets.

There were two postscripts to the chase: Officer Langstroth, in a case that would drag on unresolved for years, sued David Lee for more than $1 million, because of back injuries he had received in the collision with the car which Lee owned. And when drugs were found in the other car that Langstroth collided with during the chase, a passenger was arrested for possession of illicit drugs.

. .

Daulton's long-pending arrest warrant had finally caught up with him. Yet within two days of the arrest, he was out on bail. Over the next year, in a curious demonstration of the workings of the American judicial system, he would constantly be able to postpone his return to jail. Perhaps the system worked precisely as it was supposed to by giving Daulton every constitutional protection, every opportunity for rehabilitation—not only a second chance but third and fourth chances. Perhaps the system was abused. But because of a compliant court and the skills of an effective attorney, Daulton was able to avoid his final denouement on the drug charges for many months while continuing his transactions with the Russians.

His lawyer, Kenneth Kahn, was, like Daulton and Chris, a product of a particular time and place that had left a mark on him. Thirty-three years old, he had grown up in a poor family in Los Angeles, become a politically conservative American Legion "Boy of the Year" in high school, gotten high marks at the University of California at Los Angeles and entered Boalt Hall Law School at Berkeley. And there, like so many students at Berkeley in the sixties, he was radicalized. He joined the Free Speech Movement and other student protest groups and, after passing the bar, twice gave up his law practice—once to spend six months in the Federal prison on Terminal Island in California on a hashish-possession charge, and once to travel around the world. When he finally settled down, Ken Kahn discovered a lucrative specialty: defending the young drug dealers and users from the Palos Verdes Peninsula—a crop of defendants that, for many years, seemed inexhaustible, and many of whom became his friends.

With dense, curly brown hair, a curly moustache and muttonchops, Kahn was facetiously called "the hippie lawyer" by some of his col-

leagues. He looked the part and liked the allusion. In court, he had a feisty style that some judges called abrasive—but he was very good at what he did, agilely challenging the constitutionality of police searches, seizures and arrests in order to keep his clients out of jail—or at least postpone their day of reckoning.

25

As 1975 ENDED, each of the two young friends from Palos Verdes was facing a personal crisis that would make him more desperate.

There weren't any problems for Chris on the job: he was continuing to impress his TRW superiors as a likely candidate for promotion, and the CIA offered him another job—this time as a courier between the United States and the bases in Australia. He turned down the offer, realizing that before the CIA hired him he would have to take a lie-detector test that almost certainly would reveal his thefts from the Black Vault. Chris still hated the agency and what it stood for—more now than ever. But what had begun as an impulsive slap at a system he hated was becoming a nightmare. He constantly asked himself, Why haven't they caught us? Chris knew that Lee Harvey Oswald had visited the Soviet Embassy in Mexico City—the *same* embassy—and had been photographed by U.S. agents before John F. Kennedy was assassinated. He knew Daulton had entered the embassy twice. Surely, he told himself, someone must have spotted Daulton and discovered his transactions with the KGB.

There were not only the CIA and the FBI—and possibly the KGB —to worry about; there was Daulton himself. Somehow, the shape of his protest was being distorted. He now realized that Daulton was using some of the money he earned selling secrets about the satellites to expand his heroin trade, and occasionally Chris saw what it did to his customers: there were reports of two customers who had died from heroin overdoses and rumors of a third. One day, near the end of 1975, when Chris dropped by Daulton's home he found a girl, a high school student, lying on the living-room floor. Daulton and several friends were looking down at her, uncertain what to do. Heroin had trans-

muted the young girl's complexion to an ugly shade of bluish green; there was a gurgle originating somewhere in her chest, and gray saliva had foamed around her mouth. Chris mobilized two other girls in the room, and they undressed the overdosed adolescent and stood her up in a shower. He left the Lee house as soon as that was accomplished, but as he drove away he felt guilt for not having the courage to stay longer, and even more guilt for allowing his protest to be twisted into a medium for killing young people. He asked himself then, as he would many times in the following months: What have I done? What monster have I helped to create?

. .

Chris realized that he had set a trap for himself—and it was beginning to squeeze around him. One of the first things Chris did in 1976 was buy a .25-caliber automatic. He didn't know if, or how, he would use it.

Sometimes when Chris became depressed, he wondered, *Is what I am doing so wrong?* At night, when he was lying in bed and thoughts of the espionage scheme weighed on him, Chris would recall later, he could hear the creaky artificial leg of Rick, and then he had nightmarish visions of orange-and-white mushroom clouds rising into the sky, and he thought, once again, of the insanity of the superpowers—of mankind itself.

In his contempt for the empty nationalism and the CIA dirty tricks of which he was a part, Chris found an anchor to rationalize his decision to continue—and it was reinforced daily as he read of still more CIA activities of which he disapproved.

The communications operators at Pilot were sloppy; they frequently sent messages on the circuit to Pedal that were supposed to go to other stations on the CIA circuit. Some of the messages told of CIA operations and machinations that spanned the globe. When Chris saw the messages clack over his machines, he immediately signaled back: PEDAL CANNOT PROTECT.

The operator at Langley would then request destruction of the message and a tight lip about his goof. Chris responded that he was complying with the request, but sometimes he held a copy of the errant message, to show to other members of the TRW security organization who enjoyed reading the agency's missent mail.

Chris increasingly found solace for his confused, ambivalent conscience in drugs and drinks. Early in 1976, Daulton told him that if he

was not careful he might become an alcoholic. When all else failed—when even alcohol didn't work—Chris always had one other escape to fall back on. He went to the hills and flew his falcon.

. .

Other demons were taunting Daulton. He feared that he was losing his on-again, off-again struggle against heroin. Unlike some addicts, he occasionally managed to kick the addiction by himself; he would keep himself off the drug for two or three months, then be drawn back to its pleasures. A lot of the money he was getting from the Russians was going for heroin, sometimes at a rate of $1,000 a week—not injected but snorted. Daulton had prided himself that he could always "turn off" his addiction when he wanted, but as he confessed to Betsy Lee Stewart, it was becoming harder and harder to do so; he also dreaded the prospect of returning to jail, and was depressed because he was not getting what he wanted most—the respect of his father.

Dr. Lee had continued to let his son live at home during his frequent encounters with narcotics officers, but did not conceal his displeasure over what had become of Daulton. His disappointment surfaced particularly painfully for Daulton in an ugly scene on Christmas Eve.

All of the family had been home for the holidays. The Christmas tree was surrounded, as usual, by a mountain of packages. There were cocktails and then champagne with dinner, and both father and son were close to being drunk when the confrontation began:

"For God's sake, why don't you get out of this dope racket and do something constructive? Be useful," Dr. Lee pleaded.

"Jesus Christ," Daulton exploded angrily. "Do you know what I'm doing? I'm working for the government right now. I'm working for the goddamned government right now."

"Oh, sure."

Dr. Lee's sarcasm clawed at Daulton.

"I am, I am," he insisted.

His father grew angrier and angrier and finally left the room. Daulton broke into tears. "Why don't you believe me?" he said sobbingly. "I'm working for the CIA!"

. .

Daulton concocted a plan that he believed would convince his father that he was a success: he would buy him a vacation home on the coast in Mexico—at Puerto Vallarta or Acapulco. He'd also get off smack

and put some money into a legitimate business—maybe the Golden Cove Deli. David had learned it was available for $10,000.

Now he had to get the Russians to pay for both.

But he wondered again about Chris; he wasn't as free as he'd been at first with the stuff the Russians wanted. Daulton felt that he was in a squeeze: on one side he was being squeezed by the eager Russians, who had an insatiable appetite and were willing to pay sums that potentially could dwarf his income from drug dealing; and on the other, Daulton thought he was being squeezed by Chris, who wasn't giving the Russians some of the stuff they asked for. When he could not decide how to deal with his many problems, he retreated to heroin or cocaine yet again; more and more, drugs became the only refuge that gave him peace.

26

"YOU'VE GOT A LETTER HERE," his sister said over the telephone from Santa Cruz.

The news excited Daulton. "Open it," he said.

Inside the envelope, Daulton's sister found only a picture postcard. She noticed that the handwriting on the card was unusual—lots of Cyrillic flourishes, which made her wonder if it had been written by a woman or a foreigner. The message was brief:

Dec. 22

Am anxious to look at your book of antique rugs, Luis. Looking forward to seeing you on your next visit.

Your friend
John

Daulton was delighted to receive the card. He needed cash to finance his escalating legal battle to avoid going back to jail. He flew to Mexico City on December 29, seven days after the date on the card, and following instructions received at his previous Mexico City meeting, met The Colonel that evening at the Bali Restaurant. The city was

ablaze with the glow of neon lights depicting the Holy Family, the Christ Child and other tableaux that were a fixture in Mexico City during the holidays. Because the meeting had been called on short notice, Daulton told the Russian he had not had a chance to get much new information; he presented to him several KG-13 ciphers he had received several months previously from Chris and held for a future delivery. There was also another coded message from Chris. Later, when they decoded it, the KGB men discovered that they were accused of being "incompetent" by their secret source in California. Chris was piqued that the Soviets had taken so long to set up a phone link, and he told them so.

It was a routine delivery. The only problem was a clash over Daulton's living style. The Colonel complained that he was living too capitalistically and deplored Daulton's affection for Mexico City's fanciest hotels. Not only was such high life too conspicuous for a secret agent, he said, but—and this seemed to bother him even more—it was unbecoming for a servant of socialism. He gave Daulton the name of another hotel. Daulton had never heard of it, but reluctantly, he agreed to move; he checked out of his $50-a-day room in the Holiday Inn and rode in a taxi forty-five minutes to the outskirts of the city, each moment growing more unhappy. Spy or not, Daulton told himself, he wasn't going to live in the slums. He checked into the hotel, a small, two-story workingman's hotel in an industrial part of the city, and an hour later, without even opening his bag, he checked out and returned to the Holiday Inn. When he saw The Colonel the next morning, he ridiculed the Russians' choice. "It was a fleabag," he protested. The Russian laughed but didn't try to change his mind; he was beginning to realize that Andrew Daulton Lee was not an easy agent to control.

Even though he didn't have much new data to offer the Russian, the trip proved to be one of Daulton's finer hours as a con man. He was, by now, getting the hang of dealing with the Soviets. He had learned how to whet their appetites with persuasive promises. With sky's-the-limit optimism, he confided to The Colonel that his friend believed that he had finally found a means to get information about the TRW infrared sensors. Moreover, he boasted, his friend was also optimistic about getting the frequencies used in the code-room transmissions. Both were lies, but they seemed to impress the agent. Finally, Daulton said that he was willing to go to Vienna for training and consultation—but only after he wrapped up some personal legal problems. They could

discuss the timing of his trip after the first of the year, he added. Steely Teeth said he was delighted. In observance of the Christmas season, he presented Daulton with three bottles of French brandy and $5,000 in $100 bills. But the night did not produce a one-sided victory. Daulton got drunk, and under probing by the KGB man, he disclosed the full name of his friend in California.

.   .

Daulton didn't have to feign optimism when he returned to California.

"Look at the beautiful Benjies," he gloated, fanning the bills in front of Chris. "Benjies" was his personal nickname for $100 bills. "Benjamin Franklin," he once said of the man whose face appears on $100 bills, "is my favorite person." Two years later, Chris would say of Daulton, still with a trace of grudging admiration, "He was really a talented huckster. All he needed, he'd say, was one more month and he'd have President Ford's own diary."

.   .

When Daulton returned from Mexico City, his most pressing need was some legal magic. His hearing before Judge Donahue was scheduled for January 7, 1976, and it was certain that the district attorney's office would try to have him remanded immediately to prison. Furthermore, the narcotics agent who had been burned by Daulton in March —when he'd made the deal to act as an informant and then skipped to Mexico—had refiled charges of selling cocaine. Ken Kahn told Daulton that the policeman was furious and was out for blood.

"Kenny, get me out of this, whatever you have to do," Daulton implored. Kahn said he would try, but it wouldn't be easy.

"We could send you to a shrink," he suggested. And with that a plan took shape.

Judge Donahue had a reputation as a compassionate man who would give defendants every chance to rehabilitate themselves if there was the smallest chance of success. A defense strategy emerged: an attempt would be made to prove that Daulton had become, first, a drug user and, second, a drug pusher because of *treatable* psychiatric problems.

On January 7, Kahn urged Donahue to postpone the disposition of Daulton's case until he could undergo a psychiatric examination to determine if there was a chance he could be rehabilitated without

prison. This was a turning point in a human life, the lawyer argued; it was an opportunity to save a young man from an exemplary family, a young man who had become trapped in the quicksand of drugs and now needed the court's hand to help pull him out. The judge agreed to an examination.

Two days later, Daulton returned to court to answer the charges of illicit drug sales that had been refiled by the undercover narcotics detective. But after a hearing at which the betrayed detective testified, Kahn won a ruling that the police raid in March had been made with a search warrant issued without sufficient grounds. Daulton was off the hook. As he walked out of the courtroom, Daulton was approached by the angry lawman.

"Lee, as long as it takes," he said, "I'm going to get you. I'm going to burn you."

Daulton looked up into the eyes of the detective, who stood almost a foot taller than he did, and decided that he meant it. But Daulton was not one to give anyone the edge, and not long afterward, when two Federal Drug Enforcement Administration agents approached him with an offer that he work as an informant for *them,* he said he wouldn't think of it; lying, he said that he'd agreed to work for a Los Angeles County Sheriff's Department narc who had busted him once, and then the cop had leaked the knowledge that he was an informant to another pusher. The DEA men then complained to the Sheriff's Department about the bungling officer who had blown a potentially valuable informant.

•   •

Arrangements were made for Daulton to see a psychiatrist in Beverly Hills, and two weeks after the January 7 hearing, Judge Donahue read his report:

Preliminary Psychiatric Report
Re: Mr. Andrew Daulton Lee
Age: 24
The above was seen in one hour psychiatric interviews on 1/15/76 and 1/19/76. He presented as an extremely tense young man who says he suffers from a peptic ulcer, a nervous rash (he shows me on his back) and is depressed and pessimistic about the prospect of spending a protracted period of confinement in either a prison or a mental institution as a result of probation violation.

For a similar reason he has spent a year in Mexico to avoid the

consequences of an alleged violation, returning last November to visit his family but getting involved in trying to escape police investigation in a car chase which ended in his arrest. He denies drug involvement in that incident, or significant use of drugs other than occasional smoking of marijuana for a couple of years, although he has been involved since his teens in drug peddling and using it with much legal consequences.

On examination he seemed intelligent and articulate and began to attempt to justify his difficulties by various rationalizations. Before long, however, he was able to communicate more freely and came across as a seriously depressed young man who is unsure whether he can rehabilitate himself into anything like a normal life. He is extremely tense although becomes less so as he settled into the interview.

He is intelligent and showed no evidence of organicity. Altho somewhat suspicious and paranoid this was not to any psychotic degree, nor were there any indications of any other thought disorder.

Impression: Anxiety state severe with depression and psychophysiologic concomitants, drug use in the past, not however apparently under any drug influence now despite severe insomnia.

Recommendations: Would seem to have reached a crisis of identity and is in conflict whether or not he can rejoin society and at the moment would seem a suitable candidate for intensive psychotherapy to begin within a supervised hospital setting. (I have reserved a bed at the Westwood Psychiatric Hospital for him). Rapport with myself seemed good.

It is my clinical opinion that this course of action under probation supervision offers what may be the last chance this troubled young man has to rehabilitate himself.

There were other items in the file of Andrew Daulton Lee on January 21, 1976, when Judge Donahue was to decide whether he should be sent back to jail, including letters from friends and his family, including one that read:

I am willing to do everything within my ability to rehabilitate my son, Andrew Lee.

Sincerely,
Daulton B. Lee
Pathologist

Kahn, emphasizing that there was now medical evidence of hope for Daulton, asked Judge Donahue to give him a chance and allow him to

undertake psychotherapy before making a final decision that might deprive him of his last chance at rehabilitation. Consenting to the proposal, Donahue placed Daulton on probation once again, conditioned that he stay out of trouble, that he neither take drugs nor associate with people who did, that he take periodic tests to determine if he was using narcotics, that he enroll in school or seek employment and "enter forthwith the Westwood Psychiatric Hospital."

Five days later, Daulton was admitted to the clinic in Westwood, the community best known as the site of the University of California at Los Angeles. After six days, he was discharged with an agreement to continue twice-weekly sessions as an outpatient.

Daulton told Chris about his experiences with the psychiatrist after he got out.

"You wouldn't believe me in action," he boasted. "I conned the shit out of him, and he believed me. You know what he told me? He said he'd give me the same kind of advice he gave to a prostitute—'if you really like what you're doing, do it.' " Daulton said the psychiatrist continually interrogated him about his feelings about being adopted and wouldn't believe him when he said he didn't have any hang-ups about it. When the psychiatrist asked Daulton why he made so many trips to Mexico, Daulton told Chris, "I told him I couldn't take the city here and all the people and had to go by myself all alone in Mexico and think, and he bought it."

27 A POSTCARD requesting another meeting in Mexico City had arrived at his sister's home while he was in the hospital, and two days after his release, Daulton boarded an early-morning Western Airlines flight at Los Angeles International Airport bound for Mexico City. This time he had a traveling companion, his old friend Barclay Granger.

Like Daulton, Barclay was waging a court battle to stay out of prison. He had been arrested by Federal agents in October for cocaine trafficking and was free on bail pending his trial. Two things had hap-

pened to Barclay the preceding December: he had had a run-in with the Mafia, and he had finally broken up with Carole Benedict. Carole had flown to Hawaii to live with Barclay's mother, who had taken her side in the couple's fight. But the handsome surfer wasn't lacking for female company. Darlene Cooper had now moved into the Redondo Beach apartment that he'd previously shared with Carole.

The encounter with the Mafia had had less pleasant aftereffects. Many South Bay drug traders knew that the owners of an Italian restaurant in Redondo Beach claimed to have ties to a New York Mafia organization. Theirs was a minor-league operation, in terms of organized crime, but the family did wholesale drug peddling.

One member of the family, a young man in his early twenties with limited ambitions, had entered the South Bay retail drug trade. At a point sometime in September, 1975, one of his customers had gotten into debt with him for more than $3,000 worth of heroin, and the Italian had decided to cut off the addict until he paid his bill. He had sent word to other local pushers to cut him off too.

Barclay, like Daulton, had received the message not to sell to the youth, who was a teen-ager living in Redondo Beach. But he ignored it.

One night, about 3 A.M., Granger drowsily opened the front door of his apartment. Before he could see who his callers were, two men attacked him and broke his jaw.

. .

At the time Daulton and Barclay boarded the jetliner bound for Mexico City early in February, Granger's jaw had been wired for two months; his doctor had just removed the wire, and the trip was partly to celebrate this milestone. Barclay had seen Daulton regularly during the past few months, usually when Daulton had sought a place to hide during his quick trips to the States. Granger thought he had noticed some changes in his friend. "He wasn't the same guy anymore—he was scared all the time—afraid of strangers, anybody." Granger figured that he had become paranoid because he was afraid of being busted again by undercover narcs. "You couldn't even discuss the weather with him without him looking around to see if someone was listening," he would recall. Once, when he watched Daulton try to roll a marijuana joint, Barclay said, "Look at your hands: they're shaking all over the place."

"I'm just getting old," Daulton said.

Granger didn't like to fly, so he swallowed two large barbiturates just before they took off. Daulton was lost in an espionage novel as the Boeing 727 droned south toward Mexico City when he noticed that a stewardess was shaking Barclay.

"He's on fire!" she said.

Daulton then smelled smoke and discovered that the smoke was coming from Granger. Quickly, he helped the stewardess arouse his friend, and they discovered he had gone to sleep with a lighted cigarette in his hand, and it had burned a large dark hole in the inside left elbow of his jacket. Granger woke up and they laughed about it and he lit another cigarette. Daulton went back to his novel. A few minutes later, the stewardess was standing over him again. This time, the cigarette had burned a hole in his right coat sleeve. "You wake him up this time," she said.

•   •

Daulton had bragged to Barclay that he knew Mexico "like the back of my hand" and promised to show him a good time, tantalizing him with descriptions of Mexican prostitutes he had done business with on previous trips. The jetliner landed in Mexico City shortly before 11 A.M., and they rode in a cab to the Holiday Inn. Daulton hurried Barclay to their room, which they immediately left after dropping their suitcases.

"I've got to tell my people I'm in town," Daulton said as their taxi pulled away from the hotel.

Granger noticed that they were headed outward from the center of the city toward what appeared to be a residential area. He was unfamiliar with the geography of Mexico City and asked Daulton where they were headed. Daulton ignored the question, but with a touch of mystery that seemed to give him pleasure, Daulton said, "I've got to set up a meeting with my uncle."

At Daulton's instruction, the cab driver stopped in what Barclay took to be a neighborhood of expensive homes, a quiet street with not much traffic.

Daulton took out a roll of adhesive tape and told him to watch. He ripped off two short strips of tape and attached them in an X to a utility pole, then walked on to another pole and repeated the process. Then he gave a second roll of tape to Granger and told him to mark the next

four poles in succession while he did the same thing on the other side of the street.

"What the hell are we doin'?" Granger asked.

"It ain't nothing," Daulton said; and then he added, "It's just my spy thing." Granger took the remark as a joke, and decided the taping of the poles had something to do with his friend's traffic in stolen securities. They flagged a cab and returned to their hotel, where Daulton changed his clothes from a business suit to slacks and sport shirt and left with two cameras hanging around his neck. "Do I look like a tourist?" he asked smugly. "When I get back, we'll get laid."

After two hours, Granger's lust got the better of him, and he decided to stop waiting for his traveling companion. He took a cab to a whorehouse that had been pointed out to him by Daulton, and when he returned to the hotel, Daulton was waiting for him. Daulton had hoped to expedite a meeting with the Russians by waiting near a spot not far from the construction site of a new hotel, a route that he knew Okana frequently passed on his jogging runs. But Okana did not appear, and Daulton returned to the hotel. Granger gave him a detailed report of his experience at the bordello, and then they went to bed.

About one o'clock the next day, Daulton woke up to the glow of fuzzy sunlight pushing through the window of the hotel room and shouted, "Jesus Christ, I'm late."

Hurriedly dressing in a business suit, Daulton left Granger in bed and slammed the door of the hotel room. Daulton's schedule for meetings was changed regularly, and according to the current schedule, he was supposed to rendezvous with the Russians at 1300 hours—1:00 P.M. At 1:15, his cab pulled up to a spot in Chapultepec Park that had been previously assigned for this month. According to plan, he knew the Russians were supposed to leave after waiting fifteen minutes.

Music from a merry-go-round calliope filled the park. Daulton scanned the faces all around him. But the only people he saw were children—hundreds of them; brought, he guessed, as part of a school tour to Chapultepec Castle, which sat atop the mountain in the center of the park and where Emperor Maximilian had lived with his tormented bride, Carlota. Then he spotted the face of Karpov in the crowd, walking with another man who was wearing the same kind of dark chauffeur's suit. Daulton recognized him from the embassy.

Karpov seemed suspicious and annoyed. He said Okana had been there but had not waited for him. The chauffeur, however, offered to

return to the embassy and inform him that Daulton had arrived after all. Daulton, he said, should meet them at 1600 hours at a spot near the Bali Restaurant where they had met previously. Daulton handed Karpov his merchandise—two rolls of film containing a package of advance ciphers from the Black Vault and other documents photographed by Chris. Daulton returned to the hotel and told Granger there had been a delay in the receipt of his payment for securities and, after a while, left again.

Okana was waiting for him at four o'clock. They walked a block to a *cantina* and ordered a beer. The Russian said the film had been developed. Some of the photographs, he said, were of poor quality, but overall, he had done well. Once again he said they wanted the frequencies used in the CIA transmissions. And once again, Daulton promised to get them—"next month." Daulton asked about The Colonel and was told he had gone back to Moscow because his visa had expired.

When Daulton returned to the hotel room, he proudly held up three fat yellow envelopes in front of Granger.

"Everything's done," he said. He had passed the stolen securities, he said, and had received his commission of 10 percent.

Then he threw down the envelopes on a bed, and what seemed to Granger like a green avalanche of money poured out—stacks of crisp, new $50 bills. He helped Daulton count the money. There was $10,000.

• •

That evening, two $75-a-night prostitutes entertained them in their hotel room. The following day, his business now taken care of, Daulton gave Granger a tour of the city that he was coming to know so well.

The short misfit and the aging surfer circumnavigated the sprawling central square of the city, the Zócalo, then explored the huge Mexico City Cathedral that dominates the square, before strolling like tourists along Reforma. That night, there were cocktails, dinner and two more prostitutes in their hotel room. On the morning of their fourth day in Mexico City, they flew to Mazatlán. Daulton picked up $1,500 for an hour's work by serving as intermediary for a marijuana buy by a Los Angeles dealer, and they bought a pound of cocaine and a small amount of heroin to take back with them. Their idyll continued with sunbathing, parties and more prostitutes.

After two more days, they boarded a commercial airliner for Tucson

at the airport in Mazatlán. As Daulton had done many times before, he got up and went to the bathroom not long after their jet was in the air. He pried open a bulkhead in the lavatory, hid the cocaine and went back to sit beside Barclay, who once again was out cold from a barbiturate. This time, however, Daulton had persuaded him not to smoke.

They cleared Customs at Tucson, got aboard the same plane two hours later, retrieved the cocaine and landed in Los Angeles. Daulton, who had already missed two appointments, had a date with his psychiatrist.

But as he walked through the crowds of people at Los Angeles International Airport, he was less concerned about the meeting with his shrink than he was in making sure that Chris got some good stuff for the trip to Vienna.

28

"VIENNA?" Chris said, surprised.

"Those are my orders."

"Don't give me that bullshit; since when do you take orders from anyone except yourself?"

"Since they told me they were going to give me lots of cold, hard cash," Daulton said in a happy mood. They had also promised him, he added, a carpet from the Caucasus. The conversation in the living room of Daulton's home in Palos Verdes was typical of those the old friends were having these days—cordial, but increasingly shaded by sarcasm and mistrust. "Why Vienna?" Chris asked.

"I'm not authorized to tell you," Daulton said.

"Then why tell me in the first place? They want you there so they can stroke you."

"Just so they do it with Benjies."

Daulton poured Chris a glass of Moselle wine and brought up the question that was most important on his mind:

"What about the frequencies? That's what they're going to ask me. When am I going to get 'em?"

Chris shook his head.

"I bet they're not going to put up with that shit any longer," Daulton said. "They're getting sick of waiting, and I'm running out of excuses. I'm telling you, man, it's getting worse and worse every time."

Chris passed Daulton a plate of cheese.

"Fuck the cheese! Man, I'm serious," Daulton said.

Chris didn't say so, but he *couldn't* get the list of radio frequencies on which the encrypted CIA messages were sent. In order to limit opportunities for a security breach, the list of frequencies for the CIA transmissions was in the custody of the Western Union company, a contractor to the National Security Agency, and Western Union kept it in a special safe under NSA surveillance until the frequencies were needed to program computers used to scramble the communications.

"There's too much riding on this, asshole," Daulton said. "Can't you just get part of it?"

"Tell 'em it takes time."

"What do you think I have been telling the clods?"

"Well, tell 'em again; they paid you for junk before and they'll pay for junk again," Chris said. "They're stupid."

"It can't work forever," Daulton protested.

"Keep your voice down. Your brother is in the hall," Chris complained.

"Don't worry about it," Daulton said. He said that he was thinking about inviting David into the enterprise.

"Insanity," Chris said. "You'd do that to your own brother?"

"How long do you think *I* can keep up this back-and-forth, back-and-forth routine without getting busted?"

"How long could *he?* You're sick," Chris said.

Daulton flared at the remark: "This is a business. Get it into your head!"

Attempting to change the subject slightly to ease the tension, Chris urged Daulton to drop another plan he had mentioned—the recruitment of Larry Potts, a Palos Verdes sailor who was serving on the U.S.S. *Midway*, an aircraft carrier. Daulton had talked about recruiting him as a kind of subcontractor to take photos of the carrier, the planes it carried and military facilities it visited around the world. Indeed, Daulton had already given Okana some details of the ship's complement of planes on the basis of comments by the sailor at a party.

"What else can I do? I've got to diversify; you could ruin me," Daulton joked.

"You could quit," Chris replied.

"I can't quit."

"Why not?"

"This is my living now," Daulton said.

"You mean you don't want to quit," Chris said.

In the fog of his heroin trip, Daulton then outlined for Chris a grand design for the business: he would recruit Potts for military information and David could serve as a courier-subcontractor assigned to Russian customers, and Barclay Granger would be brought into the operation to be a subcontractor selling secrets to the Red Chinese embassy in Tanzania.

It was like old times. Once again, Daulton's business mind was planning, organizing, expanding; his grand design was very much like the strategy he applied to expanding his drug business, collecting commissions off the top and passing part of the risks to couriers.

"If the Russians find out you're playing with the Chinese, God help you," Chris said. "*No* one else will."

"I've got to expand; besides, how are they going to find out?"

"It's inevitable, you idiot," Chris said.

"Wrong. They won't catch us; look what we've already done; look how much money we've made already."

In truth, Chris did not know how much money they had made. The Russians had not yet answered his coded message. By this stage of their commerce with the Soviet Union, Daulton was keeping about four dollars for every dollar Chris received and was spending most of it on drugs—for his own use as well as others'.

"These are only the beginnings; in ten years . . ."

"In ten years you'll be dead," Chris said. "More like ten months."

Daulton was getting high from the combined effects of heroin and wine, and made an admission to Chris:

"By the way, I had to give 'em your name."

The disclosure didn't surprise Chris, because he figured Daulton had probably done so months earlier.

"I bet you were drunk when you did it," he said.

"I had to tell them. They forced me."

"Look, I've got to bring something to Vienna," Daulton continued. "*Please* make it worth their while this time. Something flashy. . . ."

"Leave your brother at home? And Barclay?"

"They stay."

"I'll think about it."

"Will it be important? Please."

"It's *all* important," Chris said.

"I know, but these idiots I have to deal with don't understand how important it is."

Chris said, "They pay like all the rest of the addicts you've hooked. They won't stop."

•   •

It was quiet in the underground garage near Fourth and Mission Streets in San Francisco on the last Saturday of February, 1976. Chris and Daulton found the telephone booth; Daulton checked the number on the phone—(415) 362-9727—and confirmed they were at the right place. Chris was certain they were being watched; he sensed the presence of others in the garage and wondered if the KGB had sent any agents from the Soviet Consulate in San Francisco to watch them.

Their voices echoed loudly across the garage as they spoke, and they tried to lower their conversation to whispers, wondering if the Russians would call. Six o'clock came and the phone was silent. . . . At two minutes past six, it rang.

"This is Luis," Daulton answered.

"This is John." Standing close to the phone, Chris could hear a voice with a heavy foreign accent.

"We have your carpet," the voice continued. "Will you come and get it?"

"Yes," Daulton said.

"My *amigo,* Cristobal, is here. Would you like to talk to him?"

There was a brief pause.

"No," the Russian said.

The telephone call to the San Francisco phone booth was the final confirmation: Daulton would fly to Vienna.

29

EVER THE GENEROUS HOST, Daulton, saying he had important business to look after in Europe, asked Betsy Lee Stewart and Carole Benedict to go with him to Vienna. But both turned him down, and he went ahead with his plans to make the trip alone, disappointed that he wouldn't have a lovely girl beside him to share what promised to be an adventure like the ones he devoured in spy novels.

On March 10, 1976, Daulton applied for a passport under his own name; on the application, under a section that asked PURPOSE OF TRIP, Daulton answered, "Pleasure—Business." He gave the expected length of his trip as a week and the countries he planned to visit as Switzerland and Germany. After telling a travel agent in Palos Verdes that he was an "art dealer," he bought a round-trip ticket via TWA to Vienna and paid $1,040 in cash for it. There'd been a minor dispute with Chris about the cost of the ticket. Chris had seen an advertisement in the newspaper for a $600 round trip to Vienna and said Daulton ought to buy one of those discounted special fares. But Daulton prevailed. "Jesus Christ," he said, "if I use an excursion fare I'll have to stay in Vienna three weeks, and it'll cost three thousand dollars just to stay over there."

After stops in London, where he changed planes, and Frankfurt, Daulton landed at Vienna's Schwecht Airport on the morning of March 16. He had arrived a day earlier than his scheduled rendezvous with the Russians in order to see some of the city that was so often the setting of the espionage novels he loved. After clearing Immigration and Customs inspection, he took a taxi to the Inter-Continental Hotel in the center of Vienna, checked in and went sight-seeing.

As the cab made its way into the heart of the city, Daulton felt vulnerable so close to Eastern Europe and the Communist bloc. The reason the Russians had given for wanting him to make the trip was to meet some Soviet representatives who could not go to Mexico as well as take some specialized training in espionage: "tradecraft" was the

term Daulton knew from his novels. Before leaving Palos Verdes, Daulton told his brother that he feared the Russians might try to kidnap him for some motive he couldn't figure out—why else Vienna? Daulton remained suspicious even as he boarded the airplane in Los Angeles. But he was going because of the lure of money—and the excitement.

Now, as he walked the streets of the old city, Daulton's fear ebbed and was replaced by a euphoria that reminded him of a high from heroin: The people who glanced at him as he walked through Vienna couldn't have any idea about the nature of his mission, and this thought excited him. And the realization that he was a spy on his way to meet Russian spies in an exotic city also excited him. Even when a light shower sent other pedestrians off the street, Daulton kept going, enjoying his adventure. He made it a point to inspect the Rembrandts and other Old Masters in the Kunsthistorisches Museum, spent a relaxing few minutes in a Viennese coffeehouse and, like any other tourist, toured Schönbrunn Palace, the old seat of power of the Austro-Hungarian Empire.

Chris had kept his promise and given him a large load for this delivery, although Daulton didn't know the nature of the documents he was carrying. It didn't really matter; to Daulton, it could just as easily have been a package of heroin. They were merely goods to be marketed, and his only concern was that they would "turn on" the Russians. He had ten rolls of film, each with thirty-six exposures. There were a month's worth of KW-7 ciphers; scores of Rhyolite messages between TRW, Langley and Australia and a long TRW technical report describing plans for the new Argus system. Chris had taken the documents from the vault in the large case designed to hold the camera that was used to make employee badge identification pictures. He took the camera case from the vault on the pretext of making a booze run. That night, the friends had taped the documents to a wall at Chris's home and photographed them. Chris had returned them the following day, some of them concealed in a plastic bag buried in the dirt of a potted plant that drew an admiring glance from a guard.

• •

The evening after Daulton's arrival in Vienna, he took a cab to Donaupark as instructed. A lush preserve of lawn and old-growth trees covering almost half a square mile northeast of the Ring, the center of Vienna, Donaupark was on the Danube.

From his taxi, Daulton looked out at the lights of the *Riesenrad,* the city's towering 210-foot Ferris wheel, which was becoming more prominent on the horizon as dusk approached. The taxi crossed the muddy Danube, and he got out at the park. Daulton didn't know it was the Danube and asked the driver, who spoke a little English, "what canal" it was. It was chilly, and Daulton regretted he had not brought warmer clothes as riverboats chugged along beside him in a steady stream.

In the distance, beyond the river, he saw the lights of the city, and he heard the sound of traffic and music playing far away. Above him the Danube Tower, a landmark of the park, loomed like a precarious spire. Beyond the trees were the shadows, under a distant moon, of the Balkans and Eastern Europe.

A familiar figure approached from the darkness. Daulton recalled the meeting later this way:

"It was my old friend The Colonel with steel teeth; no code was necessary. He was my mentor."

"Es goot to see you, comrade," the Russian said.

A limousine found the two men as they walked near the river, and Daulton learned that the Soviet chauffeurs in Vienna drove just like the ones in Mexico—rapidly.

The driver threaded his way into and out of alleys and narrow streets, doubling back, checking his mirror to be sure they weren't followed. Daulton had no idea where they were when the car finally stopped at a low-slung building, within sight of the Ferris wheel, that vaguely reminded Daulton of a barracks. It was a KGB "safe house," apparently in a Vienna suburb.

Daulton's uneasiness continued to wane in the friendly atmosphere of reunion. A woman brought the two men caviar and three bottles of vodka; then she brought a stew of beef, potatoes, carrots and cabbage while Steely Teeth sent out the film to another part of the building to be developed.

As the drinking and eating continued, Daulton became ill and asked for a bathroom. Steely Teeth showed him the way and stood by him as he used it.

Little work was necessary tonight, the Russian said, and Daulton was driven back to the Inter-Continental Hotel after midnight. They met the next morning near St. Stephen's Cathedral, the seven-hundred-year-old Gothic masterpiece that is the spiritual center of Vienna.

"The peectures were nod so goot," the Russian general protested after they arrived again at the safe house.

Some of the pictures were decipherable, he added, but others were fogged and out of focus. The Russian seemed to be growing exasperated with his two young spies.

Then, with the patient condescension of a teacher to his pupil, he said they would have to start again: The Colonel took a Minox-B—exactly like the one back in Palos Verdes—out of his pocket and began a long day of lessons in how to photograph documents. The KGB officer presented Daulton with a metal chain that, he said, was precisely forty centimeters long; his friend must use it to measure the distance from the camera to the documents in order to get sharper pictures. Moreover, the Colonel said the film should be developed in the United States—that way, the Americans could see for themselves if the photographs were of high quality. He taught Daulton how to develop the exposed film and went over each detail of the process again and again; they photographed typewritten pages and pages from books, then processed the film. When the lesson was over, the Russian smiled as if to say, You see, it's really not that difficult, is it?

He gave Daulton advice on how to avoid being followed, including instructions to change taxis or buses often and to duck into stores or other crowded places and other techniques that the Russian said Daulton should use to ensure that he wasn't tailed to their meetings.

In the evening after the photography lesson, Daulton was introduced to two middle-aged Russians; from the respect servants paid to them, he gathered that they were important, but he learned little else about the pair of men in dark suits who seemed so hyperactive that they could have been on amphetamines and seemed to know all about Daulton and his friend. They interrogated him about TRW, and he told them everything he knew. He met a third Russian whose name was "Boris."

Daulton decided that he was enjoying the experience. By now he had all but forgotten his fears of being spirited away to Czechoslovakia. The patience and deference of the Russians gave him self-confidence, and he knew he was important to them. Daulton slowly began to realize that he, not the Russians, had the upper hand in the game they were playing.

The Soviets obviously prized this mysterious source of information about the clandestine satellites. But they were also frustrated by this

perplexing American drug pusher and their inability to get more information from him.

There were more questions to Daulton about the means used to transmit messages: shortwave radio, UHF, VHF, telephone circuits, Western Union? Again and again they pressed Daulton to provide more technical data about infrared sensors, and photographs of the Rhyolite and Argus payloads. Daulton assured his mentor that he shouldn't worry: they would get the information. But it would cost $50,000. The Russian emphasized that money would be no object.

After a while, Daulton began to recognize something familiar in the intensity of the Russian's appeal for information: a hungry look in the stony eyes of the man with the bristle-cut iron-gray hair that he had seen before. It reminded Daulton of someone begging him for dope. Daulton had known that hunger for years; he had used it to whittle the niche he had made for himself in life.

As he had done with girls at Palos Verdes High, Daulton played on this dependency; he tried to exploit it, giving a little and promising more.

"They wanted what I had; I was basically dealing with addicts. But I knew they'd kill to get it, too."

. .

Daulton left Vienna after agreeing to a suggestion from the KGB control officer to apply for a job at TRW or Lockheed. The Colonel handed Daulton three envelopes full of American money and, fulfilling a promise made in Mexico, gave him a handmade rug from the Caucasus that he said was worth more than $10,000. Daulton said good-bye to Muzankov, not knowing whether he would see him again or not, and decided that he would miss the sly old man.

En route to Los Angeles, Daulton had to change planes in Paris. For reasons he never discovered, the rug was seized by French Customs officials, and he never saw it again.

When he arrived at his home in Palos Verdes on March 19 in a taxi from the airport, there was a party going on hosted by his brother; their parents were gone, visiting one of their daughters in the South.

Daulton walked in the door with a smile on his face and told the dozen or so guests at the party that he had just come from Vienna. He went into his bedroom and opened his suitcase, and dozens of packages of new American currency spilled out.

Some of the people at the party would say later there was $40,000; Daulton would insist it was $10,000, but admitted, "It looked like all the money in the world."

The arrival of Daulton and his money created more than a ripple of interest, but after a while the party went on as before, and Daulton called Chris and gave him a report on the trip.

A few days later, Daulton saw Peter Frank, the friend who had jumped out of the speeding MG during the chase.

"What's new?" Frank inquired.

"I've just come back from Europe," Daulton said casually for shock value. "I just sold the Statue of Liberty to the Europeans."

The same week he saw one of the P.V. girls to whom he supplied drugs and told her he'd just been in Europe.

"You must be moving up in the world," she said.

"Uncle Sam paid for it," he said.

"I didn't know short people like you were allowed in the Army," she joked.

• •

When Daulton made his first trip to Mexico City after the meeting in Vienna, there was a new control agent waiting for him to succeed The Colonel, whose diplomatic visa in Mexico had expired. Moscow had apparently decided that if it was to continue mining the potential of this young American, a new handler was needed. And, it had apparently decided, new tactics were also necessary in dealing with him.

Daulton was not surprised when, in response to the X marks he made on lampposts, Boris Alexei Grishin was waiting for him the following day near a downtown subway station. He was the "Boris" from Vienna.

Daulton expected to go immediately to dinner. But instead they proceeded down into the subway station and boarded a train, with Boris leading the way. They rode for at least twenty minutes to the outer reaches of the city as the rubber tires of the high-speed train hissed soothingly in the background. The new Russian said nothing and studied the faces in the passenger compartment. The train stopped and he motioned to Daulton to get off, with Daulton wondering where he was being led now. A few seconds later, they boarded another train and rode ten minutes in a different direction, before the Russian motioned him off again and they boarded still another train which they

rode to a station in a suburban neighborhood. This guy likes to play subway tag, Daulton thought. He clearly didn't want to be followed, but he seemed to enjoy it as a sport. After the final subway ride, the Russian led him up a flight of stairs to a restaurant.

Like The Colonel, Boris was a KGB officer masquerading as a Soviet diplomat—in his case as science attaché at the embassy. He had been trained as an engineer and knew about satellites.

Whereas The Colonel's style was stiff and severe—a style that matched his drab, dark suits and his favorite meals, stew and cabbage soup—Boris liked stylish American clothes, especially the blue denim Levi jackets Daulton sometimes wore. He was neat and well groomed, and he fancied himself a gourmet. He chose restaurants that had a good reputation for European cuisine, and like Okana, he enjoyed dawdling over the wine list before selecting an expensive vintage.

There was something distantly Oriental about the thirty-eight-year-old Soviet agent, who told his American agent that night that he came from Smolensk and boasted of having a son in the Red Army and two children with him in Mexico—a daughter, Irena, who was twelve, and George Boris, who was five.

Later on, Daulton discovered the reason for the hint of Oriental features: Boris' father was part Chinese. Boris spoke both Spanish and English well, usually with a cigarette drooping diagonally from his mouth which Boris smoked down to a stubby butt. His hair was receding over his temples, and he made an effort to cover the expanding region of skin by combing the hair over it, not succeeding completely. He was a compact man, perhaps only four or five inches taller than Daulton. He was not nearly as imposing as most of the other KGB agents Daulton had met, and seemed more open and more curious than the others. But lurking somewhere beyond the tight Oriental features of his face, there was, it seemed to Daulton, an icy quality about him.

Over dinner, the KGB agent told Daulton about his family and spoke longingly of the Caucasus. Boris said he owned an American-made 40-horsepower Johnson outboard motor which he used to tow water skiers; but he said he couldn't use it now because the propeller was broken and he hadn't been able to buy a replacement. Could Daulton buy one for him in America?

Daulton assured him that he would gladly order the part when he returned to the States.

After this first dinner, Karpov was waiting outside the restaurant

with a car, and he took them to the embassy, speeding as usual and taking such a circuitous route that it almost left Daulton dizzy.

• •

A party of some sort was going on in the embassy, and Boris explained that several representatives from the United States Embassy were in the building. Down a long hallway, Daulton could hear the sounds of a cocktail party—indeed, some people were talking so loudly he could almost hear what they were saying. Boris led him to one room, an office, and told him to wait there. But a few minutes later he came in looking agitated; he said some of the party guests might be drifting this way; the wife of the American ambassador, he said, was right down the hall.

They looked out of the room, and when Boris was sure no one was there, he hurried Daulton down a flight of stairs to a room in the basement. Here, Boris said, they could talk without worrying about the party upstairs and without being eavesdropped on. Foreign-intelligence operatives, including the CIA, he said, were always trying to bug the embassy, but the walls of this room were too thick for listening devices to penetrate. He pounded on one wall to illustrate his point; the noise his hand made was dull and unyielding.

It was a gloomy place, and it made Daulton think of a dungeon. He didn't like what was going on. This new man made him uneasy, and he didn't like the dungeon. Later he would say of this meeting, "I thought they were going to snuff me right there." But Daulton didn't let Boris see his fear; the high that was coming on from the cocaine he had snorted after they left the restaurant was keeping his senses sharp.

Karpov stayed in the room with Boris and Daulton, and they were joined by Igor Dagtyr, another KGB agent assigned to the embassy as a chauffeur. Daulton saw a bulge near the waist of his dark uniform and calculated that he had an automatic under the coat. Daulton didn't like what was going on at all.

Daulton handed Boris an envelope containing the negatives of several rolls of film he had developed at home. There were a month's supply of KW-7 ciphers and copies of scores of TWX messages between Pilot, Pedal and other stations involved in CIA clandestine operations. It was a particularly rich lode that Chris had provided: a message regarding the secret mission of an American submarine that, with CIA operatives aboard, had secretly monitored, via a periscope

and special antennae, the tests of a new Soviet submarine-launched missile that was fired from the White Sea over the Arctic . . . data on a "Chicom" (People's Republic of China) radar defense system . . . a long communiqué with a list of several of the most important U.S. reconnaissance-satellite programs and the respective performance capabilities of each, including the specifications for what engineers call "ground resolution"—the size of the smallest object on the ground, listed in meters, that the eyes of the camera could resolve from space —a measurement, in other words, of the sharpness and effectiveness of the espionage equipment.

Daulton insisted that the delivery was worth $50,000. Boris smiled and said nothing and sent the negatives away to be printed. When Igor returned an hour later with the prints, Boris was visibly pleased. But he scoffed at Daulton's demands for $50,000. "Where are the frequencies?" he asked; once again, Daulton said, "I'm working on them." But, reassuringly, he said he was optimistic he would get them soon —as well as photos of the actual Rhyolite and Argus satellites.

The cocaine and liquor were having, as usual, an effect on Daulton's courage, and the fear he'd had when he stepped into the dungeonlike room continued to slip away. And he decided to push his advantage: He looked angrily at Boris and complained that he wasn't being paid enough for the risks he was taking. "I'm risking my life to come here and you pay me peanuts!" he said.

"If you don't like the information and don't start paying more for it," he threatened, "we'll sell it to the Chinese; they'll buy."

Instantly, he knew he had made a mistake.

• •

There was a silence in the room, and the blue eyes of the KGB officer pierced the tiny Californian. The two chauffeurs standing at the side of the room made a scraping noise as they shifted their weight, but no one spoke.

Boris then reached into his coat and produced a 9-millimeter Makarov automatic pistol and laid it in front of him with a metallic clunk. He slipped the clip out of the gun, making sure Daulton could see the eight cartridges it contained. As he set it down, there was another clunk on the table, which resonated with a hollow echo in the small room.

"You don't carry a gun?" Boris asked. It was more a statement than

a question. Daulton shook his head that he didn't, keeping his eyes on the automatic. "You should," Boris said. "You should be more careful."

Even though his brain was saturated with alcohol and cocaine, Daulton retained enough of his wits to be persuaded by Boris' reaction: he would not mention China again. But after a few moments, the tension passed, and he renewed his demands for more money. He began to shout at the three Soviet agents, who studied him quietly.

Daulton felt almost intoxicated by his power over the KGB agents; he loved this sense of power. "They wanted what I had and they wanted it like crazy," he would recall later. He was convinced he could get away with almost anything. "I knew I had them by the short hairs; I had them hooked like junkies," he recalled.

Despite the miscalculation over China, Daulton *knew* they would give him what he asked; he was certain they didn't want to lose their access to TRW. And so he pressed his demands—successfully. When he returned to Los Angeles the next day, he had $10,000.

Before he left Boris, he promised again to get the frequencies, the photos and the performance specifications Boris wanted about TRW's infrared sensors. As he said good-bye, his last words to Boris were "Next month!"

30

CHRIS HAD NOW BEEN channeling secrets out of the Black Vault for a year.

He was certain that he was in love with Alana. They had talked about moving in together, but she had rejected the idea, saying she didn't want to hurt her parents. Their discussion turned to talk about marriage, but they decided tacitly to give their relationship more time. Instead, they spent as many nights together as they could at Chris's small rented house. In many ways, it seemed as if they were already married. Alana continued to nag Chris about his developing double chin and his fondness for junk food (he enjoyed the

nagging, he would reflect later), but there was one subject on which he refused to budge: *big* breakfasts on Sundays.

"It's part of my Catholic heritage," he said when Alana first protested, "not to mention my County Mayo heritage." To stand in the way of an ample breakfast on Sundays, he said, would be to infringe on the sacred practices of his religion and his family, where big Sunday breakfasts were a tradition. When Alana stayed over on Saturday nights, there was an invariable ritual the following morning: About eight, Chris would start a charcoal barbecue grill and go out for sweet rolls and a newspaper. When he got back, he put two steaks over the hot coals, and Alana had hash-browns and scrambled eggs on the range and orange juice and cantaloupe on the table.

These had been happy moments for Chris. But by the spring of 1976, stresses had begun to tear at their relationship. Alana complained that Chris had changed: "You're so moody," she said repeatedly. He was constantly breaking dates, she said. "Why? You snap at me all the time for nothing, and you're always so tense," she told him on a Saturday night in March. They had their big breakfast, as usual, the following morning, but the fissures in their romance were widening.

Much of Chris's moodiness and short temper was rooted in the ambiguity that twisted his conscience. On the day he had met Robin, when he was only fifteen, Chris had discovered the rivalry for his conscience. And now, seven years later, two voices were still arguing over his soul. On one hand, there was the ghost of Robin and what he stood for urging him on—the voice of the rebel who rejected the scenario that society had written for him and who saw things as they *really* were, not as the hypocrites and the chieftains of the corrupt corporate state *said* they were. And on the other hand, there was the looming presence of his father and of Monsignor McCarthy and all the others who had left a tenacious residue of *their* morality in him.

And so Chris wavered, a boat pushed to starboard one day, to port the next. At times, he repeatedly encouraged Daulton to sell secrets to the Russians and coached him in how to keep them off balance, serving as the mastermind of their operation and thoroughly enjoying the results of his scheme to tweak the noses of the CIA and the Russians, just as he had enjoyed tweaking the nose of the limp, dead mink in a church years earlier; at other times, the enormity of what they were doing seized him, and then he decided to drag his feet when Daulton asked for more merchandise. At times during the first year of the espionage operation that had begun in a cocaine stupor—at the mo-

ments when Chris became enraged by some new discovery about the CIA, or disgust for all manifestations of nationalism welled up in him —he let flow a tide of data that included some of America's most sensitive secrets. But at other times, he became repelled by the greed of his friend and his descent into heroin and, at times, repelled even by himself. The distant remnants of his father's ideals crashed through, and Chris answered Daulton's pleas for more secrets by taking his next batch of pictures out of focus or refusing to deliver items the Russians requested or trying to avoid Daulton when he called him asking for more secrets from the Black Vault.

But he knew it wasn't only a contorted conscience that produced the moodiness and irritability that perplexed Alana; it was also fear—and a growing sense of desperation. He continued to wonder how they had managed to get away with the scheme for so long. And whenever he thought about it—and he thought about it often—Chris always came to the same conclusion: *They have to be on to us.*

Chris knew that his inconsistency bewildered Daulton, and, he admitted to himself, he rather enjoyed this aspect of the operation. And in terms of dollars and cents, he was right: even when Daulton went to Mexico City with fogged film, he returned to The Hill with a stack of new currency. He was perhaps as skilled a traveling salesman as the KGB had ever dealt with, Chris mused.

Chris had not entered their enterprise with financial motives in mind. But he accepted whatever money Daulton gave him. He spent it on cocaine and marijuana, on weekend trips with Alana to the desert country along the Colorado River between California and Arizona, on car repairs and other things that, years later, he could not remember.

Chris was tormented by his fears, and they grew whenever he saw Daulton and realized the hold that heroin had on him. Sooner or later, Chris knew, Daulton was going to get high on heroin and boast that he was a spy, and the whole thing would be over.

As Chris felt the trap he had set for himself squeeze tighter, he made a decision: he must wrest control of the operation from Daulton and deal *directly* with the Russians. With Daulton out of the picture, he would somehow manage to find a way to ease out slowly. So far, he admitted, he had not been very successful in developing his own link to the Russians. He had attempted to do so again with a coded message to the Soviets, but decided Daulton was probably not delivering the messages.

He knew the Russians had broken his simple code. Their first reply to him had not been very kindly: using the same code for a reply sent via Daulton, the KGB had thanked Chris for his service in the cause of socialism, but whoever had answered his note had said he hadn't liked his criticism about taking so long to establish a telephone link and had called him "rude." Ignoring this complaint, Chris had responded with another coded message asking how much money Daulton had received so far for the material he'd sent with him. But it hadn't been answered, and Chris doubted if Daulton had delivered it.

Nevertheless, he continued to take information out of the vault, tape it to a wall in his house and photograph it. On occasion, to enhance the value of what he considered lesser documents, he typed FLASH/SECRET on them. Out of the vault went more ciphers and technical reports and spools of TWX messages rolled up like toilet paper. There were photographs of a study, several pages long, designated only as Project 20,030. It was TRW's concept for a new surveillance satellite system that, just as Argus had been an advancement over Rhyolite, was to be an advanced version of Argus. It was to be another precious buy for the Russians. Each trip out of the plant—and the return trip with the documents—was a risk. But Chris had always thrived on risk.

• •

There was a moment, early in April, 1976, when Chris thought their whole adventure was over: Gene Norman announced that the National Security Agency had appointed a new senior administrator to oversee the communications vaults at various companies that held CIA contracts, and he was on his way to the Black Vault at that moment. They quickly removed a marijuana plant that was growing in the vault, as well as project I.D. badges showing a monkey's face that Norman had prepared as a joke; but otherwise, there was no time to prepare for his arrival.

Chris thought of an incident a few days earlier and smiled to himself: He had gone home after finishing his shift in the vault, but at about seven o'clock he had received a call from one of the guards in M-4. Gene Norman's wife, the guard explained, had called TRW and said she was worried because her husband hadn't come home from work; the guard had peeked through the partially opened vault door and discovered what he thought was the soles of two feet—apparently the feet of a man lying on the floor beyond the draperies that divided the

vault. Because the guard wasn't cleared to enter the vault, he called Chris and asked him to drive to TRW as soon as possible. When Chris arrived, he learned the guard had decided there was a dead man on the floor of the vault, and several fellow uniformed security men were huddled outside. But when Chris went in, he found out that Norman was not dead, but drunk. He aroused Norman and told the guards that he had merely fallen asleep.

The crisis over the NSA man's visit was more serious.

In January, the agency had changed its encryption system; instead of making the daily change in ciphers with a keying machine, it had introduced a new kind of computer cipher card that was kept in sealed plastic envelopes in the vault's floor safe, with a new card removed for each day's use.

Previously, Chris had photographed the key cards while he was alone in the vault, usually before other employees arrived for work. But this became more hazardous after the new system was introduced: removing the cards from the sealed envelopes, and then returning them, took too much time. To make things easier, he began to take the packages of ciphers home with him, where he could remove the cards from the envelopes, photograph them and reseal the envelopes before returning them to the safe the following day. It was difficult to reseal the envelopes exactly as they had been. But he was usually the only one who opened the envelopes to pull out the cards, so this didn't matter.

The NSA official who was making the inspection was new on the job, and his surprise inspection was intended to assure him that the system he was taking over was in good shape. As soon as he entered the vault, Chris remembered that he had made a fatal mistake: he had replaced one set of crypto cards in its envelope *upside down*.

His heart pounded as the official crouched down near the open safe and checked the ciphers stored for use in future months. He watched as the visitor examined each one slowly. Chris tried to distract him by complaining about the reliability of the cipher machines—they were always breaking down, he said. The man was friendly, but painstaking. An hour passed, and then another hour, and Chris's head ached from the hopelessness of the situation. But he tried to seem relaxed as he waited for the NSA man to reach the questionable package of ciphers.

He saw it.

The man was holding it in his hand, and Chris looked down at it, helpless.

But nothing happened. The NSA executive's eyes passed over the package after a moment and went on to the next one.

Later that day, Norman reported that the inspector was unhappy because some components that were listed in the inventory for the code room were missing, but otherwise, he had no serious complaints about the operation.

. .

Laurie Vicker had finally persuaded her boyfriend to marry her, but the marriage hadn't stopped her from pursuing Chris, nor her husband's suspicions that there was something going on between them. One night when she and Chris both had to work late, the black-haired systems analyst made a booze run and returned with a gallon of wine. By the time all the messages had been sent to Langley, most of the wine was gone, but Laurie said she didn't want to go home yet, and suggested they go over to Chris's house.

Chris still wasn't interested sexually in the plump, if sensuous, woman, whose advances he found vulgar. But he considered her a friend and didn't want to hurt her feelings. And so he suggested that she follow him in her van to his house, where they could smoke a joint. When they reached his place, Laurie telephoned a friend and discovered that her husband had learned from a TRW guard that the two of them had left together. The friend said that her husband had gone looking for them. Chris rushed her out of the house and they left for Daulton's.

Laurie's husband, a bartender, was substantially larger than Chris and had boasted to his bride that he had once killed a man in a fight— a fact that Laurie had repeated to Chris. They got into their respective vehicles and Laurie followed Chris to the Lee home, where they found Daulton, drank more wine and smoked two joints. Meanwhile, Chris wondered how he was going to get Laurie home. About midnight, he decided upon a strategy for dealing with Laurie's husband: she was too drunk to drive, so there was only one way to get her home, and that was with her husband.

He telephoned him at their apartment and said that Laurie was in Palos Verdes and was drunk; he said he would deliver her to him in twenty minutes at the Plaza in Palos Verdes Estates. It was a Span-

ish-style square near the ocean flanked by red tile–roofed buildings that housed mostly real estate offices, the main industry of the town. Next Chris called the Palos Verdes Estates Police Station, which was located at the edge of the Plaza, and offered an anonymous tip: within twenty minutes, there was to be a gang fight in the Plaza. Then Daulton called the police with the same message.

A few minutes later, Chris drove the very drunk Laurie to the Plaza in her van and left her inside. There were five police cars, engines running, parked around the Plaza, and the unhappy husband saw them.

"Here's your wife," Chris jauntily said to her husband.

"You son of a bitch," he said. "Don't you ever touch her; I killed somebody once for less."

Chris just smiled, and Laurie drunkenly said, "Please take me home."

Under the eyes of the watching policemen, they all left then. But it wasn't the last time that Laurie went after Chris.

. .

Carole Benedict had returned from Hawaii and was living with her mother, who had remarried, and she was now dating Daulton regularly; it was an expensive courtship in terms of the gifts and expensive dinners he lavished on her, but it gave him access to her wonderful body. Although his drug habit was also expensive, the Russians were providing him with a steady income, and there was every reason to think this income would continue for a long time: the Russians were panting as never before.

The only problem Daulton saw—and it was growing more and more frustrating—was Chris. He had begun to sense that Chris was becoming uncooperative again; in fact, he was so unpredictable it was impossible to figure him out sometimes. It was bad for his drug business, Daulton knew that. Several times, Chris had promised him an important load of merchandise that he claimed would be worth at least $20,000 to the Russians, but the Russians said the material wasn't worth anything—either the photographs were fogged or their value fell short of Daulton's asking price for other reasons. Daulton always managed to bargain a few thousand dollars beyond what Boris offered. But it wasn't what he expected, and this caused problems for Daulton in his drug trade because he usually planned in advance how the money would be spent. Once, for example, before making a trip to Mexico

City with a load that Chris said ought to bring $20,000, he placed an order for two tons of marijuana. The weed was waiting for him in Jamaica at $30 a pound; he should have more than enough money for the deal. But that delivery brought only $5,000, and it was an embarrassment for him with the dealer who had set up the buy.

There were other problems, too. Barclay Granger had borrowed $18,000 from him to front a cocaine buy, but he'd lost it to a rip-off artist. Barclay said he'd pay it back, but that had been three months ago, and Daulton decided that he was through with his old friend.

• •

"Why don't you fly up to San Francisco with me for dinner?" Daulton told a group of friends who had gathered at his home for a party on a Saturday night late in April. Carole was there, along with George and Margie Fein. Daulton—he was called "Daultonomous" by the Feins in joking affection—had met George in a high school woodworking class and they had remained friends. It was the birthday of Margie Fein, and Daulton had invited them over to celebrate. Now he was proposing that they extend the party to San Francisco, with him picking up the tab; he said he had to be in San Francisco to catch a telephone call.

Before inviting them to San Francisco, Daulton explained to Fein that he was conducting a profitable new business selling stocks and bonds to an "uncle" in Mexico City. He boasted that he had made $100,000 from it, and that he made a new delivery each month, picking up an additional $5,000 or $10,000. He had to go to San Francisco, he explained, to arrange his next trip, and he showed Fein a sheet of lined yellow paper that bore a list of scheduled appointments in Mexico City and other places. Fein noticed that it seemed to be in some kind of code, and noticed "S.F." marked under the current day's date. The group all rejected his invitation to fly to San Francisco, so Daulton flew off by himself to take a call from Boris.

• •

When Daulton returned, after setting up his next meeting in Mexico City, he faced yet another crisis in his efforts to stay out of jail.

His psychiatrist had been scheduled in March to report the results of Daulton's hospital examination—the report that could decide whether he went back to jail or not. But the psychiatrist sent a note to Judge

Donahue saying that he had been ill and apologizing for having to postpone submission of the report.

Because of the delay, Attorney Kahn managed to put off the court hearing to decide Daulton's future repeatedly during the early spring. But in May, the psychiatrist finally finished his evaluation, and Judge Donahue scheduled a new hearing on Daulton's future on May 18, 1976.

After noting he had found no evidence of drug addiction during the hospital stay, the psychiatrist offered his analysis of the forces that had shaped Daulton and thrust him into trouble with the law so frequently:

Mr. Lee demonstrated anxiety, tension and considerable depression but was cooperative and responsive to the daily intensive exploratory and psychotherapeutic interviews with him during the hospitalization. These revealed the persistence of unresolved conflicts which date back to childhood and especially the adolescent years. As the oldest son he felt an obligation to fulfill what he felt were his physician father's ambitions for him, which entailed acceptance at Notre Dame University and athletic and academic success. Unfortunately for him his only average grades and below average stature frustrated these aspirations and left him with a deep sense of failure and a feeling of paternal rejection. This led to adolescent rebelliousness and acting out which entailed drug dealing and, again unfortunately for him, he was only too successful in this pursuit and it became a way for him to become a "big shot" in a delinquent way and at the same time triumph over and get revenge on his father.

The uncertain success of work and study have never matched for him his illegal endeavors which have persisted with the same neurotic component, as well as much guilt and alienation in relation to his Roman Catholic upbringing and rather harsh but ineffective conscience.

In addition then to establishing that although having used drugs he is not an addict, the hospital studies led to confirmation of the initial impression that the extra-legal behavior pattern had a neurotic substructure which would potentially be amenable to psychotherapy.

Course since Discharge from Hospital:

The hospital stay led to some symptomatic improvement but more importantly the beginning of a therapeutic relationship to be developed on an outpatient basis.

He was discharged to his family to arrange a rehabilitation period of several months, living and working as free of stress as possible while

he continued in therapy. Plans were made to work with an elderly craftsman to further his experience in the manufacture of custom furniture and in due course obtain his own apartment near a bus route.

The psychiatrist added that psychotherapy continued "approximately twice weekly throughout February and early March," but then had to be suspended because of the psychiatrist's illness, a serious case of influenza. He said psychotherapy had resumed intermittently since then and added:

During the treatment sessions it was felt that continuing progress has been made towards better self-understanding and the difficult but not impossible task of rehabilitating himself with family, friends and society, possibly as a legitimate business entrepreneur or in custom furniture manufacture.

This young man has made a good start towards rehabilitating himself and should in my opinion be given the chance to continue along this road, which though neither short nor easy, offers hope for salvaging someone with good potential from a criminal identity, which might otherwise be further and perhaps irrevocably ingrained.

There is no question that he is neither from an anti-social background, nor basically psychopathic, but rather belongs to that minority of offenders whose behavior have a psychoneurotic basis.

He is therefore amenable to individual psychotherapy and should continue it for many months. There is good support from his family, and although no guarantees of success can be given there seems to be an excellent result possible here. It is strongly urged that he be allowed to continue these treatments under probation supervision as part of his probation program.

At the May 18 hearing, Judge Donahue allowed Daulton to remain on probation until he evaluated the psychiatric report, even though the Los Angeles County Probation Department, citing Daulton's consistent failure to submit to supervision by probation officers since 1972, was less favorably inclined toward him than the psychiatrist. It had recommended that he be returned to jail. The court ordered a new probation evaluation based on the psychiatrist's report. Daulton could be free at least until early September, the judge ruled. Ken Kahn had scored another victory.

Daulton was, again, out of immediate danger of being sent to prison.

After the hearing, he boasted to friends that he had fooled both the psychiatrist and the judge and predicted he would never have to return to prison.

Meanwhile, he wasted no time in resuming his twin businesses, selling drugs and selling defense secrets. He had plenty of time to see Carole, and once Barclay Granger was sentenced to Federal prison for cocaine trafficking, he inherited another one of his girlfriends—Darlene Cooper.

31

DAULTON SENSED A CHANGE in Boris Grishin beginning in June. When they exchanged the passwords, his greeting wasn't as warm, and there was a coolness during their meals. Boris complained more than ever about the quality of the material and insisted on meeting *Cristobal*. An uneasiness that the Russians might be trying to get rid of him began to trouble Daulton. As usual, each delivery was paid for, but Boris was becoming increasingly impatient with Daulton's excuses.

Still, Daulton remained certain that they were hooked, and he continued his pattern of gilt-edged promises. Whenever Boris squeezed too much, Daulton did what he had always done with a troublesome junkie: he threatened to withhold the goods. He tacitly let the Russian know that he might not ever hear again from him or his friend if he pressed too hard. And that was enough to make Boris back off for the moment.

Daulton tried not to let Boris' change of mood bother him. After all, they were *still* paying. When he returned from Mexico City in June he got high at a party and hinted to one of the cocaine dealers who traveled in his crowd in Redondo Beach that he was doing business with the Soviets. Without giving any details, he said in an optimistic boast, "The Russians are so dumb they'll buy anything."

Nevertheless, Daulton knew he would have to come up with something better if he was going to keep stringing them on. After he returned

to California in June, he went to Chris's house and said that Boris was pushing hard for answers to the questions he had sent earlier to Chris, as well as the frequencies and pictures of the birds. Chris responded with the same reply Daulton had heard before: "Fuck 'em; we'll give 'em what we want, and that's it."

Daulton appealed to Chris to go into the High Bay area, at least, and photograph a Rhyolite satellite. The Russians, in fact, already knew what a Rhyolite bird looked like; they had purchased documents containing an artist's concept of the satellite. Unbeknownst to them, however, the satellite had been outfitted with a new set of antennae, and a photograph of the bird would have been a valuable prize for the Soviets.

Chris refused to take the picture.

"Why not, asshole?" Daulton asked.

"Tell 'em you're working on it," Chris said.

"That won't work anymore," Daulton said. "I've already told them that. Look, they're willing to pay hundreds of thousands of dollars for that shit. Can't you realize that? Green, coin of the realm. And here I sit. You're blind! Why do I have to take all the risks? You're a mother-fucking coward."

"I've heard that before; it doesn't work."

Chris, as he did most of his waking hours lately, was chain smoking, and he reached for another Lark.

"You're tearing me up inside," Daulton said angrily. "I'm not going to be responsible for what happens. I can't take it anymore. You're the reason I'm on this goddamned smack."

There was a pause. Daulton said, "There's always your father." It was a hint that he might tell Chris's father of their enterprise if Chris didn't become more cooperative.

"Yes, there always is, and if he didn't blow your brains out, I would."

"You don't have the stomach for it," Daulton said.

"Try me. I really wish you would try me."

"I couldn't care less if you overdosed," Chris added. "You more than pay for your habit with dealing and smuggling. No one is forcing you to go to Mexico City; if you have any brains left at all, quit. It can't go on forever."

Daulton had taken a whiff of heroin and decided to switch to a more persuasive approach.

"Look, you want some more money?" he asked.

"You can give me a pound of Colombian. A fresh pound."

"I just gave you a pound Saturday!" Daulton said. "What the fuck did you do with that one?"

"It's gone. I gave five ounces to Old Rasputin," he said, referring to an old friend. "You burned him for five ounces. And I gave Dennis and Margie some and the guy next door an ounce; we all took some excellent brownies to the desert."

"Hey, stay out of my business."

"You don't run a business," Chris retorted. "You rip people off."

Daulton was not ruffled. Once again, he appealed for new data from the vault. "*Please,*" he said.

"All right, James Bond. You play your game and I'll play mine." Chris said he would get some new material from the vault in a few days. "What happened to your attaché case?"

"I forgot the combination and had to pry it open."

"God, some swift spy you are. It's a miracle I'm not dead. You've used up all our luck, every last drop."

•   •

Several weeks later, on July 9, Stephen Sharp and Michael Maxwell, Los Angeles County deputy sheriffs, were riding in a patrol car shortly before midnight in an industrial section of Long Beach, the coastal city southwest of Los Angeles, when they saw a white Ford zoom past them. They could see the Ford hurtling toward the center divider strip in the road and braced for it to carom off the divider. But at the last moment, the Ford made a long, looping right-hand turn all the way from the center lane to another street. The deputies gave pursuit and clocked the Ford at 65 miles an hour.

Red lights went on behind Daulton, and this time he stopped. He stumbled out of the car and asked the officers why they had stopped him.

"May I see your driver's license, please?" the officer asked.

Under the glare of the patrol car's headlights, the deputies ordered Daulton to stand on one leg. He elevated one foot several inches off the ground, held it steady for a moment, and fell down on the pavement.

When they asked him to touch his nose with his right index finger, Daulton extended his arm, steadied himself, took aim and coaxed the

finger to his face. But instead of finding his nose, Daulton stabbed an eye.

"Where do you think you are?" the deputies asked Daulton.

His slurred voice replied with a location in Redondo Beach, fifteen miles away.

After leaving Chris's home near the TRW plant earlier in the evening, Daulton, somehow, had survived a fifteen-mile drunken odyssey to Long Beach.

Chris had embarked that night for Ensenada, in Mexico, and a weekend of falcon-spotting with Gene Norman; he still had no love for Norman, but the job threw them together, and they had planned the trip over lunch one day at The Hangar. When Norman arrived early in the evening to pick him up, he found Chris and Daulton, drunk. There were long strips of recently developed film drooping like black ribbons from the counter tops and cupboards in the kitchen. Chris was sober enough to recognize the danger of discovery by Norman, and steered him away from the kitchen. Although Norman caught a glimpse of the black ribbons, if he was puzzled by them he said nothing about it to Chris.

Daulton and Gene had met once before at a party, and they hadn't hit it off. Gene had written off Daulton as a boisterous braggart, and Daulton thought Gene was a smart-ass who thought he was still in the Marines. That evening did little to help the fragile relationship. After Norman drove to Chris's house and walked inside, Chris gave him a beer, and before long a dispute erupted between Daulton and Norman over something one of them said. Daulton grabbed the can of beer; there was a scuffle and pushing. But Daulton was too drunk to continue the combat, and he went to his car and passed out. When he woke up, Chris and Norman had left for Mexico, and he ended up arrested for drunken driving. He was released on bail two days later.

• •

Daulton had plans to make one big score and then move to Costa Rica. His brother had found out that the Golden Cove Deli had been sold, but Daulton now had a grander scheme in mind—a deal that could turn a few thousand dollars into a million and allow him to invest the proceeds in a business and retire, fish and relax in the sun, pulling the strings on his business from a fine beach home in Costa Rica, just like Robert Vesco, the fugitive American multimillionaire who lived in the Central American country.

Daulton's scheme was to buy a large quantity of drugs in Culiacán and turn it around on the streets of America. But he faced one major obstacle to realizing the plan: he didn't have the seed money to get the enterprise rolling. He had recently lost more than $10,000 he had fronted in a drug deal that was stolen in a rip-off, in addition to the $18,000 Granger still owed him. His own habit had chewed up a lot of his remaining capital, and with his incessant, extravagant spending, he didn't have much left. There was still some cash in Mexican banks, a few gold coins he had cached in a safe-deposit box and a few Oriental rugs. But he needed big money—$50,000 to $100,000 or more—to pull off this score.

His only hope was the Russians.

•　•

Daulton decided that if the scam could be carried on only a few more months, he could get the money he needed to begin his new life. Although Daulton sensed the Russians were growing colder to him, he was counting, as ever, on their addiction. There had been omens that summer that the Russians' patience with the diminutive huckster from Palos Verdes was wearing thin. But Daulton, as full of moxie as ever, was not deterred. Twice that summer, Boris failed to show up when meetings were scheduled—once, in August, leaving Daulton waiting an hour in a park after midnight.

The next day, Daulton went to Calzada Tacubaya, the overloaded expressway where the Soviet Embassy was located, and ignoring on-lookers, pasted adhesive-tape X marks on lampposts on side streets that he knew embassy cars passed by frequently. The location wasn't on the list the Russians had given him, but he was anxious for a meeting; Chris had given him more KW-7 ciphers and more message traffic from the vault. And he had only $30 in his pockets.

Daulton was waiting at the Bali Restaurant that night, but Boris didn't show up, so Daulton decided on a second plan of action: he went to the embassy and, ignoring Boris' warnings to avoid the building, waited outside the gate for a car to pass, followed it in and persuaded a guard to find Boris.

Boris was outraged at the insubordinate agent.

"You're a fool," he said, and told him again *never* to visit the embassy unannounced. Nevertheless, he accepted the delivery and, after disappearing into an adjacent office, returned with another envelope stuffed with American currency. In one way Daulton was right: the

Russians were *still* addicted to the possibility of getting more secrets about American spy-satellite operations; moreover, Boris still wanted to meet Daulton's partner, the mysterious American who had access to the secrets. Daulton continued to play on the Russian's eagerness to meet Chris, promising that he would come to Mexico and using, as always, the promise of more to come. Daulton's welcome was wearing thin, but he felt he could still keep them on the hook.

32

CHRIS HELD THE SHINY AUTOMATIC in his lap and wondered if he would have the guts to do it. Was this the way to end the nightmare, to kill Daulton? He had no regrets about his motive for the thrust against the insanities of the superpowers; he had acted, he told himself, on behalf of all the people who could no longer speak for themselves of the insanities—the victims of Ypres, Guadalcanal, Stalingrad, Dien Bien Phu, Khe Sanh and all the other graveyards of battle—but his protest had assumed a shape he had not imagined, and it had gone on too long.

He now wanted to survive.

He thought of Daulton's heroin-induced half-threat to blackmail his father and smiled bitterly to himself: his father would either shoot Daulton on the spot or handcuff him and get on the telephone to the FBI. No, he knew blackmail wasn't a problem; but if Daulton went to his father, Chris knew his own life would be ruined.

Daulton had evidence that linked Chris indisputably to spying for the Russians; somewhere, there were copies of the documents. Daulton had said he wanted to sell them a second time to the Chinese; as long as they existed, they would implicate Chris in espionage. Where were they? Daulton had said some were at his house, but others might be cached somewhere in Mexico. One evening after work Chris drove to Palos Verdes and slowed as he passed Daulton's house, weighing a plan to break in and ransack his room. But as he guided the Volkswagen past the sprawling house set back behind a big lawn, Chris realized

there was no way he could pull it off; he remembered Daulton had told him his family had recently installed a burglar alarm connected to the Palos Verdes Estates Police Department.

The only way to end it without being caught, Chris decided, was to murder Daulton.

The best place for it, he thought, would be in the desert—a couple of shots from the automatic and the scavengers of the desert would take care of his body very efficiently. He looked down at the gun and outlined in his mind, step by step, how he would lure Daulton to the Mojave with a suggestion for an early-morning trapping expedition. He even rehearsed mentally the words he would say: "Come on, it's been a long time; let's go check out the old haunts." He heard the shots and saw Daulton fall.

And then another vision flashed into his mind: he remembered the sight of Monsignor McCarthy saying Mass in the center of the altar at St. John Fisher, and the two of them, Daulton and himself, kneeling on each side of him.

The gray-haired priest genuflected, and his voice—a soft alloy of Ireland and Boston—resonated between the freshly painted walls of the new church:

Dominus vobiscum. The Lord be with you.

And then he could hear their response in the Latin colloquy, two boyish voices, almost like distant chimes, replying as one:

Et cum spiritu tuo. And with your spirit.

Chris recalled the two of them playing football, and in the wilderness, each placing his life literally in the hands of the other, as they explored eyries of falcons on a mountain ledge at the end of a rope, accompanied only by the sounds of rustling pines, the wind and a bubbling stream far beneath them.

He thought of the Daulton whom he had known before he became addicted to heroin. In a way, he knew they were alike. They had shared the same disillusionment over the infuriating gap between reality and the ideals they had been taught and the same repugnance for the hypocrisies of the Corporate State, as Charles Reich so eloquently called the country in *The Greening of America.*

Chris thought: Daulton fought against the system in the way in which he was most proficient, as a drug dealer, and before he soured beneath his addiction, he had challenged, along with Chris, hundreds of false assumptions about the corrupt world that had been bequeathed to

them. But unfortunately, instead of using pot or hash or coke to enhance his perceptions of life periodically as his customers did, Daulton had let his euphoria sweep him away and it had become his reality, until he had no reality left. Once, Daulton had shared with Chris a contempt for the mindless flag-waving of the nationalists; he had been equally disillusioned. But by the spring of 1975, when all this had begun, Chris had known that the only way to get Daulton to carry out his plan was to appeal to his greed.

Heroin, Chris thought, had left Daulton a shell of what he had been. He was often sick physically now, and overwhelmed by the enormity of his rejection of a culture that gave him no peace; yet at the beginning it had seemed so small—peddling a few joints in high school. Stoned on smack, Daulton could forget and escape to his nirvana. Daulton, Chris thought, reminded him of comedian Lenny Bruce, who had also sought a solution in heroin for problems he couldn't solve. They were both sick, he decided, but their sickness stemmed from a sick society; both had banged their heads against established norms until their junkie obsession had left them with no basic morality. Their motivations were right, but they had destroyed their "selves" in the process.

Heroin had become Daulton's orgasm, Chris thought, and then appended a thought: *I suppose I have my own, my stooping falcons.*

Even if he did kill Daulton, even if he could, Chris finally decided, it wasn't a solution. Somewhere, copies of the documents were cached and they would haunt him no matter whether Daulton was alive or dead. Who knew whom else he might have told about them in a junkie fog? Chris thought once again of the vision of Daulton's small body crumbling from a fusillade of bullets and put the gun away in a dresser in his bedroom. All he could do, he decided, was let fate run its course.

• •

"Can't I help you?" Alana asked in a voice that was part compassion, part frustration, part anger. "You never laugh anymore." Alana was complaining increasingly of Chris's dark moods; she suspected that whatever was bedeviling Chris had something to do with his job and with Daulton, who seemed to materialize these days out of dark alleys at bizarre hours and, after a whispered conversation with Chris, disappear just as suddenly. But Chris, every time she brought up his moods and inexplicable behavior, refused to discuss whatever it was that was tormenting him. And so she groped unsuccessfully to define the forces that were causing the changes in Chris.

"I can't take it anymore," she cried one night toward the end of August.

As she went on, Chris searched his mind for a course of action. And then he made a decision. Once again, he decided, he really had no choice. Chris felt as if he were riding a raft in the churning white water of the Colorado River, heading helplessly toward a precipice, a fall and disaster, and there was no place he could jump to a safe landing. Why, he asked himself, take someone with him on his inevitable trip to disaster?

As gently as he could, Chris lied to Alana that he did not love her anymore.

"You're wasting your time with me," he said, feigning a good-natured expression of logic. He wasn't ready to make a commitment, he said; his life was too uncertain. "Lana," he said, "I don't think our relationship is going any further than it is right now."

Alana began to cry. She was shocked and hurt by his declaration. But she told Chris things couldn't continue as they had been. And in a painful way, she admitted to herself, she was relieved by the lessening of the maddening pressure brought into her life by Chris's descent into a dark cosmos that she couldn't see or comprehend.

After that night, talk of marriage ended, and Chris and Alana began to drift apart.

"Our relationship had been poisoned," Chris would say more than a year later. "How can you marry someone with that kind of a situation? I had become a withdrawn, paranoid person; I lived behind a curtain; I had one life that was a normal aboveboard existence that I tried to make as wholesome as I could, and I had this poison gnawing away at me in this other life that I just totally put into a compartment and blocked off from everything else."

In July, 1976, on the second anniversary of Chris's hiring at TRW, his supervisor made a notation in his personnel folder:

Chris has been a valuable employee in our communications section. His daily work is accomplished quite well. Chris has potential for future growth within Security providing he applies himself to seeking that goal.

• •

After finishing his shift on September 3, 1976, a Friday, Chris drove his Volkswagen to the Los Angeles International Airport—it was less

than two miles from the TRW complex—and bought a ticket to Mexico City.

He had decided the only way to free himself from the bear trap he had sprung on himself was to take Daulton out of the picture; he must deal directly with the Russians and then get out of the mess, whatever way he could.

In July, the Russians had finally answered his inquiry about how much money Daulton had received: they said he had been paid more than $60,000; Chris had received less than $15,000 of the money by then. When he confronted Daulton with this information, his friend denied it; he said they were lying to drive a wedge between the two friends. Chris didn't believe him, but by then, the money no longer concerned Chris. He desperately wanted out—and he knew that as long as Daulton was his intermediary with the Russians, he couldn't extricate himself. In August, Chris sent another coded message to the Russians with a warning that his courier was "undependable," and suggesting that they contact him directly. But Daulton had grown increasingly suspicious about Chris's channel of communication to the KGB, especially after the confrontation over the money, and he hadn't delivered it.

At 2 A.M. on the morning of September 4, Chris knocked at the door of Daulton's room at the Holiday Inn in the Zona Rosa. Daulton, who had been asleep, was amazed to see his friend.

Chris didn't tell Daulton the genuine reason for his trip; he lied that he had decided on a whim to come to Mexico for the weekend just to meet the Russians he had heard so much about. Daulton said he would try to arrange a meeting the next day but it might not be possible. Then they both went to sleep.

Daulton had already made his September contact with Boris three days earlier, on the first Wednesday of the month. When Chris insisted that he try to set up another meeting, Daulton agreed to see what he could do. At several times during his long business relationship with the KGB, he had been assigned to meet his Russian contact at a construction site for a new hotel on Dakota Street near the murals at the Polyforum. He knew that Karpov and others from the embassy passed by the site from time to time and told Chris he would wait at this location in the hope that the Russians might see him and agree to a meeting that night with Chris. But an hour after he left, Daulton returned to the Holiday Inn and told Chris the Russians hadn't appeared.

Chris said he would try again the next month. The two of them went to the airport and flew back to Los Angeles. En route to the airport, Chris said he was curious to see what the Soviet Embassy looked like, and they had the cab driver pass by the big building on Calzada Tacubaya. As they drove by, Chris noticed several armed Mexico City policemen standing guard outside the gates of the embassy. On the trip back, Chris said nothing about his plan to get Daulton out of the picture —but he was as determined as ever to do so.

Monday, he was back to work in the Vault.

• •

The previous June, Judge Donahue, at Ken Kahn's urging, had extended Daulton's probation for three months so that it could be determined if psychotherapy and a job or schooling could salvage the chronic drug pusher. In early September, he received still another report on Daulton from the Los Angeles Probation Department. It pointed out that Daulton had recently been arrested for driving while intoxicated; that he had visited his psychiatrist only rarely; that he repeatedly missed appointments with his probation officer; that he was seldom home when probation officers went there to interview him; and it suggested that Daulton might still be dealing in drugs. For the third time in 1976, the department recommended that the probation of Andrew Daulton Lee be revoked and that he be sent to prison.

Early in September, a legal summons arrived at Daulton's home in Palos Verdes Estates. It ordered him to attend a hearing on September 10 before Judge Donahue, when the report was to be considered. But when the summons arrived, Daulton wasn't home; he was in Mazatlán again, working on the drug buy that he hoped would propel him into his soft new life in Costa Rica.

Because Daulton didn't appear at the hearing, Judge Donahue revoked his probation and issued a warrant for his arrest.

Once again, Daulton was a fugitive.

• •

Chris, meanwhile, was weighing a new option. In August, a TRW employee, Bob Thomas, had mentioned to him that a former TRW employee who had once worked in the Black Vault had written to him from Colorado, where he was now employed by another company involved in classified satellite developments, the Martin-Marietta Cor-

poration. The former employee, a friend of Thomas', had reported that his new employer paid considerably higher wages than TRW for doing the same kind of work and suggested Thomas apply for a job there. Thomas wasn't interested in the job; he said he didn't want to leave California. The Martin-Marietta plant was near Denver. Chris, however, saw the job as a possible way to get away from Daulton while returning to Colorado, which he had enjoyed during a short stay there following his year at Cal Poly. He wrote a letter to Thomas' friend:

Dear Gerald Smathers:

In recent conversations with Mary Phillips and Bob Thomas, it was brought to my attention that you are now living in Colorado and working for Martin-Marietta. I was curious as to your identity, as your name kept coming up in my logs. I work for security with Bob Thomas in M-4. In later discussions Bob mentioned that you had written him concerning a job opportunity at Martin-Marietta. After studying the folder he still keeps, I realized that you are located near Littleton, a suburb of Denver, where I used to live. Bob suggested I contact you concerning job openings.

I think at this point I should introduce myself. My name is Chris Boyce. I am 23 and I began working your job at TRW six months after you left. I know it's a bit irregular to write a total stranger but I would definitely love to return to Denver. Without going out of your way, is it possible for you to reply as to the existence of security openings as you described to Bob Thomas. I know this is a shot in the dark but I would appreciate your consideration.

Sincerely,
Chris Boyce

· ·

On a Saturday morning early in October, Chris flew to Mexico City again. Daulton was waiting for him at the Holiday Inn. At Chris's urging, Daulton had arranged an unusual Saturday meeting with Boris. But he told Chris the meeting wasn't scheduled until that evening. With time to kill, Daulton left their hotel room to have a manicure in the hotel barbershop. When he returned, they decided to go sightseeing.

As he had with Barclay Granger, Daulton guided Chris along the Paseo de la Reforma and took him into some of the museums in Chapultepec Park that made the park a rich Latin American showplace of

art. And like tourists, they photographed each other in front of paintings, statues, and other landmarks. Except for the moment when Daulton stumbled into a gaping, water-filled hole next to a sidewalk and soaked one leg of his pants up to the knee, it was an uneventful excursion. When they returned to the hotel, Chris decided to go for a swim in the hotel pool and fortified himself for the evening with cocktails called Harvey Wallbangers.

"Lulled by the alcohol I drifted in the water feeling a rising tension as the night came on," Chris wrote of that afternoon many months later. "I could occasionally see Lee look out the window of his room, and I no longer hated him as much as I had."

Like Daulton, Chris was exhilarated by the adventure, and was enjoying himself.

The coolness between the friends had deepened, although neither acknowledged it to the other. Daulton didn't want Chris in Mexico City; it meant he could lose his monopoly in dealings with the Russians. Chris didn't know where the meeting would lead him. But he hoped, at the least, to recapture some control over his own destiny, and—beyond that—to wrest control of their espionage operation from Daulton. After that he would decide his next move.

Shortly before 8 P.M., Daulton announced that it was time for them to go. They flagged a taxi near the hotel and Daulton ordered the driver to take them across town. "First, you've got to be sure you're not being followed," Daulton told Chris with the patronizing confidence of a tutor. The taxi dropped them in a neighborhood of brassy bars and cafés where barmaids who had emigrated from the poverty-stricken hinterlands of Mexico sold their bodies in upstairs rooms for $10. They looked around to check if they were being tailed, and then flagged down another taxi. Daulton directed it to a downtown park that Chris didn't recognize.

Mexico City had been pelted by an on-again, off-again drizzle most of the day. More substantial rain was starting to fall that evening. But the park was crowded nevertheless. After the taxi let them out, Daulton, a nervous grin on his face, told Chris to wait, and he disappeared into a dark backdrop of trees and brush. A television commercial was being filmed, and Chris watched the film crew at work from beside a high wall that afforded him a little shelter from the rain. After he had waited almost an hour, a man approached, paused and asked Chris in a heavily accented voice if he would like to share his umbrella.

The man introduced himself as "John." Chris, of course, recognized the code name.

His first thought upon meeting Boris Grishin was to wonder at how much he resembled Daulton. Although he didn't have Daulton's moustache and was slightly taller, he had the same kind of low-to-the-ground rolling gait, large head and broad shoulders. There was an unavoidable suggestion of an ape. Even Boris' face, Chris thought, reminded him of Daulton.

As they began to walk, Chris wondered: had the Russians selected him to control Daulton because there was something psychologically —as well as physically—similar between the agent and the snowman from Palos Verdes? With little conversation except comments about the weather, they continued to walk in the rain beneath the shelter of the umbrella. After a few minutes, Daulton's bantam figure emerged from behind a tree, and the three of them turned into an alley and walked across a wide street, where a big, dark limousine suddenly pulled to a stop with a squeal of its brakes and the hiss of tires on the wet pavement.

Just before they got into the embassy car, Daulton tried to lag behind Boris, and he whispered to Chris, "Tell 'em you can get anything they want." He had just had a session with Boris in which the Russian had again complained about his failure to deliver the code-room transmission frequencies and other information Daulton had promised many months earlier. Daulton was trying to get Chris to give Boris a consistent story—the old one about needing only a few more weeks to deliver what the Soviets wanted.

Chris noticed that Boris was watching them, and he wondered if the Russian had heard the whispered remark. He's trying to figure out what the relationship is between us, Chris thought. Karpov gunned the engine, and the car sprinted into motion. It was familiar stuff to Daulton. But Chris wasn't prepared for the race-car maneuvering, Karpov's darting into and out of side streets and alleys on what seemed to be a journey to nowhere. Before they had left the hotel, the two friends had smoked a joint and Daulton had supplemented his high from pot by snorting a dab of heroin; the drugs had served to soften their apprehension. But as the car careered over the wet streets of Mexico City, Chris began to get scared.

"Where are we going?" he asked.

"Deener," Boris answered with a smile.

196

"Where?" Chris asked.

"The embezze," he replied.

Chris recognized the shape of the Soviet Embassy when it loomed outside the car a few moments later. The car began to slow. "You're not going in the front gate?" he asked in amazement.

But before there was an answer, the gate swung open, and the limousine roared into the embassy compound. The two youths followed Boris and Karpov from the car into the building and were quickly escorted to the gloomy basement where Daulton had been before—the dark cavity that was an icy blend of sitting room and dungeon.

There were a sofa, end tables, a television set, a large conference table and several chairs in the room. On the conference table, several bottles of liquor—French brandy, three bottles of Russian vodka, several bottles of French wine and sweet Russian wine from Georgia— were waiting for them.

Boris asked for Chris's wallet, and he handed it to Karpov, who took it upstairs, apparently for an examination and photographing of his driver's license, TRW identification card and other papers in the wallet by other KGB agents.

Warmly, Boris welcomed Chris to the embassy and congratulated him for helping the socialist cause. Chris felt like Lindbergh on his arrival in Paris. Boris poured drinks for the three of them and a servant brought in platters of cooked beef, potatoes, carrots, cabbage, cheese and, of course, the inevitable caviar.

Chris felt his hands trembling. Perspiration began to soak his shirt. To pacify his fears, he gulped a glass of wine, and then another. He sampled the food, but didn't like the taste of the meat or the vegetables. He wondered if the Russians were trying to poison him. But even after he saw Boris eat from the same dishes, he decided not to eat any more; he didn't like this strange-tasting Russian cuisine.

With a raise of his hand, Boris signaled that it was time for business. He lifted his glass for a toast and said:

"To peace!"

To that, Daulton, glancing at Chris, responded:

"To cash!"

Boris looked disapprovingly at his agent and then thanked Chris for his services to the Soviet Union and the cause of socialism. Then, like the chief executive of a corporation reviewing the company's latest sales offensive, the KGB officer launched into a review of the two

spies' performance during the past eighteen months. He praised their successes, recalled times when communications had broken down, apologized for missed meetings, reviewed the information the Russians had received and what information they'd requested and hadn't received.

Chris studied the man. He seemed to have a cigarette in his mouth constantly, even when he spoke, and it drooped down diagonally like a stubby, fixed appendage. He had a dour, almost sad expression. In fact, Chris thought, all the Russians he had seen in the embassy looked as if they were ready to cry.

"We must have the Western Union frequencies," Boris implored in his broken English; it was *essential* that Chris obtain a list of the daily frequencies on which the CIA was transmitting his messages.

"I can't get the frequencies; I don't have access to them," Chris said; they were not kept in the vault where he worked, he said.

Boris seemed amazed.

Looking sideways at the smaller of his two spies, he said Daulton had repeatedly told him that he *could* get the frequencies. In fact, Daulton had been well paid because of his promise to deliver them.

Daulton avoided the agent's eyes and let his own roam over the room, stopping at a curious-looking coat of arms on one wall.

Boris shrugged and shifted to another subject: he asked Chris to give him an in-depth briefing of everything he did in the communications vault, including everything he knew about the satellites built by TRW. Chris answered the questions as best he could.

Each time Chris finished answering a few questions, Boris interrupted the interview and left the room—apparently, Chris suspected, to confer with technical specialists or superiors elsewhere in the building. When he returned, he usually had a new list of questions.

Chris noticed that every time Boris left, Karpov turned on the television set in the room. Although his English seemed less than completely functional, Karpov managed to convey to Chris and Daulton that he loved to watch television but was kept so busy that he didn't have time to watch it very often. This seemed to make him very unhappy. There was an American-made television program—the name of which he seemed unable to translate for the American visitors—that he wanted to see that night.

But unfortunately for Karpov, the TV set did not work well that evening and it defied his efforts to make it work. All he could get on

the screen was a kaleidoscope of horizontal lines, and it infuriated him. He pounded first on one side of the TV set and then on the other, and twisted the dials to make it work. But the flickering black-and-white lines remained. When Boris returned to the room, Karpov stiffened and turned off the set, only to pound his fists again on the impotent television receiver as soon as Boris left the room again.

Daulton felt ignored. "It was as if I wasn't in the room," he recalled later. A spectator to the discussions between Boris and Chris, he poured himself more vodka and wine as the others talked. The liquor, combined with the effects of heroin, began to turn him more aggressive. Daulton didn't like being snubbed, and after a while he started to interrupt their conversation.

He began with a protest over a promise by Boris to buy him a villa on the beach in Puerto Vallarta (the one he was going to give to his father). He was supposed to operate it as a safe house for KGB agents. He demanded to know why the Russians hadn't bought it yet.

It is not known whether in fact the KGB ever really intended to buy a beach house for Daulton. But after several of his interruptions, Boris turned to Daulton and told him not to worry about the villa: the purchase would be arranged soon, he reassured him.

When Daulton persisted and demanded action, Boris lost his temper. The two of them rose to their feet like two cocks preening before a fight. "You can't deliver," Boris exclaimed, to which Daulton shouted, "*You* can't deliver!"

The shouting continued as each held his ground, standing erect. Then Boris reached over, grabbed a bottle and poured Daulton a glass of vodka as a peace offering. Daulton downed it in one gulp and poured a glass for Boris, who swallowed his vodka even faster, and then repeated the rite.

Chris decided that Boris, as well as Daulton, was starting to get drunk.

Daulton became quiet for a moment, and the Russian turned back to Chris. He produced a list of TRW and CIA employees whose names had appeared on some of the TWX messages between Pilot and Pedal and said he and his associates wanted to know everything that Chris knew about these people: what their specific jobs were, details of their families, drinking habits, sexual proclivities and anything else that Chris wanted to add. Chris wrote down a few remarks about the people on the list, but ignored the request for embarrassing personal details.

Boris then asked for a list of other employees who worked on the satellite project, and as Chris started making a list, he excused himself to relay earlier answers upstairs. Karpov, who was disgusted with the performance of the television set, also left the room.

As Chris worked on the list of names, Daulton, now thoroughly drunk and staggering, grabbed one of Chris's arms and waved toward the coat of arms on the wall. He said, "Those bastards! Watch out—they're watching us through the picture."

Chris stared hard at the three-dimensional plaque on the wall and decided he couldn't see anything suspicious. But Daulton insisted there were eyes in the walls monitoring them, and to prove his point, he stood up on a chair and removed an outer shell from the coat of arms. Behind it there was some kind of electronic apparatus that Chris didn't recognize.

"This place has got to be bugged," Daulton said shakily. Quickly, he started feeling the walls and examining the furniture. With a yelp of triumph, he said he had discovered a microphone beneath an end table. With a firm tug, he ripped it out and proudly held it up for Chris to see, its wires dangling limply in the air.

"I've had it with this fucking hocus-pocus," he said.

Boris returned, and Daulton, surprising Chris, pulled an envelope from his shirt, thrust it at Boris and demanded money. Chris picked up the envelope and saw two strips of microfilm with photographs of documents that he thought he had given Daulton months before; Chris realized Daulton had kept back some of the data to squeeze extra money out of the Russians.

Boris looked at the microfilm and called it "garbage"—useless without the frequencies. Once again, Daulton jumped to his feet and started yelling at Boris, screaming that he'd been cheated. Boris rose to his feet. He shouted back at Daulton, reiterating his earlier theme that Daulton had not delivered what he had promised. Both periodically interrupted their debate by swilling down another glass of vodka.

Chris stared at the two men, who were now oblivious to him. They were standing perhaps two feet apart. Daulton was sticking the index finger of his right hand into Boris' chest like a hard-sell merchant in a Moroccan bazaar, and Boris was waving his finger right back at Daulton.

My God, Chris thought, it's like a Charlie Chaplin movie. They seem to enjoy it.

After a while, the debate subsided, and Daulton sat down and resumed his solitary drinking. Boris had brought with him blowups of pictures taken of the interior of the KG-13 machine showing the cipher circuit boards, which Daulton had brought on a previous trip, and Boris showed them to Chris to illustrate a point he had tried to make earlier: that some of the photographs had been faulty. The circuit boards of the machine were discernible in the pictures, he acknowledged, but the image was too fuzzy. Chris looked at the pictures and tried to act surprised. A few minutes later, Boris turned his attention to other matters, while Daulton sat in his chair and studied the pictures lying on the table. When he thought Boris was distracted in conversation with Chris, he grabbed them and shoved them beneath his shirt. It was a speculative urge: perhaps he could sell the pictures to another embassy, he thought.

When Chris saw the newest list of questions, he decided that whoever had compiled the list probably knew a good deal about satellites—a good deal more than he knew. There were more questions about the Pilot–Pedal communications link and the cipher equipment, plus a lengthy list of queries about Rhyolite, Argus and other TRW reconnaissance satellites, about infrared sensors and on a variety of other technical subjects. When he gave him the new list of questions, Boris also returned Chris's wallet to him. Writing in longhand, Chris answered some of the questions. But others either were too technical or applied to projects that he did not know about, and some he simply ignored.

On one of the sheets of blank paper Boris gave him to answer the questions, Chris wrote a note to the KGB agent: He said that Daulton was so addicted to heroin that he was jeopardizing their whole operation. Furthermore, he said, Daulton had spent much of the money sent to both of them to support his heroin habit and was too unpredictable to trust. "He's threatened to blackmail my father," Chris wrote, "and if he does my father will go straight to the FBI."

Boris scanned the note, and Chris wondered what the KGB agent would make of it. He looked over at Daulton and decided that the vodka, wine, cocaine and pot had finally conquered him: he was slumped back in his chair in the shadow-filled cell. But then he seemed to regain consciousness; he nibbled at a piece of cheese, chugalugged another glass of vodka and sat back again. Daulton's stomach had been giving him trouble again in the past few days, and the rich food and

drink that night had turned it into a painful caldron of sour bile. He announced that he had to go to the bathroom. While he was gone, Chris said again that his friend was a heroin addict; he said Daulton had to be removed from their operation or he would blow it. Boris was nodding agreement when Daulton returned.

Once again, Boris asked if there was any possibility of Chris's obtaining the frequencies.

"They want to listen from their trawlers," Daulton interjected. Boris glared at Daulton and ignored the remark. He reiterated that Daulton had assured him repeatedly that Chris could obtain the frequencies. Despite everything, Boris apparently still didn't believe what Chris had told him earlier.

Chris repeated that he didn't work with the frequencies and that the list was kept by Western Union and the CIA. He said he was willing to try, but there would be a high risk that he would be caught if he tried. Boris responded quickly: No, don't try. Chris should not expose himself to such a risk. He apologized for even asking, saying that he had brought up the question only because he had been assured by Daulton that he could get the frequencies.

Boris was still slurring his words, but Chris suspected that he still had his wits about him; there was something solicitous in the KGB agent's behavior toward him now, and he wondered why.

His motives soon began to be obvious.

Boris asked casually if Chris had ever thought about seeking a job elsewhere within the CIA or the American government. Chris answered that on two occasions he had been offered jobs by the CIA, but he had felt he wouldn't be able to pass the lie-detector test required of all agency employees.

There were ways to fool the operator of a polygraph machine, Boris said, and added that they could take up this matter later.

"How much would it cost for you to complete your education?" he asked.

Chris thought a moment. "About forty thousand dollars, including graduate school."

Boris then outlined his proposal:

Chris should quit his job and return to college to prepare for a career in the State Department or the CIA. Chris should take university courses in Russian and Chinese history and political affairs, become a specialist in one or both of these countries and master the Chinese and Russian languages if he could.

At some time in the future, perhaps years away, Boris hinted, Chris might have another opportunity to serve the Soviet Union. Suddenly, Chris realized what Boris had in mind: he was attempting to plant a *mole* in the United States Government—a young man with promise and good credentials who would join a government agency at a modest level and then begin climbing the bureaucratic ladder, perhaps to a high level of government, where he would be a Soviet spy *in situ*, waiting for orders to come someday from Moscow.

Chris would claim later that he had had no choice but to accept the Soviet offer that night. The trap he had set for himself in an impulsive swipe at what he viewed as a corrupt, cancerous system had sprung again. This time he knew it might grip him for the rest of his life. Wherever he went, whatever he did—whether he became a lawyer, a priest, a government employee, a teacher, whatever—he realized he might always be called on to work for the KGB. . . . They could find him. By threatening to disclose the secret of his youth, the KGB could blackmail him into doing its bidding for the rest of his life.

He hated Boris and what he stood for as much as he hated the CIA spooks on Rhyolite. He despised them as one and the same—fools pursuing the senseless nationalism that would ultimately end in a cataclysmic nuclear holocaust. They were fools, all of them.

Why not let the Russians pay for his education? There would be opportunities later, he told himself, to decide his ultimate plan. How would they find me? he asked himself.

Chris accepted the proposal, and Boris was delighted.

Meanwhile, Boris said, Chris should keep up the friendships he had made at TRW and be alert to the possibility of recruiting other employees to help the cause, adding that he should pay special attention to weaknesses of these people that might be open to blackmail. Chris said he would not recruit any of his associates, but Boris overlooked this insubordination and urged Chris to return once more to Mexico City in January.

The meeting broke up shortly before 1 A.M. All three of them were drunk. The anger between Boris and Daulton earlier in the evening had now shifted into the camaraderie of drunks the world over, or so it seemed to Chris.

Boris gave Daulton an envelope containing $1,000, and Chris an envelope with $5,000. When he gave the money to Chris, Boris waited until Daulton was looking elsewhere and whispered that there was an address written on the envelope where he should meet him the follow-

ing day. But when Chris later tried to read the message, he discovered that the KGB agent had been so smashed that his writing was indecipherable.

The two friends were dropped off at the hotel by the embassy car. Daulton, still feeling snubbed, asked Chris to share their take from the Russians equally, but Chris refused. Daulton was even angrier the next morning when they checked out of the Holiday Inn. Chris made Daulton pay the entire bill because of his admission in front of Boris that he had indeed received more money than he had admitted to Chris before.

They reviewed the meeting over breakfast, and Chris told Daulton that he had agreed to one more delivery.

33

"DISINFORMATION."

The idea was intriguing to Daulton. He had wondered what story he should tell if ever he and Chris were tripped up, and the idea seemed promising. It wasn't a new idea; he'd first thought about it months earlier. But as he lay stretched out with a book on a chaise longue beside the pool at the Oceana Palace Hotel in Mazatlán, where he had gone after the meeting in Mexico City with Chris and Boris, it began to seem more and more attractive. Perhaps it was the book he was reading, *The CIA and the Cult of Intelligence,* by Victor Marchetti and John D. Marks. Disinformation was *wrong* information leaked to an enemy that was camouflaged as the truth. "Disinformation is a special type of 'black' propaganda which hinges on absolute secrecy and which is usually supported by false documents," the authors had written.

Both the CIA and the KGB, he read, routinely used agents to feed false information to each other and to penetrate the other's intelligence service. It was a cat-and-mouse operation. Daulton read on and became further intrigued by the plan that was taking shape in his mind. It was common, the authors wrote, for the CIA to encourage Americans involved in espionage "to cooperate with the Soviets in order to learn

more about what kind of information the KGB wants to collect, to discover more about KGB methods and equipment or merely to occupy the time and money of the KGB on a fruitless project. CIA counterespionage specialists do not necessarily wait for the KGB to make a recruitment effort, but instead may set up an elaborate trap, dangling one of their own as bait for the opposition."

Daulton laid down the book and wondered. It would make an excellent defense if he ever needed one, he decided. Then a further thought flashed through his mind and it delighted him: maybe, he fantasized, his idea for a defense was even *true*.

From across the pool, two friends from Colorado who were also trying to convert the Mexico sun's rays into autumn tans had seen the American who was about their own age reading a paperback book that had something to do with spies. Bob Herbert and Larry Smith had decided in early October that they needed a vacation, and on October 20, 1976, they had checked into the high-rise Oceana Hotel on the beach at Mazatlán. They saw the American put down his book, get up from his chaise and walk along the edge of the pool toward the two Coloradans. He introduced himself as "Alex Lee" and said he was recuperating from minor injuries in a traffic accident. Smith hadn't known Daulton long before he decided that he had a distaste for him. "He's a cocky punk," he later told his companion; Smith was unimpressed that first day by Daulton's ostentatious offer each time a bill arrived for cocktails or food to pick up the tab, and when Daulton began to boast of exploits in the drug trade, Smith wrote him off as a bore and a phony.

Herbert, though, was less put off by the stranger; Daulton struck up a friendship with him, and they spent many hours together during the next few days, at the pool and in the hotel bar, with Herbert alternately fascinated by and suspicious of the stories spun by the diminutive stranger who was constantly scanning the faces of people around him, declaring that he was worried about Federal drug-enforcement agents' putting him under surveillance.

On the first day they met, Daulton informed Herbert that he was a member of the "Mexican Mafia." He described himself as a major-league drug dealer whose base of operation was Culiacán, up the road from Mazatlán. He hadn't meant to get involved in drugs, Lee continued. It had all started by accident because his sister had gotten in trouble with Mexican drug dealers and he'd had to go to work for them

to get her out of a jam. Daulton said he was "a lot of dead babies"—a man of many identities, with several passports and credentials for several people. The way to do it, he explained, was to obtain birth certificates of deceased children and use them to procure false identification. That was how he managed to travel back and forth between Mexico and California without being arrested, he said.

After three or four days, Daulton began to tell his new friend of riches he had been mining besides drugs. He said he took photographs of ships in American harbors and sold them to a foreign government for $50,000. "You don't go to the country where you're going to sell the film," he explained, "but to their embassy in another country."

Herbert feigned belief, but Daulton decided that he really didn't believe him, so he added more details to convince him.

"Come to my room; I'll show you," he said, as if challenged.

The first thing Herbert noticed about Daulton's room was a stack of spy novels on a dresser, along with so many containers of Valium and other pills that he wondered if he was a hypochondriac. He noticed several cameras on a table near the room's window wall that offered a spectacular view of the Pacific.

Daulton picked up one of the cameras and said he'd obtained it in a trade with one of his customers for cocaine. He showed Herbert a hiding place inside the leather case and pulled out long strips of film negatives.

"This is the kind of stuff I sell," he said.

Herbert held it up to the light, and on the first frame he noticed two words in large print: TOP SECRET.

Daulton said it was a photograph of a document he'd received from the Swiss Government and he was going to sell it to the highest bidder.

Actually, he added, this material wasn't all that good. "I've got better stuff to sell," he said.

Acting like a tutor, Daulton explained how easy it was to get into the business. "You can go to a public library and take pictures of stuff in books and sell it to foreign embassies."

When Herbert suggested it was a gold mine and asked why Daulton didn't do more of it, his new friend said he could make more money dealing in drugs with the Mexican Mafia.

"Aren't you taking a chance telling me about all this?" Herbert asked.

"All you know is that I have a real nice camera and took pictures of a shipyard," Daulton said.

When the Coloradans' six-day vacation was up, Daulton said he'd foot the bill if they wanted to stay on a few more days. They declined, however, saying they had to get back to work.

Before they departed, they noticed that Daulton was visited twice by a young, well-dressed Mexican. On the day they left, Daulton rented a car and drove to Culiacán for another meeting with the same man. He placed an order for the heroin buy. Now he had to pay for it.

• •

On October 27, 1976, Chris completed application for admission to the University of California at Riverside. He wrote that it was his intention to major in history and minor in political science.

In the essay that was required with the application, Chris outlined his aspirations:

After twenty-three years of existence, it is possible to divide my life into two distinct periods. First, my childhood and adolescence were dominated by a sense of searching. My attractions switched from monastic Catholicism to social protest to athletics. Most movements, fads and causes of that time held my complete if short-lived attention. I was continually groping in search of a purpose with which to direct my energy.

In 1974 I interrupted my education in San Luis Obispo in exchange for employment at TRW in Redondo Beach, California. It was here that I formulated the concepts which color my "second phase." I am extremely fortunate in that my daily responsibilities include interaction with middle level management of the federal bureaucracy. These working relationships have allowed me the opportunity to narrow my focus concerning my social role. It is from this group of mainly young, ambitious achievers from which I derive my direction.

Their ultimate goal is to accumulate the maximum amount of personal power through advancement within the bureaucracy. These drives are motivated by self-achievement yet they serve to further the public interest. Herein lies my aspirations. The completion of my education is the next logical step in pursuit of these aims.

My free time is spent dabbling in falconry, fresh water fishing and historical study. Through these interests I am aware of America's continued deterioration in the areas of environmental preservation and global politics. I perceive major altercations in the world at large in my lifetime due to population increases and food and energy shortages.

As the United States faces these massive challenges in the years to come, it will take competent performance within the intelligence com-

munity and foreign service to safeguard the national integrity. For this purpose I seek admission to the University of California at Riverside.

It was the essay of someone declaring his intention to work for the United States as an intelligence specialist or in the foreign service. It was just as Boris had requested. Chris mailed the application and waited for a decision.

Five days after Chris put the application in the mail, Daulton caught a Mexicana Airlines flight from Mazatlán to Mexico City with plans to shake down the Russians again.

Following the routine that was now familiar, he checked in at the Holiday Inn, taped X marks on a row of lampposts in one of the designated streets and arrived at the Bali Restaurant at ten o'clock the following morning.

The Russians did not appear.

After smoking a joint, Daulton went to a souvenir shop and purchased a picture postcard showing the Pyramid of the Sun. He printed three letters on the card—"K.G.B."—and then addressed it to "John." He signed "Luis" at the bottom of the card and went to the embassy, where he threw it past the iron bars into the compound.

At 6 P.M. on November 2, he was at the Bali, hoping Boris had gotten the message.

He was a no-show again.

Daulton decided to confront the situation head-on.

He flagged down a taxi and gave the driver directions to an intersection near the Russian embassy. En route, he sniffed a pinch of cocaine he had slipped into his right nostril, and again, the marvelous sense of self-confidence it gave him cascaded over Daulton.

As the cab moved slowly through dense early-evening traffic, Daulton looked out the window and saw small bands of adults and children in processions, some of them carrying candles that lit up the early-evening shadows with a soft flickering glow. He realized it was *El día de los muertos*—the Day of the Dead, one of Mexico's major holidays. It was a blend of Halloween, All Saints' Day, All Souls' Day, even a bit of Easter. *El día de los muertos* was rooted in Spanish and pre-Columbian traditions, a time to show reverence to the dead. In shops around the city, windows were filled with miniature human skulls made of white sugar and decorated with frosting and tinsel; bakeries had produced thousands of sweet breads called *pan de los muertos* (the bread of the dead), and pastries shaped like human bones; special

altars had been prepared and were laden with photographs of deceased family members. Samples of their favorite foods had been left on the altars beside the pictures. And throughout the city, there were processions of families flocking to cemeteries bearing candles, incense and more servings of dead family members' favorite foods, which were to be left at their graves while the family sang traditional songs of the holiday.

Daulton paid the driver and made his way through several processions of celebrants before reaching the high fence of iron bars outside the embassy. Deciding that there was just one way to accomplish his goal, he positioned himself near the front gate and waited. When his chance came, he followed a car that entered the gate. He introduced himself to a guard and said in his poor Spanish that he wanted to see Boris Grishin.

Boris was furious.

The tight expression that Daulton had learned to be wary of twisted the muscles around the KGB officer's mouth, as he angrily denounced Daulton for violating orders not to enter the embassy unannounced and for throwing the card through the fence. He accused Daulton of being incoherent because of drugs. "You're stupid," he said in Spanish.

In defense, Daulton whipped out several strips of microfilm ciphers given him months earlier by Chris, and demanded $10,000. Boris ridiculed the demand. The material was worthless, he said, and scolded Daulton for again failing to bring information he had promised. Daulton stood his ground; he said again he was tired of risking his life for the Russians and getting nothing for the risk and began to wave his finger at Boris and raise his voice. On this occasion, however, Boris was sober and not in a mood to debate his undisciplined spy: without any warning, he grabbed him by the back of his jacket and pulled the garment over his head, and with the help of two embassy chauffeurs, he marched Daulton to a limousine with the jacket draped over his face like a blanket. Daulton was pushed into the back seat and ordered to lie on the floor so he couldn't be seen. Within seconds, the car roared out the embassy gate with the KGB man Igor Dagtyr at the wheel, Karpov in the back seat and Daulton crouched on the floor. From the sounds of the streets, Daulton knew they were moving away from the center of Mexico City, but he couldn't tell in which direction they were headed. Sitting above him, Karpov told Daulton not to speak.

He had been lying on the floor of the back seat of the limousine for

perhaps fifteen minutes when, suddenly, it began to slow. Daulton's confidence was still buoyed by the drugs. But he retained enough of his inherent sense of cunning to be panicked by the tug of inertia he felt as the car began to slow. In his last words to Boris before he was escorted out of the embassy, Daulton had promised to return soon with some of the data the Russians had wanted all these months. But now he was disoriented; he wasn't sure whether he had his former power over the Russians. As the car slowed, he wondered: Had his promise been enough to plant seeds of hope in Boris? Or had they at last called his hand and decided to eliminate him? The car continued to slow; Daulton heard the familiar squeak of the limousine's brakes and braced for it to stop. But then he began to realize Dagtyr didn't plan to stop. He heard the two men conversing in Russian. Something in their voices suggested they weren't going to stop. Then Karpov opened the back-seat door next to him and suddenly pushed Daulton out.

Daulton fell out on what felt like a cobblestone street.

The car sped off and disappeared into the evening traffic. The car had been going slowly enough so that Daulton wasn't hurt. He caught a cab and returned to the Holiday Inn, where he wondered if the scam had finally run its course.

• •

Chris, meanwhile, had discovered a new field, and it was to provide him with a few minutes of escape from the sense of doom that weighed him down the remaining hours of each day. It was fifty acres, spared somehow by the subdividers and the shopping-center builders, in the city of Compton, a twenty-minute drive from the beach and TRW.

Chris was eating little these days and, he told himself, drinking too much. There had been no response to his letter about the job in Colorado. There had been no reply to his application to the university. He was sure of one thing: he would leave TRW now. But it would be a miracle if he got a chance to go to the university or make a new start in Colorado. Whatever would happen now was inevitable.

How insane the world had become, he reflected; he thought of ancient Greece and Rome, about the great cities man had built, his great works of art, and then he thought of the cities smoldering in the darkness of a civilization that had snuffed itself out in atomic warfare. What madness man had created!

His mind focused on the silos that pocked Siberia and the base of

the Urals and other areas of the Soviet Union; he thought of identical silos dug into the plains of Wyoming, North Dakota and Arizona and other stretches of the prairie, where, less than a century before, American Indians had fought for survival with bows and arrows. Each silo on both sides of the world had a missile with enough energy to destroy several cities. These were not abstract illusions, he thought, but reality. They were *there*. In each silo was a missile with a nuclear warhead; each missile was alive, with the gyrocompass in its guidance system spinning relentlessly twenty-four hours a day, awaiting a signal to carry the warhead to a target that had already been chosen by men and their computers.

How had man come to this brink? Civilization was so close to annihilation. Why weren't other people as panicked as he was? The missiles were in the silos, ready to be launched at an instant . . . ready to extinguish in minutes what man had taken thousands of years to build. Didn't people know that?

As Chris looked at the field, he wondered where the missile was that was targeted for this piece of earth. It was crazy! How had man arrived at this moment where a mistake, a false move or a fragile human ego had the capability to turn *everything* into ashes?

He thought again of the crazy quest for manhood that war fulfilled for so many men, that blindness he had first discovered in *Lee's Lieutenants*, the blindness he had seen in the eyes of Boris, which he could see every day in the eyes of the CIA spooks at Pedal and Banjo. They were adolescent boys trying to prove themselves to one another. But didn't other people realize what this mindless groping for manhood was going to do to the world?

There was talk in the papers about the SALT negotiations to limit nuclear weapons. There's no hope, he thought. Hadn't the generals always *used* every new weapon they acquired? Hadn't all of the wars for at least a century been preceded by just such disarmament negotiations?

In the field in Compton, Chris managed to forget some of his fears, because of Nurd. Nurd was a tercel—a male hawk—that Chris had trapped on a weekend trip to Arizona, and in the shortening days of early November, Chris brought Nurd often to the field to hunt rabbits. He set his alarm clock for 4 A.M., went to the plant, set up the coding machines for the day, accepted whatever traffic had accumulated from CIA headquarters and then went home, picked up Nurd and drove to

THE FALCON AND

the field with him for an hour or so. Almost every day Nurd got a cottontail, and one morning he caught two.

How long, he wondered, would it be before he was caught?

• •

On November 12, Chris was advised by the University of California at Riverside that he had been accepted for admission in the winter quarter, beginning in January, 1977. He informed TRW that he was returning to college and requested termination on December 17, after the company had had time to train a successor.

Now that he had made this decision, Chris decided to make one final gesture. There was no pressure from Daulton, no threats of blackmail. But he had promised Boris to make one last delivery, and he intended to keep it.

"They're catching on, I'm telling you, man, it's getting spooky," Daulton said when Chris told him they should make a final delivery. "They say the recent stuff isn't any good," he said. Chris said he shouldn't worry and then motivated Daulton with the kind of words that, as always, he knew would do the job: he said he had access to documents that he *knew* would be worth at least $75,000 to the Soviets. Daulton listened and agreed. The documents were about a project, Chris said, that sounded as if it were "something out of the movies."

34 THE ESSENCE OF RUNNING an espionage network in a foreign country is communications. Whether an agent is recruited or planted in an unfriendly nation, whether his mission is to obtain secret information or to bring down a government, reliable communication between the agent and his intelligence service is essential. What good is the work of a spy who gleans warning of a coup d'état or an invasion if he can't transmit the information to his control? What good is an agent whose supervisor cannot control the spy and direct an espionage operation?

Spies during the Napoleonic Wars used invisible ink to write messages concealed on harmless-looking public documents. German spies during World War I used hollowed stones to leave messages. Hidden radio transmitters in the Low Countries of Europe flashed reports of Nazi research on rockets during World War II.

The cameras, infrared heat sensors, radio antennae and other instruments on spy satellites revolutionized the collection of strategic intelligence information during the nineteen-sixties. But the science of communicating with individual agents remained rather primitive. The KGB gave Daulton a spool of adhesive tape to place on lampposts; it sent him coded postcards at a mail drop and gave him a schedule of prearranged telephone calls.

Late in the nineteen-sixties, the CIA began to fashion a scheme for a global grand design of espionage communications. It was to be the ultimate method of controlling and exchanging information with operatives working undercover in what the agency, euphemistically, called "denied areas of the world."

Earlier in the decade, the agency had begun using Pentagon communication satellites to exchange information with agents. With portable radio gear, spies could broadcast and receive information via the satellites. But these systems were only partially satisfactory. Agents in some regions of the world did not have access to them because, geographically, they were out of range of the satellites. Agents in other areas could use them only at limited times of the day, and the technology was such that a sophisticated counterintelligence service might eavesdrop on the signals and discover the spy.

The grand design that began to take shape within the Central Intelligence Agency was a new kind of satellite system designed for, and dedicated solely to, espionage—a push-button system of communications that was to enable agency officials in Langley, Virginia, a suburb of Washington, to maintain, twenty-four hours a day, undetected communications with a spy anywhere in the world.

A spy was to be given a miniature, portable transceiver disguised in any number of ways: as a wallet, a pocket calculator, a cigarette case, an ashtray, a flashlight or something similarly mundane. No matter where he or she was located, the agent would be able to communicate secretly and instantaneously with Langley.

It was a concept with ingenious possibilities: a CIA officer could come to work after a morning round of golf in Virginia and hold a

two-way conversation of encrypted telegrams with an agent located on a roof in Cairo, then switch to an exchange of data with agents in Kiev, Peking or Entebbe.

In November, 1972, the CIA sent Lockheed, TRW and several other companies a Top Secret letter disclosing that it was considering implementation of a series of research studies aimed at developing a "world-wide cover communication satellite system."

In the language of the aerospace industry, such a letter is called an RFP—a Request for Proposal.

TRW responded that it would submit a proposal in an effort to win a CIA study contract on the project.

The CIA's RFP read:

The principal requirements for the satellite network are as follows:
  * Provide maximum protection of the user against signal detection and direction finding leading to determination of user location.
  * Minimize dependence upon overseas ground stations.
  * Provide multiple simultaneous access capability to users employing different types of traffic, data rates, modulation techniques and radiated power levels.
  * Provide communications on demand with essentially no waiting time regardless of type and location of user.
  * Provide protection against traffic analysis, which could imply numbers, types, purpose and location of users.

The CIA said it wanted a design that could not only provide a clandestine avenue of communication with agents, but also relay information from robot transmitters that were to be dropped secretly on foreign soil to transmit intelligence information by remote control— seismic measurements, for example, disclosing the incidence, time and magnitude of nuclear-weapons tests. There was also a third desired capability—the capacity to serve in an emergency as a conduit for communications between Washington and American embassies around the world.

The intelligence agency dictated that the system had to be able to handle up to about one hundred agents at one time, a daily volume of some fifty messages to Langley and about twenty messages sent from Langley to agents. Some of the transmissions would be as long as two hundred words, but most would be in short bursts, the equivalent of about ten words.

There was to be one fundamental requirement for the system, the

CIA told TRW: the chance of transmissions' being detected was to be less than 1 percent.

The CIA letter stated:

This study effort is classified TOP SECRET and has been assigned a code-word designator, "PYRAMIDER."

All contractor personnel working on this study effort must have a current TOP SECRET clearance and must be approved by Headquarters prior to being briefed on PYRAMIDER.

Contractor personnel proposed for clearance access to this study must qualify by holding a currently valid BYEMAN security access approval.

While this study effort will be conducted within the contractor facilities as TOP SECRET, and while only those personnel holding active BYEMAN access approvals are eligible for consideration, the effort is not a BYEMAN study, but is to be conducted in all aspects of document control, physical security standards, communications within Headquarters, and the like, as if it were BYEMAN.

Security officers will assure documents within the contractor facility are stamped TOP SECRET/PYRAMIDER only, and are not entered into the BYEMAN system.

The highly sensitive nature of this effort cannot be emphasized enough. Personnel submitted for access approval will be submitted via cable message which shall fully outline their need-to-know. No Form 2018 will be submitted to Headquarters. A list of those persons approved for access to PYRAMIDER shall be maintained by Headquarters Security Staff. Cable messages shall be sent via secure TWX and shall be slugged PYRAMIDER on the second line. PYRAMIDER shall enjoy limited distribution within Project Headquarters.

In February, 1973, a Top Secret TWX arrived at the Black Vault from Langley notifying the company that it had been selected to develop a design for the Pyramider project. A few weeks later a formal contract arrived from the CIA. It was signed in a broad scrawl with the name James Cranbrook, a pseudonym assigned to a CIA official to give him anonymity. The initially authorized spending for the study was only $50,000. But as was common in the aerospace industry, TRW would invest considerably more than this in the study in the belief that it would lead to a CIA production contract worth hundreds of millions of dollars.

•   •

MULTIBEAM SPACECRAFT

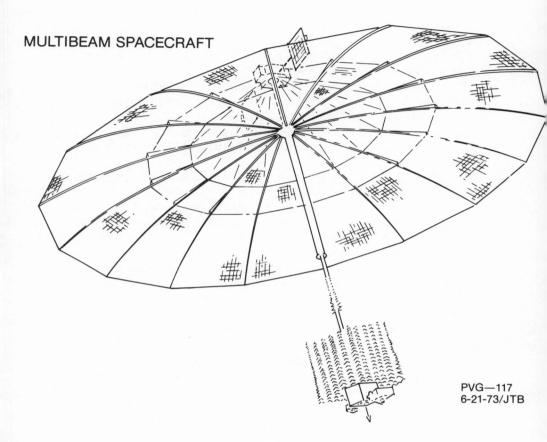

PVG—117
6-21-73/JTB

EARTH COVERAGE SPACECRAFT

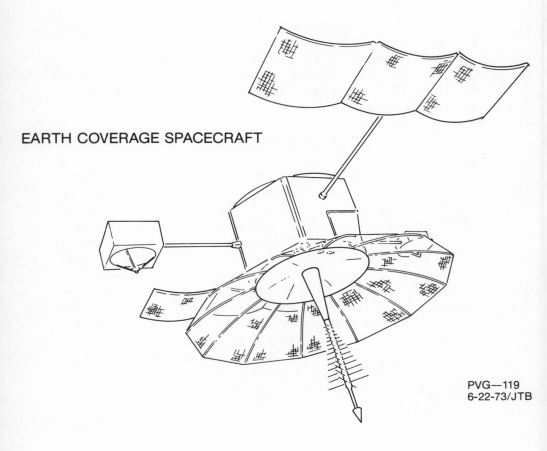

PVG—119
6-22-73/JTB

Sketches of the proposed TOP SECRET Pyramider satellites.

A specially cleared team of forty engineers and technical specialists, working in a sealed area in M-4, was assigned to design the global covert-communications network in the spring of 1973, a year before Christopher Boyce became an employee of TRW. In July, the team submitted its plan for the system.

It concluded that the CIA's ambitions for the espionage switchboard were realistic: such a system, it said, could be provided between Langley and its far-flung agents at a price of between $355 million and $442 million, depending on technical variables to be decided later as development proceeded.

The plan envisaged launching three satellites 22,000 miles from the earth in so-called "stationary" orbits, in which their movement through space would be synchronized to the earth's own rotational speed and, thus, seem to remain over the same point on earth. One satellite, positioned over the Indian Ocean, and another, over the Pacific, were to be always within broadcast range of Langley; the third was to be positioned on the other side of the globe above Southeast Asia. The messages it handled would be relayed by one of the other two satellites or by an earth station on the Pacific island of Guam.

The report emphasized that advanced radio-frequency-interception equipment in aircraft and on the ground could pose a threat to the CIA's goal of providing absolute secrecy for the agents during communications. But TRW outlined a technical strategy—such as constantly shifting the frequency on which messages were broadcast, a technique called "frequency-hopping"—that, it said, would provide large "safe areas" within cities where signals could be hidden among random urban radio transmissions. Such methods, it said, would also "reduce aircraft intercept radius in remote areas to twenty nautical miles."

TRW designed a satellite that, more than anything else, looked like an umbrella for a giant man in space. Its most striking component was a one-hundred-foot-wide concave antenna; extending from the center of this "dish," like the staff of an umbrella, was a long boom, and at the end of the boom, where the umbrella handle might be fitted, was attached a large package of electronic equipment. The satellite was to be launched from Cape Canaveral folded in the nose of a rocket booster; once in space, the antenna was to unfurl like a slender umbrella suddenly popped open in the rain.

By the time TRW had completed the design study, it had billed the CIA for $66,000.

It submitted its bid and waited for a decision to proceed.

But in the fall of 1973, the CIA made a decision: it realized it would not get the money from Congress for the next fiscal year to build Pyramider and so it shelved the project at least temporarily.

However, it continued exploring the use of similar covert-communications technology with other companies and in projects with other code names. Eventually, with certain variations, the CIA launched an alternative program to provide instantaneous communication with spies around the world using satellites similar to Pyramider.

After the Pyramider design was completed, a copy of TRW's final report, containing more than thirty volumes of documents, was locked in a safe at TRW. According to the gossip in M-4, Pyramider was a dead project.

Not long after Chris submitted his resignation, the Pyramider documents were removed from the safe where they had been held, and they were left out in the open on a file cabinet in the Black Vault.

• •

The clerk at the Hacienda Airport Hotel looked across the desk at the two young men who were registering to spend the night together on the evening of December 7, 1976, and tried to retain his poise.

The Hacienda was a popular trysting place for stewardesses and pilots during airline layovers in Los Angeles, but it didn't attract many homosexuals. Chris said they needed the room only for the night and would depart the following morning, December 8. The clerk signed them in and watched from behind as the short, curly-haired youth and the tall, thin one walked away.

They had driven the Lees' Cadillac to the motel and carried a six-inch-thick stack of papers to their room—the Pyramider papers.

It was by far their biggest night of photography—13 rolls of film, more than 450 exposures. (If either remembered that it was the twenty-fifth anniversary of the Japanese attack on Pearl Harbor, he did not mention it.)

Earlier that day, Chris had stuffed the papers into a satchel and left the plant at four thirty, attempting to lose himself in the throng of homebound employees. Chris spotted a guard looking at him; and when he didn't look away and seemed ready to say something, Chris braced himself to run. But then the guard turned his attention to someone else, and Chris put the satchel in the back of his Volkswagen.

The following day, he went to work earlier than usual and placed the

Pyramider documents back where they had been stored, unlocked, in the vault.

Meanwhile, Daulton had taken the film home and had already begun developing it.

. .

"This is my last trip," he told his brother, who saw him developing the film in the family kitchen. Daulton told Dave that he dreaded another confrontation with the Soviets after his run-in with Boris in November. But he said that Chris had told him the documents he would be delivering this time would be worth at least $75,000 and the Russians would jump at them. Daulton said he planned to parlay the payment into really big money; they could try again to find a legitimate enterprise and Daulton would be able to get out of the drug business for good.

Daulton placed a call to his friend in the Mexican Mafia and suggested they get together; he was about to come into a great deal of money, he said, and wanted to set up the heroin buy for early in January.

. .

Chris felt certain now that the CIA had to be on to him: it was inconceivable, he thought, that it had not discovered Daulton's latest visit to the embassy; and he thought: What about the NSA inspector? He must have noticed the improperly sealed ciphers; he had probably ordered a secret investigation. In November, Chris heard through the office grapevine that one of his supervisors had been called to Washington to discuss "problems in M-4," and wondered what that meant for him. Three weeks before he quit, Chris would insist later, he was drinking with Norman and a friend of his, who told him, "You're going to spend the rest of your life in jail." Another friend from TRW approached him in a bar and said Chris was in trouble: "You're on everybody's list."

I'm really getting paranoid, he told himself.

. .

Chris left the Black Vault for the last time on December 17, 1976. There was a final sign-off to Pilot, followed by a lunch at Putney's, a restaurant in Redondo Beach that was fabricated of old railroad box-

cars and decorated with railroad memorabilia. Gene Norman, Laurie and others from the Project toasted his coming success in college and presented him with a gray sweater. As was the requirement at TRW, his supervisor made a final notation on Chris' personnel folder after he quit:

Reason for termination: Chris has been accepted at Calif. State Riverside, where he will continue his studies toward his degree in History and Political Science.

Overall Evaluation: He has been a dependable, conscientious, capable employee. He has been an asset to this staff. Termination voluntary and he is definitely eligible for re-hire.

Chris's salary when he left TRW was $163.50 per week.

•   •

It was common, if illegal, for California falconers to trap a passage in their own state, where trapping was rigidly controlled, and take the young bird to another state, such as Wyoming or Utah, where the laws were more lax and where more trapping permits were available, and then bring the bird back to California under a permit from the other state.

Chris trapped his last—and best—falcon, the one he was to call Mr. Pips, in the California Coastal Range mountains near Morro Bay. Shortly after he turned in his badge at TRW, he drove the bird to Wyoming to "legitimize" it. As he guided his yellow Volkswagen out of Southern California, across the deserts of California and Nevada, he was happier than he had been in more than a year. The burden was off his back. He returned home from Wyoming in time for Christmas, and he showed off his new bird.

Pips, he bragged, was as tame as a parrot when he was on Chris's gloved wrist. But when he was on the wing, pursuing game, he could dive in a stoop probably—he estimated—at 150 miles an hour.

Despite Chris's happiness over his new bird, his mother knew *something* bothered him. She noticed that he didn't exchange Christmas gifts with Alana and wondered if his moodiness had something to do with a lovers' quarrel. But she suspected it went deeper than that. She asked her son if there was anything wrong, and he said there wasn't. But he said he wanted to talk with Monsignor McCarthy to ask his

advice on how to handle a problem. "Well, call him up," his mother, who recalled how much Chris had always respected the priest, said. But Chris never found the courage to lay out his problem to him.

His only choice was to wait. And from time to time his dark mood began to brighten. He was out of the vault; and most important: *it seemed as if they had gotten away with it*.

• •

In the Lee family, other kinds of questions were being raised. Dr. Lee, the pathologist in whose practice he frequently analyzed the tissue of other physicians' patients to determine if it was cancerous, had been troubled by certain symptoms in himself. He elected, however, not to tell his family about his concern.

• •

Shortly before the Christmas holidays, Aaron Johnson decided to visit his former partner; he knew Daulton was hiding out at his home because of the warrant issued the previous September and didn't leave there often except to go to Mexico. Johnson parked his car in back of the Lees' ranch-style house and went to the back door; he opened it and saw a middle-aged, muscular man talking to Daulton in a hallway. The man was unforgettable. At one time he had been handsome. But there was an ugly scar that swept from his right temple across his cheek in a broken curve all the way to the base of his jaw, and the white-and-pink swath of scar tissue contrasted grotesquely with the golden-bronze color of his natural complexion. He was dressed in a brown leisure suit, white patent leather shoes and a matching white belt that made Johnson think of a Chicago gangster, an impression enhanced by what he thought of as a sinister, thin moustache. When Johnson started moving toward them, Daulton looked up and seemed startled. He waved him back and led the Mexican into the living room.

"Wait in my room," Daulton yelled at Johnson.

The door of the bathroom next to Daulton's room was ajar. Johnson looked in and saw black strips of film hung almost like crepe paper from the towel racks, a mirror and the counter. Curious, he raised one strip of film up to a light and saw diagrams, tables of numbers and typing.

Daulton pushed open the door. Johnson knew Daulton; he knew that if Daulton had pictures hanging in his bathroom, it had something to

222

do with making money. That was the way Daulton was. They were technical drawings, and Johnson recalled the vague boasts that Daulton had made about being a "spy." But when Daulton came into the room, Johnson pretended he hadn't seen what was on the negatives and asked, "What are you doin', makin' porno pictures?"

"I was just messing around with my cameras," he said.

Johnson tried to change the subject: "Who was that guy?"

"He's my uncle," Daulton said with a sly grin, but explaining no further. He did not want to identify the Mexican with whom he was negotiating his biggest drug deal.

• •

A few nights later, Daulton and Chris arrived for a party at the apartment in Redondo Beach that Johnson shared with Beverly Zyser, another refugee from Palos Verdes. One of the guests at the party was Larry Potts, the Palos Verdes sailor whom Daulton regularly tried to pump for information about his ship's activities. Around midnight, he noticed Chris and Daulton huddling in a corner, and he was close enough to hear their conversation.

"It's about time," Chris said.

"For what?"

"Boris."

"John," Daulton corrected, but then agreed: "It's time for Mexico."

The sailor lost the drift of the rest of their conversation, but heard one of the friends mention a word that was unfamiliar to him: Pyramider. He wondered what it meant.

On New Year's Day, Johnson and Beverly Zyser went out for dinner at El Toro's, a Mexican restaurant near the Peninsula, and found Daulton dining with several other youths with long hair whom Johnson recognized from the drug trade. Chris wasn't there, but that was no surprise to Johnson because he knew Chris tended to avoid Daulton's buddies from the drug trade. As usual, Daulton was without wheels. After dinner he headed for a pay telephone to call a taxi; but Johnson offered to give him a ride home.

It was just after midnight when Johnson's car passed into Palos Verdes Estates on the winding drive covered by a canopy of eucalyptus trees that links the Peninsula with the beach communities to the northwest. Suddenly, red lights of a police car flicked on behind him,

and Johnson was pulled over for speeding. The policeman looked at Johnson's passenger and noticed that he seemed nervous; after asking for Daulton's identification, he placed a call on his radio to the Palos Verdes Estates Police Station and asked if there were any arrest warrants for either of the youths. After a minute, the dispatcher informed the patrolman of the warrant in Daulton's name. There weren't any outstanding warrants in Johnson's name, and he got off with a speeding ticket. Daulton was immediately placed under arrest.

. .

As Daulton rode to jail in the back seat of the black-and-white patrol car, he could think of only one thing: he had two appointments waiting for him in Mexico that were the key to his future—first with the Russians for cash, and then with his friends in Culiacán to consummate the deal that would extricate him from all of his troubles. From the police station he called his attorney, Ken Kahn:

"Kenny, can you get me out? It's *really* important."

The following day, Daulton looked up once again at the familiar face of Judge Burch Donahue. And once again, the judge granted Kahn's request for his client's freedom on bail. Daulton was released on January 4, after posting $2,500. The judge ordered him to return to court January 20, when he was to answer all the assorted charges that had piled up against him, including even the revoked probation stemming from his first arrest in 1971; six years later, it was still, amazingly enough, pending against him. When Daulton posted bail, he promised not to leave the Palos Verdes area. But the next day—January 5—he bought a ticket and flew via Mexicana Airlines to Mexico City.

"Now, remember, you get back here, you've got a court date," his mother told him the night before.

"Don't worry," Daulton said. "This is my last trip to Mexico."

35

ABOUT ELEVEN O'CLOCK on the morning of January 6, 1977, Eileen Heaphy, a Foreign Service officer assigned to the United States Embassy in Mexico City, arrived at the Soviet Embassy in the Mexican capital for an appointment with Victor Kroptov. Like numerous members of the staff at the Russian embassy, Kroptov was a member of the KGB, although his official title was "political counselor."

An attractive woman in her twenties, Miss Heaphy had been in Mexico City less than seven months. Before joining the Foreign Service four years earlier, she had been employed by the National Security Agency at Fort Meade, Maryland, the same agency that supervised the cryptographic systems in the Black Vault, as an information analyst and training instructor.

As a Foreign Service officer in Mexico, she was assigned to the Political Section of the U.S. Embassy. Her assignment was to monitor Mexican foreign policy as it related to nations other than the United States and to compile reports evaluating these diplomatic relationships. The main source of her information, besides official pronouncements and the newspapers, was personal contacts with diplomats from the other embassies in Mexico City. There were about sixty in the city, and Miss Heaphy, in the few months she'd been there, had become acquainted with someone at most of them, including Kroptov. Periodically she exchanged lunches with her counterparts at the other embassies, swapped gossip and otherwise kept in touch.

These were important times in Mexico. In December, the country had inaugurated a new president, José López Portillo, and the professional Mexico-watchers in the diplomatic community were still trying to get a fix on what his policies would be. To the United States, Mexico, a poor friend that had always been more or less taken for granted, was taking on a new, if still undefined, importance. Almost daily there were new reports of oil riches in Mexico, and it was becoming clear

that Mexico might someday become a major alternative source of petroleum to the Organization of Petroleum Exporting Countries cartel. American diplomats were being forced to have some second thoughts about Mexico. The United States had neglected its southern neighbor for many years despite its proximity; moreover, American diplomats knew that Mexico, despite some gains in the development of a middle class, had a huge population of extremely poor people who might be easy prey for Communist agitators who might, someday, remove the oil from the reach of the United States.

Beginning in the fall of 1976, there had been several published reports of new agreements between the Soviet Union and Mexico, principally involving trade. Several days earlier, Miss Heaphy had called Kroptov and said she wanted to pay a call and discuss these agreements and Mexican–Soviet relations in general as part of her assignment to monitor third-country relations with Mexico. Kroptov had invited her to meet with him at 11 A.M. The meeting went as planned, and about eleven forty-five, she passed through the gate of the Soviet Embassy and began searching for her car and driver.

As she did, she spotted a short man surrounded by a group of Mexican policemen in front of the embassy, who was gesturing animatedly with his arms; his face was flushed and he was shaking his head, apparently trying to deny whatever it was the policemen were saying to him. He looked like an American, and she walked over to the group to overhear what was going on.

"Do you speak English?" Daulton immediately asked her, and she said she spoke English and Spanish and was from the U.S. Embassy. "Can I help you?"

"I was just walking by and stuck my head in the gate of this building to see what it was. Then I threw down an empty pack of cigarettes and a piece of paper—it was just a book jacket from an old dictionary!—and these guys came running after me and said I was under arrest."

Daulton was heartened by the sight of the American woman who had come to his rescue and began to relax. As persuasively as he could, he dismissed the encounter as a silly mistake. He said he was an American tourist who had been visiting his former fiancée, who was now married to a Mexican who taught at the University of Mexico. His old girlfriend and her husband, he said, had been walking with him, but somehow they had become separated and he had gotten lost.

Miss Heaphy asked one of the policemen, a corporal who seemed to

be in charge, what had happened, and he confirmed the chronology of events. But the corporal said he'd seen a Soviet guard pick up one of the items thrown by the American, and when he was asked for it the Soviet guard refused.

Miss Heaphy identified herself as an official of the U.S. Embassy and asked why it was considered so serious to throw a piece of paper on the ground. The policeman explained that his unit had been assigned to keep the embassy under surveillance because they had been alerted for visits by representatives of Mexican terrorist groups. Only recently, he said, a member of the Twenty-third of September Communist League—a violent Mexican antigovernment terrorist organization —had passed a message to a foreign embassy by throwing it through a gate.

For this reason, Daulton had to be detained for questioning, the corporal explained.

Overhearing their conversation, Daulton protested heatedly, saying again that he was merely an American tourist. Convinced that he was getting nowhere, Daulton, with a motion of his head, summoned the corporal to his side and said in the best Spanish he could muster, "I have five hundred dollars; if you forget this, you can have it."

There was no response from the policeman, which surprised Daulton because he had long known the power of *mordida* in Mexico.

Two police cars arrived in front of the Embassy.

Miss Heaphy reentered the building and asked to speak to the Soviet chief of security. The Russian who greeted her said that while the American might have been rude in throwing trash on the grounds, he saw no need to press charges.

Using the radiotelephone in her car, Miss Heaphy called her embassy to report that an American citizen had been arrested at the Soviet Embassy and he needed assistance from an officer in the embassy's consular division who specialized in helping arrested Americans. A police sergeant was now on the scene, and he said he was willing to wait for the arrival of an American consular official. Miss Heaphy, deciding that he looked even more nervous now than he'd been before, then returned to Daulton, who was surrounded by policemen. He said he was outraged; here he was, an American tourist being manhandled by Mexican police. Then he whispered to her that he was afraid of being sent to a Mexican prison, where prisoners were tortured and starved. As they waited on the sidewalk, Daulton turned his back

on the woman; he was trying to hide something in his jacket or pants, she suspected. But a few moments later she discovered what he had been doing.

One of the policemen had motioned Daulton toward a police car. When Daulton moved, the policeman spotted a half-smoked marijuana joint near one of his feet. He shouted to his associates that he had found contraband carried by the young man.

Until the reefer was discovered, Miss Heaphy thought some of the Mexican policemen had seemed to be wavering between taking this litterbug to headquarters and letting him go. But the discovery of the joint prompted the sergeant to order Daulton into the back seat of a patrol car.

They would wait, he said, for the *comandante* of police.

Within minutes, other cars drove up, some of them containing plain-clothesmen from the Mexican secret police, the Federal Bureau of Security.

Miss Heaphy went to the Soviet Embassy guardhouse and asked a guard to let her see the chief of security again. She said she wanted to use a telephone to try her embassy once more. The security man, another KGB agent whom Daulton had met, reappeared and was nasty. He accused her of trying to "penetrate" the Russian complex with a ruse. He did, however, consent to let her use the phone; but before the call went through, two Americans arrived from the U.S. Embassy: Thomas Ferguson, a vice consul whose assignment was to help Americans in trouble with the Mexican law, and Benito Iarocci, an agent of the Central Intelligence Agency who was attached to the U.S. Embassy.

Ferguson noticed that Daulton's fingers were shaking badly when they shook hands.

Daulton explained to Ferguson that he was an American, employed by a California advertising agency, on vacation in Mexico, and once again he protested the treatment he was getting. A Mexican policeman came up and showed Ferguson the joint; Iarocci, meanwhile, had gone to see the Soviet security chief inside the embassy. When he returned, he reiterated to the Mexican police *comandante* that the Russians didn't want to press charges against the young man.

The Mexican *comandante* then made a decision: they would *all* go to Metropolitan Police Headquarters, where they could iron out every-thing. Miss Heaphy returned to her embassy, and Ferguson said he'd

follow the police car to Police Headquarters in the center of Mexico City.

• •

Daulton was ordered by Inspector Reynaldo López Malváez to empty his pockets in a second-floor office in the huge, noisy complex, whose halls were jammed with uniformed policemen, citizens in trouble with the law and people filing complaints about other people's transgressions. He was a dark-haired, middle-aged man with smoked glasses, a thickening waist and dark bags under his eyes that suggested he worked long hours. Ferguson watched curiously as the nervous American complied with the order to put all his belongings on a desk.

Daulton laid out his passport, his wallet containing $340 in American currency and more than 1,000 Mexican pesos, a paperback book, a picture postcard and a business-size envelope sealed with plastic tape.

At first the only thing that seemed to catch the inspector's eye was the postcard. He stared at it for a long moment, then asked Daulton in Spanish what his occupation was. Ferguson translated the question.

"I'm a photographer," Daulton replied in English. He explained that he worked for an advertising agency and had been vacationing in Mexico when, for no reason at all, he had been arrested by Mexico City policemen. Ferguson translated Daulton's reply into Spanish.

Without reacting to Daulton's protest, the inspector turned his attention to his other possessions on the desk. He picked up the envelope that was sealed with plastic tape, removed the tape and opened it. Inside he saw there was a stack of black filmstrips. He picked one at random and held it up to the light that was radiating from a ceiling fixture in the sparsely furnished room. Taking his time, the inspector tried to make out the images on the strip of celluloid. For a long time, López Malváez didn't say anything. Then he lowered the negative strip, looked at Ferguson and said:

"*Documentos.*"

"These are negatives for a commercial we're making," Daulton shot back. His employer, the advertising agency he worked for, he explained hurriedly, was making a documentary film for the General Electric Company about communication satellites because G.E. was "trying to sell worldwide satellite-relay franchises." Daulton tried to sound like a tourist who had just happened, almost accidentally, to have brought some of his work from home along with him.

López Malváez asked an assistant to find a magnifying glass. After one was located in an adjoining office, the inspector scrutinized the film again under the soft light in the small room. He was silent as he went from frame to frame on the thin black ribbon. Then he offered one of the shiny black strips to Ferguson along with the magnifying glass.

Squinting, Ferguson could make out two words printed on each of the frames: TOP SECRET

Ignoring Daulton, the two men looked at each other without smiling. Then López Malváez said he would send the negatives to a police laboratory where they could be blown up into prints. It would take an hour or two. He suggested that Ferguson come back to Police Headquarters in a couple of hours, and the American left.

Then the inspector turned his attention to the picture postcard that Daulton had been carrying when he was arrested, and he began speaking rapidly in Spanish. Daulton appealed to him to speak English so that he could understand. But Daulton *did* hear one word that he recognized—"*asesinato*"—and it stunned him. It was the Spanish word for murder.

López Malváez told Daulton he was being held for murder.

36 DAULTON HAD LANDED at Benito Juárez International Airport at four o'clock the preceding afternoon, the first Wednesday in January. He was a day later than he had originally planned because of the arrest in Palos Verdes. But he had thought he could make up for the lost time and decided to expedite matters. In almost two years of commerce with the Soviet Union, this decision was his most foolish.

The schedule previously set for January called for a meeting either on the first Wednesday or, alternatively, on the first Saturday of the month at the Viva Pizza café at Coyoacán and Matías Romero avenues.

230

Normally, to summon the Russians for a meeting on Wednesday, Daulton placed his X marks on one of the currently designated rows of lampposts on the day before, the first Tuesday of the month. The Russians would drive by the designated intersections (the location was changed periodically) on Wednesday to learn if Daulton was in town.

Arriving so late on Wednesday afternoon meant Daulton had little time to place the marks, and even less for the KGB agents to see them. But Daulton had been in a hurry and had been anxious to arrange a meeting that night even though he had made a late arrival. He didn't want to wait until Saturday: he needed the money, now.

Daulton had taken a taxi from the airport to the intersection of Patriotismo and San Antonio streets, at the end of the Miguel Alemán Highway. It was a busy intersection about fifteen minutes' drive from Reforma. He had affixed the tape marks and, promptly at eight o'clock that evening, had been waiting at the Viva Pizza, thinking with amusement about the incongruity of meeting Soviet agents in an Italian pizza parlor in Mexico City. Boris hadn't shown up, so after fifteen minutes Daulton had left. An hour later, he had come back, eaten a pizza and drunk two beers. But again, no one was there to meet him. He had tried a third time at ten the next morning, but no one had appeared. Thinking that Boris might be at the Bali Restaurant instead, he had taken a cab there, but no one from the embassy was at the Bali either. He snorted a pinch of coke and wondered what to do next.

Friends were waiting for him in Culiacán the next day to sew up the heroin buy, and he desperately wanted the money from the Russians. So he had decided to go after it. He had hailed a cab near the Holiday Inn and directed the driver to a side street near Chapultepec Park, gotten out and walked three blocks to the embassy, planning to wait nearby until he spotted someone he knew. Daulton stood near the gate in front of a plaque with a hammer and sickle and the identity of the building printed in Spanish on it. There was a similar plaque with the building's identity printed in Russian as well.

A curtain at one window moved and he thought he saw a face at the window, but it vanished. Then he saw an embassy car approaching, and he shaded his eyes with one hand and tried to identify who was inside. It was Boris.

Daulton began walking faster, and was almost jogging as he tried to intercept the car. It slowed and Daulton looked squarely at Boris, but Boris kept his head fixed straight ahead. The car went into the embassy

compound and the gate was closed quickly, leaving Daulton outside the gate, alone. He was furious. Maybe Boris hadn't seen him, he thought.

Still hopeful of drawing someone's attention, he had marked "K.G.B." on the cover of the Spanish-English dictionary he carried and thrown it defiantly inside the iron bars. Then he had walked on.

About thirty yards away a Mexican policeman—one of three or four visible in the immediate vicinity of the embassy—had been watching the short man curiously, wondering why he was lingering so long outside the building. Then he saw him toss *something* through the bars. (Afterward, he said he hadn't been sure whether it was a big wad of paper, an envelope or a small incendiary bomb.) The policeman sprang into action and ran after Daulton—and at that moment Daulton's long, quixotic business relationship with the Soviet Union came to an end.

Whether any Russians *were* looking out at the awkward American while he loitered so conspicuously in front of their embassy is still not known. But if they were, they made no response. After all, a member of the U.S. Embassy staff was in the building at the time.

• •

"You murdered a policeman," Inspector López Malváez said angrily in English (not much better than Daulton's Spanish) after Ferguson had left and the microfilm had been sent out for processing.

Startled, Daulton denied killing *anyone*.

"*Turista,*" he said.

The inspector was unmoved. On December 28, 1976, just a week or so before, he said, a uniformed Mexico City police officer had been murdered. The assassination, he continued, had occurred at the intersection of Patriotismo and San Antonio streets, the very same intersection pictured on the simulated postcard that Daulton carried. There was a knock on the door and the interrogation was interrupted by the return of Vice Consul Ferguson. López Malváez left Daulton, and in another office he handed Ferguson a stack of 8-by-10 glossy photographs.

On each was a reproduction of a page of typewritten information, graphs, tables and the words TOP SECRET and PYRAMIDER.

Daulton was brought into the office by two armed policemen. When he was shown the glossies, he repeated his claim that they were unimportant, just films for use in an advertisement.

232

"This material is classified; it could never be used in advertisements," Ferguson said, ridiculing Daulton's defense.

Daulton then lowered his voice and gave a look to Ferguson which meant that what he was about to say was intended only for the two of them.

"There's more here than meets the eye," he whispered. "A lot is riding on this. Here we are trying to do a service for the free world and now we get in trouble."

Ferguson couldn't fathom what Daulton was trying to tell him, but it was clear that something serious involving U.S. national security had occurred. López Malváez dismissed Ferguson, saying he would investigate the matter further, and Ferguson returned to his embassy and told Benito Iarocci about the photographs he had just seen.

After Ferguson left, López Malváez renewed his charge of murder and outlined what he claimed had happened: Daulton was a Soviet agent who was funding operations of the Twenty-third of September Communist League and had killed a policeman who had found him out.

"I wasn't even in Mexico City on December 28," Daulton tried to explain in Spanish. The inspector ignored him and repeated the charge.

Daulton didn't like the shape of what was coming down. The charge was stupid, but the policeman wouldn't *listen* to his story. So, as effectively as he could in a flawed hybrid of Spanish and English, Daulton then told the story he had prepared for such an occasion: he said he was an American agent who was part of an operation to spread false and misleading information—"disinformation"—to the U.S.S.R. He was on assignment, he repeated, for the United States Government, participating in a scheme to deceive the very country that he was now accused of helping. He tried to make López Malváez laugh at the irony. The postcard, he said, had no connection whatsoever with the dead policeman. It had been given to him by the Russians—it was the method they used to advise him where to make markings with adhesive tape and let them know he was in the city and ready for a meeting. López Malváez, upon hearing more about the Russians, listened on.

That very night, Daulton lied, he was scheduled to meet them, and he would be able to prove the postcard had nothing to do with the policeman's murder. Daulton pleaded with the inspector to go with him to the Viva Pizza Restaurant so that he could show him—he'd also

233

prove what he had said about the X marks he'd placed on the lamp-posts. López Malváez quickly agreed to his request, and they went in a police car to the intersection of Patriotismo and San Antonio streets, where López Malváez saw for himself Daulton's signal to the Russians.

At eight o'clock that evening, Daulton was waiting outside the Viva Pizza. He seemed to be a lone American patiently awaiting an appointment with a friend for dinner, but Mexican plainclothesmen were staked out inconspicuously all around him.

The small figure of Andrew Daulton Lee fidgeted nervously under the glow of neon lights for almost half an hour that night. No one approached him. Then López Malváez called the endeavor off. Daulton was returned to Headquarters for more questioning about the murder, and at midnight he was still denying that he was involved. The following morning, he begged López Malváez to let him try just once more. At ten o'clock they went to the Bali Restaurant and Daulton stood near a bus stop, hoping in vain to see one of the familiar embassy cars while Mexican detectives watched. Again, no Russians.

After twenty minutes, they returned him to the police station, and López Malváez said he was now certain that Daulton had killed the policeman and was a member of the Twenty-third of September Communist League.

Daulton struggled with his poor Spanish to answer the charges.

"*Bueno, es precisamente en ese lugar,*" the inspector said. The scene of the murder was the exact spot shown on the postcard.

"*Sí, entiendo, es muy, muy, muy,* ah . . . ah," Daulton replied; he understood the inspector's concern, but he had nothing to do with the murder.

"*Unas personas,* ah—two people—*iguales a tí mataron a un agente de la policía.*" Two people just like you killed a police officer, the inspector insisted.

"*Pero, pero yo no tengo* pistol," Daulton lied, trying to explain he owned no guns.

"*Todo misión aquí es vender la información a los rusquis,*" Daulton continued, saying his whole mission in Mexico was to sell information to the Russians. "*No tengo tiempo para más problemas; es necesario para mí todo tiempo con los rusquis y los Estados Unidos.*" Daulton said he didn't have any time for more problems; he was too busy working with the Russians part of the time and pursuing his duties in the United States at other times.

The interrogation continued through a second day, with the police inspector going over the same ground again and again. On the third day, Daulton was turned over to the Federal Bureau of Security—the Mexican secret police—and its interrogators proved to be pointedly less tolerant of Daulton's heated denials.

During the preceding six years, Daulton had been arrested seven times in the United States and had served less than seven months in jail. He had become a master at avoiding jail by exploiting constitutional safeguards of civil liberties, the mistakes of arresting officers and a sympathetic court.

He found Mexican justice different.

•   •

Daulton was led out of Metropolitan Police Headquarters with his jacket pulled over his head so that he could not see where he was going. Before he left, he had signed a statement that condensed his denial of the murder. A police official had said he would be released soon. Daulton had felt good, relaxed, thinking his detention was over. But without warning his jacket was yanked roughly over his head and he was bundled into a car and driven somewhere in Mexico City. He could hear traffic and the sounds of the city, but he didn't know where he was headed. The car stopped and he was walked into a building where the jacket was replaced by a blindfold. His escorts during the trip had said only a few words in Spanish. Daulton as yet had no inkling that he was being turned over to the secret police.

The blindfolded murder suspect was led into an elevator, and soon Daulton knew that it *wasn't* over. The elevator rose for a few moments, Daulton was escorted into an office and the blindfold was removed. He looked around and saw a desk with several phones, each a different color. Around the desk sat several Mexican men in civilian clothes. Others, grim-faced, stood behind it.

The new interrogators were disarmingly friendly at first, saying that they intended to let him go soon, but first wanted to ask him a few questions.

He repeated the story he had told López Malváez—he was an American disseminating worthless information to the Soviet Government in a scheme sanctioned by the United States. He told his story at length in his fractured Spanish. At 1 A.M. they let him go to sleep.

Four hours later, he was awakened and led back to the same office; this time there were more questioners and they were not as friendly.

A middle-aged Mexican who seemed to be in charge of the investigation said in Spanish that they had been soft with him the night before, but they had known all the time that he was lying about the murder.

"This is not the United States," a man next to him said in Spanish. "This is Pancho Villa land."

Angrily, standing around him in a circle, a half-dozen interrogators ordered Daulton to confess that he was a Communist agent working with subversive terrorist groups to overthrow the Mexican Government. He was a Russian agent, they said, an enemy of the Mexican people. One questioner, in fact, noting that his name was Lee, wanted to know if he was Chinese.

They showed Daulton photographs of Russians assigned to the Mexico City embassy, and he identified Boris Grishin as "John"—the man, he said, who had failed to meet him as planned and abandoned him outside the embassy.

Tightening their vise, the secret police officers began flinging questions at Daulton one after another in such rapid Spanish that he became hopelessly confused. But when he said he didn't understand the questions, it only made his interrogators angrier. They shouted in Spanish that he was lying, that he did understand them. "We're not stupid Mexicans," one said. Amid the machine-gun fire of questions, Daulton felt like a man descending deeper and deeper into water in which he was unable to swim. After a while when he asked them to repeat a question, someone behind him began to bang him on both ears at once.

Slowly, a story emerged from the stormy interrogation: Daulton said that his mission in Mexico had begun in 1975 when a childhood friend, Christopher Boyce, had asked him to collaborate on a plan to sell secret information from his place of employment to the Chinese Government through its diplomatic missions in Africa. The information, he said, was to be deceptively changed to get the Chinese "to go around in circles on absurd projects." After he rejected this proposal, Daulton said, his friend had persuaded him to sell "false information" to the Soviet Embassy in Mexico City. And indeed, he had begun doing so, and the process had gone on for almost two years until his arrest.

The answers were ridiculed by the Mexicans. They laughed and said he was lying, and the banging continued on his ears by someone he couldn't see. His head was throbbing with pain, and the ringing in his ears was like a duet of sirens.

"Whom do you work for?" a Mexican asked in Spanish.

"The United States."

"Doing what?"

"Disseminating erroneous information."

"Who hired you?"

"The CIA through Christopher Boyce."

"Where's Boyce?"

"I don't know."

Daulton received another slap on his ears.

"Quit lying! Tell us why you murdered the policeman."

"I didn't."

"Yes, you did. We have a witness who saw you."

"No, I didn't do it," Daulton pleaded. "No, it's not true."

The questioning went on for three hours; then Daulton was blind-folded again, handcuffed and left lying on the floor of a storeroom. Three hours later, the questioning resumed:

"Why did you kill the policeman?" It began all over.

One of his interrogators said to another that the murdered policeman might have had a chance to fire a shot at his killer before dying.

"Take off your clothes."

Daulton stripped naked and the men gathered around him, scanning every inch of his body. Aside from red and purple blotches of acne on his back, the Mexicans couldn't find any wounds: there was no evidence of gunshot injuries, they agreed.

When Daulton started to put on his clothes, one of the Mexicans ordered him to stop. He went to a wall and removed a mounted sword, and with a flourish and a perverse giggle, he held the broad-bladed weapon three inches from Daulton's genitals and said:

"Why did you kill our policeman?"

"I didn't." Daulton trembled.

Theatrically, the officer made a broad sweep with the sword, feigning a swipe at his penis, and shouted in Spanish that unless he talked and stopped lying they were going to "hang your testicles from a flagpole."

At noon there was another respite from the questioning, but it resumed at 4 P.M. and lasted until after midnight.

His interrogators covered the same ground, and Daulton continued to say that he couldn't understand some of their questions. This time, when he professed not to hear the question, someone behind him slammed him in the kidneys at each missed answer. And as the after-

noon became evening, this person didn't even wait until he missed an answer.

With Daulton continuing to deny any involvement in terrorism, the interrogators again left him alone, blindfolded, in the room. But after a short while, the guards came for him, and the questioning began all over again. When he repeated the same story, two of the secret police-men each grabbed him by a leg and carried him across the office upside down to an adjoining bathroom, and held him over the toilet with his head dangling a few inches above the foul-smelling white bowl.

"Tell the truth," one of the agents demanded.

"I am, I am!" he shouted. "I *am* telling the truth! I didn't kill anybody!"

The two men who gripped Daulton by his ankles let his head descend slowly into the stinking water in the toilet bowl, and the last thing he heard before his head was submerged was their derisive, taunting laughter. He screamed as his head went under.

"This will clean out your ears," a voice shouted in broken English when he was lifted up a moment later. They lowered him into the toilet again. "This will help you understand the questions," a second voice said. Then they did it a third time.

. .

The questioning, with occasional intermissions, continued for four days. Whether representatives of the FBI or the CIA were invited to audit the interrogation is not known. Most of the questioning was done under the glare of bright lights, and Daulton couldn't see everyone in the room.

Between the periods of questioning, Daulton was handcuffed, blind-folded and left alone on the floor of a closet. As he lay helpless in this black prison, he managed to find a little humor in his predicament: it occurred to him that he was manacled like a human pretzel—his right foot handcuffed to his left hand and his left foot handcuffed to his right hand.

Thirst was his biggest problem now, along with turbulent stomach pains. When his complaints of thirst were finally listened to, a guard brought him a glass of water. But Daulton refused it; he said he would get sick if he drank it. Despite all of his traveling in Mexico, Daulton still couldn't consume untreated Mexican water without coming down with diarrhea; he always used bottled, purified water. The guard laughed at his appeal for bottled water, as if to say it was tap water or

none at all. Daulton gulped down the glass of water to suppress the thirst that gnawed at him, and before long, as he had known he would, he had a severe case of diarrhea. And he stank from his own feces. Eventually, however, he persuaded a guard to escort him to the toilet when he asked to go. Not all the guards were so accommodating: one in particular enjoyed waking Daulton by sticking his pistol against his head as he lay blindfolded and clicking the hammer, and another came into his cell and kicked him at random.

After four days, Daulton sensed that the senior secret police officials were beginning to lose interest in him, and he guessed that they had given up on him as a suspect in terrorism and murder activities. Again and again, they threatened to bring a witness who would identify him as the murderer, but the witness never materialized.

On the sixth day, a doctor came to see him and gave him medicine to curb the bowel trouble and lessen the stomach pain. On the evening of January 14, Daulton, unshaved and sticky from not having showered since his arrest eight days earlier, was ushered into an office and introduced by a senior secret police official to two agents of the FBI who were legal attachés at the U.S. Embassy.

"Do you want to talk?" one inquired.

"*Please* get me out of here," Daulton said.

The FBI agents said they thought they could help Daulton. But first, they said, they wanted to ask him some questions.

Daulton was not unsophisticated when it came to understanding the workings of American law. He could have recited by heart the text of the "*Miranda* Warning" carried by policemen, who, according to a mandate by the U.S. Supreme Court, must advise suspects after their arrest of their rights to remain silent and to consult a lawyer. Exhausted, ill and desperate to leave the Mexican interrogators, Daulton agreed to sign a waiver of his *Miranda* rights, and at 7:09 on the evening of January 14, 1977, he began to tell his story.

"My only desire is to get this straightened out," he said. "I got in this to screw the Russians. . . ."

• •

When the interview was over, one of the agents, Robert B. Lyons, closed his briefcase and said with a smile to Daulton, "We'll see you in a couple of days." He was sure, he added, that they would be able to get him out of Mexico.

Early the next morning, a coded teletype message was sent from the

U.S. Embassy in Mexico City to the Director of the Federal Bureau of Investigation, Clarence M. Kelley:

SUBJECT LEE INTERVIEWED BETWEEN 7:09 P.M.–9:39 P.M., JANUARY 14, 1977, AT MEXICO CITY HEADQUARTERS, MEXICAN FEDERAL SECURITY SERVICE (DFS) BY ASSISTANT LEGAL ATTACHES ROBERT B. LYONS AND WILLIAM J. HOY. LEE EXECUTED WAIVER OF RIGHTS FORM AND EXPRESSED DESIRE TO COOPERATE FULLY AND WILLINGNESS TO TESTIFY IN A U.S. COURT. DESPITE THIS, HIS ANSWERS SEEMED VAGUE OR EVASIVE REGARDING SOME FACTS AND MANY DATES. THEY DID NOT INSPIRE CONFIDENCE AS TO HIS COMPLETE TRUTHFULNESS.

IN THE COURSE OF THE INTERVIEW, LEE MADE THE FOLLOWING ADMISSIONS:

(A) HAS KNOWN SUBJECT CHRISTOPHER JOHN BOYCE FOR ABOUT TEN YEARS SINCE THEY ATTENDED HIGH SCHOOL TOGETHER IN PALOS VERDES, CALIFORNIA. THEIR ACTIVITIES REGARDING SOVIETS BEGAN IN SUMMER, 1975. DESCRIBED BOYCE AS A "COURIER" AT THAT TIME BETWEEN TRW AND CIA.

(B) SIX CONTACTS WITH SOVIETS BETWEEN MID-1975 AND NOVEMBER, 1976. FIVE IN MEXICO CITY AND ONE IN VIENNA, AUSTRIA. BOYCE ACCOMPANIED LEE TO MEXICO CITY DURING ONE OF THESE, IN AUGUST, 1976.

(C) RECEIPT OF OVER THIRTEEN THOUSAND SEVEN HUNDRED DOLLARS FROM SOVIETS AND DIRECT PAYMENT BY SOVIETS TO BOYCE OF AMOUNT DESCRIBED AS A "COUPLE OF THOUSAND."

(D) DELIVERY TO SOVIETS OF VARIOUS DOCUMENTS AND MATERIALS, INCLUDING A PERFORATED COMPUTER CARD, A FIVE OR SIX INCH SEGMENT OF "TICKER TAPE" MARKED "TOP SECRET"; TEN "KW-7" CRYPTO PUNCH CARDS MARKED "TOP SECRET"; FIVE TO TEN TYPED PAGES OF MATERIAL DEALING WITH COMMUNICATION SATELLITE; SHEET OF PAPER APPROXIMATELY FOUR BY SIX INCHES CONTAINING EIGHT TO TEN LINES OF NUMBERS WHICH HAD BEEN DESCRIBED BY BOYCE AS A CODE WHICH WOULD BE RECOGNIZABLE TO THE RUSSIANS; MICROFILM OF "KW-7" CRYPTO CARDS; PICTURES OF BOYCE'S OFFICE; A QUANTITY OF MICROFILM DELIVERED BY BOYCE DURING AUGUST, 1976, MEXICO CITY VISIT.

(E) TRAINING IN VIENNA BY A SOVIET IN THE USE OF THE MINOX CAMERA AND, ESPECIALLY, DOCUMENT PHOTOGRAPHY.

(F) ON AT LEAST ONE OCCASION, MET BOYCE IN A LOS ANGELES AREA MOTEL WHERE DOCUMENTS IN POSSESSION OF LATTER WERE PHOTOGRAPHED BY BOTH. LEE LATER DEVELOPED THIS FILM IN HIS OWN HOME.

CORROBORATION:

LEE DENIED HAVING SIGNIFICANT SOCIAL CONTACT WITH BOYCE WHICH MIGHT BE SUBJECT TO CONFIRMATION BY THIRD PARTIES.

HE STATES HE HAS AT TIMES DISCUSSED HIS CONTACTS WITH THE SOVIETS WITH HIS BROTHER, DAVID, BUT THAT DAVID WAS IN NO WAY INVOLVED. DAVID LEE, AGE 21, RESIDES WITH SUBJECT LEE'S FATHER AND MOTHER, PALOS VERDES ESTATES, CALIFORNIA.

LEE STATES HIS FATHER IS DR. DAULTON B. LEE WHO IS AFFILIATED WITH SOUTH BAY HOSPITAL IN THAT AREA. IN DECEMBER, 1975, LEE MENTIONED TO HIS FATHER THE FACT THAT HE WAS INVOLVED IN DISSEMINATING "FALSE INFORMATION" TO SOVIETS. FOLLOWING LEE'S RETURN FROM VIENNA, BOYCE AND LEE TOGETHER PURCHASED A MINOX CAMERA AT A SMALL CAMERA SHOP LOCATED ON HAW-THORNE BOULEVARD ADJACENT TO THE SAN DIEGO FREEWAY.

TWO PRINTS FROM MICROFILM DELIVERED BY BOYCE AND LEE TO SOVIETS IN MEXICO CITY IN AUGUST, 1976, WERE TAKEN BY LEE SUR-REPTITIOUSLY BACK TO UNITED STATES AND NOW LOCATED IN BLACK CAMERA CASE IN THE CLOSET OF HIS BEDROOM AT HIS PARENTS' HOME.

OTHER BACKGROUND:

LEE'S MOTHER, ANNE CLARK LEE, ALSO LIVES AT THE SAME AD-DRESS. LEE STATES HE HAS BEEN SELF-EMPLOYED FOR TWO YEARS AS A CUSTOM CABINET MAKER, AND PREVIOUSLY, WORKED PART-TIME REPAIRING BOARDS FOR THE SCUBA-DUBA COMPANY, NEWPORT AND LONG BEACH, CALIFORNIA.

LEE STATES HE IS SCHEDULED FOR A COURT HEARING AT TORRANCE, CALIFORNIA (SOUTH BAY COURT) ON JANUARY 20, 1977. HIS ONLY SPECIFIC REQUEST WAS THAT HIS ATTORNEY BE NOTIFIED THAT HE MIGHT NOT BE ABLE TO APPEAR. THE ATTORNEY IS KENNETH KAHN, 1003 MANHATTAN BEACH BOULEVARD, MANHATTAN BEACH, CALI-FORNIA.

ADDITIONAL DATA:

THROUGHOUT THE INTERVIEW, LEE MAINTAINED THAT HE HAD DONE NOTHING WRONG DURING ANY OF HIS DEALINGS WITH THE SOVIETS BECAUSE HE UNDERSTOOD THROUGH DISCUSSIONS WITH BOYCE THAT HE WAS PERFORMING A SERVICE "AS A SUB-CONTRAC-TOR" FOR THE CIA IN DISSEMINATING FALSE AND MISLEADING INFOR-MATION TO THE SOVIETS. HE SAID HE HAD CONSIDERABLE CONFI-DENCE IN BOYCE AND THAT DURING LATE 1976, BOYCE INFORMED HIM THAT HE, BOYCE, HAD BEEN ACCEPTED FOR EMPLOYMENT WITH THE FBI.

LEE LAST SAW BOYCE IN EARLY DECEMBER, 1976. BUT THEY SPOKE BY TELEPHONE IN LATE DECEMBER. IN THIS LATTER CONVERSATION,

BOYCE TOLD LEE HE HAD "SOME MORE THINGS" AND NEEDED TO SEE HIM BEFORE LEE LEFT FOR MEXICO. THIS MEETING DID NOT TAKE PLACE AND LEE, THEREFORE, BELIEVES BOYCE HAS SENSITIVE OR CLAS-SIFIED ITEMS IN HIS POSSESSION AT THIS TIME.

LEE SAID HE WOULD BE WILLING TO FURNISH A SIGNED STATEMENT CONCERNING THE ABOVE.

DUE TO PRIOR FIRM WEEKEND COMMITMENTS, DFS SUB-DIRECTOR MIGUEL NAZAR HARO STATED THAT HE WOULD BE OUT OF THE CITY AND THAT LEE CAN BE MADE AVAILABLE FOR FURTHER INTERVIEW ON MONDAY, JANUARY 17, 1977.

Not all of the details in the report were accurate, and many were missing. But the official unraveling had begun of one of the most damaging espionage conspiracies against the United States in the postwar era—one perpetrated by two young men who had begun life with what seemed to be the best that America could bestow on its children.

Over the next few days a torrent of messages flowed between the FBI, the CIA, the embassy in Mexico City, the Pentagon and the White House as the magnitude of the loss became apparent. Among those who would be eventually apprised of the damage was the new American President Jimmy Carter, who would later play his own role in the drama.

· ·

For Daulton, conditions at the secret police headquarters improved miraculously after the visit of the two FBI representatives. The doctor came more often, the meals were better and Daulton's handcuffs were removed.

Two days after the visit, Daulton was summoned back to the office of the official who had led the marathon interrogation. He announced that Daulton was being deported from Mexico, and he asked whether he wanted to be deported to the Soviet Union or the United States.

"*Los Estados Unidos,*" Daulton answered.

FBI Agent Lyons came into the office and said he had arranged to get Daulton back to the United States. He shook Daulton's hand and said they'd be seeing each other in a few hours. "He smiled like he was pulling me out of the fire and into the furnace," Daulton later would ruefully recall of this meeting.

That evening he left for the United States.

· ·

242

Sandwiched in the back seat of a car between two policemen substantially larger than himself, and drowsy from codeine he'd been given to ease his stomach pain, Daulton tried to sleep. From time to time he regained consciousness in the dark automobile, and his mind drifted, accompanied by the rumble of the car's engine and the babble of the policemen gossiping in Spanish about girlfriends and bosses.

He wondered if Chris had been caught, and then he thought of his parents and wondered if they knew about his arrest. He had always phoned home at least once a week, and Mom and Pops would probably be worrying by now. And he wondered what his associates had thought when he missed the meeting in Culiacán. But, he reassured himself, that deal might not be lost forever; he had survived crises before.

More than anything else, Daulton thought about *survival*. He puzzled over how he could get out of the mess—and about how he had gotten into it in the first place. For God's sake, it had begun with a *littering* charge! He thought about Chris's strange, unpredictable behavior—first insisting that he sell the stuff to the Russians, then holding back on him; giving the Russians some of the stuff they wanted, then telling 'em to "Go fuck themselves."

What was going down? Daulton asked himself. He thought again of Chris's strange behavior. Maybe, he mused dreamily, Chris *was* working for the CIA all this time.

After the guards on either side of him fell asleep, he retrieved six grams of hash that were hidden in his bag which had been saved for him at the Holiday Inn after his arrest. He swallowed the hash and let his thoughts wander some more before he drifted back to sleep.

37

A FEW MINUTES AFTER 7 A.M. on January 17, 1977, the car reached the southern side of the international bridge that spans the Rio Grande River between Nuevo Laredo, Mexico, and Laredo, Texas. On their respective sides of the border the flags of Mexico and the United States were flattened against the wind by a strong breeze.

One of the four Mexican secret police agents who had accompanied Daulton on the fourteen-hour drive from Mexico City shook his shoulders to wake him. As they let him out of the car, each said "*Adiós*" to their passenger.

Carrying the small suitcase he had so often used on his trips back and forth over the border, Daulton walked alone across the bridge. He was a lonely figure. His mouth tasted like sour milk, he had a two-week growth of beard and he felt weary and haggard.

Waiting for him with smiles and outstretched hands were FBI Agents Robert B. Lyons, Frederick A. Slight and John W. Smith. They shook his hand and said they hoped he had had a good trip.

A few minutes later, the agents presented him with a typed statement recounting his interview of two nights earlier in Mexico City. Daulton signed the statement, and it was immediately stamped TOP SECRET. Then Daulton was offered breakfast.

• •

Nine days before Daulton crossed the bridge at Laredo, the telephone rang at the Lee home in Palos Verdes, and a man with a Mexican accent asked to speak to Daulton's mother.

The caller introduced himself to Mrs. Lee as "Rafael Vargas," a friend of Daulton's, and said he was calling from Mexico. He said Daulton had had an appointment with him in Mexico—an important business meeting—and had failed to appear.

"Do you know where he is?" Vargas inquired.

"As far as I know, he's in Mexico," she said. "He left several days ago."

The caller seemed satisfied and said he would continue waiting for Daulton. But Mrs. Lee was growing alarmed.

"You know, this is the first time Daulton has ever been gone so long without calling," she told her husband that evening. "I think Daulton's in trouble."

• •

Chris was also curious about what had happened during Daulton's trip to deliver the Pyramider papers.

On January 7, the day after his friend's arrest, he placed a person-to-person call to the Holiday Inn in the Zona Rosa from Riverside, where he had moved for the beginning of the college term.

244

The operator in California informed the hotel operator that the caller wanted to speak to a hotel guest, Andrew Daulton Lee.

There was a click, then a pause, and a male voice answered in English.

"Mr. Andrew Lee?" the Riverside operator asked.

The man who answered said his name was Brown. Chris asked the operator to try again. The operator complied and Brown answered again. Growing apprehensive, Chris requested the operator in Riverside to ask the hotel operator to "try the right room." The hotel operator agreed to investigate. After a long, empty pause on the international telephone line, the operator came back on and said there had been some confusion; Mr. Lee was no longer registered at the hotel. She said a hotel assistant manager told her that Mr. Lee had apparently been arrested. She said if the caller needed more information, it could probably be obtained at the American embassy.

Chris thought: *Finally, it's over.* They had caught Daulton. And then he thought: or did he get busted for dope? Either way, Chris calculated, it was a matter of time before the FBI found its way to him. Chris quickly evaluated his options: if he stayed, the FBI would almost certainly arrest him within a few days, perhaps a few hours; if he ran, where would he go? Time was too short to waste. He got into his Volkswagen with its oversized tires and off-road equipment and drove fifteen minutes to Ontario Airport, the nearest public airport. On the way, his mind groped for a possible escape route . . . he thought of Mexico; the wild mountains of Wyoming, where he had been last month; the desert he knew so well, where he could get lost for days without anyone's finding him. . . .

He parked his car outside the airport terminal and went inside. Aimlessly, he looked around. He paced in front of airline ticket counters, studying their flight schedules and the destinations they offered, then moved on to study the schedule of another airline. Dazed and indecisive, he strode back and forth, first selecting a destination and then rejecting it. Finally, he came to a decision; it really didn't matter what destination he chose, the FBI would track him down wherever he went.

Chris returned to his car. He started the Volkswagen and drove home. He had known from the first night, the night after Daulton made his first contact with the Russians, that eventually the sand would run out on their game. Now the sand was almost gone, and he knew there

was nothing he could do about it. Indeed, he thought, once it had begun, there had *never* really been anything he could do to halt what was now inevitable. Chris went home to the shack he rented in Riverside and began to wait.

Nothing happened.

The weekend went by and it was eerily, inexplicably normal. He flew Pips in the foothills behind Riverside, and as he admiringly watched his bird practice the instinctive skills that tens of thousands of years of evolution had honed so superbly, Chris reached out for hope. He began to wonder if—hope that—somehow he had escaped. It seemed that way. But then, bitterly, he felt reality overcome hope. As he tramped through the brush, Chris added up the circumstances of Daulton's arrest once again and decided that he had been attempting to fool himself, and once again, the pounding at his temples and the angry throbbing of his heart began.

He returned to class on Monday. Sometime during the week, Chris noticed that there was a new student sitting two seats behind him in his class on Soviet Foreign Policy. Chris had never had any trouble spotting cops. He had grown up around them. Cops and FBI agents had been fixtures around his house when he was growing up—coming for dinner, smelling up the living room with their cigars, regaling each other with war stories from law enforcement. This new student, he decided, wasn't a student.

As his professor droned on about Russia's place in world affairs, Chris raised an arm gently and held up his wristwatch and studied the face of the stranger reflected in the crystal of the watch. Every time Chris looked at him, the man was staring directly at the back of his head.

Chris was aware now that time was running out on him rapidly, and he decided that there was something he needed to do: he wanted to see Alana one last time.

He called her, and they went out dancing. Chris whispered to Alana that he had always loved her and still did, that he had been wrong when he'd said he didn't love her.

"I didn't mean it." His voice choked. Tears were brimming from his eyes. "I love you," he said.

"You stupid," she said. "I know. I always knew."

As they danced, Chris held Alana tightly and he wanted to stop time. But the evening sailed by quickly. As he drove back to Riverside from

her home, Chris realized that the memory of the evening was all he had left now to hold on to—except Mr. Pips. And he vowed to fly the socks off Pips until they came to get him.

• •

On January 12, five days before Daulton crossed the bridge and six days after his arrest, the Black Vault at TRW was shut down. That morning, two FBI agents called on Regis J. Carr, TRW's director of security for Special Programs, and said that they wanted to discuss Project Pyramider; the arrest in Mexico of a man named Andrew Daulton Lee; and a friend of Lee's, Christopher John Boyce, a former TRW employee.

Carr was stunned. A former FBI agent and a respected professional in the small world of special-projects security, he told the agents that Christopher Boyce had had "access to Top Secret intelligence information which would cause very grave damage to the United States if it were ever published or fell into the hands of a foreign country." He asked the agents if they thought there was any chance that Boyce might have passed information from the vault to the Russians, and they said that, unfortunately, they believed he had.

Then Carr gave the agents a detailed assessment of the potential damage to the United States. As an agent jotted down his comments, he said, "Christopher Boyce had access to the entire inner workings of the intelligence community, with daily access to intelligence communications, documents and hardware. He's had this privilege for two years. He's operated as a courier within the plant and outside, operated a secure voice communication system and an encrypted TWX network on line with government contractors and overseas stations, and he talked to the CIA directly by TWX." As the investigation proceeded over the next few days, the realization of the enormity of the loss became even more apparent; copies of the pictures of the Pyramider documents furnished to the FBI by the Mexican Government were shown to Carr. The documents, Carr said, "were classified Top Secret, and the disclosure of any of the information could have very grave and irreparable damage to the national defense."

An agent asked where the Pyramider documents had been stored, and Carr said they were locked in a safe in the communications vault, where Boyce normally wouldn't have access to them. Another TRW security officer was dispatched to the vault to retrieve them, and he

found the Pyramider papers not locked up, but lying on top of a cabinet. Gloomily, TRW officials told the agents that Chris had had not only access to the Pyramider documents, but intimate knowledge about two very secret satellite programs, Rhyolite and Argus, as well as NSA encryption ciphers that the Soviets could use to decipher CIA messages. Carr said that Boyce had had access to the High Bay Area in M-4, where two satellites were in storage, and could have photographed these satellites, as well as new antennas that were being prepared for satellite launching. He urged the agents to find out if Boyce had taken photographs of this hardware, whether he had transmitted any data to the Russians "about lasers" and whether he had given the Russians copies of TWX messages from the vault or the list of "slugs" that were used to identify stations on the CIA's Secret Communication Network.

When the FBI agents first arrived at TRW, it was six days after the CIA had learned in Mexico City of Daulton's arrest with the Pyramider papers. But Carr would testify later that he had not been told of the damaging security breach in the vault he supervised until the FBI brought him the news. Indeed, his first reaction after receiving the news was to tell the CIA. Instinctively, he started to use the encrypted voice link in the Black Vault to reach Pilot, but then checked himself. He feared that it might have been bugged by the KGB or that other TRW employees might have been compromised by Soviet spies. Still, he felt he had to get the word as fast as possible to Langley, and he elected to call CIA Headquarters over a conventional, nonsecure line. He informed the agency what the FBI agents had just told him, using the initial "P" to describe the missing Pyramider papers.

• •

Two days later, on January 14, two other FBI agents paid a call at the Redondo Beach apartment that Aaron Johnson shared with Beverly Zyser and inquired about their friend Andrew Daulton Lee. The couple figured the agents were investigating Daulton's drug business, although they couldn't understand the agents' intense interest in Daulton's relationship with Chris Boyce. Johnson told the agents he knew Daulton traveled often to Mexico but didn't know why. He said Daulton was "into heroin," a "hard core" criminal who made his living through pushing drugs, and always had lots of cash which he flashed around. He mentioned the scar-faced man he'd seen at Daulton's

248

house a few days before Christmas; as for Boyce, Johnson said he was Daulton's best friend but that he didn't see him as being involved in any of Daulton's illegal dealings. "He's straight; he doesn't hang around the same crowd as Daulton," he said. "I'm sure he's not into anything illegal."

After the agents left, Johnson telephoned Daulton's brother and told him FBI agents had just been at his apartment asking about Daulton and Chris. Dave Lee realized now why the family hadn't heard from Daulton since he'd left for Mexico. Johnson then called Chris's house and told his mother that it was urgent that he get in touch with him.

Chris never got the warning.

38 ON JANUARY 16, 1977, ten days after Daulton's arrest, a yellow Mazda station wagon approached a small pink house made of concrete blocks on a turkey ranch 1,600 miles north of Mexico City. It was little more than a shack in the rural outskirts of Riverside, sixty miles south of Los Angeles, with a decaying old windmill beside it.

A year earlier, the twenty-five-acre ranch had vibrated with the noisy energy of thousands of turkeys. But the owner had given up turkey ranching because it wasn't profitable anymore, and he supplemented the family's income by renting the small blockhouse for $100 a month to students from the nearby campus of the University of California.

The same evening that Chris had gone dancing with Alana, Florence Carlson had remarked to her husband, Walt, that the new tenant who was sharing the cabin fifty yards from their own home was "very nice." He was not only warm and polite, but quite intelligent, she said. The Carlsons had first met Chris two or three years earlier, when he'd knocked at their front door and asked if he might use their property to hunt sparrows with an air rifle. (Brown, rolling hills rose up behind the Carlson place, and they abounded in wildlife.) Chris explained that he

needed the sparrows for his training of falcons, and the Carlsons had been impressed by the intensity of his interest in falconry, and they'd encouraged him to come back whenever he wanted.

Around Christmastime, he had arrived at the Carlsons' home again with news that he was going to enroll at the university, and he had inquired if they still rented the small cabin. They said they did, but that it was not available because another young man was staying there. But Mrs. Carlson suggested the tenant might be willing to share the place and divide the rent. Chris moved in a few days later.

• •

There were two young men in the Mazda that arrived at the Carlson place shortly before three o'clock on the afternoon of the sixteenth. But the eyes that followed the approaching vehicle from between cracks in the corrugated-steel walls of the turkey pens were interested only in the young man in the passenger seat.

Chris, wearing Levi's, a sport shirt and the sweater that had been given him as a good-bye gift by his friends at TRW, looked like any other college student on a Sunday afternoon. With his boyishly handsome face pinched slightly at the cheekbones, and his conservative short dark hair combed back over his forehead, Mrs. Carlson would say he looked more like a product of the fifties than of the seventies.

That morning, Mrs. Carlson had spotted a car driving down the dirt road from the top of the knoll where her daughter and son-in-law had built a new home. This had puzzled her, because she knew they liked to sleep in on Sunday mornings.

Mrs. Carlson hadn't known it then, but FBI agents had moved into her daughter's home the night before. They had politely asked if they could use the home while they looked down on the pink concrete blockhouse beside her parents' house. The agents refused to explain their interest in the cabin, but the couple agreed.

Shortly before 8 A.M., a half-dozen cars carrying FBI agents had careered down the steep hill and stopped outside the shack. Agents, guns outstretched, had burst into the room and found two young men asleep.

"What's your name?" one agent said as he roused one of the sleeping youths.

"Joe Shmo; what's yours?" Steve Rasmussen, Chris's roommate, said into the muzzle of a revolver.

"Where's Boyce?" the agent had demanded, ignoring the remark.

Chris wasn't there because he had left the night before on a falcon-trapping expedition in the hills behind Riverside with George Heavyside, a falconer he knew from Palos Verdes. Steve had asked his brother, Gary, to spend the night at the cabin; in the morning, they planned to drive to Lytle Creek, in the mountains beyond Riverside, to pan for gold. Finally, the brothers had convinced the FBI agents that neither of them was Christopher John Boyce, and they said they planned to go ahead with their trip. Okay, the agent who was in charge of the raiding party had said; but he assigned two of his agents to go with them. The other agents had remained, resuming a vigil from atop the knoll, which looked down on the Carlson property and the twin concrete ribbons of the Riverside Freeway beyond it. Some of the agents had moved into the old turkey pens, and they were there, watching, when George Heavyside and Chris arrived, joking about the night and day they had spent and the wise hawks they had tried—and failed—to entice into the trap resting on Chris's lap.

As the station wagon pulled to a stop next to the shack, one of the FBI cars that had been waiting at the top of the hill suddenly raced up from behind, passed the windmill and skidded with an abrasive slide on the sandy driveway. Two agents lunged out, and each pointed a revolver at the head of one of the two youths in the Mazda.

"Freeze!" they shouted at once as other agents cascaded out of the turkey pens and surrounded the car. Chris had lived with stories of arrests such as this for as long as he could remember. He had heard about stakeouts and FBI busts from his father, his uncle and all their friends who used to visit the Boyce house, and the thing he remembered most was not to move; if he did, one of the trigger-happy agents might shoot him.

"Who's Boyce? Who's Boyce?" one agent shouted.

Heavyside, trembling and trying to gather his senses so that he could fathom the bizarre events that were happening all around him, raised his hands in shocked semiparalysis. He was led away and searched, and once the agents established that he was not Chris, they let him go.

Chris said nothing. But when he was convinced they were calm enough so he wouldn't be shot, he methodically placed the hawk trap on the seat beside him and got out of the car. As he did, one of the agents grabbed his shirt and spun him around.

"Get out, you fucking traitor!" he screamed.

"Do you know what you're charged with? Espionage!" he said, and wedged Chris against the car and snapped handcuffs on his wrists behind his back.

"Where are the documents, you fucking traitor? Where are the documents?" he demanded.

And then he said it again and again: "You fucking traitor, tell us where the documents are!"

· ·

When the FBI agents entered the small house with their prisoner, Mr. Pips looked up from his perch on a dresser and began to screech wildly at the strangers' intrusion. He flapped his long wings furiously and for a moment seemed ready to lift off and attack the intruders, before Chris talked to him and calmed him down. Later, as the agents ransacked the cabin and peppered him with questions, Chris sensed a presence behind him, and he looked around to discover the dark eyes of Pips boring into him like sabers. His eyes were wild with fury, and Chris translated instantly what his bird was trying to tell him: *You betrayed me.*

He felt ashamed and chastened by Pips's angry stare. But at the same time, he felt proud of his best falcon—as wild and as defiant as it had been on the day he first trapped it.

39

"IS THERE ANYONE HERE from the CIA?" Chris asked as he dried his hands in the men's room at the Los Angeles regional headquarters of the Federal Bureau of Investigation a few minutes after six on the evening of January 16, 1977.

"We don't have any of those people here; why?" asked George J. Moorehead, an FBI agent who had helped arrest Chris at the turkey ranch three hours earlier. Moorehead had liked him, and had seemed to develop an almost paternalistic interest in the prisoner.

"I can't discuss some things with you," Chris responded. It was one of the more bizarre remarks in the records of espionage investigations: a young man who had just been arrested as a Soviet spy said that he couldn't discuss with FBI agents the secrets he had sold to the Soviet Union because the agents weren't cleared for the projects.

Moorehead was a big, beefy man in his middle forties with light-colored curly hair and horn-rimmed glasses that gave him a vaguely professorial look. There was a casual warmth in his personality that contrasted with the chilly efficiency of some FBI agents, and when Moorehead had seemed to extend an arm to lean on, Chris had accepted, and he gravitated to the soft-spoken agent who had seemed kinder than the other agents during the confrontation at the turkey ranch. Moorehead had been puzzled during the ride in from Riverside by the discovery that Chris's father and uncle were former FBI agents. A twenty-five-year veteran of the FBI, Moorehead would later say that he hadn't forgotten he was dealing with an accused Soviet spy. But he had been impressed by his quiet good manners—what some adults referred to as his "sweetness"—and he had wondered what forces had brought Chris to where he was now. Chris might have been his own son, Moorehead thought.

"We have agents here who are cleared for anything you were working on," he replied when Chris said he couldn't discuss certain information without violating the law. Chris didn't respond. As they walked out of the men's room, Chris said he needed time to collect his thoughts. "Is there some place I can sit and think for a while?"

"Sure," Moorehead said, and he led him down a hallway, giving him a guided tour of the functions of the various specialized offices they passed.

The FBI headquarters in Los Angeles could have been designed by Kafka. Occupying most of the sixteenth story, and parts of other floors, of a high-rise building on Wilshire Boulevard not far from U.C.L.A., it is a big, sterile warren of rooms, many with partitions, that look out at a central bull pen of seemingly endless rows of desks lined close together, each with its own telephone. The several hundred rank-and-file agents assigned to the L.A. office used this central bull pen as their base of operations.

Chris had $744 in cash in his wallet when he was arrested in Riverside. His wallet was taken from him when he was booked, and he was photographed and fingerprinted. During the fingerprinting, a young

woman clerk had such trouble rolling legible prints that Chris offered to do it himself, saying that in his last job he had fingerprinted lots of people. Joking that Chris was out of money now, Moorehead bought him a pack of cigarettes and a cup of coffee from vending machines, and he escorted him to the office of the FBI's chief stenographer. It was empty on a Sunday evening, and Moorehead said he could collect his thoughts there. Before they reached the office, Moorehead asked Chris how many children were in his family, and Chris said there were nine, including himself. Moorehead shook his head and said he felt sorry for Chris's father. "This will really rip him up," he said.

. .

"It's inconceivable," Charles Boyce told the two FBI agents who had knocked on the door of the Boyce home in Rancho Palos Verdes, about the same time that Chris was sitting by himself in the office of the FBI chief stenographer, and said that his son was under arrest for espionage. A newspaper reporter had already called the Boyce home with a report that Chris had been arrested as a Soviet spy, and his parents had been immobilized by disbelief when the agents arrived with a search warrant for the Boyce home.

They told the FBI agents that it was impossible Chris was involved in any way in espionage. If anything, Chris was a political conservative. "He voted for Gerald Ford last year," his father said. And he had been considered a conservative for as long as anybody could remember. Mr. Boyce told the agents about the priest who, when Chris was a child, had said he was more conservative than Cardinal McIntyre of Los Angeles. It was true his son was interested in history and had talked once or twice about the Soviet Union and the future international balance of power, the father added, but "his attitudes on the surface were conservative—unless they were a subterfuge.

"It's not a political act unless he's really been fooling us for a long time," the father said of the alleged treason. His wife agreed. "I have no idea what would have prompted it," Mr. Boyce said. It couldn't have been drugs. Although Chris had smoked marijuana once in high school, his parents said, it had made him sick, and he didn't have a drug habit. The agent showed the Boyces a photograph of Andrew Daulton Lee; they identified him as a friend of Chris's who they knew had had problems with the law as a drug pusher. But they said they'd urged Chris not to associate with him because of the drugs, and Chris

had stopped bringing him to the house. But they agreed Chris was probably still seeing him because of a shared interest in falconry.

•   •

Six miles away on the other side of The Hill, shortly before the FBI agents had knocked at the Boyce home, four other agents rang the doorbell of the rambling Lee residence in Palos Verdes Estates. Dave Lee opened the door, and the agents showed their credentials and asked for his father.

"Do you have a warrant?" Dave asked. Agent George S. Bacon, as if he had never heard the remark, asked again if Dr. Lee was in. Almost instinctively, Dave slammed the door of the house. One of the agents quickly rang the doorbell again. After about thirty seconds Dave re-opened the door and said his father would be there shortly.

Dr. Lee had been napping when the agents arrived. He was not surprised by the callers. Over the years there had been many policemen who arrived at the same door. But he expected such calls to deal with Daulton's narcotics enterprises.

The agents informed Dr. Lee that his son had been arrested in Mexico, that he was being deported and that he was going to be charged by the United States Government with violation of espionage statutes; furthermore, he said that Daulton's friend Christopher John Boyce had just been arrested for the same offenses. Before Dr. Lee could react to this news, Agent David Reid said Daulton had told U.S. officials in Mexico there were photographs in his bedroom which the FBI believed were related to the case and requested him to sign a consent allowing them to search the home. Dr. Lee signed the statement. Then another agent produced a search warrant. Dr. Lee was annoyed. "If you have a search warrant why did you have me sign this?" he asked. The agents said it was the government's policy that occupants of premises should first be allowed to give their consent to a search. In fact, Justice Department lawyers had decided to seek both the search warrant and Dr. Lee's consent agreement to reinforce the legality of the search if evidence seized at the home was later challenged in court. The same strategy was followed at the Boyce home.

Like the Boyces, Dr. Lee said that it was impossible that his son was involved in espionage, although he knew he was involved with drugs.

"It seemed strange to us that he never worked but seemed to have

money," Dr. Lee said in the statement he gave Agent Reid and Agent André L. Knightlinger while Bacon and Agent David Smith began searching the house.

"Mrs. Lee and I questioned him about this," he continued, "but he never answered our questions. I assumed that he'd obtained the money through his involvement in drugs."

Asked if Daulton had ever said anything about furnishing false information to the Soviet Union, Dr. Lee said he hadn't.

"A long time ago," he said, when Daulton was in high school, "he told me that he was tired of doing things my way. He said that from then on he was going to do things his way."

After that, Dr. Lee added, Daulton had simply refused to discuss his activities outside the home with his parents. "I suspected that when he went off somewhere, he was up to something illegal," he said, "but I thought it was drugs."

Despite his son's frequent brushes with the law, Dr. Lee went on, Daulton was "still my son, and I wouldn't kick him out of the house."

Anne Lee, who had recently obtained a license as a real estate agent to occupy herself after her children were grown, walked in the door then, arriving home after a day of trying to sell property on The Hill. The length of time without a telephone call from Daulton had caused her to half-expect official callers inquiring about her son. But like her husband, she said she knew relatively little about her son's recent comings and goings. When she'd asked Daulton about his trips to Mexico, she said in her statement to the FBI, "he told me not to worry about it." Once, when she heard Daulton had made a trip to Vienna and she had asked about it, she said, "he wouldn't tell me anything about the trip." An agent inquired about the two youths' friendship. Daulton and Chris Boyce, she explained, were best friends; the friendship went back many years and had continued because of their mutual love of falconry. Chris's father had helped him get a job at TRW, she said, but Chris had called it a "flunky job."

"He said he was involved in cleaning up after everybody," she said.

David Lee was also interviewed. He told the agents that Daulton had told him months previously that he and Chris Boyce were involved in a scheme to sell false information to the Soviets. Daulton claimed to be working for the CIA, he said, and had shown him a Minox camera. "My brother said it was a misinformation program and he was doing it for the money; he said each roll of film he brought was worth approxi-

mately ten thousand dollars.'' In a camera case in Daulton's room, David helped the agents find the two photos of the encryption equipment Daulton had retrieved from the Russians in October.

Four hours after they had arrived, the FBI agents left the Lee home. They had a Minox camera found in a rolltop desk in Daulton's room (a room they described on their official report for the day as ''in extremely cluttered condition'') and so many other items from his room that it took twenty minutes to load their cars.

• •

A half-hour after Chris asked to be left alone in the chief stenographer's office at the Los Angeles FBI office, he asked Agent George J. Moorehead, who was waiting outside in a corridor, if he could ask a question.

''Sure,'' Moorehead said. ''I'll do my best.''

''Has anybody else been charged with the same thing as me?''

Chris suspected that Daulton had also been arrested for espionage because of his call to the Holiday Inn, but he couldn't be sure. It could have been a drug bust.

''Do you mean in the past or now, this case?'' Moorehead asked.

''This specific case,'' Chris said.

Moorehead said that he didn't know.

In that case, Chris said, he would have nothing to say. He didn't want to say anything because he didn't know what Daulton had—or hadn't—told the authorities. After his refusal to talk more, Chris was handcuffed again and led out of the room by Moorehead, who said they were on their way to the Los Angeles County Jail. In the hallway, they met James E. White, another member of the FBI's Los Angeles Espionage Squad. Moorehead told White that Chris had asked if anyone else had been arrested in the case. White left them in the hall and checked via telephone with Richard A. Stilz, an Assistant United States Attorney who had already begun preparing the government's case against Andrew Daulton Lee and Christopher John Boyce. Stilz advised him that Chris could be told of Lee's arrest in Mexico and that his friend would soon be deported to the United States.

When he heard this news, Chris thought a moment, and shortly before seven o'clock, four hours after his arrest, he said:

''Let's talk.''

The agents told Chris that if he wanted to say anything, he would

have to sign a *Miranda* waiver of his rights. Earlier in the day—after the raid at the turkey ranch—Chris had refused to do so. This time, he agreed to sign the waiver. Moorehead asked him to write out a statement declaring he had not been coerced into consenting to interrogation. But Chris told Moorehead that his hands were shaking so much that he couldn't write anything more than his signature.

His heart was pumping so hard that later he said he felt as if it were about to burst.

One of the agents said he would write a statement in longhand for Chris to sign, and he did so. The statement read:

I, Christopher John Boyce, requested from Special Agents G. J. Moorehead and William M. Smith that at 6:25 P.M. this date I be given a period to collect my thoughts regarding charges for which I was arrested today. At 7 P.M., 35 minutes later, I decided by my own free will, and without any promises, threats or inducements, to furnish a statement to the FBI regarding this matter. Any delay experienced at the Los Angeles Headquarters of the FBI, therefore, was specifically at my request and strictly voluntary.

Chris signed the handwritten statement, and during the next hour or so he surrendered any chance he might have had to avert what he had decided almost two years ago was inevitable.

As he began his monologue, Chris explained why he had asked about Daulton: "I just wanted to know if he was off the streets."

40

"I WORKED IN THE BLACK VAULT at TRW, handling encrypted communications for the Central Intelligence Agency," he began.

On his first day on the job, he continued, a co-worker had joked with him about selling ciphers used to encode messages to the Soviet Union and speculated that they might be worth $20,000 a month. A few weeks later, after a night of drinking and pot smoking with friends—"I was extremely high," he said—he had hinted at the nature of the job. After

a while, he continued, "it just kept rolling out," and he and his friend
Daulton Lee had begun joking about selling the material to the Russians. The idea that Chris had access to information worth a great deal
of money, he said, "excited Daulton."

"It just got more serious as the conversations kept going."

"Whose idea was it to sell documents to the Soviet Union?" White
asked Chris.

"It was a combination of seeking each other out," he said. "Security
was so lax you could walk out with hundreds of documents. I was
always drunk.

"I worked on the Rhyolite project for the CIA," he went on. "I
handled all communications between the people who built the satellites
and those who used them." An agent asked how much information had
been delivered to the Soviets. Chris said he wasn't sure, but thought it
"numbered thousands of documents." Most involved projects Rhyolite and Argus, he said, but there were others. "Sometimes," he said,
"the CIA fucks up and sends naval traffic and military traffic and stuff
about other programs and projects with other companies, and about
submarine activity."

The agents asked who, besides Daulton, had been involved in the
operation, and he said Daulton was the only one. They asked if Chris
had a girlfriend and whether she knew about it. Chris refused to give
them Alana's name, but acknowledged that he had a girlfriend "who
was aware that I had been given sums of money, and she knew I
worked on a secret project." But she didn't know the whole truth, he
said. "She is law-abiding, a Christian Scientist." He said he had become fearful and distraught and moody because of his involvement
with the Russians, and finally it had broken them apart.

"It was more than she could handle," Chris said.

"Did you ever tell Andrew Daulton Lee or anyone else that you
were in a project to furnish false information to the Soviet Union?"
White asked.

Chris shook his head.

"Did Lee understand what you were doing?"

"Totally," he said.

• •

In considerable detail, he described Daulton's meetings with the
Russians in Mexico City, the purchase of the Minox camera, the booze

runs, the surreptitious trips with secret documents in potted plants—and the day the NSA inspector had nearly tripped him up.

"He blew it; I was right in front of him, and he really blew it."

"I thought they were on to me long before now," Chris told the agents. It "amazed" him that they had not been caught sooner. Chris recounted his long friendship with Daulton, which, he said, had begun in elementary school, and their mutual interest in falconry. "His parents were very wealthy."

Daulton, he added, was a "hoodlum" who had "cheated" him—"he lied and would use me"—and kept samples of everything sold to the Russians to hold against Chris. After he described Daulton as a hoodlum, he was asked to describe himself. Chris said that perhaps he might be called "an adventurer."

"I got involved with the Soviets through drugs," he said, and he added, "Politically, I'm very disenchanted with this government; it's done many things wrong."

The name of FBI Agent White was paged on the public-address system, and he left the room to take a call from another agent calling from Chris's home. He returned and asked Chris if he wanted to speak to his father. Chris felt the agents suspected his father might be involved with him; in any case, he was not in any mood to talk to his father now.

"No," Chris said, and the questioning went on.

He described some of the documents he had photographed—the ciphers; data on Rhyolite, Argus, the 20,030 project study; and the message traffic—thousands of documents in all, he admitted. He said the Pyramider documents had been left out unlocked in the vault just before he left TRW, which surprised him, but said other TRW employees had called it a "dead project." Chris recited the details of his two trips to Mexico, Boris' instructions to return to college and eventually get a job in the diplomatic corps or the CIA and his fears he would become indentured forever to the Soviet intelligence service.

"The whole thing has been a nightmare," he said. "Once it began, there was no way to stop it . . . except for the way it did end."

After the interview, Chris was handcuffed again and Moorehead led him out of the Wilshire Boulevard high-rise office tower to begin the twenty-minute automobile ride to the Los Angeles County Jail. Chris was silent. As they walked together, Moorehead looked over at the curious young man. His head was canted toward the ground and there

was a blank expression on his face. Then Chris turned his head slightly
to look at the FBI agent, and he said:

"I fucked my country."

. .

The following morning, the newspapers were filled with reports of
the arrests of the two young men from Palos Verdes. At the Boyce
home, a familiar figure approached the front door. It was Msgr.
Thomas J. McCarthy.

Charles Boyce had not slept much the previous night. The arrest of
his eldest son had seemingly shattered his life. His own values were
relatively simple: he believed in his country, in his family, in obedience
to the law, in following the rules and in punishment for those who did
not. All that he had really expected of his son was that he be honest
and loyal to his country, and he was overwhelmed by the hurt and
humiliation.

Monsignor McCarthy told Mrs. Boyce that he wanted to talk to
them, to offer whatever help he could. She went into the bedroom
where Charles Boyce was sitting alone, but he refused to see the priest.

"I can't see anyone," he said.

He was sobbing. The only other time his wife had ever seen Charles
Boyce cry was at his mother's funeral.

The next few days were not any easier on the family. When the
youngest Boyce children went to school they were called "Nazis,"
and the youngest Boyce sons were set upon by classmates who sent
them home with bloodied faces.

. .

On January 26, 1977, a Federal grand jury in Los Angeles indicted
the two friends from Palos Verdes for espionage. Although twelve
counts were included in this original indictment, they would subsequently be consolidated into eight counts:

* Count One charged Andrew Daulton Lee and Christopher John
Boyce with conspiring to transmit national-defense information to a
foreign nation, to wit, the Union of Soviet Socialist Republics.

* Count Two charged Andrew Daulton Lee with attempting to transmit national-defense documents entitled "Proposal for Covert Communication Satellite Study No. 24151.0000, dated December 14, 1972,

marked Top Secret—Pyramider," and other Pyramider documents to the U.S.S.R.

* Count Three charged both defendants with conspiring to gather national-defense information.

* Count Four charged both defendants with the act of gathering national-defense information—specifically, the Pyramider documents —intending, or having reason to believe, that such information would be used to the advantage of the U.S.S.R.

* Count Five charged Daulton with receiving national-defense information—the Pyramider documents—from Christopher John Boyce knowing, or having reason to believe, that such information had been obtained illegally.

* Count Seven charged Daulton with having unauthorized possession of national-defense information—the Pyramider documents—and attempting to transmit such information to unauthorized persons, to wit, representatives, officers, and agents of the U.S.S.R.

* Count Ten charged Daulton with acting as an agent of a foreign government—the U.S.S.R.—without prior notification to the Secretary of State.

* Count Twelve charged Daulton with receiving stolen government property—the Pyramider documents—valued in excess of $100.

Upon conviction, according to Federal statutes, the charges carried the possibility of death sentences. Five days after their indictment, Chris and Daulton pleaded not guilty on all counts.

The two friends, independently, had already begun to line up their legal defense. Daulton quickly retained Ken Kahn, the moustachioed "hippie lawyer" whose specialty was defending Palos Verdes drug pushers.

Because it was a capital case with a possible death penalty, Federal law required Daulton to have a second lawyer. Donald Re, a thin, thirty-year-old Princeton-educated trial specialist from Los Angeles, was appointed by the court to help with Daulton's defense. Re's patrician, Ivy League courtliness would provide a stark contrast in the courtroom to Kahn's flamboyant style.

Chris retained George Chelius, a lawyer who had never handled a criminal case before. A big man in his late thirties with a prominent black moustache and receding black hair, Chelius worked under Chris's father as a security specialist in the aerospace industry. He had attended law school in his spare time, had passed the bar exam less than a year before Chris's arrest and planned to leave industry soon to

go into private law practice. Like most adults who knew Chris, Chelius couldn't comprehend the news of his arrest. When he heard the reports that Sunday afternoon, he immediately called Chris's father at the Boyce home and offered his sympathy and legal help.

The Boyces, besides being distraught, were worried about the cost of a defense. Chelius agreed it would be expensive, possibly costing as much as $100,000. The Boyces were prosperous by upper-middle-class standards, but not nearly in the same economic league as the Lees. Theirs was a large family, and the prospect of such a huge bill for legal fees loomed impossibly large.

Chelius said he would see what he could do. He called a partner of a well-known law firm in Orange County, south of Los Angeles, that he had been thinking of joining after leaving the aerospace industry. Chelius outlined the Boyces' concern over the costs of mounting a defense, and at Chelius' suggestion, the partner agreed to take on the case without a fee; there ought to be plenty of free publicity in a major espionage trial, he said.

About midnight on the day of Chris's arrest, George Chelius arrived at the Los Angeles County Jail, a large, noisy, overcrowded human zoo that was located in central Los Angeles. Chris was apprehensive about accepting Chelius' offer to defend him. "Are you here to represent me or my father?" he demanded to know, suspicious that Chelius had the same politically conservative views as his father. But the two men—the troubled twenty-four-year-old accused spy and the intelligent, sensitive, green lawyer—hit it off, and they talked until eight o'clock the following morning.

•   •

Within a month, the Orange County law firm had second thoughts about representing Chris without a fee. Although members of the firm received some newspaper publicity during the first few days after the arrest, they realized that an enormous amount of work would be required to provide a defense for Chris. Backing away from the earlier deal, they told Chelius it would cost $100,000 to defend him. Chelius was stunned. He couldn't tell that to Chris's father. He knew he couldn't afford it. Moreover, as a matter of honor, he decided he couldn't break his word to the Boyce family. The inexperienced lawyer resigned his job in the aerospace industry and said he would defend Chris without a fee.

Like Daulton, Chris was required to have a second attorney, and

William Dougherty soon joined his defense team. A transplanted New Englander who had never been fully at home in the sunny, materialistic climate of Orange County where he made his home, Bill Dougherty was a brilliant fifty-three-year-old criminal lawyer who had spent three years in the Justice Department's Organized Crime and Racketeering Strike Force prosecuting Mafioso and garment-industry racketeers. His gray hair was cropped so short that he looked like a slightly over-weight Marine drill instructor, and indeed he was an ex–Marine fighter pilot who still carried around occasional hurts from a broken back suffered when the engine of his Corsair had quit at five hundred feet and he had slammed into a stand of trees. When Dougherty was grounded after the crash, he had gone to law school, then taken a job with the Justice Department before moving to California and opening his criminal law practice. He was still a colonel in the Marine Reserves. By the time he became co-counsel for Christopher Boyce, he'd been involved in more than 250 criminal cases and had been on the winning side in more than 85 percent of them. Like Chelius, he agreed to help defend Chris without a fee—largely, he said later, because it seemed likely to be an interesting case.

. .

Meanwhile, the United States Government was lining up its legal talent. Richard A. Stilz and Joel Levine, like most members of the staff of United States Attorneys' offices around the country, were young, relatively inexperienced, bright, highly motivated if not highly paid, and investing a few years in government service to gain experience before going into more remunerative private practice.

Although both were thirty-one years old, they were a contrast phys-ically. Stilz, a graduate of U.C.L.A. and the Loyola University School of Law, was only a few inches taller than Andrew Daulton Lee and shared with him the same kind of nervous intensity. He had a retentive mind which amazed colleagues and a reputation as a merciless cross-examiner. Levine was dark-haired, tall and thin and wore glasses that gave him a slightly owlish look; a former New Yorker who had at-tended Brooklyn College and the Case Western Reserve University School of Law, he was more the legal scholar of the two. The two lawyers were regarded as the sharpest young criminal prosecutors in the Los Angeles Justice Department office and, between them, had won a string of convictions in heavily publicized major narcotics and

fraud cases. Both were assistants in charge of the criminal division of the U.S. Attorney's office in Los Angeles; Stilz had the additional rank of chief of the Criminal Complaint Section of the office. They were prosecutors, but as it turned out, they would also have to become detectives in the case of *The United States of America v. Andrew Daulton Lee and Christopher John Boyce*.

41

AS THEY SAT ALONE in their respective isolation cells at the Los Angeles County Jail in the days following their arrest, Chris and Daulton were both tortured by thoughts of what lay ahead. Their lawyers said that conviction for treason carried the possibility of a death penalty, and at the very least, there was the likelihood of a long prison term. But if the two friends had known about a debate that was boiling in Washington over their fate, they might have begun each day with at least a sliver of hope that the charges against them would be dropped.

Unbeknownst to them or to their lawyers, the United States of America was not at all sure that it was going to prosecute the two spies.

If they were placed on trial, it meant that potentially damaging national secrets might have to be made public; it meant that the Central Intelligence Agency would have to disclose that it was involved in the operation of clandestine espionage satellites—something it had never done publicly. Moreover, there was the risk that intimate details of the space-reconnaissance operations and methods might have to be made public, something the CIA and other elements of the American intelligence community concluded was unacceptable. To get a conviction, the Justice Department would have to produce evidence that a crime —the theft of classified information—had been committed. Virtually every item from the Black Vault that Chris had photographed was Top Secret, and samples would have to be offered as evidence.

As CIA and FBI agents went over the materials, including copies of

the TWX traffic to which Chris had had access, it soon became evident to senior officials in the National Security Council that the loss was among the worst in the history of the CIA; never before had the KGB penetrated actual American surveillance-satellite operations. This review of the information that Chris had handled reaffirmed the initial decision that none of the data could be exposed at a trial. Moreover, some CIA administrators, already worried about the precarious political status of the bases at Alice Springs and other American facilities in Australia, warned that a Boyce-Lee public trial could present a political minefield.

Nevertheless, the Justice Department said it believed there might be a way to deal with the dilemma: the prosecution would tailor its case very narrowly to avoid revealing the most sensitive information, although inevitably some classified information would have to be used. The Justice Department asked the CIA to determine if any of the data stolen from the vault could be used as evidence without serious harm to the country. There was a chance, the government lawyers said, that a cooperative judge would be assigned to the case and would seal the evidence from public scrutiny. However, they said the defendants' attorneys might have to be apprised of all information, and this meant the possibility of a leak, either accidental or otherwise.

Zbigniew Brzezinski, President Carter's national security adviser, had been told of the potential magnitude of the security breach shortly after the Mexican secret police had given American representatives in Mexico City copies of the photographs carried by Daulton. Brzezinski informed the President of the loss and warned of the possibility that the Soviet Union had compromised at least one major satellite system that was used to monitor Russian military activities and which, as a verification tool, was an important element in upcoming Strategic Arms Limitation Talks. Implicit in the warning was the possibility that once the Soviet Union learned intimate details of the satellite systems it might be able to develop countermeasures that could blunt their effectiveness in verifying Soviet compliance with an arms-control agreement.

In spite of the deep concern over the risk of disclosing intelligence secrets at a trial, officials in the National Security Council, the agency headed by Brzezinski, agreed with the Justice Department on one thing: it was unacceptable to let the two spies go unpunished; and thus a *provisional* decision was made to prosecute Christopher Boyce and

Andrew Daulton Lee. Justice Department specialists had developed a strategy: they would attempt to present a strong case against the youths utilizing only portions of the Pyramider documents as examples of the thousands of documents they had stolen.

Some CIA officials initially resisted, but finally agreed that they could live with disclosure of some of the Pyramider documents. The National Security Council staff agreed that if there was *any* chance that secret details of Rhyolite, Argus or other satellite projects were to be made public, or other details about CIA or NSA covert operations would surface, the decision to prosecute would be withdrawn.

Once the decision had been made to prosecute the two youths on the relatively narrow grounds of stealing the Pyramider papers, it fell on the shoulders of Levine and Stilz to prove they had done it. And this turned out to be less simple than it might have seemed to those who had heard damning broadcasts about their arrest on January 16.

Stilz and Levine were convinced that Chris's statement after his arrest gave them a solid case against him. Dougherty and Chelius were sure to try to have the statement ruled inadmissible on the ground that it had not been made voluntarily; his initial refusal to sign a *Miranda* waiver was a soft spot for the prosecution, and the defense was likely to contend that Chris had been too exhausted to make a rational judgment when he later consented to do so. But the prosecutors felt confident that they could defend the confession as proper. There was a related problem with the confession: it had been classified Top Secret by the FBI, and the prosecutors would have to find a method to bring out some of its contents that were damaging to Boyce at trial while keeping out the sensitive specifics regarding Rhyolite and Argus. Nevertheless, the young prosecutors felt reasonably secure in their case against Chris. They were less confident about the case against Daulton. He had been arrested in a foreign country without being afforded the constitutional safeguards that American courts require. And the statement he had given to the two FBI agents in Mexico City would probably not be an effective prosecutorial tool; not only was it too classified Top Secret: it contained exculpatory statements by Lee —his claims that he was acting as an agent for the CIA.

The prosecutors had to link Lee unequivocally to the Pyramider microfilm to get a conviction. And this didn't look easy. True, the film had been in his possession when he was arrested in Mexico City. But reality and admissible proof were not the same. The original arrest had

been made by Mexican authorities who might—or might not—have handled the evidence in such a way that it could be proved conclusively that the photos found on him were those of the Pyramider papers; there had to be no doubt that the Mexican police hadn't planted the photos on him, or that the pictures hadn't been switched. Moreover, they had to prove that Daulton had had access to some of America's most sensitive defense secrets in the first place and that, after getting possession of them, he had photographed them and taken them to Mexico with the intention of selling them to the Russians. Because of these problems, another strategic step in the prosecution emerged: Stilz and Levine would use the well-worn prosecutor's stratagem of getting one conspirator to turn on another with the promise of a concession in his sentence. Getting Boyce to testify against Lee became the foundation of their case against Lee. They didn't have any doubt Boyce would testify; the case against him was so strong, it seemed certain he would go for a deal—a guilty plea with a recommendation for a shorter sentence than was likely if the case went to trial.

Stilz and Levine prepared to wait for Chelius and Dougherty to seek a deal. They couldn't make the first move because they didn't want to appear anxious; they didn't want to tip the defense to the doubts they had about the case against Daulton.

· ·

In his cell in the Los Angeles County Jail, Daulton was preoccupied once again with survival. And with the help of Ken Kahn, a line of defense began to emerge: Daulton would argue that he had been a hapless puppet of the Central Intelligence Agency, used and discarded by a nation just like those he had read about in *The Spy Who Came In from the Cold* and other spy novels. Daulton told Kahn that Chris had never *told* him that they were working for the CIA to disseminate erroneous information. But, he asked, *doesn't everything point to that?* Why else would Chris have proposed the plan in the first place? How had he been able to cross the border so often without being caught? The story he had prepared as an alibi if he was ever arrested began to take the shape of reality in Daulton's mind. As he waited out his fate, he groped with Ken Kahn for a solution to his predicament and attempted to rationalize his choice of a defense:

Hadn't Boyce said in his confessions that Pyramider was a dead project? That was exactly what he had told Daulton—and that was

exactly what Daulton had told the Feds in Laredo. Wasn't that proof that the whole thing was a disinformation gambit? "Now [Boyce] says we were fucking the U.S. But how, if Pyramider was a bogus project?"

Even Boyce's agreement with the Russians to go back to college smelled. The CIA was probably planting him as a double agent. Boyce would learn what information the Russians needed and then go straight to the CIA and reveal weak spots in Soviet defenses.

"God, I wish I knew what the hell was really going down," Daulton wrote to Kahn in a letter that went on for several pages. "Espionage is one of the human activities where truth and fiction are closely interwoven. Only someone with deep and mystic love for country can serve the way I have, or thought I was."

•   •

Plea-bargaining talks on behalf of Chris had begun, and like the initial footwork in a prizefight, the first movements consisted of more style than substance.

The prosecutors had no interest in seeking a death sentence for the spies, realizing that there was little chance that any judge would order their execution, given public sentiment toward capital punishment, the circumstances of the case and the nature of the two young defendants. But for horse-trading purposes, the prosecutors did not immediately reveal this predisposition. In initial meetings with Chelius and, later, Bill Dougherty, they compared the espionage committed by the two youths to that of Julius and Ethel Rosenberg, the Soviet spies who were executed for giving American atomic secrets to the Russians.

The defense lawyers, rightly, concluded they were bluffing, and soon the prosecutors got to the threat they really intended to hold over Chris: life imprisonment. The defense lawyers maintained their composure at this disclosure. Dougherty ridiculed the quality of the prosecution's case and said that he would subpoena former Secretary of State Henry A. Kissinger and a score of other high American officials to testify at the trial. Dougherty sensed that the prosecution needed Chris, and wasn't going to plea-bargain totally from weakness; he claimed that Chris's confession had been extracted from him involuntarily—that he had been too tired and overwrought to make a genuinely voluntary confession. Any judge could see that the FBI had, in effect, coerced him to confess, Dougherty charged.

The initial plea-bargaining talks ended inconclusively; the minimum

prison sentence the prosecutors would accept for Boyce if he agreed to testify was forty years; the defense lawyers held out for ten.

The prosecution was having other problems. The State Department advised the Justice Department in early February that the Government of Mexico was resisting its request to allow the policemen who had arrested and interrogated Daulton to testify. The news was troubling. Their testimony was an important link in the prosecution's case; it was vital to prove that Lee had had the contraband filmstrips in his possession when he was arrested. Stilz and Levine sent word to Washington that the policemen's testimony was a must, and the Justice Department relayed this message to Brzezinski.

Meanwhile, the prosecutors had begun looking for other routes to link Daulton to the filmstrips. If they could prove that the Minox camera found in Daulton's home was the same one that had taken the photographs of the Pyramider documents, they could build a separate route to link the microfilm to Daulton; the camera and the negatives from Mexico City were sent to the FBI Laboratory in Washington in hopes they could be matched.

· ·

Chris was finding it difficult to sleep as the first days of February came and went. It wasn't the noise at the County Jail, although that might have been the reason: at night, the overcrowded jail was seldom quiet; it sounded incessantly with the hollow echo of drunken moans and anguished wailings, much of it a cacophony of Spanish that Chris didn't understand. It wasn't the noise that kept Chris awake; it was the throbbing despair in his heart that had taken the place of the perverse initial relief he had felt when the tension of waiting for the FBI was finally broken. He felt too ashamed to see his parents ever again; he had lost Alana; his conviction for espionage was certain, and so was the prospect of a long sentence in a wretched cell like the one he was in right now.

Chris weighed his options and concluded that death would be infinitely better than what lay ahead for the rest of his life.

42

"AT LEAST YOU COULD have bought Larks," Chris tried to joke as he took the cigarette offered by Daulton at their first meeting since their arrests. It was during the middle of February in a police van en route from the Federal Courthouse in Los Angeles to the County Jail following hearings over the admissibility as evidence of the statements they had made to the FBI.

The meeting was not a warm reunion of old friends. By now, Chris and Daulton had embarked on a collision course: each had chosen a different path to survival, and if either was to succeed, it meant dynamiting the escape route of the other.

Except for the passing of the cigarette, their communication consisted of nervous glances at each other.

Daulton was amazed by Chris. *He didn't seem to be worried about anything.*

"In no way did he seem troubled, or ill at ease," he later told Kahn. "He wore a smile that could be interpreted as either complacent or idiotic. For a person who is accused of such gross implications, he seemed awfully reserved. His complacency could be attributed to knowing he's backed by 'the company' [the CIA] or someone in his own company [TRW]. Or he could have the mind of a schizophrenic, possibly a psychopathic mind. Or fearing the worst, I could see him believing that he could buy his way into a Russian-US takeover. He'd want to be on top when Russia buries us."

• •

Joel Levine put down the phone in his office at the U.S. Attorney's office and stared in amazement at Richard Stilz. "That was Kahn," he said. "He wants to cop a plea for a *misdemeanor!*"

"I told him 'no,' " he added sarcastically. That was as far as the plea-bargaining negotiations went for Daulton.

The prosecution continued to be much more interested in making a deal with Chris. But it was getting nowhere. Talks with Chelius and Dougherty were continuing on an almost daily basis, but the gap between the negotiators had narrowed only marginally. The prosecution was holding out for a minimum sentence of thirty years for Chris. The defense, which had attempted to sweeten its bid by offering Chris to the CIA for a "debriefing," in which he could let the agency know exactly what information the Russians had purchased, was holding out for only ten to twelve years.

The case wasn't going well for the prosecution in other ways either. The CIA had conducted its own investigation of the Boyce-Lee espionage operation and, apparently through secret sources in the Soviet Union and elsewhere, had gleaned information that confirmed the two youths' commerce with the Russians. Stilz and Levine wanted to use part of the information to mount the prosecution. But the CIA was refusing. Levine made a trip to Langley to discuss the problem. But senior officials of the agency refused to make public any of its secret files on the case. However, the CIA officials, with the concurrence of the National Security Council, agreed to consider an alternative to revealing the information in open court: They would release certain information to Levine and Stilz (who had received Top Security clearances from the agency) and would allow them to show it to the judge who would try the spies. But if the judge decided the defendants must also see the information for a fair trial, the prosecution of Boyce and Lee would be dropped.

• •

Daulton decided to write another letter, this time to his maternal grandmother, with whom he had been close since his childhood. It was a gentle, tender letter which revealed a side of Daulton that his family knew well but that was seldom exposed to his associates in Culiacán and the drug underworld. He expressed his deep love for his grandmother and his sympathy for problems that she was experiencing as a result of her advancing age and noted that the Chinese revered the years between seventy and eighty as precious ones "to be savored and enjoyed, like fine wine.

"For what it's worth," he wrote, "I am sorry for all the trouble my problems have caused everyone. I think it quite inexcusable of me to have brought down havoc on my relatives and parents." There was a

brief prayer in the letter in which Daulton asked God for pity and to save him from death. He asked for his grandmother's compassion and prayers and then said that he was confident that his attorney, Mr. Kahn, would help him. "He will bring out the truth, and the truth will make me free.

"Everyone should have the privilege of rewriting his youth, also reliving it; if not that, then at least rectifying it."

He ended with another expression of love and gratitude to his grandmother for standing by him.

• •

Every day during February, it seemed to Stilz and Levine, they were getting a different report from Washington regarding the testimony of the Mexican policemen. On one day, it was a communiqué from the State Department that the Mexican Government had approved their testifying; the next, a refusal; the next, a compromise proposal to submit written statements from the policemen for submission in court —a worthless proposal because in American courts defendants were entitled to challenge their accusers. In mid-February, a senior Justice Department official, after a conference at the State Department, told his colleagues, "The Mexicans are afraid to let 'em testify; they don't want to get the Russians' noses out of joint."

Brzezinski, who had monitored the negotiations closely, sent word to the Justice Department that he had a plan that he hoped would break the impasse: President Carter would personally ask Mexican President José López Portillo for the cooperation of the Mexican Government in the prosecution of Christopher John Boyce and Andrew Daulton Lee. López Portillo would be coming to Washington within a few days—it was to be the first major diplomatic visit for the new Carter Administration—and President Carter would make his request to the newly elected president of Mexico at this meeting.

• •

Daulton, in one of several long, rambling statements to a friend on the outside, said Boyce had to be pressured to help get Daulton out of this nightmare. Boyce must testify in his behalf so that at least one of them got out of the mess. Boyce *must be* a Government agent. As he put down his thoughts in a torrent of scribbled words, Daulton mused about the nature of his friend:

273

"Is it possible Boyce is so obsessed with birds he lost touch with reality? Birds: Peregrine, Rhyolite, Argus?" he asked in one letter. In another communication he wrote, "I never pressed Boyce about his work. He used to lay it on me, like he was trying to clear his conscience."

"You broached the subject of whether Boyce would accept a bribe and stand pat," Daulton wrote in another long letter to the same friend. "One of two things would induce him. First and most, a prize falcon; or lots of money, so he could get his own falcon—in that order."

Other times his thoughts turned to other sentiments:

The government we've got now—mealy-mouthed, milk-and-water socialists—are leading the last of capitalism and free enterprise to the grave. Our country now is besieged by ten cent politicians pushing socialistic measures to acquire votes from the masses. How irrational for our country to give it all away. . . .

To hell with socialism, long live free enterprise and capitalism. I will not equivocate. I will not retreat a single inch and I will be heard. The more I think about it, the more I see I'm a pawn in a game with no rules or morals. Boyce has manipulated me like a maniquen [*sic*]. God damn fool I am!

Daulton said the more he thought back on the past two years, the more he was convinced that Boyce was either crazy or covering up a secret operation. He was so *flippant* about the whole thing.

Boyce, he said, must be forced into helping him. He must be told that "they don't divide the time—two into 20 years is not ten apiece but 40 total. . . . Men such as me have seen too much of life and considerable more of depression and destruction than the average man. Controlling my emotions is my chief stock in trade. . . .

"Does it make sense that an alcoholic and a Polack pot head could do this on their own?"

43

As February drew to a close, the prosecution's case was ambushed twice, and the optimism of Richard Stilz and Joel Levine plummeted: President López Portillo rejected President Carter's personal appeal for the help of the Mexican Government in prosecuting the two spies, and the plea-bargaining talks with Chris's lawyers ended without an agreement.

The final negotiations were held on February 28. By now, stresses were appearing in the previously cordial professional relationship between the prosecutors and Boyce's defense lawyers. During the pretrial hearings, Dougherty had repeatedly hinted that Stilz and Levine were concealing CIA reports of the case that might help his client; Levine interpreted the remarks as an attack on his personal integrity and had begun to smolder each time he heard the charge renewed. For their part, Boyce's lawyers were convinced that the prosecution was in fact using the cloak of official secrecy and "national security" to impede fair access to information they might be able to use in defending Chris.

Thus, there were now deepening personal animosities at the lawyers' bargaining table besides the fate of Christopher John Boyce. When the plea-bargaining talks finally broke down, the defense was still holding out for a maximum sentence of ten to twelve years, while the prosecutors said they wanted a sentence of thirty years. Secretly, the prosecutors, who still desperately wanted Chris's testimony, were willing to settle for a twenty-year sentence. But they never got a chance to show their final card in the negotiations. Amid the mounting personal bickering between the two sides, the talks collapsed.

• •

After the double setback of losing the testimony of Chris and that of the Mexican police officials, Stilz and Levine had to regroup and develop an alternative battle plan. They would have to link Lee to

espionage without Boyce's testimony and forge an indisputable link between him and the film without testimony from the police who had arrested him and seized the film.

To do so, they began what became, more than anything else, an anthropological expedition into the world Andrew Daulton Lee inhabited—his world of drug pushers and users, of smugglers and dropouts. For most of a month, often working twelve hours or more a day, they met with fellow pushers, Daulton's friends and customers, and the hangers-on in his crowd from The Hill and its environs, searching for clues that would implicate him as a Soviet spy. They assured the young people that they weren't interested in drugs or any transgressions they might have made against Federal or state narcotics-abuse laws. Whatever they said about drugs would not be used against them; the attorneys were interested only in Daulton's possible involvement in selling American secrets to a foreign country. Some of those they approached refused to talk; others, after resisting for several days, gave in. After a while, Stilz and Levine began to sew together a case made up of strands of information from many of the young people. One of the first breakthroughs came at the end of two days of questioning of Darlene Cooper. She spent most of the interview recalling bitterly how Daulton had turned on Palos Verdes girls to heroin and then "used" them. Stilz and Levine pressed for any memories she had of Daulton ever discussing anything about spying. Finally, she recalled a party, more than a year earlier, when Daulton had popped a tiny camera out of his breast pocket and bragged that it was a "spy" camera. Then she said, "Oh, I remember now; once he said he was working as a spy 'for the Russkies.' "

Then came an admission by Barclay Granger, who was promised help by Levine and Stilz in having his sentence for cocaine trafficking reduced if he cooperated. He said he had accompanied Daulton during the purchase of the Minox-B camera, and he described their trip to Mexico and the mysterious tapings of lampposts, and Daulton's joke about being a spy. Carole Benedict denied ever using drugs, but recalled the trip she had made with Daulton to Mazatlán and Daulton's frequent furtive meetings with Chris. Carole—and virtually everyone else Stilz and Levine interviewed—told about the wads of money that Daulton seemed to have all the time.

The pieces began to fit together. Sometimes, after a long day of wading through this subculture, Stilz and Levine would have a drink

together and wonder with amazement at what they had seen and heard. "It was so decadent," Levine would say later. *"Nobody worked. Everyone got up at ten or eleven, played a couple of sets of tennis and made drug deals. They all had so much money, but they never worked. They either got it from their families or through drug dealing. They were just aimless. I thought to myself, My God, what an *empty* life."*

Although the prosecutors were now lining up an effective battery of witnesses who could implicate Daulton, at least circumstantially, as a spy, there remained the critical need to prove beyond a doubt that he and Chris had photographed the Pyramider papers and that there had been an unbroken chain of custody linking the photographs and Daulton; President López Portillo's refusal to cooperate with the prosecution meant that neither Inspector López Malváez nor the arresting officers would be available to testify. Aaron Johnson would testify he had seen film negatives drying in Daulton's bathroom that appeared to have technical drawings on them, and Eileen Heaphy and Thomas Ferguson, the Foreign Service officers in Mexico City, could testify about observing, respectively, his arrest and the removal of an envelope containing microfilm from his pocket at López Malváez' office. But that wouldn't be enough; a more conclusive link between Daulton and the documents had to be found.

• •

In Washington, D.C., Kent Dixon looked through a microscope at an enlarged photograph for a long time. Someone who did not know what he was doing might have wondered about the state of his mental health: there seemed to be absolutely nothing on the photograph he was scrutinizing. It was a picture of white light.

Dixon was a forensic scientist at the FBI's National Crime Laboratory. He wasn't interested in the glowing, blank center of the picture, where images of faces and scenery were usually savored by eager photographers. He was interested in the tiny, almost invisible permutations in the shape of the blank picture frame. It was one of hundreds he had taken with the Minox-B camera found beneath the tambour doors of the rolltop desk in Daulton's bedroom. A criminalist who had worked eight years for the FBI, Dixon believed that virtually all mechanical devices have a personal signature unique to themselves and as individual as a fingerprint. They have defects left at their birth in a

factory, whether they are automobiles, typewriters, cameras or computers, that make them different from other machines that appear to be identical. And once they leave the factory, each device is used differently, evolving an even more singular identity: daily wear and tear, time, weather, usage all leave their imprint. Dixon was looking for the distinctive fingerprint of the Minox that would link it to the film seized in Mexico City; if the link could be made, it would substantially bolster the prosecution's search for an unassailable connection between Daulton and the Pyramider papers.

From experience, Dixon knew of several places to look first for the unique character of the camera. There was the possibility of peculiarities in its lens and shutter; in the framing area where the film was held behind the shutter; in the sprocket wheels that advanced the film and sometimes left marks on the film itself; the pressure plate behind the film that can scratch the film or leave deposits of dirt. Dixon often looked first at the framing area of a camera in cases such as this. In his experience, many cameras had burrs or imperfections left during manufacture that affected the shape of the photograph made by the camera. Also, dirt tended to accumulate around the edges of the framing area after being forced there by film rolled through the camera.

Dixon peered through the microscope at the photo he had made of the blank white image. He noticed that the edge of the frame at one corner was not perfectly square; there was a slight curvature. His eyes followed the edge of the frame of the picture and began to see small black dots and projections. They were barely as large as a pinhead sticking up into the edge of the photograph, but magnified, they appeared as enormous anomalies in the seemingly sharp lines of the picture. They could have been burrs in the metal, scraped there during manufacture, or just blobs of dirt, Dixon thought. He wasn't sure. He noticed a tiny imperfection at another spot on the picture's edge, then more tiny specks which he concluded were bits of dust or dirt. Dixon had found at least part of the unique character of the camera.

Now he turned his attention to another set of pictures—blowups made from the strips of negatives seized in Mexico City. Scanning one of the photos through his microscope, Dixon ignored the center of the picture—the typewritten data, the technical drawings and the words TOP SECRET. He was interested instead in the outer edges of the picture.

He found what he was looking for: there was a perfect match.

Dixon had discovered the same pattern of irregularities and flecks of dirt on the photograph from Mexico City that he had found on the photos made with the camera found in Daulton's rolltop desk.

Stilz and Levine got the news and decided they were ready for trial.

•   •

The trial was scheduled to begin March 15, 1977. But the defendants' attacks on the constitutionality of their arrests and efforts to block use of their statements to the FBI caused Robert J. Kelleher, the Federal judge who had been assigned to handle the case, to order several postponements.

If Superior Court Judge Burch Donahue had a reputation as a compassionate man ever willing to give a defendant still another chance, the reputation of Judge Kelleher probably leaned in the opposite direction. A tennis nut who was a former captain of the U.S. Davis Cup team and former president of the U.S. Lawn Tennis Association, Kelleher was considered implacably honest and evenhanded in his treatment of defendants, although a few defense lawyers who practiced in his court complained that he tended to side with the prosecution on toss-up calls. Kelleher was well known for his impatience in dealing with lawyers whose knowledge of the law was deficient according to his standards, and he seldom hesitated to tongue-lash lawyers who he decided were getting out of line. Educated at Williams College and Harvard Law School, Kelleher, aged sixty-four, had been a Beverly Hills lawyer for twenty years before being appointed to the Federal bench in 1971 by President Nixon. A tall man with graying hair, Kelleher was an aristocratic-looking figure on the bench, and there was never any doubt when he was sitting there who was running the courtroom.

When, after weeks of on-again, off-again pretrial hearings, Kelleher ruled that the arrests, the seizure of evidence and the statements made by the youths were admissible at trial, few people who knew Kelleher were surprised. He said the FBI had acted lawfully and properly. His decision meant that the trial would proceed now with the prosecution's large quiver of evidence against Chris and Daulton virtually untouched.

Ken Kahn, arguing that his client's interests were different from those of Christopher John Boyce, sought and received a severance of

the cases; Judge Kelleher ordered that the two friends be tried separately.

. .

Daulton was still confiding his thoughts to a friend outside the jail. Boyce, he continued to insist, had to be convinced of his foolishness in dragging Daulton down with him. Boyce was the only one who *really* knew what had happened, the only one who could really implicate Daulton. "Boyce was the malevolence behind this entire nightmare," he said. He had informed Boyce the previous November, after being ejected from the Russian embassy, that he didn't want to continue the operation, but Chris, he maintained, had insisted on one more delivery.

In the early stages of their operation, Daulton said, Boyce had told him they could squeeze the Soviets for $50,000 a month. When the Russians gave him only $5,000 for some of the codes, Daulton said, he had considered them a fraud. The Russians, he said, invariably wanted more and different information—details about infrared sensors, the names of company executives, photographs of the birds and other stuff that Chris refused to supply.

"Infra red. That's what the Russians wanted but didn't get. They're really paranoid about the superior quality of our Recon Birds. They must be in the dark ages ('pun') with their infrared cameras."

In effect, Daulton said, his role in the scheme had been to make the Russians believe that they could keep up to date on the accuracy of American infrared sensors. Yet, he said, they had sought this information for a year and still hadn't received it. But he had managed to keep them on the hook. He said he had told the KGB agents that there were "thousands of birds" going over their country daily. "If they wanted to know what we knew," Daulton said, "they'd have to play ball."

If nothing else, Daulton said, if his case was brought to trial he would make a "laughing stock" out of TRW. Here was a company, he wrote, that had sent the Viking probe to Mars and yet "can't control alcoholism in their own internal security."

Daulton repeatedly returned to his theory of disinformation. It was commonplace in espionage, he insisted, for one country to leak erroneous data to its enemies, but in order to make the information believable, everything had to be done in a way that gave it credibility. "What better way to leak information than through an edifice like TRW, using

a young clerk and a capitalistic pot head?'' By leaking intelligence to the Soviets about the flock of reconnaissance birds secretly flying over Russian and Chinese territory, the United States quietly ''makes it known to the Russkies that we're hep to their charades of peaceful coexistence. . . .''

If this wasn't a carefully orchestrated plot by the CIA, he asked, then why hadn't Boyce given the Russians the information they wanted? ''The Russians wanted photos of Argus and Rhyolite. Boyce had easy access, but he never would do it for them. In Mexico [after] Boyce and I left the embassy, Boyce said they're never going to see pictures of Rhyolite or Argus. Joke: Boyce claimed Rhyo might see them instead. . . .

''Obviously, there is a more complex and demented side of Boyce that alludes [sic] us. Or else why would he refuse the Russians any photos?''

On one of his letters Daulton appended an afterthought. How, he asked, could he even be considered to be a Soviet spy? He had always voted Republican, he said, and he had never even taken a political science course.

• •

Judge Kelleher and the attorneys for the two defendants agreed Chris would be tried first.

As his trial approached, he and Daulton saw each other only rarely, and briefly, when their paths crossed during pretrial court appearances. But the chasm between them was growing daily, and whatever remnants of their friendship had been left in January had all but withered by April under the heat of their respective efforts to survive. Chris blamed their arrest on Daulton's foolishness in his frontal attack on the embassy, but, more, he was enraged that Daulton had turned on him now.

He made the discovery during pretrial hearings: Daulton's lawyers announced that their client intended to prove his innocence by showing that he had been enticed into spying by Christopher John Boyce under the pretext of working for the CIA—and that he had been abandoned by his friend and the CIA after his chance arrest by Mexican police. Chris was further antagonized against his old friend when a mutual acquaintance sent a message to Chris from Daulton urging him to take full blame for the espionage operation. Chris ignored Daulton when

they saw each other, and when he did speak, his few words were a caustic denunciation of Daulton's stupidity for getting arrested and his betrayal of him.

Further pretrial hearings and other procedural delays consumed the final weeks of March and the first few days of April. Shortly before Chris's trial was finally scheduled to start, Chris and Daulton encountered each other at the jail again, and afterward, Daulton told Ken Kahn about the meeting:

"I managed to have a few preliminary words with Boyce to break the ice; it would have gone further, but a marshal stopped us," he said. Boyce's spirits, he added, seemed somewhat improved. "After court, in the transfer cells, I walked past and he said, 'cheerio.' He's beginning to weaken." He asked Kahn to counsel him on "what to say to him or what to ask him. Our present diplomatic aura is very shaky. I must tread carefully."

Daulton also revealed some doubts about the strategy for his defense:

"If there is no CIA involvement, then aren't we putting ourselves out on a limb? I mean, all this could be coincidence."

• •

Since the night of his arrest, George Chelius had implored Chris to write to his parents. Chelius had known Chris's father as an initially standoffish boss with a conservative point of view who, after a while, warmed up to his friends. He knew that he adored his eldest son, and he had known of the many trips they had taken together and the many afternoons he had spent coaching teams on which Chris played. And so he had been amazed to discover the depth of Chris's philosophical estrangement from his father during the long night they had spent in his cell after Chris was arrested. Later, he had delivered a message to Chris from his parents: they loved him and would stick by him and wanted to see him and help with his defense. But Chris told his jailers he did not want any visits from his parents.

Finally, on the eve of his trial, at Chelius' continued urgings, Chris consented to write a letter to his father. In the letter, he wrote that he did not want any members of his family at the trial.

44

THE ESPIONAGE TRIAL of Christopher John Boyce started at 10 A.M. on April 12, 1977, in the United States District Court for the Central District of California. A jury of seven men and five women was selected to hear the case in a wood-paneled courtroom on the second floor of the Los Angeles Federal Courthouse, an imposing monolith of concrete and glass a block from the city's landmark City Hall tower.

There were unusual aspects of the trial from the beginning. Judge Kelleher immediately ordered his bailiff to prevent spectators, except reporters with official credentials, from taking notes at the trial. Although the judge did not explain his reasons for the unusual order, it was evident that he anticipated that sensitive defense information would be discussed at the trial and wanted to prevent, as best he could, agents of hostile countries from recording the facts unraveled in his courtroom.

Chris's face was pale from life in the shadows of his cell. Nevertheless, as he was escorted into the courtroom, he looked, as ever, the scrubbed, all-American boy. He was dressed in a corduroy suit that was the color of polished copper and an open-necked sport shirt. He sat down at the defense table with Chelius and Dougherty, and a Federal marshal was nearby.

At the prosecution table, Stilz and Levine sat with FBI Agent Jim White, the bureau's case officer assigned to the prosecution; sitting near them were other Department of Justice lawyers and close behind, in the spectator gallery, a lawyer for the Central Intelligence Agency.

Ken Kahn was auditing the trial in preparation for his defense of Daulton. Ken Kahn's mother was there too. A petite woman with gray hair and intelligent eyes, Fay Kahn would remain throughout Chris's trial as well as Daulton's. "This is the biggest case Kenny's ever had," she replied proudly when a reporter inquired about her devoted attendance at the proceedings. Sitting near Mrs. Kahn on the opening day of the trial was a curious-looking man wearing what appeared to be a

military uniform—a blue tunic similar to the kind Air Force officers wear and a matching cap. But on close examination it proved to be something else: the tunic and cap were festooned with toy rockets and plastic airplanes and a collage of badges issued by political candidates of years past and assorted commercial enterprises, and he introduced himself as "General Hershey Bar." The general was a court buff, the kind of spectator who can be found in any major court around the country on any given day, monitoring the drama of other people's lives.

• •

Several days before the trial began, Joel Levine had carried three large cardboard cartons into the chambers of Judge Kelleher. The boxes were stuffed with some of America's most sensitive secrets, detailing how the Central Intelligence Agency and other agencies collected photos and other information about the Soviet Union, China and other countries from far out in space. There were documents about Projects Rhyolite and Argus and other reconnaissance satellites, and they described how much of the data from the satellites flowed through the Black Vault at TRW. There were also reports of the CIA's own investigation of the Boyce-Lee case.

The delivery had been a critical juncture for the prosecution: if the judge read the papers and then decided it was essential that the defense lawyers also be given access to them, the Department of Justice, on instructions from the National Security Council, planned to suspend prosecution of the two youths. But Judge Kelleher, after reading the documents and the CIA's investigative reports, decreed that they were *not* vital to the defense. With that, the prosecution had gone forward, despite strident objections from lawyers for both defendants.

It was now up to Stilz and Levine to prove that Chris and, by inference, Daulton had conspired to steal the classified Pyramider documents with the intent of selling them to the U.S.S.R., and then had actually done so. The CIA had declassified portions of the Pyramider papers for use as evidence and had allowed copies to be made available to each defendant.

• •

With Chris's statement to the FBI on the night of his arrest now certain to be used against him, his lawyers began the trial with a piti-

fully thin hand of cards to play. They retreated to a strategy that they believed gave them their only chance of an acquittal: to argue that the Pyramider documents were "overclassified"; that they had no value to the Russians because the project had never been implemented, and moreover, that the technical data in the study were essentially common knowledge available to any sophisticated electronics engineer. The strategy was to convince the jury that the material really didn't deserve a top security label and that Chris had not sold secrets to the Soviet Union that would harm the United States. "We'll have testimony that the government could have gone to any Radio Shack to get that kind of thing," Dougherty confided to a reporter on the opening day of the trial.

The trial began with a summary by Joel Levine of the prosecution's allegations. In itself the opening argument was newsworthy: it was the first public admission by the United States Government that the CIA and TRW were involved in clandestine satellite operations. Levine told the jury that the case he would present involved a secret project called "Pyramider," purloined secrets in potted plants, miniature cameras and other elements of intrigue that he made sound like a James Bond thriller. He told the jurors they would be hearing a lot about a man named Andrew Daulton Lee, a childhood friend of Christopher John Boyce. "From that friendship," he said, "the seeds of an espionage conspiracy were born."

• •

FBI Agent White was the first witness and presented a long review of Chris's statement on the night of his arrest, including the damaging allegation "He told me that they had delivered to the Soviets the contents of thousands of documents."

"Thousands of documents?" Stilz asked.

"That's right, thousands of documents."

White did not mention Rhyolite or Argus or the other classified projects Chris had discussed during his interrogation by White. Dougherty, in his cross-examination of White, did not mention them either; Judge Kelleher had already advised the defense attorneys that he would not allow any mention of the other projects.

There was testimony from the FBI agents who had arrested Chris, and who maintained that his confession had been made voluntarily; from Thomas Ferguson, the Foreign Service officer, who described

Daulton's arrest and the film in his pocket with the words "Pyramider" and "Top Secret" on them; and from Regis Carr of TRW, who described Chris's job in the vault and said he had not been briefed on Pyramider and therefore had not had legal access to information about it. To link Chris and Daulton, Stilz and Levine presented Barclay Granger, Darlene Cooper and other friends of Daulton's as witnesses.

After a week of testimony, the jury for Daulton's trial was impaneled by Judge Kelleher and immediately sequestered in a hotel to await the outcome of Chris's trial. The judge took the unusual step of sequestering jurors in a trial even before testimony had begun because he did not want them exposed to news reports of the Boyce trial that could influence their judgment of Daulton.

Before Chris's trial had been under way very long, reporters began to notice a man with reddish hair and a ruddy complexion monitoring every session with what seemed to be extraordinary intensity. He sat alone in the back of the courtroom, his chin resting on the back of the pewlike seat in front of him, following every word of testimony. Initially, it seemed he was just another court buff watching an unusual trial. But after a while, reporters noticed that during each recess or lunch break, he promptly went to a pay telephone down the hallway from the courtroom and spoke animatedly in a foreign language that sounded Slavic to some people who overheard him. After one such call on the third day of the trial, a reporter introduced himself to the man and asked if he was Russian or if he was observing the trial for another foreign country.

Caught off guard by the question, he answered, "I am Polish." Eyeing the reporter warily, he refused to identify himself further or otherwise explain his interest in the trial.

"I'm not representing anybody but myself and my shoes," he said when the reporter persisted. And then he fled into an elevator moments before the door closed.

He was back the next day. Identifying the man and his purpose became a contest for reporters covering the trial, and after an article mentioning the mysterious Pole appeared in *The New York Times,* the Columbia Broadcasting System assigned an artist to sketch him, and for several nights a week he was featured on the six-o'clock news with Walter Cronkite. But reporters never managed to find out who he was.

• •

Kent Dixon, using large photo-blowup comparisons for illustration, testified that tests in the FBI Crime Laboratory had forged an indisputable link between the Minox camera in Daulton's home and the photos of the Pyramider documents; an FBI fingerprint expert testified that Chris's fingerprints had been found on the Pyramider documents and those of Chris and Daulton had been found on circuit boards for one of the encrypting machines. A Palos Verdes travel agent testified that Daulton had made airline reservations with her to go to Vienna—one of many such examples which illustrated that Daulton, as much as Chris, was on trial here, even though at the moment only Chris's fate was being debated.

Leslie Dirks, the CIA's deputy director for science and technology, a tall, gaunt, balding physicist with the sterile aura of a pathology laboratory, traced the history of the Pyramider project. He testified that even though the TRW design had not been implemented, the disclosure of data from the study to the Soviet Union would be a serious setback to American intelligence. Communicating with secret agents, he testified, was vital to fulfilling the CIA's fundamental responsibility —to avert another Pearl Harbor. "Agents around the world are our primary sources. Only from the minds of men can we find out what is going to happen in the world," he said. Knowing the state of American expertise in covert satellite-communications technology at the time the study was made and the kinds of options that were considered for providing secure communications with agents would be invaluable to Soviet analysts, he asserted emphatically. In more than four hours of cross-examination, George Chelius did not knock any significant holes in Dirks's testimony. He had left a solid impression with the jury that Chris's actions involved grave harm to the United States.

With Dirks, the prosecution rested its case.

•   •

By this point in the trial, Bill Dougherty and Joel Levine were no longer talking to each other except through the judge. With little ammunition to work with, Dougherty had repeatedly hammered at the prosecution's refusal to give it access to all the information it possessed from the CIA regarding the vault and the agency's investigation of the case. Judge Kelleher invariably upheld prosecution efforts to keep the trial from wandering into national-security matters beyond the bare essentials of the Pyramider papers, frustrating the defense

attorneys. In open court as well as private discussions, Dougherty had assailed Levine and Stilz for not giving the defense access to all of the information it had, and Levine was furious at what he perceived as assaults on his integrity. After one such encounter outside the court-room, Levine threatened to punch Dougherty. The confrontation cooled before any punches were thrown, but Levine's anger had subsided only for the moment.

. .

Skillfully, the defense began to lay out its meager cards. Dougherty and Chelius presented a witness from Stanford University, an engineering professor named Martin Hellman who asserted that much of the information in the Pyramider documents was common technical data known to any well-informed electronics engineer. William Florence, a onetime Pentagon classification expert who had presented effective testimony along similar lines at the trial of Ellsberg and Russo four years earlier, claimed that the Government routinely overclassified documents. And Victor L. Marchetti, the former senior CIA staff officer and coauthor of *The CIA and the Cult of Intelligence*, was called to provide an unusual look at the internal CIA planning process.

He testified that a covert communication system for spies similar to Pyramider had secretly been proposed by the agency to Congress in 1968. But he claimed it was only part of a "dog and pony show" meant to impress the members of a Congressional subcommittee that monitored the agency with an insincere, exotic proposal from science fiction. There had been resistance in the agency to actually developing such a system, he added, because it would have been a violation of a tacit agreement with the Soviet Union that the espionage satellites both countries used were to be restricted to passive missions like reconnaissance and were not to play an active role such as communicating with spies.

On cross-examination, however, Marchetti acknowledged that he had not been privy to CIA decision-making processes for more than five years and admitted he might be unaware of more recent work on such projects.

Alfred J. Oliveri, a public-school teacher who lived near the Boyces in Palos Verdes, was called as a character witness, and he testified that he had known Christopher Boyce since 1959, and "his reputation has always been one of honesty and integrity; it was above reproach."

The next person who took the witness stand also knew Chris very well.

"I've known Christopher Boyce since he was an altar boy and a student of mine," Msgr. Thomas J. McCarthy said in the gentle Boston-Irish voice that was one of his trademarks. Asked by Dougherty to describe Chris's reputation in the community, the gray-haired priest said, "To my knowledge, he has the highest reputation for truth, veracity and integrity." That was the end of his testimony.

A reporter intercepted the priest in the hallway outside the courtroom and asked him if he had any explanation of why Chris and Daulton were both now accused of being Soviet spies.

"For idealism? I don't know. When I heard about their arrest on the radio in my car, I had to pull to the side of the road and stop," he said. "I couldn't believe it. And then I thought about it: These kids have come through a revolution. They had tremendous pressure on them, peer pressure; there were drugs; they had the moral filth of Watergate, the war; they went through that whole era when national leaders were playing footsie with crooked people. Chris is most surprising; he always loved the underdog. I admired him so much. But he grew up in a different ambiance than I did. Maybe he was disillusioned."

Monsignor McCarthy died less than a year later. Two weeks before his death, he told an acquaintance that he still prayed for his two former altar boys.

45

"KENNY, I'M SCARED," Daulton wrote to Ken Kahn as Chris's trial appeared to be winding up and his own loomed closer. "If our defense is based in its entirety on CIA involvement and this assumption should prove wrong, what is left for defense?"

Kahn reassured him again that the defense they had agreed on—that Chris had enticed him into a CIA scheme to spread false information

—was the best they had. Furthermore, he said he believed it was true; he was convinced, he told Daulton, that Chris was a CIA agent.

.   .

On the afternoon of April 25, 1977, George Chelius and Bill Dougherty decided to make a final attempt to make a deal with the prosecution.

They agreed they'd probably not scored enough points for the defense to undermine the strong prosecution case anchored in Chris's own admission of guilt. They still maintained from a constitutional standpoint that Chris's confession had not been voluntary according to the Supreme Court's *Miranda* decision, and therefore shouldn't be admissible as evidence; but this was now a moot point. It appeared that Chris was going to be convicted, and his only hope now was a deal.

They met with Stilz and Levine in the offices of the U.S. Attorney on an upper floor of the same building where the trial was being held. The defense lawyers proposed that if the prosecution agreed to a maximum sentence of ten years, Chris would plead guilty, testify against Daulton and tell everything he knew about their espionage operation to the CIA. Otherwise, they said, Chris would take the stand the following day.

"Ten years!" Stilz said sardonically.

"We already turned that down," Levine said.

Things were different now, the defense lawyers suggested. Unless there was a deal, they hinted, Chris might say embarrassing things from the witness stand the next day.

"No deal," Levine said. "We told you we wouldn't take that deal two months ago!"

"You weren't going to lose a ground station in Australia before," one of the defense lawyers snapped.

"Get the fuck out of here," Levine said, and that ended the final round of plea-bargaining negotiations for Chris.

.   .

While this scene was being acted out by the lawyers at the courthouse, Chris was being transported back to the Los Angeles County Jail.

The trial had confirmed what Chris had expected from the moment

he saw the carloads of men swarm around him at the turkey ranch—indeed, what he had expected from the moment he got the call from Daulton on the night of his first contact with the KGB. Chris *knew* that he was going to be convicted—and he had decided to make a final stab at the system he hated now more than ever. He had decided to plot his own murder.

Many times during the past few weeks, in the solitude of the tiny isolation cell, he had told himself suicide was the only reasonable ending to what had begun two years before. But if he was going to commit suicide, shouldn't he give his death some meaning? Why not stick it to them where it would hurt when he did?

It really didn't matter, he mused, who got the blame for his murder. Some people would blame the CIA, others the KGB. To Chris, they were one and the same. Most people, he thought, would probably blame the CIA. He was going to kill himself and make it appear that he had been murdered by someone who didn't want him on the witness stand the next day.

The basic plan had taken shape in his mind over the past week: He would hang himself with the electric cord from the radio in his cell. But before he did, he would arrange the cell like a stage set bristling with clues to murder—a murder committed by someone attempting to make his death appear like suicide. His resources to carry out the plot were slim, he thought, but they would be enough.

The first thing that occurred to him was to leave an ample amount of toothpaste in his mouth when he placed his makeshift noose around his neck—who would commit suicide with a mouthful of toothpaste? He would throw his toothbrush under the bed to make it appear that it had been flung there when Chris was overpowered while brushing his teeth; he would leave notes in the pockets of his pants, written to a friend and to Bill Dougherty, saying he was extremely optimistic about the way the trial was going and expressing hopes for the future.

Methodically, Chris began arranging the set in the small cell: He pulled out the edge of the blanket on his bed so it looked as if it had been yanked out during a struggle; he ripped open a package of cigarettes and stomped on it to make it appear as if it had been smashed during a fight; he laid out the toothpaste and toothbrush like a craftsman neatly arranging his tools before starting a job; and then he wrote the letter to his friend on fancy tissue-paper stationery and got ready to carry out the simulated murder sometime after midnight.

Midnight approached and passed. In the dim light of the jail, Chris stared at the materials he had assembled to stage his murder and cursed himself for procrastinating. Was it the old dichotomy that had haunted him for as long as he could remember?

He tried to resist the doubts that were keeping him from his final step of preparation—pulling the wire from the radio and tying his noose. But he couldn't fend off the doubts; they taunted him, and his mind groped for alternatives: perhaps, he thought, there was still a chance of acquittal; if he was convicted, wasn't there a chance he could escape?

Chris thought at length about a conversation he had had with Victor Marchetti. He had sensed in Marchetti the same disgust he felt for the dirty tricks of the agency; perhaps, he had told Marchetti, the way to get his revenge on the agency was to say in public something the CIA spooks did not want to hear.

Chris didn't go to sleep that night. As the implements of his suicide/ murder plot lay beside him, he read and reread the statement he had made to the FBI on the night of his arrest, memorizing it so that he would not trip himself with inconsistencies. Then he prepared a list of questions that he would give Bill Dougherty to ask him the next day.

From time to time as he wrote the questions and rehearsed his answers, Chris's thoughts went back to suicide and he scolded himself for lacking the final measure of courage to implement his plan. But ultimately this sense of guilt was overpowered by a different kind of guilt: he realized he could not shake off the belief that he felt planted deep somewhere in him, that it was a mortal sin to commit suicide— and to die with a mortal sin on his soul meant burning in the eternal fires of hell.

Besides, he admitted to himself, he wanted to live.

But, it was more than that: he had decided he could hurt the evil he hated more by taking the stand than by killing himself.

Since his years at St. John Fisher, Chris had loved public speaking and debate. He had never minded taking a risk. Now he had a chance to speak for his life.

. .

After his night without sleep, Chris took the stand shortly after 9 A.M. on April 26, 1977, and was sworn in.

Under gentle questioning by Dougherty, Chris began by sketching the details of his life until the middle of 1974: his youth in Palos Verdes; his attendance at Harbor College, Loyola and Cal Poly. In July, 1974, he said, his father had helped him obtain a job at TRW; he traced the first few months on the job, his introduction to "black projects" and his assignment to the Black Vault.

And then Chris got ready to give the story that he had sketched out the night before of how—and why—he had become a Russian spy.

"Do you know Andrew Daulton Lee?" Dougherty asked.

"Yes."

"How long have you known Andrew Daulton Lee?"

"Since I was a child. A long time."

Dougherty asked Chris if he could recall a conversation he had had with Daulton shortly after he took the job in the Black Vault, and Chris said he could.

"I was at a party over at his house. Not too many people—a fairly small party." After everyone else had left, "we were sitting down in the back of the house and we were drinking, smoking pot, and he began to talk about . . . He was on—he had violated his probation—and . . ."

"Well, were you discussing politics before he got into this?"

"We were discussing problems with the government in general and his particular problems."

"Were you discussing any major problems of national interest?"

"We were discussing Watergate and Richard Nixon, and he had read a book and he was talking about how the Central Intelligence Agency had killed President Kennedy, and that I didn't believe. You know, it was just up for discussion, and we talked about Chile, and he said he was leaving the country to escape arrest. He didn't want to go back to prison, and he said that his probation officers were really giving him a raw deal, that they were really giving him the shaft."

The conversation turned back to Chile, he continued. "A democratic government had been overthrown," he said, and they agreed the CIA had probably been behind it.

"He said that the government, as he knew it, was really giving him the shaft, and I said, 'If you think that's bad, you should hear what the Central Intelligence Agency is doing to the Australians.' And he asked me what, and I told him that—"

293

Stilz lunged from his seat.

"Your Honor, at this point, I'm going to object. That conversation is irrelevant."

"Sustained."

Chris continued to try to make a point about Australia, but Stilz battled to keep him off the subject. Slowly, however, in his interrupted answers and Stilz' hurried objections, it was becoming apparent to spectators in the courtroom that Chris knew something sinister about America's dealings with Australia.

What wasn't yet apparent was that Chris was establishing the foundation for the defense he hoped would keep him out of prison: he was about to charge that he had been an unwilling spy, that he had been blackmailed by Daulton into being a spy.

Chris continued his testimony under Dougherty's probing. Shortly after the initial discussion with Daulton, he said, the subject of Australia had come up again. Once again, Stilz recognized possible disaster ahead and started to rise. But he was too late. Chris said:

"And I informed him that part of my daily duties . . . I worked in a communication room . . . part of my daily duties were to continue a deception against the Australians."

There was a stir in the courtroom. The television-network artists and reporters seated at the press table looked at each other as if to say, What did he mean by *that?*

"Your Honor," Stilz said urgently, "at this point I'm going to object. Irrelevant."

"Sustained."

There was a banging noise in the back of the courtroom, and heads turned instinctively to see who it was. It was General Hershey Bar in full regalia pushing open the doors of the courtroom and reclaiming his seat after visiting the rest room. The tension of Chris's testimony was broken momentarily.

"All right," Dougherty continued. "Did you tell him you wanted to do something about this information?"

"I said I would like to make it known, but that I didn't want to get in trouble for it. I didn't want anything to come back to me. And he said his father knew many influential people. . . ."

"At this point did you have any intent or desire to hurt the United States in any way?"

"No, sir, not at all."

Chris then lied that he had agreed to write a letter documenting the still undefined grievances about Australia and that Daulton had volunteered to have his father make it public through unnamed influential friends, thereby exposing official shenanigans as Ellsberg and Russo had done. Subsequently, Chris claimed, Daulton informed him that he had not passed the information so that it could be made public, as he'd promised, but that instead, he had sold Chris's letter to the Russians in Mexico City, and demanded more information from the Black Vault under the threat of exposing Chris. If he didn't give him more secrets, Daulton had threatened to blackmail his father, he said. Chris said that he had agreed to go along with Daulton's demands—but only because of his threats—and he had responded by giving him worthless, outdated information.

"I never—never planned for this to happen," he asserted.

"Did you ever willfully transmit information relating to the national defense to anybody at all with the belief that it would be used by—to an advantage by a foreign nation?" Dougherty asked.

"No, sir," Chris lied. He spoke surely, decisively. There was a plaintive, boyish aura to his testimony that gave it verisimilitude. At times, he seemed on the verge of tears. He seemed to some in the courtroom a child trapped by forces he could not comprehend or control.

"And did you ever willfully or knowingly act as an agent for a foreign government?"

"Not willfully, but I knew that's what I had become."

The interrogation had lasted more than two hours, and it left the courtroom in shocked silence.

•　•

Stilz' cross-examination was brutal. He started by getting Chris repeatedly to admit that he knew he was transmitting *classified* information to the Russians in violation of the law and secrecy pledges he had signed. Stilz showed him signed copies of his project-briefing security pledges from the CIA archives.

"You admitted to the FBI that you received fifteen thousand dollars?"

"Yes, sir."

"And did he [Lee] coerce and pressure you into taking this money, Mr. Boyce?"

"Coerced me and pressured me into the whole organization, the whole system," Chris answered.

"Including receiving money for the classified materials given to the Russians?"

"No, he did not."

. .

The trial was recessed after a full day with Chris on the stand.

The next day, the morning newspapers carried his allusions to mysterious deceptions against Australia, and when the trial resumed, the press gallery had grown to include a delegation of correspondents from the Australian press.

Stilz brought up Chris's acceptance of $5,000 from Boris during his trip to Mexico City.

"Mr. Boyce, isn't it a fact that the reason they thought that you were valuable is because you were going to go back to school and study Soviet history and policy with the eventual aim of working in the State Department?"

"I said I was going back to school," Chris answered, "and they suggested that I study that, and they said that it would be a good idea to go to work for the State Department. And I agreed to do that, knowing that there was absolutely no way I could ever go to work for the State Department; and I was accomplishing not having access to classified documents; I was getting out of TRW, and what possible good would I be to them?"

"Did you not begin to take a course in Soviet policy requested by the Soviets?"

"It was a Soviet foreign policy class," Chris said. "I had just gone through an experience with them, and there it was. I took it. It's not illegal to take that. What if they checked up on me, Mr. Stilz?"

"Mr. Boyce," the prosecutor hammered back, "you knew that your actions over the two-year period, by causing classified materials, Top Secret materials, to be transmitted to the Russians . . . you knew you were doing an extreme disservice to your country, didn't you?"

"I dragged my feet the whole time and I don't think I gave them anything they could use."

Stilz had finished his cross-examination. Dougherty moved in for one last attempt to demonstrate the defense's theory that Chris had had compelling, ideologically motivated reasons for his behavior. Re-

calling his earlier testimony about the party at which Chris claimed to have discussed with Daulton the possibility of making public a letter, Dougherty asked Chris to recount the conversation.

"We talked about—" Chris began. Stilz jumped up.

"Your Honor, if I may interrupt for a moment, may counsel approach the bench?" he said urgently.

"No," the judge said. "You may answer."

"You talked about politics, you talked about Lee's arrest warrants," Dougherty said. "Now, what else did you talk about?"

"Labor unions."

"Specifically, what labor unions?"

"Australian labor unions."

Stilz and Levine looked at each other, puzzled and surprised. They had been prepared for the possibility that Chris might attempt to talk about certain facets of the Australian CIA operation; but labor unions? They didn't know what he was talking about.

"In what sense did you talk about Australian labor unions?" Dougherty continued.

Stilz rose to his feet. "Objection. Irrelevant."

"Overruled," Kelleher said.

"The suspension of strikes—the suppression of strikes by the Central Intelligence Agency of Australian labor unions."

Stilz was now on his feet shouting his objections. But Kelleher had allowed Chris to make his point: he had been revulsed by the discovery of American manipulation of Australian unions and unspecified deceptions against the same country.

That ended Chris's testimony.

• •

For the next month, reports of CIA activities in Australia dominated the front pages of several Australian newspapers. Using Chris's disclosure of CIA tampering in Australia as a springboard, the newspapers initiated investigative series which suggested that the ouster of Prime Minister Whitlam might have been orchestrated by the American intelligence service, and there were fresh reports almost daily of different alleged CIA manipulations of political, economic and labor affairs in the country. None of the Australian journalists managed to discover the "deception" that Chris had alluded to—the Rhyolite-Argus deception. Nevertheless, the close Australian–American alliance that had

been cemented in World War II was suddenly buffeted by a political tornado, and the incident touched off day after day of stormy sessions in the Australian parliament. There were demands for a complete investigation of the CIA's role in Australia. But the government managed to ride out the storm. It simply remained aloof from the crisis, refusing to respond to the allegations and biding its time until they subsided.

Precisely what transpired in hurried talks between Australian and American diplomats in the aftermath of Chris's testimony has never been disclosed. But a few months later, the two governments announced that they had renegotiated and renewed the Executive Agreement under which the American bases were operated on Australian soil. No details of the new agreement were ever made public.

The political storm was suppressed for the moment. But perhaps for decades to come, the long shadow of the CIA would loom over relations between two old allies.

46 "WE REQUEST no lunch today," the jury foreman wrote on the torn scrap of yellow legal-size notepaper sent to Judge Kelleher at 11:21 A.M. on April 28, 1977, shortly after the fate of Christopher John Boyce had been placed in the hands of the jury. On the Boyce defense team, there was a glimmer of hope that Chris's eloquently told story of blackmail and coercion might have swayed at least one juror. "All you need is one woman on that jury who'd like to mother that nice kid," a reporter speculated, and Dougherty agreed.

As soon as the Boyce jury left the courtroom to begin deliberations, the jury that had been chosen to hear the case against Daulton was ushered into the room, and his trial began before Chris's was over.

In his opening argument, Kahn broadened further the rupture between the two friends:

The defense in the case of *The United States of America v. Andrew Daulton Lee,* ne said, would prove that Daulton had been employed by

298

the Central Intelligence Agency to disseminate false information to the Russians as part of a calculated intelligence scheme, and that Christopher Boyce had recruited the defendant for the mission. His client, he said, was not a spy. "He is an outright capitalist—he's a right-on American."

Sitting near the front of the spectator gallery were Dr. Daulton Bradley Lee, who looked thin, extraordinarily gray and very tired, and his wife, Anne. The mysterious Pole did not appear for Daulton's trial.

At 1:17 that afternoon, the foreman of the Boyce jury sent another message to the judge, scrawled on yellow paper: "We would like a definition of 'willfully and knowingly' in reference to Count One and the admonition of duress in reference to Count One."

The note paralyzed the court. Testimony against Daulton, which had been scheduled to resume after the lunch recess, was suspended as Stilz and Levine fought to convince Judge Kelleher that no further directions need be given the jury. Dougherty urged compliance with the request, seeing a message of hope in the sheet of yellow paper.

Whether the information should be provided the jury was still being debated heatedly at 2:40 P.M. when the question became moot. The jury sent another note that read:

"In regard to our previous request, please disregard it."

Eleven minutes later, there was a fourth note: "We have reached a unanimous verdict."

Chris was ordered to the courtroom from a holding cell on a lower floor. He entered the courtroom with a U.S. marshal, and the verdict came quickly:

Guilty on all eight counts of espionage and conspiracy to commit espionage.

It had taken the jury less than three and a half hours.

Chris listened to the verdict at the defense table. The muscles of his cheeks tightened when the jury filed back into the room, but when the bailiff read the verdict, there was absolutely no expression on his face. He turned to his attorneys and said resignedly, *"C'est la vie."*

After the jury was discharged, Judge Kelleher declared a recess until the Lee trial could be resumed. Chelius and Dougherty shook Chris's hand and said they were sorry. Chris managed a smile and thanked the lawyers, and he was escorted out of the courtroom, now emptying of reporters and spectators. Daulton was outside, waiting for his trial to continue; he had heard the news of Chris's conviction from another

marshal. When he saw Chris leave the courtroom, Daulton's face was empty and grim. The two old friends passed but did not speak.

Then Daulton's trial resumed.

• •

The prosecution's case against Daulton was essentially a rerun of the one against Chris. The main exception was that it elected not to use Daulton's statement made in Mexico City containing his claims of working for the CIA. Instead, it offered a case based on the testimony of witnesses linking him to espionage and forensic evidence from the FBI.

Eileen Heaphy described the scene outside the Soviet Embassy in Mexico City and pointed out Daulton, who was sitting in the same seat that Chris had occupied a few minutes earlier, and said he was the man she had seen being arrested by Mexican policemen.

Vice Consul Thomas Ferguson described how Daulton had removed a white 4-by-8-inch envelope from his pocket at the Mexico City Metropolitan Police Headquarters and recalled the removal of ten to fifteen strips of photographic negatives from it and his inspection of the negatives marked PYRAMIDER and TOP SECRET. Under cross-examination by Kahn, Ferguson acknowledged that Daulton had told him he was involved in doing something for the "free world," but he said he didn't believe him.

The FBI agents who had searched Daulton's home in Palos Verdes described their discovery of the Minox camera, airplane tickets between Los Angeles and Mexico City, and photographs of Chris and Daulton taken in Mexico City.

Darlene Cooper, Carole Benedict, Barclay Granger and others from The Hill recalled his boasts of making big money in Mexico by selling what he said were stolen securities; they described him brandishing what he called a "spy camera" and wads of money, and his frequent requests that they fly with him to Mexico to serve as couriers of cash.

Leslie Dirks of the CIA and Regis Carr reiterated the testimony they had given at the Boyce trial, and Kent Dixon of the FBI gave his damaging testimony again that linked the Pyramider microfilm to Daulton's Minox camera.

Stilz and Levine had affidavits from CIA personnel officers asserting that Daulton had never had *any* working relationship with the agency; but the prosecution lost ground when Kahn succeeded in impeaching

the testimony of another CIA representative who first denied Daulton's connection with the agency and then admitted that he didn't know the identities of all the CIA's secret operatives. Re and Kahn hammered away at the prosecution witnesses, claiming that there was nothing in the government's case that was inconsistent with Daulton's claim that he had been duped into spying for the CIA by one of its agents and had been abandoned when the espionage agency no longer needed him.

Frequently and sarcastically, Stilz and Levine scoffed at the theory, and from the frequency of objections made by Kahn and Re that were overruled, so did Judge Kelleher. But one person in the courtroom appeared to be paying attention to the theory—a woman in the front row of the jury box named Peggy Fuller. A twenty-two-year-old college student who had plans to become a lawyer, she watched and listened to Kahn carefully as he ridiculed the affidavits from the CIA. The word of the CIA, he sneered again and again, was "worthless." It would be *expected* to leave its spies out in the cold. Andrew Daulton Lee was nothing more than an American patriot who had felt he was serving his country and was being thrown to the wolves, Kahn said. A spy, he said, doesn't go to his neighborhood travel agency to buy tickets for an espionage rendezvous in Vienna. A spy doesn't brag about selling secrets while sitting around in Mazatlán or developing espionage pictures in the family kitchen.

• •

When the defense opened its phase of the trial, there was a surprised murmur in the spectator gallery: the first defense witness was an FBI agent.

Robert Lyons, one of the agents who had interviewed Daulton at the Mexican secret police offices on January 15, acknowledged that one of the first things Daulton had said that night was that he worked for the CIA as a "subcontractor" to Christopher John Boyce. John Foarde, the second agent, then corroborated this; thus, the defense had managed to salvage the one point favorable to Daulton from the Mexico City interview that the prosecution had elected not to use against him. However, under cross-examination by Levine, the two agents said that when they had investigated Daulton's claims, they had been told by the CIA that the agency had never heard of Andrew Daulton Lee prior to January 6, 1977.

Kelleher invited the defense lawyers and prosecutors to a confer-

ence near the bench; as he did from time to time, he asked the lawyers for an estimate of how long they expected the trial to continue. Kahn and Re said they expected to be able to wind up the defense in a day or two. It was the first indication that Daulton would not testify. They had decided that he wouldn't make a good witness; they were afraid he might cross himself up under the heat of cross-examination, and had decided there was nothing he could offer that would justify the risk. The lawyers, of course, didn't give any reasons to the judge; they just said Daulton would not be called to testify.

The defense began its final efforts to save Daulton the next day.

Borrowing an idea from the Boyce defense team, Kahn and Re decided to try to persuade the jury that the Pyramider documents were worthless—not the prize defense secrets claimed by the government. Professor Martin Hellman of Stanford reprised his testimony from the Boyce trial, but Kelleher refused to permit William Florence, who had been one of the star witnesses in the Ellsberg-Russo trial, to testify as he had in the Boyce trial; the judge ruled that Florence was not qualified to give expert opinion on the matter of whether the Pyramider documents were properly classified.

"The defense calls Myrtle Clarke." Stilz and Levine looked back in the rear of the courtroom and saw a gray-haired woman who appeared to be in her seventies walking slowly down the aisle, seemingly barely able to walk. It was Daulton's grandmother.

Solicitously, Kahn asked her if Daulton, during the summer of 1976, had ever mentioned to her his plans to make a trip to Mexico. She said he had. "And did he tell you that he worked for the government?" Kahn asked.

"Yes, he did," she replied. Kahn sat down, certain he had made a point supporting the theory that Daulton worked for the CIA.

Levine rose to cross-examine Mrs. Clarke.

As he did, Stilz, sharing a lawyers' joke over having to interrogate the kindly-looking woman, smiled at him and said, "Go get her, Tiger."

"I'll eat her alive," Levine grinned, uncomfortable with his assignment.

"Did defendant Lee ever tell you *which* government he was working for?"

"No, he didn't," Mrs. Clarke said.

• •

Daulton's future was placed in the hands of the jury in midafternoon on May 12, 1977.

Stilz and Levine had studied the jury's response to the testimony, and they expected a conviction within a few hours.

But the day ended without a verdict. The jury had sent a note to Kelleher requesting copies of the original indictment against Daulton, so that jurors could review them in their hotel rooms. Kelleher granted the request.

The following morning, at 9:15, another note arrived from the jury:

Good morning your honor!

Thank you for the copies of the indictments. Is it permissible to make notations, etc., on our individual copies of same? If possible we would like copies of your instructions to the jury.

Are parts or all of the trial transcripts available to us? Are we able to make enquiry of you without generating action by yourself . . . I suppose an "off the record" type inquiry?

We would appreciate it if something could be done about the total lack of ventilation in the Jury Room. We have no air conditioning, nor do the windows open.

> Thank you
> Jane Lyon
> Foreman

Los Angeles was in the midst of a modest spring heat wave, and temperatures were in the eighties. But that was only one reason the atmosphere in the jury room was so warm. The second reason was that the jury was engaged in a pitched battle.

Before adjourning the night before, the jurors had taken an informal straw ballot. It was 8 to 4 in favor of convicting Daulton. They had decided to get some rest and try again the next day. The following morning, after Kelleher denied the request for the transcript, jury instructions and off-the-record advice, the foreman conducted a review of the testimony and evidence, and the jury took its first formal vote; the decision went against Daulton 10–2.

The majority then went to work on the holdouts, both women. Within an hour, one changed her mind and voted to convict. But Peggy Fuller, the prelaw student, refused to change her vote.

"There are grounds for *reasonable doubt* to believe he's innocent," she insisted.

It was obvious, she continued, that the CIA could have been manipulating the two young men. "You can't believe what they say," she said when other jurors pointed out the CIA's denial that Daulton had been in its employ.

Outside the jury room, the lawyers waited impatiently.

Stilz and Levine were puzzled and starting to worry; Kahn and Re offered hope to Daulton. "The longer they stay out, the better chance you've got," Kahn told Daulton. "You may be home free." Daulton's lawyers also encouraged Dr. and Mrs. Lee, who were keeping a vigil at the courthouse, to have hope.

Miss Fuller now found herself alone at one end of the jury table looking out at eleven unhappy faces—antagonists who were beginning to lose their patience and raising their voices. When the jury took its lunch break, some of the jurors seemed to want to avoid her; at dinner, the other eleven jurors refused to sit with her and she dined with one of the Federal marshals who were guarding the jury. Again and again, the other jurors reviewed the evidence and argued that Daulton's guilt was obvious. But Miss Fuller stood her ground, unrelenting, through the second day of deliberations and into the third. She would recall later: "I wanted to hold out forever; I was under terrible pressure; you're cut off from all contact with other people; you're alone, and they refused even to *listen* to my arguments. They were cold and laughed at me. They just didn't understand the concept of reasonable doubt."

"Finally, I said, 'All right, I'll say he's guilty,' but I didn't think he was."

At 11 A.M. on May 14, 1977, a Saturday, the jury reentered the courtroom.

Without looking in Daulton's direction, the foreman handed a note to the court clerk, who in turn showed it to Kelleher and then announced the verdict:

Guilty on all counts of espionage and conspiracy to commit espionage.

Daulton shook his head in bitter disbelief. And then in a gesture that recalled his tormented glances toward his father years before when he had dropped a fly ball or swung at a third strike, he looked quickly in the direction of his parents, both of whom had tears in their eyes.

47

AFTER HIS CONVICTION, Chris had been transferred from the Los Angeles County Jail to the Federal Correctional Institution on Terminal Island, a prison fortress set on a rocky jetty that thrust into Los Angeles Harbor near the southern foot of the Palos Verdes Peninsula. As Chris traveled to Terminal Island along the Harbor Freeway in the back of a prison car, he could look out the window and see the rolling hills where, not many years before, he had first met Robin and Mohammed.

He was assigned to D Block, T.I.'s maximum-security wing, where prisoners were locked in individual cells, measuring eight feet by five feet, around the clock, except for weekly two-hour exercise periods. Prison administrators told Chris he was being isolated because they feared other inmates might try to murder a man convicted of treason. His only regular communication with the prisoners was through the bars of his cell—a shout across a corridor or quieter words with an inmate in one of the cells next to him. Prison guards warned him not to accept food from the other prisoners: they had picked up reports of a plot to poison him from their informants, they said. But Chris thought the inmates were friendly, and he didn't worry about the warning.

Lonely, Chris groped for ways to use up his many hours by himself. He began reading six and even seven books a week from the prison library—mostly history and biographies—and worked to keep in good physical shape by doing 1,200 pushups a day. The subject that was on his mind now more than anything else was escape.

One morning there was a commotion in the corridor outside his cell, and Chris looked out inquisitively; the arrival of a new inmate was one of the few happenings that broke the lonely monotony in D Block; and he saw that the new prisoner was being moved into a cell beside his.

Vito Conterno was a husky man with olive skin and silver hair at his

temples. From that first day, Chris was fascinated by him: he was utterly self-confident, and seemed to be completely in command of himself, maintaining his dignity even in a prison cell. Here he was in a Federal penitentiary, where the prisoners wore denim uniforms, and Vito had a silk robe and leather slippers. To Chris, the robe and slippers were somehow equivalent to papal finery that elevated him above the other inmates. Through their respective walls of prison bars, Chris began to learn about his new neighbor. Vito said his parents were from Sicily; they had emigrated to America more than sixty years before, and because there was no other line of work as lucrative, his father had gravitated into the Mafia, and Vito had followed later. Chris was fascinated by his stories of growing up in a big-city Italian neighborhood, of running numbers when he was still in grade school, of later graduating to bigger money with work in bookmaking parlors, of killing his first man when he was eighteen. It was like a novel, and Chris was spellbound.

Vito said he was in prison because of a minor parole violation. He'd been locked up in D Block, he said, because other Mafiosi in the prison had heard of his reputation as a hit man and he had prevailed upon the warden to isolate him.

As the hours shared in isolation by the young man and the old Mafioso wore on, Vito tutored Chris on prison ethics and how he'd learned them himself at the Federal prison in Leavenworth, Kansas. The lowest scum in a prison, he said, was the stoolie; he told about a snitch at Leavenworth who had gotten a shank stuck in his chest and bled to death in front of Vito's cell; about another who had had gasoline thrown into his cell—"burned to death in his own grease"; and about still another whose charred bones had been found in a prison incinerator.

Vito fretted about being in prison again; it was bad for his heart condition, he said, and he had business deals to look out for on the outside. He lived in a big home in Beverly Hills, he explained, and he'd pumped some of the money he'd made in the rackets into buying liquor stores which, he said with a twinkle, would support him handsomely as he advanced into old age. The only reason he was in the joint now, he said, was that he'd gone to Las Vegas without telling his parole officer, and the Feds had been lying in wait for him when he'd landed at the airport—waiting for an excuse to lock him up.

"Fuckin' Feds," he said. "You'll never leave the fuckin' prison

system alive. You ought to think about getting out of here. I have a friend—my lawyer; he can do some things, maybe.

"Think it over," Vito said. "Maybe I can help you."

•   •

Chris's lawyers had pressed him to cooperate with the CIA in its efforts to pinpoint exactly what information the Russians had obtained from the Black Vault. At first Chris had rejected the request and refused to even discuss it. But Chelius and Dougherty said that if he was to have any chance of getting a light sentence, he had to do it. On May 18, Chris and the lawyers met with Stilz; Rodney Leffler, an FBI agent who served as a liaison officer between his agency and the CIA, and a pipe-smoking man in his early forties who introduced himself as "Jerry Brown of the CIA." The meeting was in a starkly furnished office in a Los Angeles County Sheriff's Department building. Also present were a polygraph-machine operator and a Federal probation officer who had been assigned to formulate a report on the defendant to guide Judge Kelleher when he sentenced Chris.

The debriefing was almost aborted before it began: Chris had been ordered to the meeting wearing his denim prison uniform, but he refused to go unless he was allowed the dignity of wearing his corduroy suit. He was allowed to do so.

For eight hours, under persistent questioning by Brown, Chris recounted his experiences as a spy. He told essentially the same story he had given the FBI on the night of his arrest, but offered more details, including as much as he could remember about the nature of the data he and Daulton had sold to the KGB. This day was to be the first of six such sessions, spaced over several weeks, that Brown (not his real name) called a "damage assessment debriefing."

Chris labored to recall everything he had transmitted to Daulton and the Russians, but said he simply couldn't remember *everything*. He said he had been so intoxicated sometimes that he couldn't remember everything he had photographed. But he volunteered an idea he said would help the CIA solve part of the mystery: he said that he and Daulton, in the later stages of the espionage operation, had taped the TWX message traffic they sold to the Russians to a wall and photographed the messages before returning them to the vault in a potted plant or other conveyance. Chris suggested that the CIA assign a technician to test the rolls of TWX messages that were still in the vault for

307

residue of adhesive from the tape; this would help identify some of the TWX messages that had found their way to Moscow, he said.

The CIA man liked the idea and did what Chris suggested. The test helped the agency discover that Chris had photographed the teletype messages from the vault for at least two full months; there was a spool of messages—as thick as a roll of toilet paper and twice as wide—for each month. Brown said grimly that the CIA had discovered, among other things, that one message on the spool included details of most American intelligence-collection satellites and their performance capabilities.

Chelius and Dougherty told Chris they thought his willingness to participate in the debriefings would probably help him when the time came for his sentencing. But Chris wasn't counting on a light sentence now. He had made other plans.

. .

Back at Terminal Island, he decided to write a response to Vito Conterno:

I have been turning over what you said in my mind. Thinking back over the last five months and listening to your conversation, you appear the most-together inmate I have come to know so far. I know nothing about you other than what you say. I don't think you would bullshit me. I intend no insult with the following, but you're not just trying to bolster my morale and give me hope by mentioning your lawyer, are you? I mean no insult but you came off the wall rather fast with it. Seriously, the heat would be intense with that type of action concerning a Soviet spy. I hate the Feds as much or more than you do. Your problems with them appear to cover a broad spectrum of activity while I specialized in a narrow scam. No doubt your connections have a varied assortment of skills.

I am a realist. I am going to get more time than I can handle. Furthermore, I have no hope of action on appeal with my case. I would wait until that was resolved, which my lawyers tell me would be finalized within a year and a half before I would seek an alternate solution. I cannot end up like poor Tim. I would rather be dead.

Chris was referring to a wretched prisoner in D Block who had been returned to the block after a liver operation in a nearby public hospital. He had made the mistake of attempting to escape from the hospital, and when he was caught he was returned to the prison, rather than the

hospital, to recover from the operation. As Tim twisted in pain on his bunk, moaning, the sutures on his wound popped open and he began to bleed. Prison doctors sewed the wound, but the same thing happened again. Chris listened to Tim's groans at night and watched flies swarm around the wound. Time and again, Tim ripped pus-and-blood-soaked bandages off the wound and threw them out of his cell into the corridor. From his own cell Chris watched a column of ants a half-inch wide feed on the bloody matter adhering to the bandages.

I have no qualms about taking risks. This would just be one more. If you mean what you say, I am interested as hell. Again, please don't take that as an insult. I don't mean it as such. I am just feeling you out.

What you suggest would put my life in hands of people with whom I have no experience. I would have to go forward on trust alone. I would be out on a limb with my cash on the line. But anything would be better than the life the Feds have planned for me. You don't sound like a person who stabs in the back unless crowded first. All I could do is rely on my judgement that you are a honorable man and that those with who you do business are of a like kind.

Once again, to be honest, it does not seem to me that O.C. [Organized Crime] would want to cross CIA. I would have everything to lose, nothing to gain, in a double cross. I once prevented a termination on a courier by the KGB for his duplicity because he was a boyhood friend and I had a big heart. I now regret it. I don't think I would be here now if I had let them go ahead. I totally am aware of the implications you mention. Meaning no insult, I would be acting completely on trust and would be open to rip-off.

Either one of us could be moved at any time and after that we will never see each other again. Believing you are sincere I will rely on your word. You are probably wondering where does this brat get off questioning me. It's just that I was burned bad and here I sit. This is to me a new ball game. I would imagine espionage operates on the same principles.

No way are the Feds going to give me any slack. I am not a socialist and the Soviets no doubt would feel safer with my mouth closed permanently. I am between a rock and a hard place with both systems. My only hope would be to go into deep cover. You mentioned the availability of an initial set of I.D. I am interested as hell. I hope you mean it. I would put all my resources on the line.

Once again, I mean no offense.

•   •

In May, five months after his arrest, Chris held a reunion with his parents. His only communication with his family since the arrest had been the letter to his father on the eve of his trial asking his family not to attend and a brief, inconclusive phone conversation with his mother shortly after his arrest. But Chelius had not stopped urging him to see his parents, and they had repeatedly sent messages through the lawyer saying they wanted to see him. Chris, now that the ordeal of the trial was over, consented to see his parents.

The reunion took place in a small office at the Terminal Island prison, and it was the beginning of a precarious truce.

His mother hugged Chris and almost immediately broke into tears of love and sympathy for her eldest son. His father extended his hand, and Chris did the same.

"How are you, sir?" Chris asked.

"Fine," he replied.

It was a meeting with about as much overt affection as the father and son ever showed.

They visited for more than an hour, and after a while some of the stiffness thawed. His parents brought Chris up to date on family news, and Chris asked about his dog, Magyar.

During the next few weeks, there would be frequent meetings between Chris and his parents, brothers and sisters. Once his father even brought Magyar to the prison, and Chris visited with him through a chain-link fence. It appeared that the wounds in the relationship between Chris and his family were healing.

Meanwhile, the thoughts of all the members of his family turned to his sentencing, which was scheduled for the middle of June.

48

CHRIS LAY BACK on his bunk and remembered the first time he had seen Fawkes.

They had met on a December morning in 1973 in the California coastal range near San Luis Obispo. One of her blue feet had been tucked in her belly feathers as she peered out from atop a

perch on a high-voltage-transmission-line tower. As he watched, she twisted her head around and looked down the brown mountainside at the sparkling reflection of his binoculars, then lifted off the wire with a defiant snub and rose higher and higher until she was only a black speck in the sky and Chris lost her in a cloud.

The vision of Fawkes and the blustery morning filled his cell.

After the first sighting, he went back to the Volkswagen to water and feed the pigeons in the back seat. As he leaned against the car to rest, a roadrunner ran, hopped and flew through the broken chaparral, stabbing at mice. And then he waited.

After a while, Chris decided to return to the mound, his lookout, hoping for another sight of the young prairie falcon. But she was gone; the only birds he spotted with his binoculars were an occasional mourning dove and tight formations of teal flitting between puddles.

There was a pair of ravens circling in endless spirals to no purpose while coyotes, far in the distance, barked from the foothills. The shadows of twilight were beginning to stab over the jagged edge of the mountainous horizon, and as Chris admiringly watched the panorama of pastels change from rose to orange-streaked gray, he saw the prairie falcon approaching up high, two hundred yards away. Planing her wings flat and taut, she glided down and settled into the dusk with a small tug on the wire. On his mound of rocks, Chris froze, afraid to move his hand or turn his head. When at last the final streaks of twilight had given way to darkness, he cautiously made his way down the hill to the Volkswagen for cold stew out of a can and a can of cold beer. It had to be at first light or not at all.

He cursed himself for not bringing help, but then he thought again: These are my towers. No one else knew the prairies came here, and no one was going to know.

Before dawn, he was out of his down bag quietly stamping his feet, awakened by the mental alarm he had set for himself in his final moments of consciousness the night before. His toes ached from the cold.

Chris went to the car and grabbed one of his pigeons from the cage and wrapped a leather vest, with nylon nooses bristling almost invisibly from it, around the bird. Then he lit up a joint of Thai and waited.

As dawn broke, Chris wasn't sure if it was the joint or his imagination, but as the morning's first lark announced the arrival of sunrise, he looked up and saw the young prairie moving slightly. She was restless, slipping her head out from under a wing—probably, he

thought, struggling to regain her wits for the day, just as Chris himself had done a few minutes earlier.

In the mantle of gray half-light, Chris tensed, bracing himself, as the pigeon struggled in his left fist. The prairie was now growing more restless on her perch, and Chris decided it was time. He started the engine of the Volkswagen and gunned it, startling Fawkes. She swiveled her head in dismay and suddenly bumped off the perch, rising not far from Chris in a tight ring. He had to act quickly. He kissed the pigeon for luck, whispered, "Keep your head down!" and launched it out of the Volkswagen.

The pigeon recognized its peril from the spiraling falcon immediately. It began to struggle frantically for altitude, flapping its wings and moving diagonally away from Chris. Fawkes forgot the chug of the Volkswagen. She turned and dived rapidly for her breakfast. It was a beautiful stoop. Fawkes seemed to hit the pigeon with only a glancing blow—but that was all it took: in that instinctive pass, the falcon's blue foot had become ensnared in a noose. Chris yelped in triumph.

The falcon beat her wings furiously to gain level flight. Just as furiously the terrified pigeon beat its wings to escape in another direction. Finally they fell to the ground in tandem, four wings flapping against each other in helpless desperation. Chris sprinted the quarter-mile to the screeching birds, hoping every second that Fawkes wouldn't extricate herself from the thin thread and escape. He approached the flailing birds from behind and quickly popped a hood over the passage, sending her into darkened tranquillity. Then he stripped the pigeon of its vest and let it fly free.

. .

Vito wrote a reply to Chris: Everything could be handled. His associates in Chicago should have no trouble springing him. "My friends will look out for everything," he said. "You get plastic surgery on your face and nobody will ever see Chris Boyce again." Chris burned his note and flushed the ashes down the toilet.

He then wrote a second letter to the aging Mafioso. As always, he seemed to show deference to his elders:

I don't mean to pry or get personal; what would be the broad, general mechanics of an exit? In transit? In what way would my movement to Ill. be handled? This would appear to be most crucial. What type of

summons could bring a spy there without arousing Fed suspicion? Would the crew know my true identity?

What would be the total bill? Exit, facelift, I.D., passport, credit cards, the works?

How much time between exit and completion of facelift?

Would not my meeting of your attorney previous to an exit lead to an investigation of a connection between the two? Are you worried about CIA heat? I know nothing about O.C., drug dealing, etc. I respect a man who holds the agency in contempt. In all probability counter intelligence would think the KGB is responsible.

Would you ever broaden your horizons? Would all relationship between us cease at the completion of an exit?

Two weeks after she plummeted to earth with the pigeon, Fawkes was back in the air. For three months, Chris and the falcon hunted, man and animal in the marvelous partnership that always had such a hypnotic effect on Chris.

He would never forget the last time:

Chris removed the hood near a pond of cinnamon teal, and Fawkes, as usual, exploded from his fist to gain altitude, eager for the kill. Poised for his own assignment in the partnership—flushing the teal— Chris waited for Fawkes to relax and level off. But to his surprise, Fawkes didn't stop. She climbed higher and higher, oblivious of the teal, confusing Chris. To his horror, Chris soon understood why: a large orange-footed wild hawk—a haggard—had spotted Fawkes poaching on his territory, and he was preparing to expel her. Chris saw the big old hawk rising to gain the advantage; then both of them were rising in parallel corkscrews. Chris rushed forward on the ground to be closer, but he knew he was only a helpless spectator in the impending combat.

Fawkes and the haggard, in a spectacular double corkscrew that could only have been choreographed by nature, fought stroke for stroke to achieve the dominant altitude from which one would soon launch its opening attack. Chris leaned on a post and did the only thing he could do: watch his falcon battle for her survival. They pushed hundreds of feet into the air, and after a while, Chris could no longer tell one bird from the other. When they were only barely visible from the ground, Chris saw that one bird had opened the attack. The dark speck was above its antagonist and let loose with a diving stoop. Chris strained to see which of the birds had the advantage.

It was the old hawk.
Fawkes was fleeing for her life. Chris never saw her again.

.   .

God, how he missed his birds, his outdoors, Chris thought. Except for Vito and a few other prisoners in D Block, Chris didn't have contact with anybody except his lawyers and the CIA spook named Jerry Brown who still called him downtown periodically to go over more documents. Chelius and Dougherty visited often and tried to keep his spirits high until the sentencing. They said they would try to have him sentenced under a Federal statute that gave judges the flexibility to show youthful offenders—those under twenty-five—more leniency than older defendants. First, they said, there might be a short sentence for a psychological evaluation, possibly at the Federal Bureau of Prisons' Metropolitan Correctional Center in San Diego. There were a few rays of hope, they said encouragingly.

But Chris had decided that he had seen enough of prison to convince him he didn't want to do *any* more time. He was, like his birds, he thought, not meant to be caged, and he vowed to escape.

Isolated and lonely, Chris had only one friend: Vito Conterno.

Vito had warned him that the guards could overhear prisoners' conversations in D Block, so the escape negotiations had to continue via the prison "kite" communications network—notes secretly sent between cells, usually wrapped around a heavy object like a razor or piece of soap that was tied to a string. The sender flipped the weighted missile down the corridor, then retrieved it after the intended recipient had removed the note. Vito sent Chris a kite trying to quash his worries about the escape and said they should plan it for as soon as possible. Chris replied:

Talking to you in my position is like getting close to a cobra. Once again no offense. You're right, once I get settled in a pen it would be all the harder. My lawyers are completely straight and of no use to me except for legal advice. Sitting here I can not contact anyone but my lawyers and my family, which is straighter even still. My old network is down. They would not even consider contact. In fact I am considered a threat to them as long as I'm incarcerated. After an exit I revert to an asset.

You just told me I was too easy to get close to. Okay, I will be above board with you. Jesus, I wish I had heard of you before. I wish I had

some knowledge of your reputation. I am a babe in the woods as far as O.C. figures. But to hell with it. I bury these thoughts. You offer me my life.

Anyway, I am isolated. I cannot touch my links nor would I even consider trying. Even exited I would have to establish new ones. I do not know what slots I would fill after that. Obviously my cover was blown as a direct source within the CIA. There are many other roles to play. I don't work *for* any men and I never will. I work for the KGB. The U.S. government is not going to collapse in our lifetimes. It would seem to me that there would be mutual interests that could be exploited between O.C. and the KGB to the advantage of both parties. No doubt such connections might already exist although that was not my specialty and I wouldn't know.

I did hundreds of millions of dollars worth of damage to the NSA and the CIA over the last two years. I am not trying to brag or impress you, I am merely stating a fact. I delivered the agency's crypto codes, cipher machines and the Pyramider Project. These came out in court so I don't mind telling you. The diplomatic relations between the U.S. and Australia are poisoned at their worst ever through my efforts. For this the Soviets are grateful. It means the main base for monitoring of Chinese and Russian telemetry by satellite surveillance will be shot down and kicked off the continent by the Australian government. Can you put something soft besides that razor on the line so it doesn't make noise when you throw it? Why don't we say *matches* when we want to pass something?

Until I receive my sentence I cannot see anyone that I trust. I think I will be moved out of here very quickly after that.

Chris said his lawyers had told him chances were good that he would be sent to a Federal prison in San Diego for his psychiatric evaluation.

It would mean I would be transported between here and there by the marshals, probably in a sedan.

I want out. I will raise $15 [$15,000] as soon as I can talk to a friend. The study in San Diego would be perfect. I could have visits and I would have to be transported. $15 is cheap, very cheap. Perhaps at the end of the study. How long does this type of thing take to arrange?

•   •

George Chelius was on the phone to Bill Dougherty: "Bill, something terrible has happened. I'm going to withdraw from the case."

Chelius had just been called into the office of Assistant United States Attorney Richard A. Stilz, who had handed him the notes Chris had written to Vito Conterno.

Chelius had believed in Chris. He did not understand his psyche, his curious sense of disillusionment and anger at his country; but he had believed that Chris had become a spy not out of pro-Soviet sympathies, but through an enigmatic act of bad judgment whose consequences had snowballed and eventually smothered him. He had not even been sure that Chris was not a secret agent for the CIA. Chelius was now bowled over by the admission of loyalty to the KGB and its implication that he had been working for the Russians all along.

Stilz told Chelius that he planned to give the notes to Judge Kelleher. The implication was clear: any chance of leniency toward the troubled son of his former boss would probably vanish.

"Take it easy, George," Dougherty advised Chelius, urging him not to withdraw until they could discuss the affair with Chris.

When Chris learned that Vito had given his notes to the warden at Terminal Island, he became physically ill in his cell. Once again he had trusted in something—this time, the Mafia—and it had let him down.

Like Fawkes, Chris had been trapped by a pigeon—a stool pigeon. Vito Conterno was a professional snitch—a Mafia hit man who had agreed to testify before a Federal grand jury against other mobsters in return for a light sentence and, eventually, a new identity in a distant city. He was a murderer–turned–government witness whose life in prison was gilded by a silk robe and slippers. From the beginning, Vito had given Chris's notes to the Federal agents.

His precise motive for entrapping Chris is uncertain. Perhaps it was patriotism or outrage against the egghead kid who had spied for the Communists against his country; or perhaps it was merely an act of gutter survival, throwing Chris to the wolves so that he could curry favor with his keepers.

When Chelius and Dougherty asked for an explanation, Chris admitted that he was the author of the incriminating notes, and seemed close to tears when Chelius said he was afraid the notes had destroyed any chance he had had for leniency. After all, Chelius said, Chris had now *admitted* he worked for the KGB; it was sure to be used against him.

Chris insisted that he had not meant what he said in the notes. Yes, he said, he had feigned loyalty to the Russians, but it was because he thought that was what Vito wanted to hear; he wouldn't help an *inno-*

cent man, would he? Yes, Chris said, he did want to escape, but, no, he was not loyal to the KGB. The notes were elements of a charade. After Chris presented his defense, Chelius agreed to stay on the defense team with Dougherty; but doubts had been planted in the attorney's mind, perhaps never to be exorcised completely. Once more, Chris had left the people around him wondering what really went on behind his thin face and probing eyes.

After meeting with his lawyers, Chris, still shaken, had another session with Jerry Brown of the CIA. While riding back late that afternoon to Terminal Island, once again passing the mountainous southern face of The Hill, he thought of one thing: he would spread the word that Vito was a snitch. He relished the idea. But when he reached the prison, Chris discovered that he had been preempted: Vito had told other inmates in D Block that *he* was a snitch and had just come from squealing to the Feds.

"Hey, you fuckin' snitch," one inmate taunted him as he was led down the corridor to his cell.

"Hey, look what's back! Joe Valachi," Vito Conterno shouted.

"You son of a bitch!" Chris screamed.

Then other inmates took their cue from Conterno, and Chris could hear their chant, "Joe Valachi . . . Joe Valachi . . . Joe Valachi . . ." ringing in his ears until he finally fell asleep.

•   •

Daulton also was depressed much of the time these days as he awaited his sentencing. He had evaded jail so often, for so long, that he found it impossible to accept that he might now actually go to prison, possibly for a long time. And then something happened that gave him hope—and still another chance at survival.

It was contained in a postscript to the bitter strife among the jurors who had decided Daulton's fate. It was written six days after his conviction and filed with Judge Kelleher by Kahn and Re:

Peggy Fuller, being first duly sworn, deposes and says:

1. That prior to the commencement of the trial, several jurors expressed the belief that Mr. Lee was guilty.

2. That the majority of the jurors became aware of the conviction of Christopher Boyce on the same charges during the course of the Lee trial.

3. The fact of the Boyce conviction was discussed in the Jury Room.

4. That other jurors discussed the case outside the Jury Room.

5. That pressure was applied on me outside the Jury Room to change my vote.

6. That I do have reasonable doubt as to the guilt of Mr. Lee and had the jury been polled, I would not have agreed with the jury verdict.

Affiant says nothing further.

Executed this 20th day of May, 1977, at Los Angeles, California.

(signed)   Peggy Fuller

Miss Fuller told a reporter several jurors had seen a newspaper headline reporting Boyce's conviction on May 14, the night of his conviction, while they were dining in a Holiday Inn restaurant. It was a serious allegation. If it was accepted by Judge Kelleher, it could mean a new trial for Daulton. It would mean that the jury might have been prejudiced against Lee because his case was so closely intertwined with that of Christopher Boyce.

Stilz and Levine contacted other members of the jury and were told a story different from the one related by Miss Fuller. Joan Lyon, the housewife who had served as foreman of the jury, wrote a letter to Kelleher stating that she had contacted nine of the other ten jurors (besides herself and Peggy Fuller) and had found none who had seen the newspaper headline.

"We are dumbfounded as to what has prompted Miss Fuller to make these statements," she said, calling the assertions "absolutely false."

"We are satisfied that our performance of duty was in keeping with our oath as jurors. Because of the total lack of truth in the affidavit," she said, "we felt you should be so informed and I was delegated to write to you for the group of jurors."

Judge Kelleher held a hearing to determine which of the statements addressed to him was accurate. Miss Fuller took the witness stand and testified that she had seen the news headline and that another juror—whose identity she could not recall—had told her, "Well, if Boyce is guilty, then Lee must be guilty too."

Eight other jurors who had been subpoenaed to the special hearing before Judge Kelleher followed her to the stand. They all denied her charges. Kelleher ruled that there were not grounds in the affidavit for a new trial, and then he turned his attention to the next matter pending before him.

49

THE SENTENCING of Christopher John Boyce was scheduled for June 20, 1977. The night before, Chris began a letter to his parents. Neatly, slowly, he wrote in longhand:

Dear Dad and Mom:
    My thoughts are a jumble. My emotions are bled white. I have become callous. I have been dancing on a razor. I close my eyes and I feel my falcon beating hard into the wind. . . .

Chris laid down his pencil. For a long time he looked at his words under the dim light of his cell, which was partially blocked by the shadow of his trousers. The trousers were knotted into a noose and hanging from the bars above his head.

Chris was writing a suicide note.

Once again he had weighed his options and concluded that dying was better than living.

His sentencing was tomorrow, and he was certain to get a life term.

He felt the lowest that he had felt since the day of his arrest. His sense of doom had kept him awake most nights since he had learned that Vito Conterno had turned his letters over to the prosecution.

Vito was still in the cell beside his, and as Chris looked up from his words he occasionally yelled an epithet at him. Lately, he had gotten a small measure of revenge on Conterno. Other inmates in D Block hadn't believed him when he shouted that *he* wasn't the snitch, Conterno was! But luckily, Bill Dougherty had another client in D Block, a drug dealer; Dougherty had told him the story, and this new prisoner had corroborated Chris's account. Now most of the other prisoners weren't speaking to Conterno.

Conterno also was awake in his cell on the night before Chris was to be sentenced: Chris could hear him pacing and groaning. He knew the

old Mafioso was having heart pains again and tried to enjoy the thought. "I hope your heart bursts, Conterno!" he said loud enough for him to hear. "I hope you die!" Moments of pleasure were rare in his cell, but this was one of them.

Chris wanted Conterno to go to sleep so that he could go ahead with his suicide, but Conterno continued to moan and pace the floor in a monotonous thump.

Chris looked back at the few words he had written and wondered what he could say next. He wanted to say that he was not ashamed of what he had done, that he would do it over again. But mostly, he sought the words that somehow, against all the odds, would convince his father that he was right. He wanted him to *understand*. But what could he say? They were two people living in the same world who spoke different languages, each indecipherable to the other.

At dawn, the letter was still unfinished, and Chris removed the pants he had tied to his bars that were to serve as his noose.

As it had in the days when Chris had plotted to murder Daulton and on the eve of his testimony, his courage failed him again. Somewhere, through the night, he had heard the distant voices of Monsignor Mc-Carthy and the sisters of St. John Fisher preaching that it was a mortal sin to take one's own life—as grievous as taking another's life. He ridiculed himself for his weakness.

His courage failed him that night in another way, too. Chris wanted to tell the judge what he *really* believed about the nation-states and their blind march toward self-destruction. Mentally he composed a script that would lay it all out right between the eyes.

But he decided that if he was going to have any chance of escaping prison for the rest of his life, he couldn't say what he believed.

He began to write a speech to the judge.

•   •

"If ever there was a case in which a person presented himself in total puzzlement, your client is it," Judge Kelleher told George Chelius and Bill Dougherty a few hours later.

Kelleher had before him a presentencing report from the Federal probation officer who had been assigned to evaluate the defendant and report any special circumstances the judge should weigh in his behalf. It was a long and detailed exposition on the life of Christopher John Boyce—twenty-six pages, single-spaced, that tracked Chris from St.

320

John Fisher to the three colleges he had tried before going to work at TRW, and his subsequent arrest. The probation officer had talked to Chris's family, many of his former teachers and neighbors, and had found no one who would say anything negative about him. It was as if he were a surgeon, responding to symptoms of a malignancy, who had gone looking for a tumor and had found the organ normal, and it seemed to befuddle him.

At the probation officer's request, Chris had written an account of his experience—essentially the same one he had told at the trial—and answered so many questions about it that one day following a session with the P.O., he told one of his lawyers: "This guy's a spy freak. He wants to hear all the dicey details." In a rambling, sixteen-page handwritten memoir, Chris recounted for the probation officer the story he had told from the witness stand, but added some details. He first described how he purportedly had blurted out the information about Australia and the CIA to Daulton, while he was high, and then continued:

A couple of weeks later under similar circumstances I had another private conversation with Lee at his father's house. Our discussion again drifted to Australia, and he inquired how I had come by that knowledge. I informed him I worked in an encoded communications room and that I was also aware of treaty violations perpetuated [sic] by the CIA against that government. I stated that I wished that and all other instances of CIA abuse could be made public, but to do so always left one open to a lawsuit. He stated that that sort of activity could best be handled by a third party. I replied that that had been the problem with the Pentagon Papers. He stated that his father, an ex-colonel in the Army Air Corps, had many influential friends, including many lawyers and business men. He said without revealing the source of the information a la Deep Throat he could make public the information. Sitting there stoned on hashish the idea sounded plausible and I told him it might work but that it would have to be documented. He suggested I outline in writing in general terms what I had told him. Later in the evening he informed me that his parole officer had issued a warrant for his arrest and that his father had given him money to leave the country and he had decided that soon he would go to Costa Rica. He stated that he would try to take care of the letter before that and would do what he could. I left the Lee house at about one in the morning and went home to my father's. I learned later in the week that he had left the country. I was surprised that he had not said goodbye.

A few days later I received a call from Lee at my parents' house and

I took it in my father's bedroom. Lee sounded belligerent and mentioned that he had taken my letter to his people. I asked, "what people?" He asked if I was sure I wanted to know. I answered in the affirmative and said, "come on tell me." He said "I gave it to the Russians." I said, "Come on, really, who did you give it to?" He replied again that he had given it to the Russians and informed me that he had taken it to the Soviet embassy in Mexico. I hung up on him and sat down on my father's bed. I couldn't believe what I had just heard. . . . The phone rang again and I took it off the hook, replacing the receiver and then setting it on the floor. I left my father's house and went to my apartment in Hermosa Beach. I began to drink and consider my next course of action.

Chris's story then described how Daulton had threatened him and his father with exposure unless he fed him more information from the vault. "I told him to drop dead and in no uncertain terms would I cooperate with him. He told me for $200 he could have me taken care of if I didn't want to play ball. He said he had copies of my letter and asked me how I would like to have them mailed to TRW. I hung up on him."

Chris wrote that a CIA technician had told him that much of the equipment in the Black Vault had been compromised when North Korea had captured the American spy ship *Pueblo,* and other NSA equipment had been seized by Communist agents in Africa during racial strife.

Lee continued to call me at work and threaten me with exposure by mailing my letter to my employment. I also learned at this time that he was a heroin addict.

With this knowledge I decided I had two options. Kill him outright or destroy his credibility with the Russians. I did not know who his real employer was and even now I am not sure. If I successfully murdered him I still had the problem of recovering the copies of my letter he retained. I would also have to contend with his narcotics connections with whom he was threatening my life. Not even owning a gun I decided on my second choice. His demands continued on my line at work.

Chris said that he had bought a gun, but had tried to satisfy Daulton's demand with outdated materials from the vault, photos of training manuals and materials he'd been told had been compromised.

322

I began to lead a reckless life. I drove like a maniac on the freeways with no regard for my safety. I would go alone to falcon cliffs and climb down my lines hand over hand to the nesting ledge not really caring if I fell. I slipped from a raft in the Colorado River in the turbulence and came close to drowning. I frequently considered shooting Lee and then myself but I could not bring myself to go through with it. I became moody and depressed and escaped more and more often with pot, hashish and cocaine, all of which Lee gave me. I realized that under the circumstances my girl friend and I could never be married and she finally left me. I began to drink heavily and by October, '76, Lee had given me a total of $10,000 all of which I spent in quick sprees, considering even the money incriminating. Lee attempted to turn me into a heroin addict by lacing the cocaine he freely supplied me. After getting sick and realizing another one of his ploys, I refused further narcotics from him. I began to go over to his house armed with my automatic looking for an opening but I could never pull it out of my pocket and if I did I wasn't sure whether I would stop and who I would include. I never willfully committed espionage and what was supplied was useless. Perhaps that was the CIA's intention from the start. What I am guilty of is being a coward, although had I become a killer I had no idea who in the end I would have to settle with.

It was a well-reasoned tale of espionage by extortion, a blending of lies and reality.

•   •

The probation officer's presentencing report was sympathetic and compassionate, and appeared in almost every line to be straining to believe Chris. Once again, Boyce had made a conquest. The report said in part:

In his written and oral statements, the defendant notes a deep personal and societal disillusionment with the centralization and abuse of power by the Government and several of its agencies and specifically, the CIA. To him he became a witness to, and an instrument of, this abuse, which was all the more shocking as it involved CIA activities in Australia, "a true friend and ally."

The defendant is the product of a stable, moral oriented middle class religious family, having the physical, intellectual and personal wherewithal to be successful. With no prior law violations but this one, he continues to command the respect of his family and friends, whose

unwavering faith in him is remarkable. A pattern of radical changes emerge from the defendant. Having a strong Catholic religious upbringing in which he fully identified, his teens saw him at first question and then ultimately reject the fundamental precepts of that religion. Having a Catholic centered conservative view of politics, society and authority, this too was disturbed during his teens and rejected. The defendant, before entering high school, seemed to identify with authority figures in both the home, school and in society. Although the defendant never underwent a rebellion against a domestic authority, it is clear that he did reject other such sources. His acts in this offense are a manifestation of his rejection of Governmental authority.

Chris's actions, he said, had been influenced by Watergate and by revelations of official corruption and of abuses of American power abroad. "The defendant pursued his understanding of 'corruption' and held rather deep rooted opinions concerning them; to some extent the defendant's motivation was an attempt to expose what he considered to be unjust and unlawful activities of the CIA," the probation officer said.

Richard Stilz, the prosecutor, would say later that he had given copies of the letters Chris wrote to Vito Conterno to the probation officer, but, curiously, there was no reference to them in the probation report. Stilz also said the probation officer promised to send the letters to Judge Kelleher before Chris was sentenced.

The probation officer concluded in the report that he believed Chris's story of being dragged into the espionage scheme because of his Ellsberg-like impulse to expose evil in government. He accepted Chris's lies as the truth, but his report also contained a good deal of insight into the puzzling young man:

The defendant had two important motivating factors: 1) His desire to attack central authority by virtue of his loss of faith in central government; 2) At the same time to expose the Central Intelligence Agency with an implicit faith in Government. These contending factors, it is suggested, were both operative with the defendant, and are consistent with the views set forth above, namely, that the defendant had developed these two attitudes toward authority in general. The reason why the defendant engaged in writing the letters exposing the Central Intelligence Agency, and handing them to Lee, lies in these two motivations. If the defendant were purely intending on exposing

324

the Central Intelligence Agency, he probably would have engaged in a more direct and less dangerous route.

It is felt that the defendant's continued cooperation with Lee arose out of a personal fear of Lee. This is suggested by the reputation that Lee had in the community. Although the defendant may have been coerced by Lee, it is not felt that the immediacy of Lee's threats excuses the defendant's actions. On the one hand we have the threat of exposing Boyce, with a possible harm to his family, and on the other hand we have the compromising of the United States concerning national defense and sensitive communications information. As between the two it is fairly evident that the implied threats do not justify his actions.

However, the defendant did apparently make a good faith attempt to resolve the dilemma that he was placed in in a way which would harm neither the United States nor himself or his family. The defendant apparently felt that he could control the flow of information, as he was the only person with access to it, and that he could thereby control both Lee and the Russians. To some extent the defendant drew incorrect inferences concerning the potential harm involved in his actions, and thereby did not correctly appreciate the harm involved, but nevertheless it appears that in most instances the defendant was attempting to resolve the dilemma that he found himself in without injury. When the defendant states that it was never his intent to injure the United States, it is felt that he is being basically honest.

The fact that the defendant received money tends to suggest his pecuniary interests in his activities. It is felt however that the defendant's motivation was not financial, but that his interest is more consistent with what has been discussed above.

What is perhaps the most shocking aspect of the defendant's activities is the continuity of it and the fact that there was much time to reflect and to consider alternative means to resolve the dilemma that he describes. It simply strains credibility that the defendant was at all times being threatened. Nor is this his position. His own statements reflect that the threats were no longer immediate, but were only implicit.

In assessing the defendant generally, it is to be noted that there is nothing in his past to suggest that he would engage in this type of activity. His prior record and general community adjustment, his personality and relationship with friends and family all strongly indicate that this is out of character with the defendant.

Because of these facts, the defendant was given the benefit of the doubt in many close factual questions. By and large he has been very

open, candid and fundamentally honest. This is consistent with his general reputation and with the assessment made here.

Without making a recommendation for a sentence, the report concluded:

It adds little, but it must be said that the defendant has derived a lifetime of experience by virtue of this episode, his detection and processing through the courts. It is felt that the defendant will eventually return to society and function as an asset in it, with a rather unique appreciation of himself, his motivation and his future purposes.

Judge Kelleher seemed utterly perplexed over the decision he faced on sentencing the young man who had so obviously impressed his probation officer. The probation report had been sealed from public scrutiny, but the judge alluded to it in remarks to Chelius and Dougherty, emphasizing that the probation officer had suggested there was a strong chance their client could be rehabilitated, and there was "some good" in him. Chelius asked the judge to consider sentencing Chris on an interim basis for ninety days so that he could be examined in depth by the Federal Bureau of Prisons psychiatrists and then the judge could decide on the final sentence. Before ruling on this request, Kelleher asked Chris if he had anything to say before sentence was passed.

• •

Chris had looked into a dilemma the night before: Should he tell the court how he *really* felt about the United States, the nationalists and their crazed march toward oblivion? Or should he plead for his future? It was, he would recollect later, a one-sided struggle with his conscience, and a brief one. He opted for survival.

50

His face reddening, Chris rose and walked slowly to the same lectern that had been used by the lawyers who had argued his guilt or innocence.

"I stand convicted of a great offense," he began. "I have had much time to consider what I believe to be my primary error in thinking in this matter.

"There have been times in my life when I have been caused to face intense dilemmas. My judgments, my mistakes defy explanations. I address myself to that which I fail to understand." He paused, letting the words resonate in the quiet courtroom.

"I have witnessed a lack of trust in this country between the governed and their government. As I grew older, I became aware that the overwhelming majority of young people of my age placed little or no faith in our established institutions. It was not that we failed in our commitment to democratic principles. It was that we no longer were confident of the direction our government had taken."

Chris's voice thickened as he spoke. Reporters sitting at the press table saw moisture glistening in his eyes that reflected the soft lights of the crowded courtroom.

"What I failed to understand," Chris went on, looking up at Judge Kelleher from the words he had written the night before, "was that it didn't matter if the President was a criminal; it didn't matter if the land was filled with prejudice and bias; it didn't matter if law enforcement could be lawless or that we could kill and maim in Vietnam for eight years. It didn't matter if we could assassinate and topple elected governments.

"What I failed to grasp," he continued, "was that while these and other things disgusted me, none of them individually or even their sum total were the central issue. What was vitally, indispensably important was that we had ideals. That we based our society on law. . . ."

Chris turned to the next page and started to continue. But as he

began to speak the words, he was momentarily stunned. The page read:

"Dear Dad and Mom: My thoughts are a jumble. . . ."

It was his half-finished suicide note from the night before, written on the back of a sheet of the tissue-paper stationery on which he'd drafted his appeal to the judge. Quickly, he flipped over the piece of paper and continued:

"No matter that our history was flawed . . . There are those who strive to be correct, to heal, to persevere toward those goals upon which we base our government.

"And when the time arrived, in the face of pressure, my decision was colored in the back of my mind with the thought that I had been betrayed by my government. That what we were and where we had arrived were irreconcilable. I was wrong to believe that my ideals no longer counted. I believed the nation to have abandoned those commitments toward principle which have made this country unique. And when I was coerced, it left me with little strength to fall back on. It was a position I did not seek. My primary error was in failing to appreciate that my country is anchored in principle no matter what the practices of its government. On the eighth of January I was determined to remain in the United States and to account for my actions. It was no easy decision. I appreciate the court's position. I would hope that at some reasonable time I'd be allowed to contribute once again to this society. There is no possibility of a recurrence of this matter. I have never been involved in criminality. I am emotionally exhausted but not beaten. I have one goal in my life and that is to recover my reputation. I am resolved to accomplish it. I appreciate the conscientious defense my attorneys provided. I apologize to my father. I express profound regrets to the American people and their principles."

•   •

There was a silence in the courtroom that lasted perhaps thirty seconds. Then Judge Kelleher, after praising Chris's two defense lawyers for work in the "finest tradition" of the law (he seemed to appreciate how little they had to work with), sentenced Chris to a ninety-day psychiatric study. The sentence was imposed under the Federal statute designed to allow leniency for young offenders. His final sentencing was delayed until September.

There was rejoicing in the Boyce camp. "I'm delighted," Dougherty

told a press conference after the hearing ended. Without divulging its contents, he said the probation report had been "extremely favorable," and added that the judge's seeming puzzlement over Chris suggested to him that he was going to show compassion for him at the final sentencing three months hence. "Sentencing him under the Youth Act is a bellwether," he said. "I think it's possible he may not serve more than six years."

• •

Daulton returned to the courtroom of Federal District Judge Robert J. Kelleher on the morning of July 18, 1977.

He had observed Kelleher long enough now not to expect the patience he had found in the Torrance courtroom of Judge Donahue. Nevertheless, as he entered the courtroom that morning wearing the conservative business suit he had worn throughout his trial, Daulton still clung to a shaft of hope. The hope was based on one thing: he had, like Chris, agreed to be debriefed by Jerry Brown and his associates, and as Chris had before him, Daulton had given the CIA a step-by-step account of the espionage partnership. He maintained that it had been Chris's idea from the beginning and gave his interrogators a list of the documents and photographs he could remember delivering to the Russians. He couldn't recall all of them, though, he said; he hadn't bothered to read a lot of the documents he sold to his KGB contacts. He gave every impression of being a simple peddler, unconcerned about the nature of his merchandise, interested only in the money he could sell it for.

The government representatives showed Daulton photographs, many of them taken surreptitiously by CIA agents. Some were slightly fuzzy pictures of a man getting into cars; others showed men walking along streets and entering a restaurant. Daulton recognized an old friend—there was a photograph of Old Steely Teeth, Mikhail Vasilyevich Muzankov—in the full-dress uniform of a Red Army general. There were photos of Boris, Okana, Karpov, Dagtyr and a half-dozen other KGB agents whom Daulton identified for the CIA as his contacts in Mexico City. "I blew a dozen agents for the KGB," Daulton would boast afterward.

On the morning of July 18, his cooperation with the agency whose secrets he had sold to the Soviet Union was his only hope—the government had promised to take this into consideration when he was

sentenced. He hoped the judge would sentence him under the Youth Act so he could get out in six or seven years.

When Richard A. Stilz rose to address Judge Kelleher, the first thing he did was inform the court of the defendant's cooperation with the CIA, and he said it had helped the agency assess the damage from the espionage conspiracy. But it was soon apparent that leniency was not on his mind. Stilz began his argument by recounting Daulton's long record in drug trafficking. From the time he was a teen-ager, he said, Daulton had spurned the basic tenets of conduct of a civilized society.

"Furthermore," he said, "based on the evidence that has been adduced before this court, there can be no question but that defendant Lee committed perhaps the most serious crime that a person could possibly commit—espionage. A crime against one's country; in many respects, a crime more serious than murder . . . a crime, your honor, not committed against one victim, such as murder, but against millions of victims . . . here the entire population of the United States.

"And for what?" Stilz asked, looking over at Daulton, whose eyes were cast down at the table in front of him.

"Why did he do what he did? What was his motive for selling out his country? What was his motive in delivering this country's most sensitive top secrets to the Russians for over a two-year period?" Stilz asked, slightly stretching the duration of the espionage operation.

"His motive was simple, yet shocking. He did it for *money*. In other words, Your Honor, he jeopardized this country's safety and well-being for money. Not for any strong anti-America belief or for any particular ideology which he possessed. He simply did it for the money."

And then, for the first time, Stilz acknowledged in public that the loss from the Black Vault had extended beyond the Pyramider papers. Some of the documents sold to the Russians, Stilz said, were "so extremely sensitive that the government did not include them in the indictment or expose them in trial."

Daulton fidgeted in his seat and looked at Ken Kahn with a frown that needed no words to convey his fear.

"Your Honor," Stilz went on, "no value can be placed on the actual damage that defendant Lee had caused to the national defense and security of the United States, nor the damage that he had done to the CIA's covert intelligence gathering and operations. Nor can we place the value on the lives of covert CIA intelligence agents which may

have been jeopardized due to defendant Lee's espionage activities. In fact, we will probably never know the full extent or content of the damage done by defendant Lee, but may someday, unfortunately, realize its effect.'' Given Lee's long pattern of criminal behavior; his unwillingness to abide by the rules of society; the seriousness of the charges of which he was convicted; the nature of the documents he had sold to the Russians and his calculated economic motive in selling out his country, Stilz argued, there was only one choice facing Judge Kelleher: life imprisonment.

• •

Don Re stood up and approached the lectern with a seemingly impossible task. After Stilz' stinging attack on Daulton, Re had to plead for compassion. He tried gamely, but there was not much he could say.

One of the basic reasons for sending one man to jail, he said, was to deter another from committing the same crime in the future. But, he argued, espionage was not a crime in this category: the motives for espionage were so varied, so unique to the individuals who were moved by the temptation to commit it, that the traditional concept of deterrence did not apply. "It is almost inconceivable that a person can engage in that kind of conduct if he is fully aware of what the potential harm can be.

"I suppose in this case we have some indications as to the 'why.' We can see the excitement that is generated. We can see a young man in his early twenties at the time this began perhaps being attracted to the notion of excitement, the notion of adventure. But that attraction is not the attraction of a criminal to do a criminal act. That is an attraction of an immature individual who chooses perhaps the most unwise course he could ever choose. . . .''

The youthful dark-haired attorney was trying, but if he was making any points with Kelleher, there were no indications of it in the bored expression of the judge.

"I would ask the Court to give long consideration," Re continued, "to the question of whether there is anything that can be salvaged from this life or whether we just throw it away and determine to make an example, or for whatever other purpose, keep him out of society. And I think that when the balance is struck in that manner, some substantial consideration has to be given to whether there is salvageable material

331

in this defendant. And it really is salvage, because regardless of what this court does, this defendant bears a stigma which he can never erase for the rest of his life. He will bear a stigma that he is not trustworthy, that he is not loyal.

"He has stigmatized his name through this conviction," Re said.

"It is a family which is torn apart now, not only through the potential loss of their eldest son, but, I think the Court is aware, through the imminent loss of the head of the household; that since the termination of this trial, Mr. Lee's father has discovered that he is terminally ill."

• •

Kelleher asked Daulton to stand while he imposed sentence.

Daulton lifted his small body with its almost simian geometry out of his seat and prepared to hear the judge's decision. Kelleher asked Daulton if he had anything to say in his own behalf. Daulton said he did not and was allowed to sit down.

"This is a crime of great degree . . . treason doesn't occur very often," the judge began. He acknowledged Daulton's cooperation with the CIA and that he planned to weigh it as "an act of expiation" in determining his sentence.

Hope flickered in Daulton. But as quickly as the judge had ignited it, he snuffed it out:

"This Court is satisfied that the defendant made available to the Soviets—for a price—whatever he was able to obtain," and along the way passed a substantial measure of corruption to his codefendant.

"The Court is satisfied that there was a disposition on the part of this defendant to do any hurt which might result from turning over to the Soviets the materials available to him as long as the price was right. The Court has in mind also that this is a youth. When were you born, Mr. Lee?"

"January, 1952."

"That is January 2, 1952?"

"Yes, Your Honor."

"The Court is aware that this is a defendant now in his twenty-sixth year and was a youth when the crime was committed. The Court is not persuaded at all that he suffered during the period involved with any significant degree of immaturity. The Court is impressed and wholly satisfied that this was a young man mature beyond his years in the sophistication of world travel and engagement in nefarious activities

332

on a wide geographical basis." It was a tip-off that Kelleher did not intend to sentence Daulton under the Youth Act.

Looking at Re, Kelleher said he found it difficult to give weight to his argument that Lee deserved mercy because he came from a close, devoted family. He made no mention of the reference to Dr. Lee's cancer, but said, "The Court's heart goes out to the parents of this defendant." He noted that he had observed their daily attendance at his trial. He said he felt compassion for them and respected their loyalty. But in his next breath, he said that, contrary to Re's argument, treason was a crime that demanded a sentence with a deterring effect.

Daulton looked quickly over at Re and Kahn, as if pleading for help.

"The Court," Kelleher continued, "must give recognition to the compelling need to those similarly disposed that for whatever reasons —of youth, or challenge, or excitement, or otherwise—that this is a game you do not play for any such purpose. . . .

"The defendant is hereby committed to the custody of the Attorney General or his authorized representatives for imprisonment for a term of his natural life."

• •

Daulton packed the few possessions he had in his jail cell in Los Angeles and prepared for transfer to a Federal penitentiary to begin the life sentence. He had not seen Chris now in many weeks. But through Kahn, he had followed his efforts to get a favorable sentence under the Youth Act, via his defense of extortion and his participation in further debriefings with the CIA. Daulton had heard about the favorable probation report and felt a grudging admiration for Chris: it looked as if he might save himself.

When Daulton had finished packing, he was taken to a car by Federal marshals for the trip to his next prison. But en route, Daulton made one stop, arranged by Stilz at the request of Anne Lee.

The prison car climbed up The Hill from the flatlands of Los Angeles, followed the high bluffs that skirted the Pacific, and came to a stop on the big driveway in front of the Lee home.

A marshal led him into the house and then stood back, waiting, while Daulton tiptoed into his father's bedroom and said good-bye.

"Pops, I love you," he said, and held his hand a few moments.

• •

Lompoc is a small town in Central California 170 miles north of The Hill that is best known for its production of commercial flower seeds —an industry that each spring turns the Lompoc Valley into a panoramic rainbow of fragrant sweet peas, stock, petunias and a dozen other varieties of flowers. Besides flower blossoms, Lompoc's economy is rooted in the payrolls of two institutions of the United States Government—the Lompoc Federal Correctional Institution and Vandenberg Air Force Base—the CIA's principal launching platform, along with Cape Canaveral, for spy satellites.

The prison car arrived at the Lompoc penitentiary late in the afternoon of August 4, 1977, and Daulton began his life term. At 1:10 P.M. the following day, his father died of stomach cancer.

51

AT 2 P.M. on September 12, 1977, the clerk of Federal District Court Judge Robert J. Kelleher announced Item 19 on the judge's calendar that day:

"Criminal Case 77-131, *United States of America versus Christopher John Boyce.*"

Chris's parents and most of his eight sisters and brothers were seated in the second row of the crowded courtroom. It was the first time they had come to court. George Chelius had told his friend and former boss, Charles Boyce, that he was optimistic Chris would get off with a moderate sentence.

Chris had reason to be hopeful. There were now two encouraging reports about him in the possession of Judge Kelleher. Since the favorable presentencing probation report had been filed with the court in June, he had been interviewed at Terminal Island by Federal Bureau of Prisons psychiatrists and psychologists, and they, like the probation officer who had written the earlier report, had accepted his story that he had become a spy because he was blackmailed by an old friend. *Maybe his lie had worked.*

The other reason to be optimistic was Kelleher's decision in June to

334

sentence him preliminarily under provisions of the Youth Act. To the lawyers, this seemed to signal that the final sentence would also be under this provision of the law. Daulton's life sentence had not added to their optimism, but the lawyers hoped the judge accepted Chris's story of extortion.

A few days before the sentencing, Chris had told two newspaper reporters, during an interview at Terminal Island, that he hoped for a sentence of six or seven years. Then, he said, he wanted to become a lawyer. "I know that sounds funny," he said, gesturing toward his prison uniform. "But the law is something that's always interested me, and it's something by which I would be able to show society that I'm a worthwhile person and that Judge Kelleher was not wrong."

•   •

Although Chelius and Dougherty were ostensibly optimistic when they entered the courtroom, they knew there was the equivalent of a legal bomb that could detonate Chris's chances of a lenient sentence —his letters to Vito Conterno.

The clerk had barely finished reading the docket number of the case when Chelius signaled the judge that he wanted to make a motion at the side of the bench, where he would not be heard by the spectators.

Chelius, Dougherty and Stilz all approached the bench. Joel Levine had resigned from government service, and Stilz was representing the government alone.

"Yes, gentlemen?" Kelleher inquired.

Chelius said he wanted to bring up the matter of letters Chris had written while he was at Terminal Island. "We would like to see those suppressed on the basis that they would cause undue prejudice and would be only cumulative in nature as to the continuing charges for which he has been found guilty."

"I am not clear what you are saying. Specifically, to what letters are you referring?" Kelleher, like Chelius, was whispering.

"Well," Chelius said, "the United States Attorney submitted letters purportedly written by the defendant Boyce prior to the last sentencing—"

"If I may interrupt for a minute," Stilz said. "They were letters purportedly written by defendant Boyce to an inmate in prison, and these letters discuss partly about the spy trial, that in fact he still works with the KGB and that his interests still lie with the KGB."

335

"Does the record reflect that the Court is familiar with these?" Kelleher, seemingly puzzled, asked.

"No," Chelius said.

"It doesn't ring a bell with me at all. I don't think I ever saw them," the judge said.

"Well, I submitted these letters *in camera,* copies of those letters," Stilz said. "I provided them to the probation officer, and the probation officer indicated that he provided those letters to you, Your Honor. If you are not familiar, I can go get the original letters and let you consider them before sentencing.

"I think they are *extremely* important," Stilz insisted.

"No, they will be ordered suppressed," Kelleher said. "The Court will represent that it has no recollection whatever of the contents of any such letters, and if there is a recollection that comes to mind it will disregard any such matters."

"Okay," Chelius said, pleased.

"Your Honor, may I be heard for a moment?" Stilz persisted.

"Your Honor, I think it is extremely imperative that I be allowed to argue those letters, the contents of those letters. They show the state of mind and intent of Boyce after he was convicted, and they show no—"

"They are insufficient before the Court for that purpose," Kelleher snapped, "so you will not make any reference to them."

"May I submit those letters to Your Honor before sentencing?"

"No, you may not."

• •

Chelius and Dougherty returned to the defense table and told Chris things still looked good: Kelleher had refused to consider the letters in determining his sentence. Chris's spirits were lifted.

Stilz rose to begin his pleading. As he had done at Daulton's sentencing, he began by acknowledging that Chris had "cooperated fully" with the government since his conviction. "He voluntarily allowed himself to be interviewed and debriefed on numerous occasions by Federal agents; and more important, the information he did in fact provide to the United States Government proved extremely valuable to the CIA in terms of assessing the damage done to our national security and defense.

"However," Stilz continued, "even taking defendant Boyce's co-

336

operation into consideration, it is the position of the United States that defendant Boyce should be sentenced to life imprisonment.'' And then he listed the reasons:

"As he stands before Your Honor for sentencing, it cannot be questioned nor challenged by anyone that he committed one of the most serious offenses that a person can possibly commit against society: espionage—an act of betraying one's own country, here the United States of America, a country that gave defendant Boyce his very existence, his education and an opportunity; a country that gave him, above all, freedom, his liberty and his security. But apparently unimpressed by these cherished items, defendant Boyce turned against his country and jeopardized its safety and well-being; in turn, he jeopardized the safety and well-being of all Americans. Why did he do what he did?

"What was his motive in jeopardizing the security and safety of his country and selling his country's most sensitive top secrets to the Russians?

"Was it money? Was it for monetary gain? Perhaps to a small degree. But this was not his primary motive as it was with his codefendant, Andrew Daulton Lee.

"His primary motive, Your Honor, was to aid and benefit the Russians.''

Of course, Stilz continued, the defendant had said in open court that he was disillusioned by his government and had been coerced by Lee and had committed crimes that "may have caused untold potential damage to our national security and for this damage he has expressed in open court his 'profound regrets' to the American people and their principles. He then asked to be allowed to contribute once again to our society, that there was no possibility of a recurrence of his past deeds.''

The government submits, Stilz said, that his defense is "simply not worthy of belief.

"He was not coerced by Lee. No doubt his codefendant, Lee, had an influence upon him and probably at times pressured him due to his own monetary greed. But clearly not to the extent claimed and emphasized by defendant Boyce. Boyce had his own motive for betraying his country. He carried his betrayal into fruition because he had a reason to do so. His reason was to advantage and benefit the U.S.S.R.''

Chris, again wearing his rust-colored corduroy suit, but with an

open-necked, flowered sport shirt different from the one he'd worn during most of the trial, didn't look at Stilz as he spoke. He looked down at the defense table and fiddled with a pencil.

Not only, Stilz said, had the defendant systematically transmitted secrets to the Soviet Union; he had quit TRW to take a college course that would lead to a job in the State Department working covertly for the U.S.S.R. There was still another reason that this case demanded life imprisonment, Stilz continued: the nature of the documents that were sold to the Russians.

"First, there were those Top Secret documents and materials proved at trial, of which this Court is fully aware. Second, and more important, Your Honor, were those Top Secret documents and materials not charged in the indictment nor proved at trial. These documents and materials were, of course, so extremely sensitive that the government did not dare to expose them at trial. Yet defendant Boyce freely caused their transmittal for over a two-year period!"

Dougherty rose to his feet.

"May it please the Court," he said. "I dislike to interrupt, but I hardly believe my client can be sentenced on the basis of anything that was not brought before the Court or proved at the trial."

"Overruled," Kelleher said.

Stilz deplored the espionage acts of Chris for more than twenty minutes. And then he concluded:

"Defendant Boyce knew if he breached the security of his position at TRW that the lives of every man, woman and child in this country would be drastically affected. He did so notwithstanding. He must, therefore, Your Honor, be expected to pay the consequences."

• •

Now it was the defense's turn. Bill Dougherty raised his huge frame out of his chair and approached the lectern. There was a short silence while he arranged the notes he had written and put on his reading glasses. Then, having no choice, he appealed for mercy.

Referring to the study of Chris that had been made that summer by the Bureau of Prisons, he said its author had concluded "that this act never could have happened had it not been for the gross negligence of TRW. I don't say that excuses Mr. Boyce, but if we take the setting of a young boy, an impressionable young boy, in an extremely sensitive place, with absolutely no supervision, we see that the opportunity was not created by him."

He stressed Chris's willingness to spend six days with CIA representatives. "He and only he knew what had happened, and he chose to tell completely and honestly to the CIA and the FBI everything that he remembered." Finally, after appealing to Judge Kelleher to sentence Chris under youthful-offender statutes, Dougherty turned over the defense's case to Chelius. As he walked away from the lectern, the judge stopped him and told Dougherty he might want to consider two points while Chelius was proceeding.

"First: When one is awaiting sentence under a statute which, amongst other things, provides for a death penalty—the appropriateness of which has been brought under some question by virtue of some of the expressed wisdom of the Supreme Court in recent years—but facing sentence which clearly can be maximized to life imprisonment —it is understandable that he will at that time become cooperative." Nevertheless, the judge said he would not ignore the defendant's cooperation.

"But there is one thing that struck this Court very strongly concerning your client at a time when he really could have performed in vindication or perhaps in expiation, and that was perhaps to come forward as a witness to see that a disreputable codefendant did not escape with a fictitious, false, unsupported, almost insulting defense, which might have succeeded before a jury, but which would never have been done had your client been in the position where he would come forward to give the full lie to the testimony of his codefendant.

"You rise to some matter, Mr. Chelius?"

"Your Honor, I represent to this Court that defendant Boyce offered his testimony against Lee, which testimony was rejected by the United States Attorney."

"What testimony did he offer?"

"He offered to tell the whole story," Chelius said.

"Well, what was that testimony? Did it relate to—"

"It would have related, Your Honor, to the fact that defendant Lee was not a representative nor had he ever been advised that he was working for the Central Intelligence Agency; the United States Attorney rejected that testimony."

"Very well," Kelleher said.

Then Stilz, looking agitated, rose to address the judge.

"Number one," Stilz said, "we rejected the testimony because I would put no witness on the stand who I thought would lie. And number two—"

"Very well," the judge said. "That is sufficient. I think we will let it rest at that."

Resuming the pleading, Chelius argued that Chris's espionage acts had done less damage to the United States than Stilz had claimed. "Historically," he said, "such crimes would have gravely damaged the defense interests of the United States; but modern rapid scientific improvement in the state of the art makes most, if not all, information obsolete within a matter of months. Some experts, for example, believe that such information cannot be protected longer than two years." Then he turned, as Dougherty had before him, to the seedbed where Chris's acts of espionage had occurred—the TRW plant.

"One could use the cliché 'When in Rome do as the Romans do,' for at TRW the security awareness and the importance they attached to the information, which has been the subject matter of the case, begged for just such a result. This, combined with the gullible nature of the defendant, made Christopher John Boyce an easy mark for completion of the crime.

"The probation report fairly details the personal life of Christopher John Boyce. I will not discuss it in any great detail except to point out that the defendant is twenty-four years old without a prior criminal record, a good history of satisfactory work and achievement, and a very supportive family, which is present in court today. All of these factors should assist Chris in achieving the societal goal of rehabilitation."

Chelius stressed again Chris's cooperation during the debriefing sessions. "It should be noted that by giving this report he has subjected himself to personal risk of injury from other inmates, because such actions are inconsistent with the code of conduct within the prison system.

"What is the future of Christopher John Boyce?" Chelius asked, after a short pause, and then answered:

"Since the defendant's arrest and continuing through today, I have had numerous opportunities to discuss future goals of the defendant with him. One of the things that impresses me is his resolve to become a useful and productive member of society and to show this Court that he is capable of its trust and confidence. To this end I urge the Court to structure its sentence toward the goal of rehabilitation and not punishment."

52

"MR. BOYCE, you have the right to address the Court before sentence is passed," Kelleher said. "Do you wish to speak?"

"No, sir," Chris responded.

"Does the Court wish to ask my client any questions, Your Honor?" Dougherty asked.

"No. Very well, you may be seated," Kelleher said, and then began a long, often rambling monologue. Before he had spoken many words, it became apparent that the judge who had admitted three months earlier to being perplexed by the defendant was more sure of himself this day.

"This was a long and protracted trial, and much was said in the course of that trial," he said. "Much was disclosed in the course of the trial. Some of what was said was believed by the jury and some by the Court. Much was believed neither by the jury nor by the Court.

"It has been urged on the Court today, for example, that the laxity of security, in whatever degree it existed, at TRW is a factor relevant to the sentence process. I am not sure that the record here would disclose in fact that there was a significant degree of laxity in the security program at TRW." The defendant, he added, had testified about such laxity. "I don't believe a word of that."

Chris shifted in his seat.

"The difficulty that this defendant faces at the present time is whether there is any integrity within him.

"The Court didn't find any veracity in him. The attempt that he made to rationalize his reasons for embarking on this program of espionage at one time was generally to the effect that he was appalled at his government and what it was doing to Australia.

"Absolutely made of whole cloth, totally irresponsible—an act of irresponsibility not only toward the penal laws of this country but toward its international relationships—and the defendant was not de-

terred in the saying of those things, because apparently he thought they would serve his purposes.''

It hadn't worked.

"There are factors which run in his favor," Kelleher continued. "The Court has in mind the cooperation which was given in attempting to minimize the wrong that was done by telling what he knew or what he could remember, perhaps, of the sensitive material that he had caused to be turned over to the Russians.

"But the Court had the impression that he just photographed everything in sight as long as it would serve the purpose of equipping Lee with that which he needed to sell to the Russians, and that there wasn't much discrimination by the defendant as to what he was photographing. He perhaps didn't even *know* the full extent to which he thereby caused the Russians to know about the sensitive program involved.

"Just what can conscientiously and consistently be done by a court in imposing sentence here which gives adequate recognition to the need to tell Boyce and all others like him that you play this game at risk of the most severe penalty . . . not a moderate penalty, but a severe penalty?

"There was real wisdom in the Congress in providing by statute that acts exactly such as here performed qualify one for a death sentence.''

There was a pause in his monologue, and in the silence of the courtroom one of Chris's sisters could be heard sobbing.

"*That* is obviously deterrence of the highest order,'' he continued.

"I think this defendant was corrupted by an evil person. I think the defendant has within him some decency and perhaps some real potential for that decency to manifest itself and become meaningful to the community. If there were somehow disclosed to the Court a sentence which would allow this defendant to take his place at some reasonably early date in the community and still not send forth the wrong word in deterrence, the Court would embrace such a sentence.

"Even if the Court accepted as true the expressed motivation by this defendant that he was setting out to correct evil security practices by the government, the word needs to go forward that you don't do that.

"In the role he played, in the position he occupied, it was none of his business to attempt unilaterally and through criminal acts to revamp a system he didn't like, or which he disapproved, or of which he was critical.

"With all respect to Mr. Chelius and Mr. Dougherty, the Court will

say to you gentlemen that you compound the difficulties for the Court in imposing sentence by the fact of who you are, respectively. It is part of the record of this court that you, Mr. Chelius, are one of those unusual persons, unusual in numbers, who bears the highest security classifications and who, accordingly, is unusually informed concerning all matters as they relate to the security program.

"And you, Mr. Dougherty, enjoy at least a reputation which certainly has the effect of placing you somewhat similarly situated to Mr. Chelius in respect to kinds of acts which are here disclosed as having been committed." It was a reference to Dougherty's Marine Corps record.

"The Court will say at the same time that each of you gentlemen has at the very least earned the admiration and the respect of the Court for the professional manner in which each of you, under what must be unusual difficulties for each of you, discharged your professional duties."

Kelleher then rejected Chelius' contention that in an era of fast-moving technology a nation is unable to hide all its secrets for long. "We have to survive despite the weaknesses of the system," the judge said, "and we have to cope with the system and make it work better."

Kelleher's long monologue was coming to an end. It had revealed that he had wrestled with a dilemma. And then he disclosed how he had resolved it.

Reversing himself, Kelleher said that he had concluded that the defendant would not benefit from the Youth Corrections Act and then gave his decision:

"The Court has a duty in regard to the sentence that it imposes here, and it would hope by whatever means may be available there would be some expansion of the restraints which decent people must self-impose if the system is to work or, in the alternative, that inability to exercise such restraint will lead to prison. Any legal reason why sentence should not at this time be imposed?"

"No, Your Honor," Dougherty said.

And then, at the age of twenty-four, Christopher John Boyce was sentenced to forty years in prison.

53

AFTER THE ARREST of Chris and Daulton, the Central Intelligence Agency ordered surprise security inspections at companies around the country that manufactured espionage satellites and other equipment for the CIA, and Stansfield Turner, the agency's director, reported afterward that the results were "distressing, perhaps appalling."

TRW instituted a number of reforms in its security procedures after the arrests. It decreed that henceforth no employees would be allowed to work alone in the Black Vault, and that only two employees, working together, could set ciphers for the cryptographic machines.

Employees henceforth were forbidden to take packages, parcels, briefcases and other items, including potted plants, into and out of the vault. Rules were promulgated informing employees that while entering and leaving designated "secure areas," they were subject to search. Television cameras were installed to monitor certain high-security areas twenty-four hours a day, and a score of other restrictions were imposed after the trials, including rules tightening surveillance of employees' foreign travel; periodic interviews regarding employees' personal lives and random inspections for security violations in the Black Vault were ordered.

TRW also informed the CIA that it would implement new screening procedures for staffing of sensitive areas, "looking toward maturity of personnel and compensation commensurate to the responsibilities of the job function."

A new policy was put into force requiring annual rotation of employees in high-security assignments "to preclude incestuous relationships from developing." And TRW said it would "embark on a positive education program to break down the code of silence that exists among most working groups" in the hope of encouraging employees in sensitive jobs to report the misconduct of others. And, TRW told the CIA:

All personnel history statements of employees thirty years of age and under will be required to list five names of associates of peer groups for interview as to possible suitability.

• •

In October, 1978, in a speech at Cape Canaveral, President Jimmy Carter lifted the official veil of secrecy that had cloaked American espionage operations in space for twenty years: The United States owned up to using spy satellites. Carter declared:

"Photoreconnaissance satellites have become an important stabilizing factor in world affairs in the monitoring of arms agreements. They make an immense contribution to the security of all nations."

A few weeks later, after the CIA had failed to anticipate a popular uprising in Iran against the Shah, the President sent a critical memo to CIA Director Turner. Alluding to the setback in Iran and other recent intelligence failures, Carter took the CIA to task: Perhaps, he suggested, the CIA had become too dependent upon "technical" means of intelligence collection—specifically, satellites. Perhaps, he added, it had forgotten the value of old-fashioned human spies.

• •

There was never any public admission from the CIA about its grievous loss of data concerning Projects Rhyolite and Argus and the other secrets that had flowed out of the Black Vault for almost two years.

On December 8, 1978, William Clements, who had served as Deputy Secretary of Defense during part of the time Chris worked in the vault and was later elected governor of Texas, in a speech to the Philosophical Society of Texas that generally denounced what he saw as the sorry state of American military preparedness, said:

"Our intelligence community is in disarray. A major satellite intelligence system, developed and deployed at a cost of billions of dollars over the past decade, without Soviet knowledge, has been compromised by intelligence procedures as porous as Swiss cheese."

• •

A number of months after the conviction of Boyce and Lee, the CIA began to notice a difference in some of the telemetry signals the Rhyolite system was collecting from the test flights of Soviet ballistic missiles: they were in code.

345

For at least four years, the American satellites had secretly intercepted test data from the launches and transmitted the information to the Australian bases. The intercepted telemetry signals provided reports on velocity, heading, trajectory and other aspects of the test intended for Soviet researchers who used the data to diagnose the performance of their new hardware. Because of the eavesdropping by the Rhyolite birds, American technical experts also could analyze the signals and follow from afar the evolution of new Soviet weapons, including tests of advanced multiple warheads, atmospheric-reentry systems and radar-deceiving "penetration aids." Along with on-the-ground and aircraft monitoring of Soviet telemetry, the eavesdropping enabled the CIA to develop a substantial body of information about the evolving capabilities of Russian weapons and give American negotiators at SALT conferences advance knowledge about the capabilities of the weapons. It was as if Americans, playing a game of poker with the Russians, were standing behind them, looking at their hand.

When the Russians began encoding the telemetry reports, the United States lost part of its ability to look over their shoulders. Exactly what role the information provided by the two young Americans played in the Soviets' decision is not known. Only the Soviet officials who made the decision to begin encoding the signals could attest to the importance of the information. But whatever the reason, it was a major setback for the United States because it closed a window on Soviet technology at a time of rapid improvements in Russian missile hardware; and further because when such satellites were becoming increasingly important to police international arms-control agreements, U.S. listening posts in Iran would soon be closed by political turmoil there.

It is also impossible to assess fully other aspects of the damage done to the United States by the two friends' espionage scheme. Ironically, only the Soviet Union knows in full all of the secrets that flowed out of the Black Vault. Chris may have been drunk some of the time he selected the secrets he gave Daulton. And Daulton did not remember all his merchandise because it was only that—goods to be sold for a price.

At the least, the Russians obtained an unprecedented look at the day-to-day operations of American espionage satellites, particularly Rhyolite. They became privy to the function of the Australian bases and the American deceptions against them. And they learned technical details about U.S. spy satellites at a time when the two countries were

negotiating agreements to control strategic arms with the intent to use such satellites to verify compliance with them—and when each country was urgently preparing weapons, such as TRW's laser gun, to disable the other's spy satellites.

The dual loss of the data from the Black Vault and the Iranian monitoring stations came at a particularly unfortunate time for the CIA. In the spring of 1979, the Carter Administration negotiated a new SALT agreement with the Soviet Union in which the world's two superpowers agreed to throttle back development of new nuclear missiles. The issue of whether the United States could verify Soviet compliance with the agreement became the subject of a major national debate.

The Administration (which didn't publicly reveal the security breach at TRW) conceded that the loss of the Iranian listening posts was serious, but said it was confident that the United States would be able through other means to verify Soviet compliance with the agreement, hinting that satellites could take over much of the work of the Iranian stations. To help fill the gap, the CIA accelerated work on low- and high-altitude eavesdropping satellites more advanced than the four Rhyolite satellites which were then in orbit. As it did, it appeared that Moscow was in an enviable position to anticipate the United States' next move in the high-stakes game of technological one-upmanship that the superpowers play.

Not only did the Soviets have intimate knowledge of the Rhyolite system; they had blueprints and voluminous other data regarding Argus, a system that was to have an antenna almost twice as large as the one on Rhyolite; moreover, when the Soviet Union bought the Project 20,030 study from Andrew Daulton Lee, it had become privy to what some of the best brains in the American aerospace industry thought would be possible technologically in the 1980s to intercept Soviet telemetry. Certainly, the CIA's knowledge that the KGB possessed these data would be likely to persuade the agency not to build a new system exactly as it was laid out in the study.

But there are certain things in this spectrum of technology that cannot be changed if a country wants to use its technical capabilities to the fullest, and in the Project 20,030 study it appears that the Russians bought at least a partial preview of how good American abilities to monitor their missile tests would be far into the future.

The Russians had also obtained copies of numerous classified cables, including the report of a CIA submarine's secret mission to monitor

Soviet missile tests over the Arctic; they had obtained reports on the surveillance of China and other intelligence operations that cannot be disclosed here; and perhaps most important, they had received the classified TWX message listing the capabilities of many of the American satellite systems used to monitor the Soviet Union and other countries from space.

But what this information really meant to the Russians, only they know. Some capabilities of the American reconnaissance satellites had previously become known to the Soviet Union across the negotiating table at the SALT conferences. Certainly, some of the information they obtained from the two Americans about U.S. satellites was available by simple deduction through analysis of orbital data collected by their own tracking stations or supplied routinely by the United States to the United Nations.

The Russians never got the transmission frequencies they needed to use with the ciphers from the Black Vault to eavesdrop on CIA communications. Chris had seen to that. Prosecutors Stilz and Levine would argue that possession of the ciphers alone would allow the Russians to read the CIA's secret mail; again, only the Russians know the importance of the tables of ciphers from the vault they bought from Lee.

• •

Some mysteries about the affair remain.

Daulton frequently and openly visited the Soviet Embassy for more than a year and a half, and it is astonishing that the CIA did not discover his visits before January 6, 1977, if in fact it did not.

The Soviet Embassy in Mexico City is, for the CIA, one of the most closely watched foreign embassies in the world. It had been a principal target of American intelligence for decades before Daulton began making his visits.

Long before Daulton sat down for vodka and caviar with Vasily Ivanovich Okana, Lee Harvey Oswald demonstrated how convenient a destination it was for a disaffected American seeking contact with the Russians.

Phone taps and electronic surveillance techniques of the newest designs are used to monitor the embassy. Its KGB personnel are kept under surveillance by their counterparts in the CIA, some of whom are assigned to the U.S. Embassy with specific assignments to compro-

mise Russians and turn them into double agents. Attempts are made regularly to plant American agents as servants in the embassy.

There are suggestions, but only that, that the CIA might have been aware of Daulton's business dealings with the KGB, at least during the latter months of the espionage operation. Despite the bench warrants that were outstanding against him during much of his commerce with the Russians, he was never stopped at the border; there was Chris's recollection, albeit one after a night of drinking, that Gene Norman told him he had heard Chris was going to jail for the rest of his life; there was another employee's claim that he was on "everybody's list." Perhaps these were the distorted memories of a troubled young man seized by paranoia, but there are other curiosities about the case. Why TRW would place a $140-a-week, twenty-one-year-old college dropout in such a sensitive national-security position in the first place is, at least in retrospect, a puzzle. Circumstantially, TRW's decision to leave the Pyramider papers unlocked in the vault where Chris could read them shortly before his departure suggests they could have been left as bait. And there was the mystery of Daulton's fingerprints on the circuit boards. An FBI fingerprint expert testified that he had found Daulton's prints on a circuit board from one of the encryption machines in the vault. Yet both the two spies, when denials meant nothing regarding whether they might be convicted or not, insisted that Daulton had never entered the vault nor had he ever touched the circuit boards. And certainly, the presence of a U.S. Embassy official at the Soviet Embassy on the morning of Daulton's arrest added another curiosity to the case.

In the black world of espionage, it is tempting to hypothesize that the CIA discovered the two young men's cottage industry of selling American secrets to the Russians and either attempted to spread false information through them or had other motives in mind. If nothing else, the CIA confirmed through the two young men that the Russians were in desperate need of improved infrared technology for their own spy satellites. And it is inviting to speculate that the list of American satellites sold to the Russians with the specifications on their respective capabilities to spy from space might have been leaked with a purpose to the Russians on the eve of a new round of SALT talks.

At the trials of Chris and Daulton, the prosecution insisted repeatedly that the government had known nothing about their scheme until Daulton was arrested in Mexico City. This is a critical legal point: if

the CIA in fact knew about it before the arrests and didn't inform the prosecution, many lawyers would argue that it put the United States Government in a position of withholding evidence that the defense could have used to claim entrapment—a defense that might have freed the two young men.

The CIA successfully resisted efforts by the defense to obtain its internal reports of the affair. Judge Kelleher inspected at least some of the reports in the privacy of his chambers and said that he found nothing that would have been of significance to the two friends' defense attorneys. Still, the feeling that the CIA might have manipulated their clients lingered with the lawyers long after the trials ended.

If their thoughts were ill founded; if the CIA had not in fact been on to the two spies; if it had not been aware of the scruffy young man who so brazenly and so often entered the Soviet Embassy over such a long period, only one other conclusion is appropriate: the affair of the snowman and the spy who called himself Falcon was an episode that demonstrated amazing ineptitude on the part of the Central Intelligence Agency.

54

LOTS OF YOUNG PEOPLE grew up during the nineteen-sixties and early seventies, went off to college, began careers, got married, raised families and started on the road to middle age uneventfully, despite having been bathed in the emotional heat of a controversial war, assassinations, racial strife and Watergate. Many young Americans were revulsed by a discovery that America the Real did not invariably measure up to America the Ideal, and many were seduced by the instant euphoria and easy money of drugs.

Chris and Daulton were two people amid a horde—the generation of the postwar baby boom: better off materially than most, but seedlings growing in the same soil as millions of others. Bill Dougherty said of Chris: "He was like a lot of other kids. He had a high draft number, so

he never got called; but he was affected by Vietnam just the same. He saw what it did to the country, how ten years went down the drain. He saw Spiro Agnew, John Mitchell and Richard Nixon.''

Yet others like him did not become Soviet spies.

Ken Kahn, the bearded hippie lawyer who specialized in defending troubled youths from Palos Verdes, said of his client:

"Daulton was a Greek tragedy figure. He grew up with too much money. Things were too easy for him. He could have been a really brilliant businessman; he was a capitalist; he may have been amoral, but aren't a lot of capitalists? He could have been John D. Rockefeller. But he got into dope and he became a big shot, and then he just couldn't get out of it. Daulton's dream was to be a Big Man; drugs made him one.'' Palos Verdes, he added, might or might not be typical of similar enclaves of the affluent around America; many of the young people he knew who grew up there, he said, never got into trouble and began productive lives. But, Kahn said, he had worked for enough young people from The Hill to be troubled by what he saw:

"The kids get in trouble over drugs, but shouldn't the parents have to take some of the blame? The only thing those kids had, a lot of them, was what money could buy. Their fathers were into making money as fast as they could, and their mothers were up to their ears pursuing their social interests, and they just blinded themselves to what was happening to their kids. I know a lot of these kids were smoking pot and snorting coke and heroin when their parents were in the house; some of them were *dealing* right out of their houses, the parents were taking calls from their customers—and the parents were oblivious to it. It was incredible. The parents gave their children all the material things, and that made them think they had discharged their duties; it gave them a clear conscience so the father could go back to making money and the mother could keep up with her tennis and social life. Then, all of a sudden, when their kids are seventeen or eighteen and in trouble, or on drugs, they ask, 'What happened to my children?' ''

Yet there were lots of young people in Daulton's generation who used drugs and sold them. They did not become Soviet spies.

What made Chris and Daulton different was opportunity.

What brought them together in the basement of the Soviet Embassy in Mexico City with Boris Grishin of the KGB was a confluence of circumstances: Daulton's cynical pursuit of money and self-impor-

tance and his desperation to escape prison, coupled with Chris's disillusioned idealism which rejected centuries of man's concepts of nationalism and patriotism, and his almost accidental employment at the age of twenty-one in a tiny room that gave him intimate access to some of America's most sensitive defense secrets.

At their trials, each blamed the other: Chris said he had been blackmailed by Daulton, and Daulton claimed that Chris had told him from the beginning that they were both working for the CIA. The fact is that Chris never told Daulton that they were working for the CIA—but neither did he tell Daulton the real motive for his invitation to commit espionage. In truth, each entered the espionage conspiracy with different motives. In a grotesque way, each used the other.

To Daulton, secrets became a commodity to sell, like marijuana or heroin. His was the generation of the rip-off, and to Daulton, the Russians were merely another victim to be ripped off. And when the time came when the Russians asked for more secrets and Chris did not give them to him, Daulton did threaten blackmail—to go to Chris's father, striking him in his most vulnerable spot.

But this was not only a case of evil corrupting good; it was a case also of good corrupting evil.

In the end, the Russians knew they had been had. They had paid for some grains of gold in what would become an avalanche of dust. In the end, they threw Daulton out of the embassy car, and when he came back, they left him out on the street.

Chris, as he lay on his prison bunk, would muse that he had made fools of both the Russians and the Americans. He would lie back and study the ceiling of his cell and think of Robin resting in his grave, a foolish grin on his face.

To Chris, the man-boy who rejected nationalism and dreamed of One Nation, the nation of man, his job in the Black Vault became an opportunity to take a saber stroke at both the world's superpowers at once. It was, he told himself, a flimflam against the Russians and a nonviolent protest against what he believed was the corruption of his own country. And Daulton had had the greed to serve his purpose.

Or was there more to it than that? There is no evidence that his father was anything but a loving, attentive and devoted parent who idolized Chris. But somehow, the chemistry between father and son didn't work. Somehow, Chris failed to assimilate from his history books the same sense of patriotism that was instilled in other Ameri-

cans by the legends of Valley Forge, Pearl Harbor and Iwo Jima. During the years he was reaching manhood, Chris embraced different ethics from those of his father, who believed in the purity of patriotism that had galvanized his country in World War II and who stoutly defended its presence in Vietnam. When he rebelled against the CIA and his country, perhaps Chris was also rebelling against the man who ruled the home in Palos Verdes where he had grown up.

• •

Chris continued to receive visits from his parents after his final sentencing; but after a time, their precarious rapprochement ruptured again. The break occurred over what his father considered a small matter—a suggestion that if Daulton managed to win a new trial through an appeal, Chris testify against him. Chris, fearing that other prisoners would hear the conversation and brand him a snitch, refused; there was a dispute, and finally, Chris sent word once more that he did not want to see his parents again.

• •

After the trial, prosecutors Levine and Stilz entered private law practice together.

George Chelius developed a lucrative law practice in Orange County catering to businessmen and land developers.

Bill Dougherty resumed his criminal law practice, as did Donald Re.

Ken Kahn returned to defending drug pushers and began a business teaching members of the public how to represent themselves in court.

Gene Norman was transferred out of the vault and eventually left TRW.

Laurie Vicker also quit the company and moved with her husband out of California.

Betsy Lee Stewart, the girl whom Daulton loved, realized her dream and became an airline stewardess.

Darlene Cooper went to New York to pursue her dream of becoming a fashion model, but, it was rumored, she didn't make it and became a topless go-go dancer instead, before returning to California, where she entered Harbor College and joined the tennis team.

Alana McDonald dropped out of Chris's life and went away to college.

353

Barclay Granger's sentence in Federal prison was reduced after he testified against Daulton, and his former girlfriend, Carole Benedict, drifted away from The Hill.

.   .

Daulton has found a kind of peace at the Federal penitentiary at Lompoc, where, sometimes, late at night, darkness is turned into day by the brilliance of a white-hot rocket booster lunging upward from Vandenberg Air Force Base, carrying another spy satellite into space.

Other inmates gave Daulton a nickname—"Spy"—and in prison, Daulton finally kicked his drug habit after months of torturous deprivation.

Although Daulton received a life sentence and Chris was sentenced to forty years, both, under Federal statutes, could become eligible to be considered for parole about 1995 or shortly after that.

In a conversation at Lompoc, Daulton was asked if he had any regrets about his original decision to choose drug pushing as his vocation—the decision that, over time, would eventually lead him on a circuitous road to espionage.

He thought a long moment and replied:

"To tell you perfectly honestly, no. I always had more money than any of the people I knew who played by the system. I was intellectually as sharp or sharper than they were. I traveled extensively. I was in a better position to know what was really happening; I got to the point where I was enjoying the finer things in life, and I didn't have to go out and rob and steal for what I needed . . . and the drugs I used were no different than someone sitting home and guzzling Scotch."

.   .

After his sentencing, Chris was sent to the Metropolitan Correctional Center in San Diego, where a curious thing happened not long after he arrived.

An urban penitentiary, the prison is a skyscraper that rises twenty-four stories on the edge of the San Diego downtown business district. Chris was looking out a window one day at the San Diego harbor, which was crowded with Navy ships, when he saw something that amazed him.

It was a peregrine falcon, one of the rarest of falcons.

354

The peregrine made a spectacular stoop at a pigeon that had nested at the nearby San Diego City Hall; it seized it in midair in an explosion of feathers, and then disappeared somewhere above Chris.

He knew that there were perhaps a dozen or two, no more, in all of California, including the pair he had studied on the big rock in Morro Bay through his binoculars.

The spectacle of such a bird—a bird officially classed by the Federal Government as an endangered species—hunting in the heart of a city startled him. Chris saw the peregrine again the next day, and the next, and each time it vanished above him. Finally, he realized that the falcon was living in the same building that he was! It had established an eyrie in a concrete niche in the prison tower and was using the side of the building as if it were a cliff in the wild.

A San Diego newspaper heard about the rare bird and the prisoner's unusual love for birds, and it sent a reporter over to the prison to interview Chris. His story was headlined BIRD'S FREEDOM BRIGHTENS SPY'S IMPRISONMENT.

But one day Chris looked out from his cell and discovered the peregrine was gone.

•   •

At night, in the lonely confinement of his cell, Chris lives with memories of Fawkes, Pips, Nurd and his other falcons.

When he can't sleep, he closes his eyes and sees the long wings of the falcons rising gently on thermals of air, their elegance still the most beautiful thing he knows in the world. He thinks of climbing down rocky cliffs at the end of a taut rope to the eyrie of a falcon and sampling its rage as it hurtles past him as he twists in the wind. He recalls the defiant look in the eyes of Pips the last time he saw him and wonders what happened to his last and best falcon after a friend, at his request, released him back into the wild after Chris's arrest at the turkey ranch.

Chris thinks also of Alana and what might have been. He had released her too. It was best, he sent word to her after his arrest, that they not see each other again; he said he did not want her to wait for him; and the last he heard, she had found a new boyfriend. But Chris could not forget the sight of her face framed in her blond curls, and long after he was sentenced to prison, it lived with him in his cell.

Yet if Chris has any regrets, he does not express them.

Perhaps he best summarized his feelings in the letter he wrote to his father on the eve of his trial:

Dear Dad:

I thought of you all long and hard today and have decided I owe you an explanation of my feelings. In reality I owe you so much more than that, but at this point it is all I can give.

I wish I could bring myself to convey my love to my family from this place but I cannot and so I leave it up to you. I realized many dozens of months ago that there could be no coming back from the decisions made and I do not propose to pick up the pieces now. I regret none of my actions except for the deceptions I played upon you and any subsequent loss of face. For that I am truly sorry, more now than ever. If we never understood each other, the fault is mine.

I was never a socialist. I do not support their actual society any more than I support that found here in these times. I reject both equally.

To my perceptions, the foundations of this country are a sham. It was designed by the few for the few and so it will remain. Western culture is in decline now and the trend cannot be reversed. We are grasping along in a headless insanity that will continue to consume until nothing is left.

Time and time again I watched the destruction of those things and places I love and I was disgusted. I believe we are on the edge of a poisoned horrible darkness. Industrialism and technology are dragging humanity toward universal collapse and will take most life forms with it.

I used to sit on Silver Spur Road [looking out at the view] and shudder at the enormity of the lights of Los Angeles at night. To me it was always an infected spectacle. I lived in it and I breathed in it. It was not the people I hated. It was what had been blindly created, and so I just turned my back on it all.

I ran my dog through the fields and I flew my hawks and falcons and I did everything I could to shake things at their roots. I just do not accept the direction of this society. I could not sit still for what we are leading to. I didn't think so then, I don't now.

There is no possibility of my fitting back into a normal life style, if indeed I ever had one. Nor will I spend the rest of my life in prison. I will continue to fight in court till George and Bill advise me otherwise. My legal position is precarious through no fault of theirs.

Your attendance in court or any family would hinder my rationality and thus my case. I ask that you not come to court. Thank you for not coming so far. I appreciate greatly the books you've sent me and I will return them through George.

I would give anything to be out of this place and be able to feel sunshine and to just even run again. I think there is small chance of that now so I have detached myself from what goes on here.

Being alone all the time leaves one much time to turn thoughts inward. As I think back upon my beliefs that put me here in the first place, they are strengthened more than ever. I could never make of my life that which you would have wanted.

That is no reflection on you. I chose freely my response to this absurd world, and if given the opportunity again, I would be even more vigorous. Please give all my love to mom and Kathy and everyone and tell them for me to see them would just make a bad situation worse.

Respectfully,
Chris

• •

As Chris lies awake in his cell and thinks of his falcons, of Alana and of his walks alone in the mountains, he sometimes worries about growing insane because of the empty solitude of his existence.

"I am beginning to talk to myself again," he said in a letter to the author. "Slowly at first, a word here, a word there, it grows. The sound runs with itself across this cube and then bounces back at me before the final syllable has even left my throat. To read out loud is a concert. The prisoner next to me recites Dickinson in the late afternoon. His muffled tones remind me of long ago days and standing under cottonwoods with wet earth underfoot. When I sit very still I can hear my heart thumping in my chest and my stomach churning. That and my lungs pulling for breath, it makes the hair on my arms stand on end. What a simple thing life is. You can almost hold it in your hand. How very peaceful it is to be alone and silent and conscious of one's own body.

"I am not a complex man and my tenets are quite simple," Chris wrote. "I have always abhorred the national patriots and can dismiss them because their days are numbered just as surely as were those of the primordial leviathans. A century must sound to you like an age but it is actually a mere moment in the history of man. Your great-grand-children will enjoy the birth of the tranquil millennium, the one world. The evolution of a global society devoid of competing militarisms will be a green house of worthful development.

"If I am mad they are all the madder for the thousands of nuclear weapons they are prepared to unleash on each other.

"I have made my life a study of aggression and the carnivores, and

humanity is the most self-predatory species in existence. I am ashamed of the history of the nations and of my own origins and someday so will all of united humanity. To believe otherwise is to bankrupt pessimism. Not in your lifetime, nor mine, nor any living man's, but someday they will all understand. The past shall be judged as ignorant and grisly barbarity. That someday will be the dawn of mankind's redemption and the new treason is the rejection of nationalistic society and its exploitive and butchering adjuncts. These were my dreams, alone with my falcons. Do you think me deranged, too?

"Like Camus," Chris wrote, "my subconscious is plagued with life's purposelessness and therein lies my inner peace. I am neither conservative nor socialistic. I cherish friendships with the back country, wind and rain, the seasons, and the spontaneous hazards of the wilds.

"I have always viewed myself a spectator of the great human void racing towards what it knows not. I long ago excused myself from the mad dash, to find my own sanctuaries. Thus falconry and history have always attracted me."

ACKNOWLEDGMENTS

The roots of this book began in the spring of 1977 when David R. Jones, the National Editor of *The New York Times,* assigned me to cover the espionage trials of Christopher John Boyce and Andrew Daulton Lee. I want to express my gratitude to Mr. Jones and other editors of *The New York Times* for their patience in originally allowing me to pursue the story.

It is impossible to describe adequately all of the many contributions made to this book by Jonathan Coleman of Simon and Schuster; not only did he first propose a book on the story, but as its editor, he was a constant source of inspiration and good judgment that was felt on every page. My thanks also to Deborah Katsh, Lynn Chalmers and Vincent Virga of Simon and Schuster, and to Carole Zahn and Jean Brown.

This book could not have been written without the generous assistance of the lawyers in the case, and I thank especially Kenneth Kahn, William Dougherty and George Chelius. I express my deep gratitude also to the families of Christopher Boyce and Daulton Lee.

There are others to whom I would like to extend my appreciation publicly, but unfortunately, to do so would violate my pledges of confidentiality to them, and so I must pass on my gratitude anonymously.

Finally, I say thanks to the two protagonists of this story, whom, over a period of more than two years, I came to know almost as well as the members of my own family.

R.L.